The Great Vermont Ski Chase

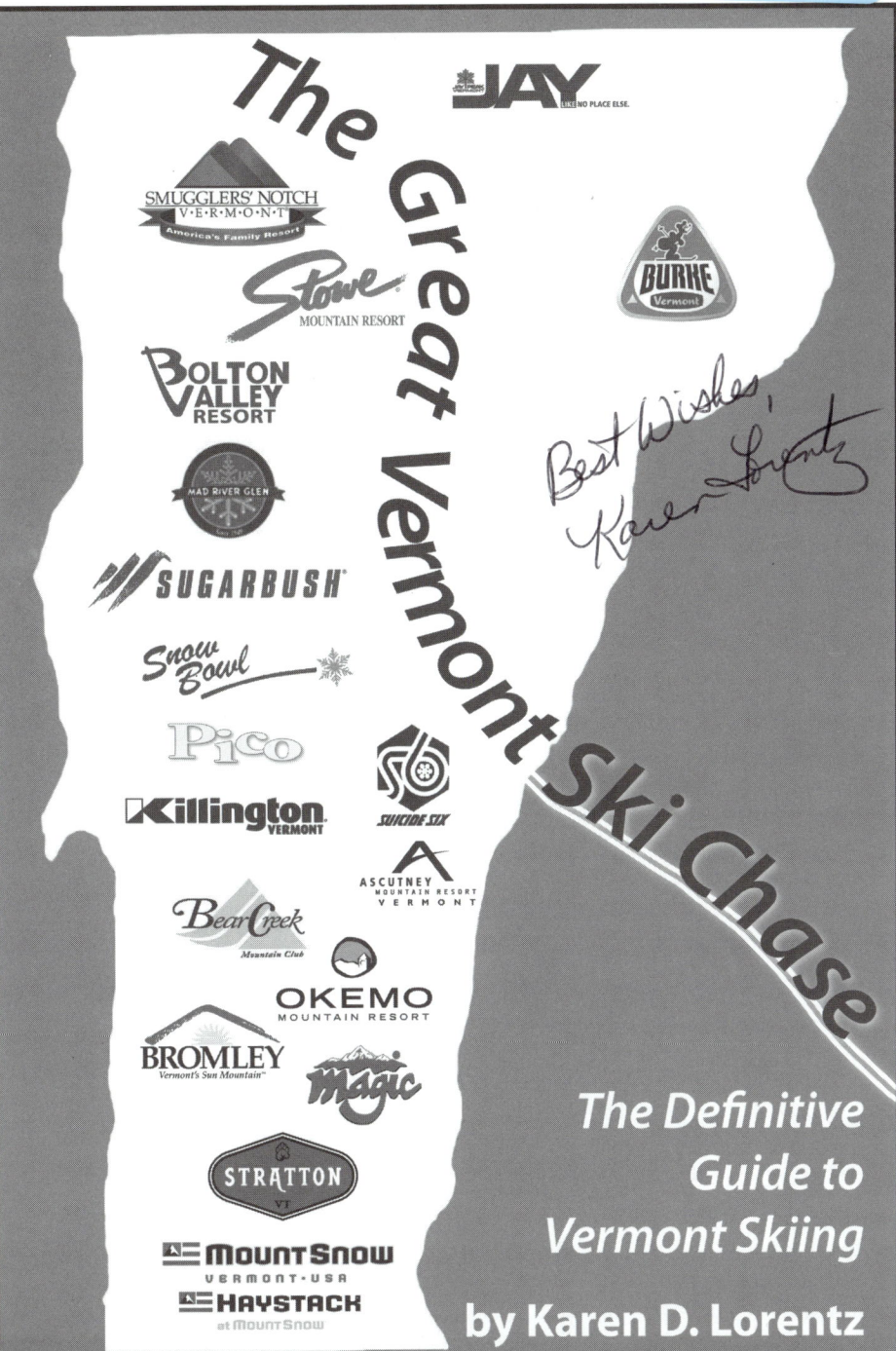

The Definitive Guide to Vermont Skiing

by Karen D. Lorentz

Best Wishes, Karen Lorentz

© 2005 by Karen D. Lorentz

All rights reserved. No part of this publication may be reproduced or transmitted in any form or by any means, electronic or mechanical, including scanning, photocopy, recording, or any information storage, retrieval system, and computer or digital medium without permission in writing from the publisher. Requests for permission should be addressed to:
Mountain Publishing, Inc.,
1300 CCC Road, Shrewsbury, VT 05738.

Although every effort has been made to present accurate information, using the most up-to-date information at the time of going to press, some details are liable to change and cannot be guaranteed. Neither Mountain Publishing nor the author accept any liability whatsoever arising from errors or omissions, however caused. If in doubt about any details, contact the ski areas for the latest information. If you would like to contact the author with any corrections or additions for future projects, please write to Mountain Publishing.

Also by the Author

Killington, A Story of Mountains and Men, Mountain Publishing, Inc., 1990.

A Vermont Parent's Prevention Resource, a guide to raising healthy, drug-free children, Prevention Works, 1995.

Okemo, All Come Home, Mountain Publishing, Inc., 1996.

Good Vermonters, The Pierces of North Shrewsbury, Mountain Publishing, Inc., 2000.

Two Harwoods in the House, A Vermont Memoir by Madeline Harwood with Karen D. Lorentz, Mountain Publishing, Inc., 2001.

ISBN: 0-9625369-4-6
Cover Design by Kitty Werner, RSB Press
Printed at Daamen Printing, West Rutland, Vermont

1 2 3 4 5 6 7 8 9

This book is dedicated to:

Dayna Lorentz and Anita Duch
in hopes that
it will help you enjoy
a return to skiing;

John, Jason, Jonathan and Jim,
the fabulous men in my life;

And to all
who enjoy mountains
in winter.

Photo Credits

Many of the photographs and all the trail maps or mountain aerials have been supplied courtesy of the ski areas. The abbreviated photo credits are explained below. Where a photographer was specified by the ski area, their names are listed; if more than one photographer, page reference to respective photographs are given. Grateful appreciation is extended to all for the permission to use these images as well as to others named below.

AMR	Ascutney Mountain Resort	page 7 Rick Russell, 9 John Miller
BCMC	Bear Creek Mountain Club	
BVR	Bolton Valley Resort	
BMSA	Bromley Mountain Ski Area	
BSA	Burke Ski Area	
JPR	Jay Peak Resort	
KR	Killington Resort	
MRG	Mad River Glen, TJ Greenwood	
MM	Magic Mountain	
MCSB	Middlebury College Snow Bowl	
MSR	Mount Snow Resort page 158 Todd Modica	
OMR	Okemo Mountain Resort	
P	Pico page 190 Jerry LeBlond	
	pages 193, 200 Don Heithaus	
SNR	Smugglers' Notch Resort	
SMR	Stowe Mountain Resort page 213 Landewehrle Studio	
	pages 215, 226 RL Photo	
SM	Stratton Mountain	
SSR	Sugarbush Ski Resort	
WIR	Woodstock Inn and Resort (Suicide Six)	
VSM	Vermont Ski Museum	
KL	Karen Lorentz	

Back Cover Skier Courtesy of Woodstock Inn and Resort
Back Cover Snowboarder Courtesy of Kitty Werner, RSB Press

Foreword

Welcome to the world of skiing and snowboarding in Vermont, the nation's third largest and most spectacular ski state! Vermont may be small in geographic size and population, but it offers genuine big-mountain skiing and riding, boasting more 2,000-foot-vertical mountains than all other eastern states combined!

Lift-serviced Alpine skiing made its debut in Vermont when America's first rope tow began pulling skiers up Gilbert's Hill in Woodstock in January 1934. Vermont's been in the forefront of Alpine skiing and snowboarding ever since, pioneering developments in the ski industry from innovative ski instruction to the advent of the snowboard.

Skiing in Vermont is a passion. Vermont skiers and riders make the most of annual snowfalls that top 300 inches at some resorts and a season that often begins in October and stretches into June. In between, they savor an unparalleled variety of trails, slopes, glades, and terrain parks that challenge and reward at every turn, whether expert or beginner. Today we have over 1,200 trails and 6,078 acres of ski terrain served by 174 lifts and state-of-the-art snowmaking so you are assured of skiing even if mother nature fails to cooperate.

The endless opportunities for great winter adventures extend to exploring the picture-postcard villages and towns that lie at the base of our great mountains. They offer a host of après-ski activities, from a massage at a sports center to a tour of a working farm. There's plenty to do for all ages, and lots of good Vermont products to sample, from syrup and cider to cheese and chocolates.

And now this book offers you the information to help find all the special delights and treats that await you. We think you'll find it a handy tool to make your ski days and trips rewarding ones.

This winter, don't hibernate—celebrate Winter in its original state!
And have a great ski chase!

David Dillon	*Bill Stenger*	*James H. Douglas*
President	*Chair*	*Governor*
Ski Vermont	*Ski Vermont*	*State of Vermont*

Acknowledgments

I am indebted to Alice Dugan for the suggestion that I write this book. Her counsel was a jump starter and her encouragement invaluable. I treasure her friendship.

I would also like to thank all the people at Vermont ski areas who helped me with my research and who so patiently answered my questions and read and re-read the chapters. Special thanks are extended to:

Killington President Allen Wilson who propelled "the challenge" with an enthusiastic "yes" to the reward idea; Kim Jackson who checked the Killington chapter more than once; also John Cole, Alex Kaufman, Kevin Leach, and George Potter for details.

Jennifer Hewitt and JJ Toland at Sugarbush for all kinds of help.

Mike Purcell, Melissa Gullotti, Kelly Pawlak, and Mike Murphy at Mount Snow.

Barbara Thomke and Karen Bushey at Smugglers' Notch Resort.

Dick Andruss, Ford Hubbard, Wayne Brown, and David Gwatkin at Burke.

Bill Stenger, Kim Hewitt, and Scott Allen at Jay Peak.

Eric Friedman, Henri DeMarne, and Andrew Snow at Mad River Glen.

Bob Fries, Mark Aiken, and Mel Croshier at Bolton Valley.

Peter Mackey at Middlebury College Snow Bowl.

The above had to do double duty because I was less familiar with their areas than those I have covered and skied more extensively in the past ten years. But even that familiarity had to be enhanced and for their being so knowledgeable and helpful, I am also indebted to: Gary Aichholz and Ethan Bins at Magic Mountain; Pam Cruickshank at Okemo; Michael van Eyck, Peter Dee and John Cueman at Bromley; John Neal at Bear Creek Mountain Club; Chuck Vanderstreet at Suicide Six; Steve Plausteiner, Bill Henne, and Cindy Osgood at Ascutney Mountain Resort; Kirt Zimmer and Jeff Wise at Stowe Mountain Resort; and Myra Foster at Stratton.

Many thanks to the folks at the SE Group for engineering information regarding gradients; to Brian Lindner for all kinds of expertise; and to skier Dick Findlay, Meredith Scott at the Vermont Ski Museum, and Jeffrey Leich at the New England Ski Museum for help with 'knotty' historical information. Appreciation is also extended to the folks at Ski Vermont who have been such a help to writers over the years and particularly to Heather Atwell and David Dillon for assistance on this project.

A sincere thank you to the ski areas for participating in the book and for extending the "challenge to ski all Vermont's mountains." I hope the "reward" will be a fun incentive to explore and experience Vermont's great mountain diversity.

Hats off to Kitty Werner for a cover design that met with my husband's approval!

Thanks to my husband John for editing, making suggestions, and bearing with the late meals and lack of brown socks in his drawer. As always, his love, support, and encouragement enabled me to make the final long dash to complete a book.

And finally, to the many skiers and patrollers I met on the lifts and trails, thank you for sharing your insights and sending me to discover trails I so thoroughly enjoyed.

Karen Lorentz

Contents

Photo Credits ....*iv*
Foreword ....*v*
Acknowledgments ....*vi*
Preface ....*viii*
Introduction ....*ix*

Chapter One	Ascutney Mountain Resort 1
Chapter Two	Bear Creek Mountain Club 15
Chapter Three	Bolton Valley 25
Chapter Four	Bromley Mountain 37
Chapter Five	Burke Mountain 51
Chapter Six	Jay Peak Resort............................65
Chapter Seven	Killington 83
Chapter Eight	Mad River Glen 111
Chapter Nine	Magic Mountain 123
Chapter Ten	Middlebury College Snow Bowl...135
Chapter Eleven	Mount Snow and Haystack 147
Chapter Twelve	Okemo Mountain Resort.............169
Chapter Thirteen	Pico Mountain 191
Chapter Fourteen	Smugglers' Notch Resort............205
Chapter Fifteen	Stowe Mountain Resort...............221
Chapter Sixteen	Stratton 239
Chapter Seventeen	Sugarbush 257
Chapter Eighteen	Suicide Six 277

Appendix A   Essentials to Good Mountain Times *288*
Appendix B   Glossary *291*
Appendix C   Helmets: Added Protection But *298*
Appendix D   Off Piste and Backcountry *302*
Appendix E   Nordic Areas *304*
About the Author *306*
The Great Vermont Ski Chase Challenge *307*

Preface

The idea for this book came from a writer friend who shared with me that she was enjoying the ski features I was doing during the winter of 2002-03. She added, *"You really should do a book."* Knowing that as a journalist she is interested in many subjects, I could understand her reading something by a fellow writer, but since she doesn't ski, I asked why the *emphatic* book suggestion.

She said she found the articles interesting and full of information that she thought would be helpful to skiers like her son. She was saving the articles for him as he lives in another state and suggested a book would be more convenient. Knowing I had written several books, she told me, "I just assumed you'd want to do a book."

But the truth was, I had undertaken the articles for a different reason, and the thought hadn't occurred to me. At the time, I was still rushing to visit ski areas, sometimes two in one week, and struggling to meet deadlines. Each time I headed north, there would be fresh snow on the roads, and I would get behind a snowplow or slowpoke crawling along Route 100 and start to worry about being on time. I was too late to catch a morning lesson at Sugarbush on one trip but miraculously made a noon lesson another time at Smugglers' after leaving at 7 a.m. (The drive took a skier from Boston less time than my Vermont trip had taken—backroads can put us "lucky" in-staters at a distinct disadvantage.)

On another trip, I pushed the pedal to the floor and passed a tanker on Route 107, and my heart pounded from the adrenaline rush all the way to I-89. Between the deadlines, appointments, and long drives, I got to feeling that I was chasing mountains. But how do you chase mountains? They don't exactly move.

What I was after was a firsthand experience; but beneath that lay a goal to ski every area in the state. As a writer for various publications, I had written about all Vermont's areas but often it was from interviews, not recent slope time. For reasons of school-aged kids, freelance work, and general demands of home and family, I just hadn't found the time to get to all of them.

Then suddenly the boys were grown, and I was somewhat free. I still had writing assignments and helped out in my husband's office two days a week, but that left me a day or two to ski. Of course, the housework, cooking, and laundry never go away.

Still, I had a strong desire to ski every area, and there's nothing like a goal to get one going (or in the case of housework, leave things undone). I asked the *Rutland Daily Herald* if they would like features on every area in the state, knowing the weekly deadlines would be just the incentive I needed.

It was a busy year, but one I shall never forget. The experiences, people, and places were all memorable. And I was truly impressed by all the mountains. I live very close to Killington, Pico, Okemo, and Bear Creek. They provide plenty of challenge and variety with no need to go further afield. But I found that I liked and enjoyed every area I visited — each was distinctive and fun. Some brought back long-ago memories; others were totally new experiences. I also found that after an absence of several months, I appreciated my "local hills" more!

I debated doing another book; books are work and to finish them you don't have a life let alone time to ski. But Alice's line of reasoning prevailed: there wasn't a current, definitive Vermont ski guide available and besides, "they would make good gifts," she said. The only thing worse than deadlines is trying to figure out what to give people for Christmas. She had me.

About this "guide"

To meet Alice's expectations, I have tried to produce a comprehensive guide to let you know what you will find at each ski area or resort. The end of each chapter contains facts and data to help you arrange a visit and phone numbers and Websites for obtaining more information. Although prices are bound to change over the years, they are included to provide you with an idea of what to expect (you can look back and chuckle years from now). I've included ticket *steals'n deals* for the wallet watcher.

Each chapter presents distinguishing characteristics about the area as well as trail highlights and suggestions on things not to be missed. I have *not* made comparisons or ranked the mountains. They are different breeds offering different adventures. If "variety is the spice of life," that is as it should be.

And quite frankly, every skier I've met has different criteria for what they want for a challenge or a family mountain. So when I'm asked "What's your favorite area?" I invariably respond, "I like them all. Just as I have three very different sons with various strengths and quirks, I love each of them and enjoy each for their special ways." What I am attempting to share with you are those "special ways." Perhaps they will enhance your skiing enjoyment. Or get you to discover areas you haven't been to before.

Nor have I critiqued snow conditions. Snowmaking, grooming, weather, trail pitch, and skier traffic are variables that make "conditions" a very subjective and serendipitous topic. I have skied long enough (45+ years) to know one day I can flawlessly schuss a slope and another flail my way down. Packed powder is fine, but I accept that Eastern skiing encompasses a range of interesting snow conditions and have learned to handle fresh ungroomed, corn, frozen granular, sticky, fast, blue ice (less of that today than in the 1960s), and all manner of permutations as part of the challenge of the sport. Thanks to modern snowmaking and grooming, I can always find a trail to my liking even on "the worst weather days."

I have included, however, some personal experiences in an attempt to share the mountain's flavor and communicate what was delightful about my discoveries. As I am interested in what others discover, especially if I missed something, you're invited to contact me with your thoughts at the address found on the publication page.

I've also included some background as to how each area got started, survived its challenges, and made its mark on the ski industry. And I've described recent changes at an area in case you haven't been there in some years or are simply curious as to "what's happening." Where pertinent I include a description of future plans.

Please don't take offense at the "generic" use of the word *skiing*. Gliding on one wide snowboard or two narrow skis, Telemark or other equipment is still about steering boards on snow and despite different techniques, that process can be most easily and simply be referred to as skiing. For economy of words, "skiing" and "skiers" are used *inclusively* and include riding and snowboarders. (The exception is Mad River Glen where snowboarding is not allowed and therefore skiing refers to getting down the hill on Alpine or Telemark skis only.)

Finally, I have tried to present enough information to make your mountain adventures good ones. I want nothing more than for this book to lead to your own personal store of memories, a kind of choose-your-own adventure—one that encourages you to get to know all Vermont's mountains more intimately so you can appreciate *all* the challenge, variety, and fun they have to offer. I hope you'll record some of your experiences on the *Adventure* page so someday you, your friends, kids or grandkids can look back on many years of wonderful winter-in-Vermont adventures.

About the "kicker"

Chances are you don't ski by deadlines, but maybe you'd like to try the sport or want to get out more often or try another area but lack the information or incentive to risk it with what little free time you have. Hopefully, this book will foster that first or extra trip—a new adventure that might lead to a super discovery or a sexy new wrinkle in your mountain life. Or, simply, greater appreciation for your favorite mountain.

To encourage you to try all Vermont's ski areas, I decided that the guidebook aspect would be a good start but thought maybe like me, you might need a little 'kick.' To add incentive, I asked the various areas what they thought about the idea of "a challenge to ski all of Vermont's Alpine mountains," and if they would participate by offering a free day at the end of *your ski chase.* They liked the idea.

If you are up for the challenge, see page 307 and send in for your free Ski Chase Card. Present it for validation when you purchase your lift tickets, save the receipts, and send them in when you finish your adventure. You'll receive a voucher for a free day as your reward.

Yes, if your family of five skis all the areas, you get five passes for a free day—makes this book a good investment or gift doesn't it? Yes, a girl or guy friend can be on your card. Ditto a neighbor or nephew you ski with. But no, you can't duplicate the last page. This book is an independent project, paid for by the author (not ski-area sponsored), so I have to pay the bills incurred to produce it.

If you know someone who wants to take the challenge, please give them the Book Order Form (okay to copy this page) or send them to a mountain ski shop or a bookstore to purchase their copy. Your support of this project is greatly appreciated.

But get busy skiing; you've got just *four s*easons to complete the challenge (from season of card issue) if you want to redeem a free day.

And even if you can't take the challenge, I hope this book will enhance your appreciation of the Vermont ski experience.

May all your ski days lead to wonderful adventures and warm mountain memories.

Karen D. Lorentz

Introduction

Everyone skis or snowboards for a different reason—for the solitude or the camaraderie, for the speed or the grace, for the closeness to nature or the awareness of technology, or just the sheer fun of it. However you choose to get through the snow of Vermont's mountains, you are part of a proud tradition. By taking the great ski challenge, you come face to face with Vermont's people, landscape, and history.

Skiing had humble beginnings. First used as a means of transportation, students often skied to school on homemade skis with leather straps and jar rubbers as bindings and neighbors used skis to get around and visit each other in winter. In 1914, Nathaniel Goodrich, a librarian at Dartmouth College, climbed up and skied down Mt. Mansfield, Vermont's highest peak, and the practicality of skis as transportation began to evolve into the industry of today as more people discovered the fun of recreational skiing.

In the 1930s, adventurous souls from Boston and New York rode the "ski trains" throughout New England to test themselves against the rigors of snow and mountains. They began by hiking up to ski down. The first rope tow went in on Gilbert's Farm in Woodstock, Vermont, in 1934. From this point on, Vermonters and the people who skied here applied technological innovations to skiing, resulting in better equipment, improved lifts, more access to the slopes, ski patrols and ski schools, and a vibrant social life.

Skiing's growing popularity in the U.S. was interrupted by World War II but mushroomed after the war when the elite ski troopers of the 10th Mountain Division returned. They started ski areas, ski schools, lodges, patrols, manufacturing firms, and raised families who loved skiing and the outdoors. This enthusiasm for skiing was also experienced in Vermont with the result that the mountains were changed forever.

Thanks to the many small ski areas built to serve local communities and schools, most Vermonters had access to the ski slopes. The numerous Nordic, jumping, and Alpine Olympians, many of whom learned to ski at the smaller areas, show how integral skiing was to Vermont life. Vermont has more Olympians per capita than any other state, and the prestigious ski clubs and ski academies throughout the state continue to produce world-class competitors.

Of course in more recent history, Jake Burton Carpenter developed the snowboard in a barn in South Londonderry, Vermont. He is one of the many who took up the mountains' challenge and changed the sport forever. Only time will tell how many more Vermonters will innovate or further advance the sport through new discoveries or technologies.

I encourage you to take Karen's challenge to ski all of the areas in Vermont. Reading the histories of the areas, you will be inspired by the pioneers who started them as well as by those who continue to make improvements.

As you visit the mountains, I hope you will look around the lodges, study the trail designs, listen to the snow, and enjoy the uniqueness of each of Vermont's ski areas.

Meredith Scott
Curator, Vermont Ski Museum

Ascutney Mountain Resort features two distinct skiing areas. The lower slopes provide dedicated learning terrain while the main mountain features a surprising diversity of trails, from groomed wide to ultra steep and natural. The runs off the summit are long with lots of combinations making for interesting routes.

Chapter One

Ascutney Mountain Resort
Carving a Family Niche to Success

It's 5:25 on a Saturday night. Do you know where your children are?

Well, if they are ages four to ten and the family is at Ascutney Mountain Resort, chances are they are at their very own "Happy Hour."

They may be coloring or having their faces painted, playing games or eating pizza, but at the stroke of 5:30 something very special happens as in walks a tall, well-fed, gray rodent.

It's Cheddar the Mouse, and he's not alone—pals Blizzy the Beaver and Rocky the Raccoon are at his side.

The hush lifts as eyes light up, giggles pour forth, and the good times roll. This is Cheddar's Happy Hour, a time when kids dance and limbo to the music they love with Cheddar, Blizzy, and Rocky.

Oops—too wound up to ever go to sleep tonight? Not a chance. The children's movie that follows allows for some chillin' and by the time parents pick them up at eight, they're ready for some shut eye.

The fun continues the next day at Cheddar's Discovery Zone, where "Mini Olympians" learn to ski at their very own park. Colorful cutout characters adorn the slopes along with instructors of all ages, and if anyone gets cold, there's a special children's lodge to duck into for hot chocolate.

Fast forward to Wednesday of the traditionally busy President's Week. We (day skiers) are on the lift with a vacationer. He's from Connecticut and his family is here for the week. He had to leave for a business day but is rejoining them now. Being easy to get to and not too long a trip is part of Ascutney's appeal, he says, adding that he and his wife like the ski programs for the kids and daycare for their youngest. Other parents tell me the same thing, with some adding, "It's affordable, too."

The young single we meet tells a different story. He lives nearby, and plays hooky from work a couple of times a week to ski for a few hours—gets "in lots of long runs thanks to the Express quad. It's convenient and the season pass doesn't cost too much. The challenge is good here," he adds, raving about the glades and diamonds and ticking off a list of double diamonds.

One of Ascutney Mountain Resort's distinguishing attributes is its small village setting. Everything is nicely proportioned and the effect is aesthetically pleasing as the buildings fit in with their natural surroundings—pristine, rolling farmland and the tiny village of Brownsville with its white-steepled church.

The amenities are modern resort, however. The slopeside housing along with the sports/fitness center, restaurants, and convenience of having everything in one place—ski shop, ski-school meeting place, beginner lift, learn-to-ski slopes, skating pond, tubing hill, country store, daycare programs, and game rooms—make Ascutney a family-friendly place. The programs, special events, and facilities for children are exceptional; the separate learning area for little ones and all age 'never-evers' means peace of mind for all.

The Mountain

The ski area provides the variety and modern lift system (a double, triple, and fast quad on the upper mountain, two chairs and carpet on the lower) that keep skiers happy, including those who crave woods and double diamonds. When you ask people what to ski, they mention a litany of trails, then lapse into why they love this area, adding "but please don't tell too many people."

What they describe is the way this mountain "hums along." It handles peak crowds with nary a lift wait and offers big mountain skiing—1,700-foot vertical for every run off the North Peak Express Quad; 1,800-foot vertical to the village base—with a diversity of trails for all ability levels. That includes everything from the wide-open acres of groomed terrain for beginners on the lower mountain (100-feet of vertical) to scenic meandering greens, cruising blues, and bruising double diamonds on the upper (main) mountain. With 56 trails on 150 acres plus another 50 acres of tree skiing, Ascutney skis big and offers the fun that comes with a ski-home bonus at the end of the day.

Beginner/Novice ●

The lower mountain 10-acre Learning Area offers wide-open, gentle terrain, and two lifts for beginners. Kids and adults can learn here without better skiers and boarders flying all around them or watching them from the lifts. Two triple chairs allow novices to progress from a few shorter slopes and trails to higher up the slope and a long run down Easy Rider.

Within this Learning Area lies Cheddar's Discovery Zone with a Wonder Carpet for the youngest learners. Close by is the Mouse House Lodge where kids and ski school classes can take a break, warm up and have a cup of hot chocolate, or enjoy a nature lesson.

Once beginners have mastered turns and stopping, they can progress to the upper mountain via the Village chair. Dipsy Doodle (●) leads to the Sunrise

The village at Ascutney Mountain Resort is part of the area's appeal. It's cozy, convenient, and comfortable for those who like resorts that are "just the right size." Above is a section of the lower mountain beginner area. KL

Double chair and a nice area with gentle trails in Honeybee (●), Ridge Run (●), Sunriser (●), and Buttermilk (●). A low intermediate slope Lower Snowdance offers a good opportunity to develop further control and then head up the mountain on the Triple Chair, which stops short of the steep top.

The Triple has a mid-station so low-level novices can try a few runs on the greens here first, starting with Catwalk which leads to more greens. From the top of this chair, there's a more challenging 2.5-mile novice route via Cloudspin (●) to Catwalk (●), Ridge Run (●), and Sunriser (●) to Buttermilk (●).

Off the top of the Express Quad, there is no easy trail but Gateway (■) is wide enough to allow a controlled, non-fearful snowplower or stem turner to access Cloudspin. Gateway can be tricky if it gets scraped off or moguled up at the end of the day and since the Triple only misses the Gateway section, it makes more sense for non-aggressive novices to use this lift.

Intermediate ■

The Sunrise Double on the main mountain offers a nice assortment of blues, some meandering like Enchanted Forest and Twister, and some straight and steeper like The Plunge, or mellow and wide like Lower Snowdance. It's a good place to get to know the mountain if you are not a beginner.

Gateway off the top of the mountain is a classic blue that leads to a number of choices, as does Trust Me. Otter's Slide (■) is a cross-mountain, long, narrow romp with sidehills and lots of turnoffs to vary your runs. Snowdance, accessed from the top of the Triple or from Gateway off the peak, is a fabulous long run to the lift with many width and terrain variations. The 2.5-mile route of Gateway to Otters Slide to Last Chance and Lower Snowdance is a delightful, varied, and fun intermediate run off the Quad.

From the midstation of the Triple, Cruise Control, The Plunge, Lower Exhibition, Screaming Eagle, and Back Home to Lower Terminator are mostly wide blues with consistent pitch—nice mile-long runs for practicing or cruising.

Advanced/Expert ♦ ♦♦

Among the diamonds that offer a diversity of short and long, wide and narrow, fun and tough without being *too* tough are: Sidewinder, a more classic narrow, twisting trail with steeps and runouts; Face, wide, steep, sometimes bumped; and Terminator, narrow and steep to start, then wide and steep with a blue cruiser finish. Add Ledges, Heartbeat, Mayday, and Hot Shot for good variety and the opportunity to up the pulse rate. Bump skiers will find their greatest challenge on Gun Barrel (♦).

Ascutney has several mean double diamonds, including: Blind Faith under the uppermost section of the Quad; Free Fall, a narrow, natural-state trail that has double fall lines and winds its way through the trees; Touch 'N Go, narrow, winding, and steeper than Free Fall with multiple double fall lines (a bit more manageable when groomed); and Upper Exhibition, steep, ungroomed with plenty of big, knee-bashing bumps. Add Cabin Chute, Dark Side, Neverglades, and Bushwacker (all ♦♦) tree skiing and that's a good amount of rough and tough. Located on the mountain's western side, and taken sequentially, Cabin Chute and Dark Side offer almost a mile of trees with chutes, bumps, rocks, waterfalls, and other extreme terrain.

Cabin Chute offers a narrow descent to an abandoned cabin (there are plans to restore the Jones Cabin to its former operating condition), but it also has a flat section before coming out at the top of Terminator or the start of Dark Side so it's not recommended for snowboarders who mind a walk. Dark Side begins with a moderate pitch but steepens quickly. Lower down it widens out into a pretty hardwood glade before exiting to a lower section of Terminator.

Impressions

Our day started at the Village, where my nephew Geoffrey Ballou (age 12) and I watched the instructors and their helpers who were attending to the tiny tots on the carpet and the other classes by the novice chair. It was definitely a lively scene! We saw more novices of all ages, including adults, on Easy Rider as we rode the Village chair up to the main mountain.

From there we began our exploration at the Sunrise Double for warm-ups on some easy greens and then sampled Twister, Enchanted Forest,

Lower Snowdance, and The Plunge—all enjoyable blues, some through the forest and some with short steep sections. We found a good variety of terrain.

The North Peak Express Quad took us to the top, where 90 percent of skiers and boarders were starting out on Gateway or Trust Me. Blind Faith, the third option, was very steep, bumped up, and too gnarly for all but true experts. Geoff and I did just about all the black and blue trails off the top, with Geoff also running several glades and then meeting up with me on a lower trail, which was very convenient as he loves trees.

Gateway to Trust Me to Sidewinder provided a great taste of challenging classic

The Ascutney Mountain Resort Village and tiny Brownsville are seen from the lower section of Terminator, a wide steep that gets the adrenaline flowing and boards a-cruisin.' KL

skiing with a long schuss on Lower Snowdance to the lift. Upper Snowdance and Face were also great discoveries, but Moment's Rest to Terminator or Gun Barrel were the real "hoots" of our day.

These trails are so far over (skier's left) that few people seem to find them and having them to yourself is the "cat's meow" in my book. Terminator starts narrow but widens out to a steep speed run that makes even wimps like me get a taste of feeling like "the Herminator" for one very thrilling moment! Geoff loved it when I got to racing him. Obviously, I was feeling like a kid again —the trail and its perfect conditions made me do it!

Ascutney was a great discovery for both of us. We noticed both the progression of difficulty as you move up the mountain and the diversity of long runs (2 to 2.5 miles off the upper two lifts). With the exception of some occasional congestion at Gateway (a couple of times in the afternoon), we had almost every advanced run to ourselves or at the very least the ample space I crave for my particular comfort and enjoyment level. Geoff especially enjoyed the challenging glades, which occasionally tripped him up when very tight or steep or both. I loved the silly sheepish grin on his face when I asked what took him so long, and he told me, "I fell."

With good uphill transportation and downhill dispersion of skiers and riders, we rarely had a wait at any lift and then it was five minutes or less. For most of our four hours on a busy Wednesday of President's week, we skied right on to the Express chair! Its six-minute delivery to the summit and the variety of trails keyed us into why this once languishing area has become so popular. Ascutney is a smart vacation choice during peak times, and it would make a great place for a family reunion with many things for non-skiers to do as well.

From First Challenge to Success

At 3,144 feet above sea level, Mount Ascutney has a long broad summit whose profile is particularly noticeable because it is a "monadnock," a freestanding mountain that is not part of a range. As one of Vermont's more visible mountains, Ascutney beckoned to be climbed for its wonderful views early on. In 1825 residents of Windsor cleared a path to the summit in anticipation of a visit from the French dignitary the Marquis de Lafayette. In 1857, D.C. Linsley surveyed and built a road over what was thought to be the overgrown Lafayette trail. He also built a Stone Hut on the mountain. The mountain proved popular during the era of "summit houses" (1880 - early 1900s) with the large stone lodge on its crest affording meals and beds to visitors who were attracted by the views and cool mountain air.

After the popularity of mountaintop excursions fell off (due to the advent of the automobile), things were quiet on Ascutney for awhile. But during the early 1900s, the Linsley trail was revived and more hiking trails were built to the summit. During the 1930s when 3,000 Civilian Conservation Corps (CCC) troops were working in Vermont under direction of the Department of State Forests and Parks, (then) State Forester Perry Merrill arranged for the state's purchase of 1,000 acres on Mount Ascutney and assigned a contingent of CCC troops to build Ascutney State Park. A magnificent four-mile auto road was built on the southeastern side of the mountain along with campsites, picnic areas, scenic overlooks, and hiking trails.

Merrill was eager to have a ski area built on Ascutney's northwestern side, but his plans were temporarily thwarted by some disgruntled politicians who didn't like the mountain purchases he had been making. Nevertheless, during the CCC's tenure, a one-mile ski trail and a 30-meter jump were built on the western boundary of the park (in 1935-36 according to CCC reports).

As skiing caught on in Vermont during its first heyday in the 1930s, local enthusiasts formed the Mount Ascutney Ski Club, and in 1938, with permission of farmer Ray Blanchard, they cut a trail on his land on the north side of the mountain. World War II interrupted their climb-up/ski-down venture. But after the war, the Ascutney Ski Slopes Corporation was formed in 1946 under the leadership of a group of Windsor citizens headed by Katherine Cushman. They leased land from Blanchard and the state, erected a ski lodge and four tows, and operated on several trails in 1947.

Poor snow years caused them to go under so Windsor Machine Products, Inc. (partners/owners Robert Ely and John Howland) bought the land leases and assets in 1953 and took over. Having heard about early snowmaking experiments, Ely experimented in the yard of the machine shop in Windsor and produced machine-made snow. Seeing its potential, he installed a primitive system at Ascutney in 1957, the first in the state.

Mark Green participates in the Antique Ski Race using vintage equipment. This annual Ascutney event benefits the Vermont Ski Museum. AMR

Eventually Howland became the ski area's owner and made many improvements. The 1960s saw ambitious expansion and mountainside homes being built as part of efforts to transform the area into a recreational resort as was then the new trend in Vermont. The 1970s and 1980s had their lean and difficult no-snow years, however, and a succession of owners could not make a go of the area.

That included Summit Ventures, a group of businessmen who bought the mountain in 1983 and began pumping $50 million into the area to transform it into a true resort with a 100-unit hotel, 114 village condo units, a state-of-the-art sports center, childcare facilities, and many mountain upgrades. But 1986 tax law changes put a damper on second-home investment and high interest rates added more problems. The late 1980s/early 1990s recession and some poor natural snow seasons took their toll, and the area closed in 1991.

The current owners, Susan and Stephen Plausteiner bought the resort for $1.1 million at a bankruptcy auction in 1993. Interestingly, the only other serious bidder was Smugglers' Notch owner/operator Stanley Snider. "He simply did not want to see Ascutney closed," Stephen Plausteiner recalled, noting that when it came to the bidding, Snider deferred to the Plausteiners.

"He told me that his wife might kill him if he bought another area so close to his retirement," Plausteiner added with a grin and appreciation of their good fortune to pick up the resort for a bargain price. If imitation is the sincerest form of flattery, the Plausteiners repaid Snider's interest in saving Ascutney by implementing the kind of family-oriented programs and service emphasis that made Smugglers' so successful.

With ski-area management and financial expertise, the extended Plausteiner family—Stephen (president), wife Susan (CFO), father John (GM), mother Lucille (hotel manager), and brother Tim (mountain operations manager)—modernized the mountain by adding more trails and snowmaking (95 percent coverage) and increased the vertical to 1,800 feet by adding the mile-long North Peak Express Quad. Thanks to the town selling them eight acres, the chair was able to reach a higher elevation at 2,520 feet above sea level.

The new owners also refurbished the hotel, implemented the programs and activities that appeal to families, and hired a ski-area marketing guru who helped them get the word out on the upgrades. With $12 million and their own hard work invested in the resort, skier visits more than doubled during a decade when ski industry visits were relatively flat—evidence that families respond to kid-friendly programs and day skiers to affordable lift tickets.

Today, Ascutney is back on top, hosting skiers all winter and vacationers, conferences, and weddings in summer and autumn, along with area residents for dinners year round in the increasingly popular Brown's Tavern. Steve Plausteiner explained the mountain's comeback and success as a family-owned and operated mid-sized area as a result of several factors.

> When we bought Ascutney Mountain Resort, we inherited a solid Master Plan from the former owner Summit Ventures that provided a good framework and streamlined the planning process. As we applied for specific permits, the process was made smoother—not easy—by having the Master Plan in place. I don't think a small or mid-sized area could afford the cost of master planning today, though.
>
> The already-built village was another tremendous asset in turning the business around, and proximity to I-91 and Boston helped. The 215-unit village gives us a substantial lodging and restaurant business, and also gave us the opportunity to sell individual hotel units for time-share ownership—the Snowdance Vacation Club program, an affiliate of Interval International. This provided a further source of income for re-investing in expensive on-mountain improvements like state-of-the-art snowmaking, grooming, and lifts. If it takes buying an $80-million ski resort for $1 million to be successful, I guess that shows how challenging the ski industry has become.

Success in today's competitive ski world also requires a savvy business approach. Realizing that it was the cost of "too quickly" building the resort village for an upscale "club type of market" that put Ascutney's former owners out of business, the Plausteiners concentrated on making slow-but-steady mountain and village upgrades for a family market. The approach worked and as the resort continued to get better with age, it also became more popular, tripling skier visits in the Plausteiners' first ten years.

Today, future plans include the golf course called for in the Master Plan; hopes are to build it within the next five years. "I don't know if we will ever build all the 600 units provided for in the Master Plan, but I do foresee some additional condos along the golf course when it's built," Plausteiner said.

Mascots Blizzy and Cheddar with friends. AMR

Good to Know

Ascutney is located on Route 44 in Brownsville, six miles from I-91 (Exit 8); about 2 hours from Boston or Hartford; 2.5 from Albany; 4 from NYC.

New for 2005: a 90-seat movie theater that will show family movies; the extension of spring operating hours to 4:30 after March 12 (due to longer, warmer daylight hours).

The old-fashioned ski-week activities (welcome reception, torchlight parades, bonfires, kids movie nights, tubing, and live entertainment) provide lots of fun things to do. Teens enjoy the Bumps Teen Center (second floor in the hotel). Sidewinder's Arcade and Game Room appeals to all ages.

The Brownsville Country Store will deliver groceries to your unit.

Cunningham's Ski Barn offers equipment, clothing, etcetera and is located at the base of the resort village right on the slopes.

Special events include bump contests, terrain park jam, snowboard competitions, Antique Ski Race, annual Ski Ball. Check Website for updates.

Steals and Deals

Ascutney has many special deals, including: a $99 college season pass (includes weekends and holidays); a $22 Sunday afternoon ticket for VT & NH Residents; Two for Tuesdays (2 ski for-the-price-of-1, non-holidays); Boardroom Wednesdays $24 tickets; and Tele-Thursdays (non-holiday) for Telemarkers ($20).

Ascutney

The Advantage (season) Pass is valid Sundays through Fridays with exceptions of a few peak/holiday dates. Early bird purchases save even more.

A Max Card ($89) provides for 50 percent off all full-day lift tickets and group lessons for adults and juniors at any time.

The Midweek Getaway Package (lodging & lifts) starts at $59 pp/night/d.o. for a hotel room; $79 pp/night/d.o. for a one-bedroom condo.

A Slide, Glide, and Ride Introductory package gives first-timers a 2-hour group lesson, rental equipment, and lower-mountain ticket for $79.

Check Website for more specials and details or call/write for a brochure.

All phone numbers below are **area code 802** unless otherwise noted.

Handy Info

Website: www.Ascutney.com
Email: info@ascutney.net
General information: 484-7711
Snow report: 800-243-0011 x 8000
Hours: 9-4 midweek; 8:30-4 weekends/holidays; to 4:30 p.m. after 3/12.
Tickets 2005 Season: Adult $52 midweek, $55 weekends/holidays; Juniors (ages 7-16)/Seniors (65-69): $37/$40; Kids 6 & under with paying adult/Seniors 70+ ski free.

Quick Stats

Season: late November into April, average 140 days.
Average annual snowfall: 160 inches.
Snowmaking capability: 95 percent; 150 acres.
Lifts: 6; 1 express quad, 3 triples, 1 double, 1 surface (carpet).
Uphill lift capacity: 5,850 per hour.
Trails: 56; 150 acres plus 50 acres tree skiing; longest trail 2.5 miles.
Glades: 5, all double diamonds.
Bumps: Gun Barrel, Upper Exhibition, Blind Faith, The Plunge.
Parks: 1 terrain park by the Sunrise chair.
Vertical Drop:
Upper Mountain area: 1,700'
Summit to Village base: 1,800'

Ascutney Learning Center   484-7711 x 3147

Group and private ski and snowboard lessons are offered daily with an emphasis on a fun, positive learning experience. The Classic Ski Week includes a daily lesson. Special clinics are available.

Children's Programs   484-7711

Reservations are strongly recommended for full or half-day options.
Ducklings Childcare: for ages 6 weeks to 6 years (ext. 3132).
Flying Ducks: childcare & introduction to skiing for ages 3-6 (ext. 3132).
Mini Olympians: ages 4-6, ski lesson & indoor play (ext. 3158).
Young Olympians: ski or snowboard program for ages 7-12 (ext. 3158).

Other Things to Do

Skating on the Village pond and tubing by the pond.

The Sports and Fitness Center offers indoor pool, racquetball, saunas, aerobics studio, weight room, personal trainers, massage by appointment.

Nordic skiing and snowshoeing at the re-opened Ascutney Mountain X-C trails; 20 km of X-C and snowshoeing. Also at: Woodstock Touring Center (457-6674) or Wilderness Trails Nordic Ski Area (295-7620) in Quechee.

Windsor: Vermont State Craft Center (647-6729); American Precision Museum (674-5781); Old Constitution House (672-3773). Call for hours.

White River Junction: New England Transportation Institute and Museum (free) at the railroad station; the Tip Top Mall for shops, arts, bookstore.

The Northern Stage Theater (296-7000) has professional theater productions in an historic Opera House with wonderful, intimate setting. Don't miss it!

Quechee: the Antique Mall at Quechee Gorge Village and adjacent Toy and Train Museum for educational fun, walks down memory lane for all ages; the Ottauquechee Valley Winery for tastings, gifts; Vermont Institute of Natural Science and Raptor Center (457-1052) on Route 4. All are wonderful fun!

Norwich: Montshire Museum for science and natural history of northern New England (649-2200); King Arthur Baker's Store (800-827-6836).

Hanover, NH: The Hopkins Center for the Performing Arts (603-646-2422) at Dartmouth College offers concerts, plays, and films.

Dining Out

At the Ascutney Mountain Resort Hotel, there's a range of options from casual to gourmet. Brown's Tavern offers seasonal contemporary fare, wine list, children's menu, and select pub menu from award-winning executive chef Ross Jones. The hotel's Harvest Inn dining room offers relaxed dining, innovative menus, theme buffets, extensive wine list. Biscotti's Café (breakfast and lunch daily) has casual fare for "food on the go."

Windsor: Windsor Station Restaurant (restored railroad station, fine dining); Windsor Pizza Chef; Shepard's Pie Restaurant and Deli (home cooking, dine in or take out, local flavor, and casual).

Springfield: Penelope's (great food, atmosphere), The Hartness House (historic, gracious inn), Shanghai Garden, Morning Star Café.

Perkinsville: the Inn at Weathersfield offers fine dining in an historic inn.

Hartland: Skunk Hollow Tavern (renovated farmhouse with casual pub fare downstairs and fine dining upstairs).

White River Junction: Café Coolidge at the Coolidge Hotel, Como Va (Italian), China Moon (buffet style), and A.J.'s Steakhouse (extensive salad bar, great seafood and big steaks in a casual setting, reasonable prices).

Accommodations

The Ascutney Mountain Resort Hotel and slopeside condos offer the convenience of a village location and an assortment of units: 800-243-0011.

There are B & B's, inns, hotels, motels, and lodges in every price range nearby, including many in Springfield, Windsor, Perkinsville, and White River Junction.

Windsor-Mt. Ascutney Region Chamber of Commerce: 674-5910.

Hartford Area Chamber: 295-7900; 800-295-5451.

Après-ski/Nightlife

Live entertainment Thursdays through Saturdays, some holidays at Brown's Tavern; Main Base Lodge at Ascutney Village every Saturday and Sunday. Bumps Teen Center (second floor in Hotel). Skunk Hollow Tavern offers live music Wednesdays/Fridays. Open Mike Night Thursdays at Firestone's in Quechee. Excellent music and theater in nearby towns.

Summer/Fall

The resort features Flying Ducks adventure camps for kids, hiking, mountain biking, tennis programs, volleyball, horseshoes, miniature golf, family billiard room, and hosts special events and concerts. The popular Future Stars Tennis Camp now includes camps for soccer and lacrosse. Vacation options include golf, Orvis fly-fishing lessons, fishing tours, horseback riding, canoeing, and kayaking with everything pre-arranged and packaged by the resort for the utmost in convenience.

You can also visit the summit via the State Park entrance (off Route 44A) and toll road. Park at a mountain-top lot. Enjoy the views as well as a good hike to the lookout tower and various promontories where hang-gliders take off. The Summit offers truly bucolic mountain and Connecticut River Valley views on a clear day.

Hiking is an historic and still popular summer/fall activity on Mount Ascutney. KL

Our Ascutney Mountain Adventure

Date:

Weather:

Companions:

Where Stayed:

Visit Highlights:

Our Discoveries:

14 Bear Creek

The Clubhouse at the unique Bear Creek Mountain Club.   KL

TRAIL MAP

● Easiest   ■ More Difficult   ◆ Most Difficult

1. Goldbrook ■
2. Roller Coaster ■
3. Coolidge ◆
4. Mogulch ■
5. Tinker ●
6. Pushover ●
7. Upper Salt Ash ◆
8. Lower Salt Ash ■
9. Route 100 ●
10. Chute ●
11. Woodpecker ◆
12. Boulder Bowl ■
13. Lower Woodpecker ■
14. Balancing Rock ■
15. Glades ■
16. Wedel Village ●

Chapter Two

Bear Creek Mountain Club
Country-Club Skiing

When it comes to mountains, Vermont has them all—world class, family fun, and some gems people know little about. Bear Creek Mountain Club, located in Plymouth on Route 100 between the big O and K, is one of the latter.

It's an old-fashioned mountain (the former Round Top) that has been reincarnated to offer some really fine skiing. There are 15 trails, a 1,300-foot vertical, and a nice variety of terrain. There's something else—uncrowded slopes on holidays and weekends. That's due to a membership-club concept with a limited-ticket, advanced-reservation sales policy. But it's also partly due to the area being new and not too many knowing about it.

Like a country club that offers golf memberships, Bear Creek offers club membership and members pay a joining fee and yearly dues for mountain privileges. And like a country club, members are allowed to invite guests. It is also open to the public by reservation when daily capacity is not met. Currently capacity is set at 450 skiers/snowboarders per day and non-members are encouraged to make reservations. (*Ski Chasers* are welcomed!)

The math alone is surprising—450 guests on 52 acres. That works out to twelve people per acre. That's a lot of space and part of the concept the owners are going for—uncrowded slopes! But there's something else. They top it all off with a fine dining experience. That's where the simple but elegant Clubhouse with a formal dining room *and* a casual Tavern come in. Not a base lodge as usual, this facility offers a special atmosphere with food to match.

One of the keys to making the winter country club concept work is that Bear Creek only operates for skiing Thursdays through Sundays—operating costs are held in line even though guests aren't. The limited number of days open and restricted numbers of participants means that trail conditions are apt to be *superb*—not just for the first run of the day, but for the last as well!

Bear Creek is still something of a "best-kept secret" with the new owners in the early stages of a long-range development plan. It's a plan that takes the environment into consideration as well as the desire to offer a top-quality, distinctive experience. They are taking it slow and steady, building a solid membership base, while at the same time making some very nice improvements to the area and overall experience, which includes both snow and food of a higher order.

Bear Creek

A Mountain with a Gourmet Touch

This is a delightful mountain with consistent pitch on long runs that all converge at the base of the summit lift. Even if your family or skiing buddies take a different route, you can still meet at the chair for the 8.5-minute ride to the top. And you get 1,300 feet of vertical for every run!

Beginner/Novice ●

Beginners have some very gentle terrain to learn on at the Pushover slope and rope tow area. From the summit, they have two easy options, Route 100 (●) or Chute (●), which connects to Route 100. Chute is a long meandering trail that gets progressively wider as it melds into Wedel Village (●) for another mile of wide, gentle skiing over rolling terrain back to the lift. A strong novice will find Boulder Bowl (■) doable and a good next step.

Intermediate ■

Intermediates have the most options. Boulder Bowl (■) is a true blue favorite with a consistent pitch but ultra width making for many routes down. Shorter trails like Balancing Rock and the blue Glades (tree terrain) add visual interest, variety, and a chance to enjoy some natural jumps. Goldbrook (■) cruises delightfully with optional dropoffs to practice short-radius turns on but nice width for GS runs, too. Roller Coaster (■) is another story as this narrow trail gives a real thrill ride through the woods, with dips and turns making it fun for the young at heart.

Advanced/Expert ♦

The Upper Salt Ash trail under the lift is straight-down, consistently diamond-pitched with sidehills and short dropoffs that make it the most difficult trail at the area. It eases up to blue for a last-minute cruise to the lift. Coolidge is another diamond with forgiving width that has racer written all over it. Woodpecker (♦) on the other hand, is tight, narrow and steep before letting up at Boulder Bowl.

Bear Creek's mountain experience is enhanced by a distinctive dining experience. Executive Chef Dan Croft, formerly of the Lacota Club in

Geoff Ballou gets air in The Glades. KL

Woodstock, prepares both tavern fare and full gourmet meals. These meals may be enjoyed in the casual Tavern restaurant overlooking the slopes or upstairs in the table-clothed, cheery dining room with views of the mountains. In either place, you will enjoy tasty, freshly prepared food and some unique creations.

The Tavern menu features such items as: baked Brie, Sesame Soy chicken wings, Nachos, shrimp cocktail, Caesar salad, chicken club sandwich, grilled marinated flank steak sandwich, and sirloin burgers.

The Clubhouse Dining Room features appetizers such as shrimp scampi with herbed polenta cake, warm mushroom and goat cheese strudel, chilled apple-smoked duck breast, and fennel and leek ravioli. The dinner entrees ($18-28) might include duck or chicken breast, pork tenderloin with pumpkin dumplings, Cajun spiced sea scallops and shrimp, Atlantic salmon, or Black Angus filet. Like the appetizers and entrees, the salads and desserts are uniquely prepared creations that vary with the season. There is also an extensive wine list.

Sports writer Mort Kail enjoys a banquet and wine tasting at Bear Creek. KL

Past, Present, and Future

Round Top was opened by Paul Goldman in 1964 during the height of the ski boom. Located in a natural snow belt, the mountain was tall and round and afforded trails for all ability levels. Following the 1970s' no snow, no gas, poor economy years, Goldman filed for Chapter 11 bankruptcy in 1974, and his son David purchased the area in 1976.

He and his wife Karen operated Round Top with two chairlifts and a T-Bar and had an old-fashioned big barn-type base lodge. It was run by a family for families and offered an alternative to the bigger areas that charged more for a lift ticket. There was support for ski racing and both race and freestyle camps were held during vacation weeks. Many youngsters trained at Round Top, and the area was well liked by its loyal fans, some of whom bought or built homes along the Wedel Village trail at the northern side of the ski area.

But like so many areas, Round Top struggled again with the difficult 1980 no-snow year. Despite adding snowmaking and offering a number of programs, the owners ran into financial difficulties and filed for bankruptcy in 1981. After another tough year, the mountain closed in 1982.

Round Top lay dormant for many years until a local former ski racer and industry ski rep with experience in mountain operations decided there was potential for an area here if it were to have a special niche. That's how John Neal became vice president/general manager of Bear Creek Mountain Club. He interested David Yurkerwich in the mountain, and seeing the potential, Yurkerwich joined forces with him, forming Plymouth Properties, L.L.C. in 1997. With Yurkerwich as owner and president and investing the necessary capital, planning proceeded.

They saw the mountain as having a series of peaks that skiing could be expanded to. They also saw a potential for offering a comfortable, relaxing environment, combining the qualities of a first-class experience with a protected mountain setting. They hired specialists in resort development and planned for ski area renewal and expansion, a village of homes, and a clubhouse that architecturally resembles a Vermont home.

Since the mountain was "nothing but weeds," they installed a double chair, revitalized the trails, put in snowmaking on two trails, and replaced the dilapidated base lodge with the new Clubhouse. The area opened for skiing on a test basis in 1999 and for weekends and holidays in 1999-2000. For the 2001 season, they went to Thursday through Sunday operations. In 2002, they hired a professional chef and opened for dining on a year-round basis. The restaurant is open to the public and is available for private functions as well.

For the 2003-04 season, a gentle handle tow was installed on a learning slope for children and first-timers, and Christopher Marks was hired to head the Learning Center. (He hails from Colorado where he spent two years teaching at Copper Mountain and worked with PSIA to develop testing materials for instructors.) A Kids Cub House program is offered on weekends and holidays for three to nine-year-olds. It incorporates ski or snowboard lessons along with sledding and games and operates out of the Cub House, which has an indoor play area and an outdoor learning slope.

Plans are to expand the mountain in conjunction with demand for the area and the sale of homes. Slopeside mountain homes are being built, and the owners envision another four lifts, a 130-acre trail network with 100 percent snowmaking, and a village of 'Vermont vernacular' homes that will match the distinctive skiing experience.

Family Fun

I took two of my grown sons and one of their friends to Bear Creek on a February Saturday, and they couldn't quite believe it. They had grown up skiing Killington and Okemo and didn't know the area existed as it was closed during the years of their youth.

What they discovered as adults was an uncrowded mountain with terrain they thoroughly enjoyed. They thought it was great to ski on to the chair without a wait. They didn't mind a slower pace of uphill transport, enjoying conversations on the chair. Having the trails to themselves (there were a few families skiing but we always had our own space) was delightful, and they quickly got into exploring the varied terrain, including some glades and the huge boulder known as Balancing Rock.

One of the highlights was the discovery of Roller Coaster. I had been skiing with John Neal and when we caught up again, they exclaimed, "You gotta do this trail with us. We've never seen anything like it."

Roller Coaster snakes down the mountain with switchbacks like I hadn't seen since the roads of Italy and Austria (where the bus drivers had to blink their lights before making the turn because they hogged the entire two lanes).

Be sure to catch the scenic Balancing Rock at the intersection of Lower Woodpecker and Chute. KL

While they cruised this "easy" natural-snow-only run, made difficult by its narrowness, sharp turns, and fast conditions, I found myself occasionally snowplowing. It is a definite roller-coaster ride. For them, it was a novelty and they loved it. For me, it was memory lane of skiing in the fifties!

They also discovered and commented on the unique and more upscale Clubhouse with flowers in the restrooms, tile floors, mahogany doors, and a cherry locker room for club members.

Their break for a rest, food, and libation at the Tavern Room was another uncommon experience with wait service and food cooked to order. They got more than they expected with plates heaping full of Nachos and sirloin burgers accompanied by handcut fries. It was all I could do to tear them away from the table and back up on the mountain for some last runs. They definitely got into the civilized aspect of Bear Creek!

On another visit after a winter storm, I skied with a friend on conditions so good (we got 'first tracks" on a Thursday morning) that we actually took a first run on Salt Ash. Although steep, it was pure heaven and an ego boost to have such a perfectly groomed trail to ourselves.

From first turns on beginner hill to stem and traverse on Boulder Bowl in 3 hours.

Since it was a Demo Day, we demoed skis and ran every trail. After a lunch on gourmet pizza and salad in the upstairs dining room, we skied some more and by 3:30 my legs gave out. My friend was so enamored that she took a last run alone. A recreational racer who is younger than *moi*, she admitted I had been right to quit as she barely made it through that last run—an admission that this mountain offers a full day of challenge that can tire anyone out.

On a February vacation day, a sister and her son skied with me. Geoffrey loved the Glades and was all over the mountain, finding lots of good jumps. He ate a huge lunch, a plateful of spareribs that disappeared so fast that we never even got a taste. Roberta marvelled at both having the hill to ourselves and the exceptional deals on Thursdays and Fridays (see tickets section).

On a warm, spring day, I introduced another sister who hadn't skied in 25 years to Bear Creek. We got her short 150 cm shaped skis at the First Stop Ski Shop, and she loved them. We took two runs on the beginner area, and the lift attendant suggested Boulder Bowl next as it was freshly groomed and she was doing controlled wedge turns. So up to the top we went to a blue trail. She quickly progressed to stem turns and good parallel traverses.

She loved the area, commenting, "When you're nervous to start with for your first time and then you have your own private mountain with such good snow conditions, you don't have to worry and that made me comfortable and more relaxed. It really took the pressure off, and I had a great time," she said, telling me I had chosen "the perfect place" to get her hooked on skiing again!

Good to Know

NASTAR Racing is offered every Saturday and Sunday and during Holiday weeks starting at 1:00 p.m. on the Wedel Village trail.

You will not find a rental shop at the Clubhouse. However, there is one just four miles up the road (First Stop Ski and Snowboard Shop in West Bridgewater) that accommodates Bear Creek's members and guests so not having equipment shouldn't be a problem if you plan ahead.

You will find delightful slopes, children's program, and private lessons for all ability levels. And bargain skiing on Thursdays and Fridays!

Visit www.bearcreekclub.com for details on club membership or new townhomes or stop in and check out the displays and plans.

Because ticket sales are limited, guests and members need to call ahead to make reservations so as not to be disappointed (802-672-4242).

Phone numbers below are **area code 802** unless otherwise noted.

Handy Info

Website: www.bearcreekclub.com
Email: bearcreek@vermontel.net
General information: 672-4242
Snow report: 672-4242
Hours: Thursdays – Sundays, all Holiday Weeks: 9 a.m. to 4 p.m.
Tickets for the 2005 season:
Thursday Race Day Special: $35 lift ticket, 2 timed runs included. Also, $1 drafts, 10 % off Tavern menu. Optional racing at 12 noon.
Fridays Lift & Lunch: a $35 lift ticket includes a hot buffet lunch!
Saturdays and all holidays: Adult $75; Junior $50.
Sundays: Morning Solution (9 a.m. to 12:30 p.m.) $30; all day $50.
Adults are 18 and up; Juniors 7-17; six and under ski free with a parent.

Quick Stats

Season: Late December to late March.
Average annual snowfall: 250 inches.
Snowmaking capability: 30 percent; 15 acres.
Lifts: 2; 1 double to summit; 1 handle tow for lower beginner area.
Uphill lift capacity: 550 per hour.
Trails: 15; 51 acres; longest trail 2 miles.
Glades: 1, The Glades.
Bumps: 1, Woodpecker.
Vertical Drop: Summit to base area: 1,300′

Learning Center   672-4242

Private lessons for skiers, snowboarders, and Telemarkers of all ages, abilities, and comfort levels are available upon request during weekends and holidays from 9 a.m. to 4 p.m. Reservations encouraged. Private lessons are predicated on the philosophy that individual attention is the key to an enjoyable, successful learning experience.

Children's Programs   672-4242

Kids Club House: ages 3-9; lessons and indoor/outdoor program (sledding, games) on weekends and holidays.

Other Things to Do

X-C skiing and snowshoeing at Hawk Inn and Resort in Plymouth (672-3811) or Okemo Valley Nordic Center (228-1396) or Mountain Meadows in Killington (775-7077).

Killington Snowmobile Tours (422-2121) offers guided tours (just four miles up the road). Tours are customized by ability levels.

Sleigh rides, ice skating, indoor/outdoor pools, fitness center, and massage are available nearby at Hawk Inn and Mountain Resort (also open to the public). Shopping in Ludlow, Killington, Rutland, Bridgewater Mill Mall, Woodstock—country stores, art galleries, craft shops, boutiques, made-on-premises furniture stores, etcetera.

Area attractions: Long Trail Brewery (Route 4 in Bridgewater), Green Mountain Sugarhouse (Route 100 in Ludlow), and Calvin Coolidge Homestead and Historic Site (Route 100A in Plymouth).

Dining Out

The Clubhouse Dining Room and Tavern offer both fine dining and casual pub fare. Nearby are: Black River Tavern at Hawk; Back Behind Saloon (an authentic railroad car with rustic interior at corner of Routes 4 and 100); the Corners Inn in Bridgewater Corners; Echo Lake Inn in Tyson; and a host of eateries in Killington and Ludlow. Take-out is available at the Plymouth Country Store with special orders accepted (672-3326).

Accommodations   672-4242

At the mountain, there are privately owned chalets, some of which may be rented. In Plymouth, there are several inns and B & B's as well as the 4-star Hawk Mountain Inn and Resort, which offers free shuttle service to Bear Creek and a health and fitness center along with indoor and outdoor heated pools and other outdoor activities.

Après-ski/Nightlife

Visit the Tavern at the Clubhouse and Black River Tavern at Hawk for après-ski libations. For more active nightlife, check out Okemo and Killington listings.

Summer/Fall

The Clubhouse is open from mid-May until late October for dining Thursday through Saturdays. It is also available for reunions, weddings, and other special functions.

End-of-day snow, still soft and groomed. KL

Our Bear Creek Adventure

Date:

Weather:

Companions:

Where Stayed:

Visit Highlights:

Our Discoveries:

24 Bolton Valley

From left to right: Ricker Peak, Vista Peak, and the Timberline area. A Nordic Center gives access to cross-country and snowshoeing trails and backcountry terrain, and a Sports Center offers tennis, swimming, exercise room, and more.

Chapter Three

Bolton Valley
A Planned Community Resort

Most ski areas begin to wind down at three in the afternoon. As winter's early darkness descends on the trails and the cold settles in, many skiers and riders begin to head for the warmth of home or après-ski fun.

Not at Bolton Valley. It lights up and livens up—literally.

That's because the area offers night skiing. And being that it is located just seven miles from I-89 between Burlington and Montpelier (two of the state's largest cities), Bolton Valley Resort attracts Vermonters of all ages, some for club racing, some for the kids' after-school ski program, and some just for the fun of "mountain recreation" after work or college classes.

However, with its picturesque, self-contained Village set in a bowl of 5,200 acres of mountain wilderness, Bolton Valley is also a destination area. You'll find out-of-state visitors attracted by the convenience of a charming Village tucked away in the mountains as well as in-staters who choose to stay over for a mini-vacation.

The kid- and adult-friendly Resort Village sports a hotel complex with shops, restaurants, and offices; a base lodge with the usual amenities; condominiums and townhouses; a large Sports Center; and a complete Nordic Center—all within walking distance of the lifts. That's because Bolton Valley was conceived as a self-contained mountain resort and was developed with base-of-the-lifts lodging from its very first season. So the loyalists who grew up loving the area come back with their families and the locals join them, making Bolton one of Vermont's community gems that hums with the sounds of school kids, adult league racers, and families from near and far.

The emphasis on being family-friendly doesn't mean this is a small mountain. Nor is it a pushover. There's a 1,634-foot vertical and a diversity of terrain that spills from three separate but interconnected peaks. Trails range from classic New England to broad boulevards, double diamonds to gentle greens. There's learning terrain for first-timers, glades for all, and halfpipe and terrain parks for freeriders and big air fans.

Bolton Valley is also Vermont's latest "comeback area." Like others that fell on hard times in the 1990s and struggled through bankruptcies and changes in ownership, Bolton has bounced back and remains independently owned and mid-sized, bucking the "bigger-is-better" trend and retaining its distinctive character as a "community resort" in the mountains.

Under owner/operator Bob Fries, who has thirty-plus years experience in the ski industry and confidence that a conservative approach will work, Bolton is being positioned as "a nice, friendly, affordable family area that can serve the greater community." He sees knowledgeable, experienced management and skier support from surrounding communities as key to Bolton's success as a "niche" area. That support was evident during his first two seasons and made them successful ones despite being record cold years. The area's long history as a good ski mountain, its reputation for year-round outdoor recreation, and Fries' knowledgeable leadership are all credited for the turnaround.

How It All Came About

In 1922, Edward Bryant, a native New Yorker, conservationist, and pioneer ski enthusiast, purchased 10,000 acres of mountainous wilderness in the Town of Bolton from the American Brass Company. The famous Otto Schneibs helped him cut ski trails, and Bryant formed the Bolton Mountain Club. Club members hiked to the top of Bolton Mountain to "earn their turns," as was the custom in skiing's formative years. Bryant began to plan for lifts in 1946 but died before he could secure financial backing. The land was subsequently sold to a lumber company.

In 1964, Roland DesLauriers sold 11 acres of his family farm for an I-89 interchange (site of the Sheraton Hotel and Howard Johnson in South Burlington) and purchased an 8,000-acre tract in Bolton from the lumber company. It was on this tract that his son Ralph saw potential for a high-elevation Alpine Village and ski area. In 1964, Ralph spent his life savings of $10,000 on a five-year master plan and borrowed $1 million to start the Bolton Valley Ski and Summer Resort.

The state built the 4.2-mile access road up through the steep woods, using tractors to haul up the heavy trucks. In 1965, nine trails and three liftlines were cut and in 1966, three double chairs, a base lodge, ski shop, and a 24–room lodge were built. The resort opened in December 1966.

Bolton was home hill to acrobatic "acroskier," free-skiing pioneer, and "Swiss blitz" Art Furrer, who trained a squad of local Bolton youngsters to be the nation's first 'acrosquad' in 1967. Acroskiing was the next step in the freestyle progression that started with Othmar Sneider's Royal Christie, Stein Eriksen's flip, and Tom Leroy and Hermann Goellner's double somersaults and backward flips. Furrer developed and popularized such maneuvers as the Charleston, the 360° Tip Roll, the Stepover, and the Airborne Helicopter. His early presence at Bolton helped to "put the area on the map." With that history, it was little wonder that Bolton became a training ground for America's extreme skiers extraordinaire Rob and Eric DesLauriers, sons of the owner.

The first townhouses were built in 1968 and tennis courts were added in 1969. The area continued to grow with more housing and a fourth chairlift (to the top of Ricker Peak), an ice rink, outdoor heated pool, night skiing, trails, and snowmaking (1976). The Sports and Conference Center was finished in 1983, and the trail-connected Timberline area debuted in 1987. By 1988, Bolton was winning accolades as a family destination area, ranking seventh out of the top-one-hundred national ski resorts in a *SKI Magazine* poll.

But in the 1990s, like many ski areas affected by weather blips and rising prices, to say nothing of a lingering national economic recession, DesLauriers encountered five difficult years. After struggling through them, he had to call it quits in 1996. After thirty years at the helm of his mountain, DesLauriers was the third-longest continuing ski-area founder/operator in the state. [Only Bromley founder/operator Fred Pabst ran a privately-owned area longer (33 years). Killington founder Preston Leete Smith was at the helm of the publicly owned Killington for 38 seasons, the Vermont record.]

Although it was a sad time, it was also a testament to what the DesLauriers family had achieved that others came along and attempted to revive the mountain (Mason Dwinell, 1998–1999; and Ned Hamilton, 2000-2002). Unfortunately, they were unable to surmount some difficult obstacles.

In the late 1990s, Bob Fries, a former president of Breckenridge, Waterville Valley, the New York Olympic Regional Development Authority, and Stratton Mountain Resort, set out to buy an area. A fortuitous meeting with the Vermont Land Trust, which wanted to see Bolton's remaining 5,200 acres preserved as a recreational and environmental resource, led to his purchase of Bolton Valley.

Fries signed papers to buy the resort in 2002 and closed on the purchase on January 31, 2003. His management team includes individuals with over 200 years of combined experience in the ski industry. In addition to "working with good mountain people," Fries' strategy is to "focus on providing affordable family skiing and riding that is memorable for its excellent customer service, cleanliness, and value. Carefree, affordable fun will be the hallmark of the Bolton Valley Resort experience," he said.

The Mountain

Bolton has four distinct skiing areas, three of which funnel back to the main Village/base area and a fourth that is connected to the main base via long ski trails. To the north is Ricker Peak with a 1,030-foot vertical and an assortment of trails that are primarily blue above and green below. The chair ends below the 3,400-foot summit at 3,130 feet. Vista Peak is predominantly black-diamond on the upper mountain. The lower section offers greens and blues that are served by the Mid-Mountain and Snowflake chairs. Timberline is a delightful complex with long trails, quad lift, base lodge, and parking lot. With tickets sold here on weekends and holidays, it makes a good second entry that gets visitors to the slopes faster. All areas are connected by trails.

Bolton is unique among Vermont's major areas in that it was one of the first to offer night skiing and continues to offer night skiing on 12 trails for all ability levels. The area also keeps other trails open later in the spring when the days are longer, enabling a midweek skier to experience both the quiet solitude of the mountain by early day and the lively buzz that begins mid-afternoon. The lighted trails are located on upper and lower Vista Peak and the Practice Slope area, all served by 3 chairs and a handle tow.

Advanced/Expert ♦ ♦♦

Vista Peak (top ski elevation 3,103') offers several upper-mountain expert trails with the steepest pitches at the area. Show-Off (♦) is bumped up, natural, and tough. Hard Luck (♦) is a wide steep with 40-degree pitch and good turns while Spillway (♦) is a wide heart stopper that humbles with a consistent pitch of 45 degrees.

The Devils Playground (♦♦) is the hardest glade on the mountain while Preacher, TNT, and Vermont 2000 are single diamonds that provide some narrow, twisty steeps—some with bumps.

Spellbinder (♦) is a run worth checking out off the Timberline midstation. With bumps and deep snow, it can set you on your backside in no time. Lost Boyz (♦♦) offers woods skiing at Timberline, while Tattletale (♦) is a nice wide steep that turns into a blue cruiser on Lower Tattletale.

From the top of Ricker Peak, Fanny Hill (♦) and Bolton Outlaw (♦) provide some challenging sections before becoming or spilling into blues. They make great "next tracks" after warm-ups on Peggy Dow (■) and Wilderness (■).

Intermediate ■

Ricker Peak (ski elevation 3,130') offers a range of low- to high-intermediate trails. The northernmost trail, Peggy Dow (■), off the top of the Wilderness Double, affords great views of Mount Mansfield; there's also an entry to the 12-mile backcountry trek to the Trapp Family Lodge off the top section of this trail. Peggy Dow offers a nice warm-up cruise along winding, undulating terrain. Wilderness, Coyote, and Cougar and lower Fanny Hill provide more blues with all spilling into nice, easy green schusses toward the bottom.

The Upper Crossover (■) provides a glorious, albeit in some places narrow, ridge run to connectors with the Upper Vista chair. Off the top of Vista Peak, Cobrass is a great classic blue that twists and turns, widens and narrows, and undulates as it follows the contours of the mountain. It shouldn't be missed! It

It leads to the Snowflake lift area, back to the Vista lift, or to trails that go to Timberline. The Snowflake chair serves a nice assortment of gentle and shorter blues for lower intermediates.

The Timberline Quad has a "mid-station" about three quarters up the mountain, offering access to two of the nicest blues you could ever hope to perfect a carve on, appropriately named Twice As Nice (a true-blue meanderer) and Showtime (straight down, mega wide, and under the chair) for spectacular GS cruising.

Off the top of Timberline Quad, Sure Shot (■) is a cruiser that joins up with Timberline Run (●) for a fast schuss to the chair. Brandywine (♦) is difficult on its top section but is wide enough to be forgiving for a strong or upper-level intermediate who aspires to improve. Its lower half becomes a blue cruiser. Tattletale is similarly black and blue and also spills into Timberline Run for the return to the chair.

Bolton Valley owner Bob Fries on the scenic Peggy Dow trail.   KL

Novice/Beginner ●

The main base area features a Mitey Mite Slope and handle tow for 'never-evers' and beginners at a dedicated (secluded) learning area so that mountain schussers can't come speeding by and unnerve learners.

The Mid-Mountain chair offers a variety of greens, with Deer Run and Bear Run to Sprig of Pine fun favorites. The Enchanted Forest Kid's Park features easy elements for younger and beginner tricksters.

Novices can also ride the upper Vista Chair to the top of this mountain area, enjoy the view, and take Sherman's Pass (●) to the bottom with access to Upper and Lower Glades (■)—trails with wide open trees that are manageable for advanced novices/aspiring intermediates—or take Lower VT 200 (●) to the chair base and connect with lower mountain greens like Deer Run.

Timberline Run (●) is accessible off the top of the Mid-Mountain and Snowflake chairs and provides a long cruise to the Timberline Quad. From the Quad's mid-station, Woods Hole (●) connects to Lower Tattletale, which is a wide blue and doable for strong, advanced novices who want a taste of a little steeper slope before hitting easy Timberline Run again. Off the top of Timberline Quad, Villager (●) is a delightful, long trail with pretty scenery back to the main base area or to Timberline for another long run to the Quad.

Community Sensations

Bolton Valley is unusual in that it has the steepest access road (not to worry, school buses make it every day) of any ski area in Vermont. What is neat about this approach is the feel of embarking on a real mountain adventure, especially after cruising on a modern highway!

After climbing for four miles, you come to the Alpine Village at the end of the road. The 2,100-foot elevation makes Bolton one of the highest base elevations in Vermont. What's particularly nice is that the buildings are architecturally interesting but scaled to fit in with the mountains, not dominate them, so you really feel like you've left civilization for an Alpine experience.

Once on the mountain, every liftie (Bolton speak for lift attendants) greets you. The trails offer a surprising mix of pleasures and surprises—steeps that intimidate (Hard Luck and Spillway) and views that take your breath away. One of the great things about this mountain is that you will suddenly come around a corner and there before you lies an expansive panorama of Lake Champlain, Camel's Hump, Mount Mansfield, or Whiteface in the Adirondacks.

A tour of the main and northern sections of the mountain left me struck by the beauty of the views, the delight of classic trails, and the dedication of its new owner. It was a most memorable moment when, while skiing with Bob Fries, he told about remarking to his family on their first lift ride after the purchase, "Well, this is really ours now." It was just the right touch of pride and joy in ownership that says here is someone who will be a good steward for this recreational resource.

It was a passion for the sport and mountains that I also saw when skiing with Mark Aiken, grandson of Vermont Governor and Senator George Aiken. Mark had previously returned to Vermont from out West to become Bolton's

The Bolton Valley Village has a secluded location at the end of the road. BVR

Ski School Director. He told of being drawn by "Vermont's pull" on his spirit as well as a desire to help this mountain achieve its rightful place among the many wonderful ski areas in this state. His comments were echoed by the people I met on the lifts. Most were locals who evinced a strong loyalty and appreciation for the area in what was tantamount to an unsolicited advertisement for the mountain.

With my own delightful experience skiing Bolton, I found myself wishing my now grown boys could have been with me to revisit the area we last skied in 1990, when we stayed in one of the condos for a weekend.

What was particularly memorable for me then—besides the fantastic dinner we enjoyed fireside in the hotel—was the Timberline Quad that enabled all four of us to ride together and the sunny trails which offered just the right mix of variety and challenge for all of us. I also remembered a great ski-school lesson on foot steering. Being able to park the car and walk everywhere and let the boys visit the Sports Center while hubby and I went to dinner was the height of comfort and convenience.

That convenience is still there, but there are more trails lit at night now and more snowmaking. Most importantly, it is still a nice mid-sized resort that exudes a cheerful friendliness and a feeling of down-home comfort.

As I drove down the long access road at 4:15, I saw more cars going up than I had seen that Friday morning. It was somehow appropriate that so many would get to keep the mountain company for a few more hours.

Good To Know

Bolton Valley Resort is located in Bolton, Vermont, just 4 miles from I-89. There isn't a direct exit off I-89 for Bolton Valley so you take Route 2 from either Waterbury Exit 10 (if approaching from the south) or Richmond Exit 11 (if coming from the north). It's an easy 4 miles to the Access Road but be sure to watch for it. The area is 17 miles from the Burlington International Airport; 200 miles from Boston, 210 from Hartford, 300 from NYC.

Timberline has its own base lodge and parking, so consider it for day trips if you don't need other services like daycare, which are available in the Village.

Visit the Wilderness Chair area and Fanny Hill for early morning sun and for late day sun, catch Rock Garden, Cobrass, and Sherman's Pass.

Off Piste happens from Bolton Valley's lift system. The routes and challenges are endless; the scenery awe inspiring. (See Appendix D, page 302.)

Kid's Night Out at the Childcare Center on Saturdays includes dinner (usually pizza), crafts, and a movie for ages 3 – 12 years, from 5 - 9 p.m.

The Bryant Cabin and the Buchanan Lodge are accessible from the Bolton Valley Nordic trail system and can be rented for summer and winter camping.

Bolton has a large "after-school ski program" with skiing under the lights for about 1,000 Vermont school kids each year.

Wednesdays' Night Rider Series/Rail Jam features fun and competition in Bolton's Terrain Park and half-pipe. Thursday nights are corporate race nights with team competitions.

Steals and Deals

Bolton's unique All-Inclusive Package includes 3 meals, room, skiing (downhill or cross-country), rentals, and even a lesson if you need one for $139 pp, d.o. weekdays/ $149 weekends.

First-Timer Special: Teens $55, Adults $65; for lesson and lift ticket (optional equipment rental, more); lessons at 9 a.m. and 12 noon.

There are discounts on multi-day lessons and tickets when purchased in advance. See the Website or call for details.

Women's Wednesdays: coffee, free lessons, camaraderie—all for $29. Childcare in the nursery (reservations required) is $15 extra.

Tele-Thursdays: $35 includes demos, lessons and a ticket.

Stay & Ski Free: stay in a hotel room midweek (non-holidays) for $79 pp, d.o. or for $89 pp, d.o. on weekends (non-holidays) and ski free!

All phone numbers below are **area code 802** unless otherwise noted.

Handy Info

Website: www.boltonvalley.com
Email: info@boltonvalley.com
General information: 434-3444 or 1-877-926-5866
Snow report: 434-7669
Hours: 9 a.m. – 9 p.m. Wednesdays – Saturdays.
   9 a.m. – 4 p.m. Sundays – Tuesdays.
Tickets 2005 season: Adults $44 midweek/$52 weekends/holidays; Teens (13-17)/College Students with ID $30/$40; Juniors (7-12) & Seniors (70+): $30/ $36; Ages six and under ski free. Night 4-9 p.m. Adults $28/$30; Teens/College $22/$24; Juniors/Seniors $20/$20.

Quick Stats

Season: Thanksgiving to April, average 135 days.
Average annual snowfall: 270 inches.
Snowmaking capability: 60 percent; 100 acres.
Lifts: 6, 1 quad, 4 doubles, 1 surface (handle tow).
Uphill lift capacity: 6,000 per hour.
Trails: 60; 165 acres; 17 miles; longest 2.5 miles.

Glades: 12, Devils Playground, Preacher, Lost Boz, and more.
Bumps: Show Off, Hard Luck, Spillway, Outlaw, Spellbinder.
Parks/Pipe: 3 parks, 1 pipe; Lighted Terrain Park with halfpipe; snowdeck park; Enchanted Forest Kids Park.
Vertical Drop:
- Ricker Peak area: 1,030'
- Ricker Peak to Timberline base: 1,634'
- Timberline area: 1,120'
- Vista Peak area: 1,003'

Ski & Snowboard School   434-3444

Group and private ski or snowboard lessons are available for adults and teens either alone or with equipment and/or lifts package. Night Group lessons (all ages) must be reserved 48 hours in advance.

Children's Programs   434-3444 x 1078

Honey Bear Childcare Center; ages 6 weeks – 6 years; structured activities and games, indoor and outdoor play, solid food lunch provided. Reservations required. 434-3444 x 1060 or 434-6866.

Ski & Play: 3 years & up, childcare and ski lesson, full or half day.

Mountain Explorers: ages 4-12 (skiers), ages 6-12 (snowboarders). Ski /ride instruction and mountain exploring.

Ridge Runners: Saturday or Sunday season-lesson tickets for ages 4-12.

Recreational ski racing program for kids ages 5-16.

Other Things to Do

The Bolton Nordic Center offers 50 km of backcounry trails and 15 km of X-C, skate skiing, and snowshoe trails; also "Doggie Trails." Rentals and instruction are available for classic, skate, and Telemark skiing. Special events schedule (races, waxing clinics, etcetera). There are several guided-snowshoe tour options, including one for children.

Different backcountry ski tours are offered daily and by appointment. Inquire about the unique Bolton to Trapps Traverse,

Cross-country and snowshoe treks to Bryant Cabin are popular outings. BVR

an 11.8 mile guided, cross-country ski that leaves the ski area and ends up at the Trapp Family Lodge in Stowe. This route goes through some absolutely stunning terrain and affords glorious views of the mountains. Great fun for the truly adventurous. The tour with guide and transportation back to Bolton is $40.

The Sports Center offers: tennis courts, exercise room, tanning, indoor pool, Jacuzzi, sauna, lounge, a large screen TV, conference space for up to 500 people.

Nearby, check out: the famous Ben and Jerry's Ice Cream Factory and tours plus the Cold Hollow Cider Mill in Waterbury; the Shelburne Museum in Shelburne; Champlain Mill Mall in Winooski for unique shops and restaurants; Burlington Church Street Marketplace (outdoor pedestrian mall); and in Montpelier (15 miles east of Bolton) the state capitol and Vermont Historical Society Museum.

Dining Out

In the Resort Village: Bailey's (creative American cuisine); Fireside Restaurant (American bistro); James Moore Tavern (classic pub menu); Deli & Grocery; Mountainside Food Court. On the access road: Black Bear Inn.

Accommodations   434-3444 x 1050   877-926-5866

The Inn at Bolton and walk-to-the-lifts condos offer traditional hotel rooms, studios, and one, two, three and four bedroom units. Total bed base is 1500 at the mountain. Accommodations are also available at Black Bear Inn on the access road and in nearby Waterbury, Montpelier, and Burlington.

Après-ski/Nightlife

Fireside Restaurant, James Moore Tavern, and activities at the Sports Center. There are clubs with live music in Burlington and Winooski. The Flynn Theater in Burlington features excellents shows and concerts.

Summer/Fall

Bolton Valley offers a variety of summer camps for kids, special events, and adult activities. The area also hosts weddings, family reunions, conferences, and seminars. There is mountain hiking on the numerous Alpine and Nordic trails, swimming, Disc Golf, an Adventure Center, and tennis (indoors and out). The resort provides a good base of operations from which to explore Vermont's lakes, rivers, Long Trail (which passes through Bolton's property), attractions, and cities. Bolton Valley is a beautiful foliage spot.

Our Bolton Valley Adventure

Date:

Weather:

Companions:

Where Stayed:

Visit Highlights:

Our Discoveries:

36   Bromley

The Bromley Mountain base area provides a convenient, centralized location for all activities and services with the base lodge, children's center, lifts, and Sun Lodge hotel (to the right on ski slope) within close proximity of each other. The "Sun Mountain" is home to many generations of families and has an active Junior Program for local children.

Chapter Four

Bromley Mountain
Family Fun in the Sun

Bromley Mountain is one of Vermont's oldest and best-loved family ski areas. Started by ski-industry pioneer Fred Pabst in 1938, the ski area is located on Route 11 in Peru and lies in the famed Green Mountain snowbelt.

Pabst was the first Vermont ski-area operator to cater to families. Arriving skiers were greeted by a big red base lodge graced by international flags and then enjoyed sunny, south facing slopes that were buffed to smooth finishes. Pabst stressed good ski instruction, hiring qualified teachers to make sure beginners learned well. He even made a day on the slopes manageable for parents by offering childcare in the first slopeside nursery.

Today, a new owner operates Bromley but that same genuine family friendliness and helpfulness still prevails. Even while modernizing with terrain parks, highspeed quad, and more expert terrain, Bromley has retained its focus on service through innovative children's programs and its modern learning center. Bromley's warmth has as much to do with a sunny disposition as it does with the mountain's rare southern exposure.

As you approach the ski area, colorful flags still greet you at the airport-styled unloading zone. The parking lot is on the other side of Route 11 so after unloading passengers and gear, you drive under the highway through a tunnel and hop a shuttle back to the base area. On weekends and holidays, valet parking is available, and the Host and Courtesy Staffs greet and assist arriving families. They answer questions, give directions, carry skis, or help get little ones to daycare or ski programs. Hosts also give complimentary mountain tours.

The base area is convenient and compact. It is laid out with the Daycare Center to the left of a broad, heated stairway, and the base lodge a snowball's throw to the right. Wisely, the rustic character of the original base lodge has been preserved as it was expanded over the years, and a real wood fire still warms you when you take a break or eat lunch in the newly reorganized main cafeteria.

The new section of the lodge has two eateries on the second floor: the Wild Boar Tavern, a modern, cheery sit-down, wait-service restaurant and lounge; and the Deli for quick self-service. Downstairs is the new Bart Adaptive Sports

Center for people with physical disabilities or other special needs. (Bromley has long served skiers with disabilities.) The Center is named for Bart Ruggiere, an avid skier who learned to ski at Bromley as a youngster and was a Bromley regular before his death as a victim of 9-11. That Ruggiere's family and friends chose to honor him through donations that made this center possible reflects on the family values that make Bromley special.

The "Sun Mountain"

Bromley Mountain has a unique, large rounded summit from which trails flow off in every direction, affording wonderful 360-degree views and the feeling that you are on top of the world at this 3,284-foot pinnacle.

On a blustery winter day with snow coming down, you feel nature in her fury, and, as you quickly leave the exposed summit, you are glad for the protection of the trails. On a sunshiny, balmy day, you can see forever and play "king of the world" as you tackle the mountain's challenge.

The trails that spill off the summit range from classic narrow and winding New England style to straight-down wide boulevards, smooth to bumps, groomed to ungroomed, easy to expert. What's particularly nice is that there is some separation so that advanced and expert skiers are not always emptying onto beginner areas. First-timers have their own learning areas and experts their own black diamond complex with a quad and glades to push their limits. There are also lots of long top-to-bottom intermediate trails with a 1,334-foot vertical served by the highspeed quad, and trail signage is very good.

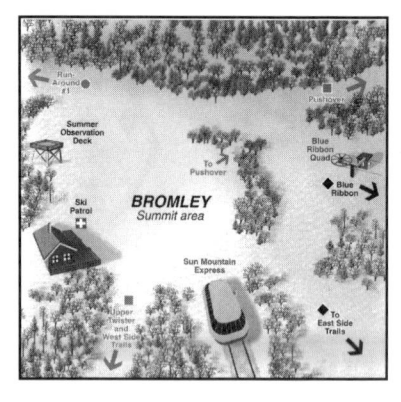

Beginner/Novice ●

Bromley has several excellent beginner areas. Toddler terrain is served by a carpet lift to the left of the Sun Express Quad. The Beginners Circle learning program utilizes two handle tows at a dedicated Learning Center away from the main flow of traffic. The Lower East Meadow (●) is a beginner slope *par excellence*. It is wide and gentle with associated trails for variety and is served by the mild-mannered, low-to-the-ground East Meadow chairlift.

Going to the top of the mountain is always a thrill, and Bromley's layout allows novices (beginners with turning and stopping ability) to enjoy this experience on a wonderful 2.5-mile, scenic run back to the base via Runaround to Lower Boulevard (both ●).

Intermediate ■

There is a wide assortment of intermediate trails (ranging from low to high intermediate) to the west side of the Sun Mountain Express Quad (left as you look up the mountain). Upper Twister has some steep pitches but is broad and forgiving before turning into a nice cruiser under the lift. Trails like Sunset Pass, Upper Thruway, Shincracker, Upper Boulevard, and Spring Trail offer an interesting mix of narrow and wide blue runs and 1,334 feet of vertical to the Sun Quad.

Off to the far eastern side of the Sun Quad, there is a classic old trail called Pushover (■) that curls around the back side of the mountain before descending in a roller coaster ride that winds through the woods—a sure kid pleaser and still a thrill for good skiers. Don't miss it!

The Sun Double Chair stops short of the summit and offers access to Twister, Liftline and Upper East Meadow among other trails, all blues that offer a variety of challenge with enough steeps here and there to invite aspirers to go for it and get better. The Alpine Chair goes halfway up the mountain and offers access to blues on both sides; Upper East Meadow (■) is a dancer's delight.

Advanced/Expert ♦ ♦♦

The Blue Ribbon Quad serves the black diamond area that lies on the east side of the Upper Mountain. Trails here drop down off the summit for 1,100 feet of heart-pumping vertical back to the chair. Havoc (♦) and Stargazer (♦) offer ungroomed terrain with bumps, and Avalanche Glade (♦) offers steep tree skiing. Blue Ribbon and Corkscrew are popular, widish groomed black diamonds with consistent pitch. Pabst Peril (♦) and Pabst Panic (♦) are narrow for a distance before joining together on a wider cruise to the lift. Sunder (♦) provides a challenging race training course and No Name Chute, Avalanche, and Little Dipper round out the diversity of diamonds at this area.

The only expert terrain to the west of the Express Quad is The Plunge (♦♦), which offers truly steep tree skiing for experts who are part mountain goat.

Parks/Pipe

For tricksters and those who like to get airborne, The Halo Freestyle park on Lord's Prayer slope, which is serviced by a T-Bar, offers BlueJ Rails, a steep 400-foot halfpipe with 17-foot walls, and various snow features. Located one hill over on the Plaza slope (served by a double chairlift) is the Unforgiven Boardercross course, which features hips, spines, and tabletops. Beginning tricksters and younger kids have their own smaller terrain features over at the Bonanza Park at the top of Lower East Meadows. Even on a midweek day, you will see lots of action in the parks with good viewing from the express quad.

Pioneering from Pabst to Present

Born in 1899 and grandson of the Pabst Blue Ribbon founder, Fred A. Pabst, Jr., was an old guard visionary, an entrepreneur who loved skiing and harbored dreams of offering a different and better product for the skiing public. After a 10-year stint in the family brewery business and some business courses at Harvard, he went to Europe to ski and learn more about the ski business, and in particular, ski instruction. Liking what he saw, he cast his future in skiing.

Pabst formed Ski Tows, Inc., in 1935 and started 17 areas in the Midwest, Vermont, New Hampshire, New York, and Quebec between 1936 and 1941. Rather than cater to the elite corps of well-to-do, rugged sports-minded collegians who populated skiing in the 1920s and early 1930s, Pabst wanted to create a sport that everyone could enjoy. What he foresaw when the snow trains started rolling in the 1930s was a bigger potential market in the workers pouring out of urban offices for trips to places where they could learn the sport.

Finding a great interest in skiing in the Manchester area, Pabst settled in Vermont in the 1930s and installed a rope tow at the Equinox Golf Course in Manchester and a J-Bar on Mount Aeolus in East Dorset for the winter of 1936-37. (He eventually moved both lifts to Bromley.)

Ski races had been held on Bromley Run in the mid-1930s, and when there was poor snow in the valley the winter of 1937, Pabst installed a rope tow below Route 11 on Little Bromley, which tow operated the winter of 1938. The next year he installed a unique 2,200-foot rope tow that had a turn in it (due to the terrain) at the West Meadow across the road on "Big" Bromley. Newspaper articles indicate that this tow began operations in January 1939. According to Pabst's accounting records, Big Bromley grossed $1,350 its first season (winter of 1938-39) while Little Bromley had revenues of $2,498!

At the same time, Pabst was installing tows and J-Bars elsewhere and still running Mount Aeolus. His idea to have a "chain of ski areas" was a little before its time, however. With World War II, gas rationing, and not enough skiers, his 17 areas failed to make money, and he began to sell them. Favoring Bromley as a good location, he purchased the Walker Farm (155 acres for $6,000) in March 1942 and began expanding his "Big Bromley" operation. He lived in a farmhouse by the side of his tows and when his new base lodge burned down in 1944, he replaced it by converting the Walker barn and painting it red (later replaced by his Wild Boar Lodge and Restaurant in 1950).

Most ski-area founders built northeast or eastern facing trails so that the sun wouldn't melt the snow. Not Pabst. As a south-facing mountain, Bromley's slopes were sunnier, warmer, and more apt to soften up rather than be hard eastern boilerplate, he boasted of efforts to create a better ski surface. He also made about half of his slopes wide and open and manicured them so that they could be skied with just a few inches of snow. To do this in the early years prior to snowmaking, he blasted out the rock (1947), bulldozed the ground, raked the dirt, and planted grass. He bought his first Tucker Sno Cat for grooming, and hired teenagers to "pick rocks" in the summer so the trails would be smooth.

With rope tows being tiring on the arms and T-Bars hard to ride for twosomes of unequal weight or height, Pabst installed J-Bars to make getting up the hill easier. He had seen the first J-Bar built at Oak Hill in Hanover, NH in 1935 and hired an engineer to improve upon its design. These "improved" J-Bars worked well, but Pabst later paid a licensing fee for use of the patented J-Bar design to Ernst Constam, its inventor.

Pabst moved the J-Bar from his East Dorset area to Bromley in 1942 and, as he closed other areas, continued to add more lifts until by 1955, he was operating five J-Bars, a Pomalift, and two rope tows (4,500 rides an hour). In 1958, he installed a 5,700-foot Riblet Double chair that ran from the base to the top of the mountain and had five J-Bars, one rope tow, and a Pomalift running. The double was named the Number One chair after its designation as the first two-seat chairlift to be licensed by the State of Vermont.

After the snowless winter of 1953-54, a cloud seeding expert was in Manchester the following winter to "seed the clouds" to make it snow. Although Project Snow didn't work, Pabst did succeed in installing a large conventional snowmaking system (starting in 1965) and committed close to a million dollars to put snowmaking on the face of Bromley Mountain. He was the first operator in Vermont to take snowmaking to the top of a mountain.

By 1967, he advertised, "The World's Largest Snowmaking System." As a marketing-savvy entrepreneur who took skiing seriously and worked hard to create a good experience, Pabst let the world know about his efforts!

The innovations continued over the years, and Bromley implemented Vermont's first state-accredited Ski Nursery (now the Kids Center) in 1946. With Pabst's desire to bring more people to the sport, Bromley boasted a large professional staff of ski instructors early on. He insisted on hiring trained instructors and

The Mighty Moosers going out for some slope time. KL

It is possible to ski to the lifts from Bromley Village. BMSA

the area became known for its ability to teach beginners. His wife, the former Sally Litchfield, was an instructor who enjoyed teaching children and had much to do with Bromley's emphasis on providing helpful services for families.

With an emphasis on instruction a Bromley strong point, the Bromley Outing Club, a group of area adults, created and sponsored Vermont's first Junior Instruction Ski Program (JISP) in 1951, making it one of the oldest and longest continuing Junior Programs in the country. It is still going strong with some 600-700 students from area schools participating each week during the winter.

Pabst began building the Bromley Village on 200 acres, but with health failing, he sold to Stig Albertsson, who had managed the mountain for him since January 1970. In a 2004 interview, Albertsson said he bought the area in the spring of 1971 and continued to build some 150 units in the Bromley Village that Pabst had started.

He also installed two more chairlifts, removing the J-Bars that had divided the main mountain in half. (Prior to this time, Little Bromley had been discontinued when the highway was rerouted.) In 1976, Albertsson installed the first Alpine Slide in North America for summer fun. He also expanded his revenue base by selling slides to other ski areas (which he still was doing in 2004).

Knowing the Village was about 60 percent built and that its revenue stream would soon come to an end with nothing to replace it, and also sensing the consolidation trend in the ski industry after several difficult snow years, Albertsson had tried to buy Okemo in 1978-79. When that effort failed, he sold Bromley to Stratton in December 1979.

Stratton, in turn, sold the area in 1987 to a small investor group that also owned nearby Magic Mountain. Today, Joseph O'Donnell, a Boston businessman, is the sole surviving owner of that group, which closed Magic in June 1991. He continues to own Bromley while experienced managers headed by President John Cueman operate the area on a daily basis.

Bromley has continued to innovate by inaugurating the first full-time Telemark Program in the East, developing innovative learning programs and kids' instruction, and introducing Valet Parking for weekends and holidays. The area has kept abreast of industry trends by welcoming snowboarders and free riders with terrain parks and a halfpipe and by replacing the double with the Sun Mountain Express Quad in 1997. It also expanded summer activities.

As a result of its long history of improving the experience for skiers and especially for families, Bromley has become an area where you ride the lift and invariably your seatmates rattle off a long association with the area that often goes back to their grandparents.

What they like about the mountain is its terrain and friendliness. Having learned to ski there as youngsters, they return as adults and feel comfortable having their kids taught to ski, or ride, by ski-school staff. They cite the convenience of all trails funneling to a single base, the wonderful kids' programs, and the area's affordability and ambiance as reasons for their long-lived loyalties. It's little wonder then, that this area has won national accolades and awards for its skiing programs and being a top family area.

Mountain Memories to Pig Dog Fun

I first skied Bromley in 1959. I had won a season's pass in the Hartford (CT) Travel Show by guessing how many rides the area's lifts could deliver in one hour. I remember skiing in a blizzard and filling in my sitzmarks on Pushover and tying a six-foot scarf around one ski pant leg when it split because I didn't want to stop skiing. We skied so hard for two days that on the way home, I felt as if I were snowplowing as the car descended Route 11. I even remember Bobby Darin singing *Mack the Knife* on the radio and the woodstove in the home we had stayed in—it was that memorable a trip!

On my most recent visits, I sampled a more modern mountain, but when I explored the base lodge, I was happy to find my old friend, the fieldstone fireplace. There is something about sitting on a wooden bench before a fireplace that warms more than hands and toes. A roaring fire is such a simple thing, but it is one of the lasting memories I have of that trip forty-plus years ago when it snowed all weekend and my dad and I dried our mitts by the fire.

Now Lord's Prayer is where the action is, and I've yet to revisit my childhood favorite because even though it was easy then, it scares me now. I saw kids getting huge air, and I figure I have to wait for a day when no one is there to sneak in and ski around and inspect the hits *without actually doing them*.

Below the park, I watched the Mighty Moosers (ages 3 to 5) as they stepped onto a moving carpet and rode it to the top. It reminded me of the first-time thrill of an escalator. Next, they did it with one ski on. Then it was follow-the-leader. Watching them, you could see why parents report being happy with the learning programs. If Fred Pabst were still alive, I am sure he would approve of this pampering and bringing kids to the sport at such a young age!

Kids ages six to twelve have the Pig Dog Ski and Snowboard program for learning to ski/ride. "What's up with Pig Dog?" I asked Peter Robertson, who is the director of Bromley's Learning Center and a PSIA Examiner.

"Pig Dog and Bruce the Moose are Bromley mascots and going to the Pig Dog Club takes away the idea of going to school and makes learning more fun," he explained. Robertson's enthusiasm in describing the children's programs was intriguing for its emphasis on fun.

Might coaching or lessons help experienced skiers to have more fun, too, I asked Peter. He replied in the affirmative but noted that with the ease of shaped skis has come a kind of complacency and lost interest in instruction among experienced skiers. In 2003, 85 percent of the Learning Center's business was in the children's programs at Bromley, he noted.

Learning to ride the carpet is done in steps. KL

Curious to see how instructors might address the issue of older learners, I took a lesson. The terrain my instructor chose was interesting and appropriate to my wish to carve versus skid a turn. She used kinesthetic, verbal, visual, and auditory cues to help me. In a short, one-hour lesson I was able to process information—extend uphill leg and thrust forward into the turn with her explanation of the motion needed (diagonal) that enabled me to have a breakthrough "aha" moment.

My other desire is to be able to shortswing down the edge of a trail in the controlled, graceful descent of "really" good skiers and instructors. Following Sue, I got a taste of this—I now strive to 'scoop' instead of zigzag.

When the lesson was over, I was excited to see that improvement is within reach and that instructors are just as dedicated to helping us "old-timers," as they are to turning on the youngsters to skiing or riding.

Over the course of two visits to Bromley, I got to know about two-thirds of the mountain well. On the third visit, a contact lens problem necessitated a visit to the ski patrol room at the top. In addition to providing the water I needed to clear a lens, a friendly patrolman answered my questions about the diamonds and then offered to show them to me, assuring me they were in good condition and that he'd keep me off the big moguls and out of the steep glades (at my request).

We cruised Blue Ribbon and Sunder, and then I met Corkscrew. It was like a guided tour of a glacier—one of those moments when fear returned as he dropped over the edge and out of sight. I had no choice but to follow—whimping out was not an option! Besides, if I wiped out big time, the sled could get there quickly.

So I stayed away from the trees and began to ski, timidly at first with big butterflies in my stomach, and then having survived the dropoff and spotted him ahead, I mustered my best effort to impress and went for it.

The smile I managed was more a 'thanks be to God,' but he took it for fun and off we went, chasing more trails and thrills, and even cruising Pushover, which was a tad fast in places. That's when the memory hit me of skiing this trail with my Dad forty-plus years ago, and suddenly, the meaning of family mountain flooded in, and I basked in the experience of a rediscovered roller-coaster ride and the joy that my legs could still take it!

Good to Know

Bromley is located 6 miles East of Manchester on Vermont Route 11 and is about 25 miles from I-91 Exit 6; about 1.25 hours from Albany, 2.5 hours from Hartford, 3 from Boston, and 4 from NYC.

Complimentary tours are given by mountain Hosts at 9:30 a.m. and 1:15 p.m. on weekends/holidays (meeting place is at base of Sun and Alpine chairlifts).

Courtesy Staff are on hand to assist guests in any way they can.

If you, or someone you know, has a disability of any kind, give the Bart Center a call (824-6498). Even if you don't require these services, be sure to visit the Bart Center and read about how one wonderful skier is being honored and remembered. This is the warm and fuzzy side to skiing that people often miss, but it says loads about how Bromley is revered in the hearts of its loyal skiers.

The Beginners Circle has an introductory special for 'never-evers.' It includes lessons, equipment, and lifts for at a special package rate—1 day for $79; 2 days for $109.

There are 100+ HKD Spectrum Tower Guns in Bromley's snowmaking arsenal. These state-of-the-art guns allow more snow to be made at higher temperatures. Snowmaking covers 90% of beginner terrain, 70% of intermediate, and 95% of advanced trails.

Customer Guarantee: Skiers will be issued a free lift ticket within one hour of purchase of their lift ticket if they are not satisfied for any reason.

The Sun Lodge has a reputation for good food and is located on the slopes overlooking the base area. Bromley Village also offers trailside access.

Bromley hosts annual NATO Telemark Workshops. Check Website for details and dates.

Lots of other events: Snojam, Jeep Owners Appreciation Day, annual Boy Scout Weekend, BlueJ Rail Fest, competitions—check brochure or Website.

Steals and Deals

Couples ski 2-for-the-price-of-1 on Valentine's Day (smooching at the ticket booth required). Moms get to ski for a $15 donation to the Susan G. Komen Breast Cancer Foundation (VT affiliate) on Mom's Day Off in February!

There are a variety of ticket packages and specials like Family Fridays, Sunday Afternoon Passports, Friends & Family Season Pass Program. See Website for details or call or write for a brochure.

Midweek Value tickets are available from Opening Day till 1/13/05 and from 3/14/05 till Closing Day, *non-Holiday only*: Adults $39, Teens $37, Juniors $34. $35 Seniors; $34 Senior Plus.

Enjoy savings for *on-line purchases of five or more* 1 and 2-day weekend/holiday Value TKTS; Adults $49, Teens $43 and Juniors $32 *if you purchase your tickets before December 8, 2004*. Two consecutive days for $95 Adult/$83 Teen/$63 Junior. There is a minimum order of five Value TKTS (any combination of Adult, Teen, Junior, 1-Day or 2-Day tickets). Value TKTS don't lose their value or expire at the end of the season.

Phone numbers below are **area code 802** unless otherwise noted.

Handy Info

Website: www.bromley.com
Email: info@bromley.com
General information: 824-5522
Snow report: 824-5522
Lift Hours: 9-4 midweek; 8:30-4 weekends/holidays.
Tickets 2005 Season: Adults, $49 midweek, $57 weekends, $59 holidays; Juniors (7-12), $34/$37/$39; Teens (13-17) $40/$49/$51; Seniors (65-69) $35/$49/$51; Senior Plus (age 70+) $34/$37/$39. Ages six and under ski free.

Quick Stats

Season: Mid-November to Mid-April, average 150 days.
Average annual snowfall: 145 inches.
Snowmaking capability: 84 percent; 252 acres.
Lifts: 10; 2 quads (1 express), 4 doubles, 4 surface (1 carpet, 2 Mitey Mite, 1 T-Bar).
Uphill lift capacity: 9,904 rides per hour.
Trails: 43; 300 acres; longest trail 2.5 miles.

Glades: 4, The Plunge, Avalanche, The Everglade, The Glade.
Bumps: Havoc, Stargazer.
Parks/Pipe: 3 parks (1 for beginners/young set); 1 halfpipe.
Groomers: 3 Bombardiers, 1 Piston Bully Winch Cat; 1 Pipe Dragon.
Vertical Drop:
Summit to base: 1,334'

Bromley Learning Center   824-5522

Privates and group lessons are available from a staff of 100+ PSIA trained instructors. Clinics are offered to work on areas of specific interest and Telemark Workshops are also available. Reservations for adult private lessons are highly recommended.

Children's Programs   824-5522 x 301

Reservations highly recommended.
Daycare: Mighty Mites for 6 weeks to 6 years, full or half day.
Mighty Moose Club: 3-5 years, on snow & indoor playtime, full/half day.
Pig Dog's Mountain Club: 6-12, ski/snowboard lessons, lunch, full day.

Other Things to Do

Wild Wings Ski Touring Center (824-6793) in Peru offers classical X-C skiing on 25 km of machine-tracked, wooded terrain. Viking Nordic Centre in Londonderry (824-3933) offers classical on 40 km of trails, 30 km machine tracked. Also XC at Nordic Inn in Peru (824-6444) or at Hildene in Manchester (362-1788). For snowmobiling, try Equinox Tours (362-4700).

Sleigh rides are available in Landgrove by Karl Pfister (824-6320); in Londonderry by Taylor Farm (824-5690); and at Horses for Hire (297-1468).

Ice skating at Riley Rink (for public hours, call 362-0150) in Manchester.

For shopping: Manchester, Londonderry, Weston, Chester offer country stores, boutiques, art galleries, antiques and craft shops, and outlets.

Visit the Northshire Museum and History Center (362-0004) on Route 7A or the Southern Vermont Arts Center (362-1405) in Manchester.

Dining Out

Johnny Seesaw's (next door to Bromley) is a classic. It is one of the longest continuing ski lodges with a restaurant in Vermont, having opened in December 1938 and continues to be a favorite with locals and skiers who return year after year (could be the ambiance and the French chef who creates his own menu).

The Manchester region offers an abundance of restaurants, representing Continental, Italian, California, French, Mexican, New England, Oriental, Austrian, and nouvelle cuisines and more. In Manchester the variety includes:

Angel's at the Village Country Inn (inspired New England cuisine), Bistro Henry (Mediterranean, classic and contemporary favorites), Black Swan (fresh fish, game, pasta, homemade desserts), Candeleros (southwestern cantina and grill), Christo's Pizza and Pasta, The Equinox (elegant dining room or Marsh Pub), 4940 Main Street (creative American Bistro), Garlic John's, Laney's (open-kitchen concept with wood fired oven, sports bar, ribs to pizza), Lilac Café (eclectic menu and take out), Mulligans (burgers to seafood, children's menu), Panda Garden (Chinese), Sirloin Saloon (a popular classic featuring steak, seafood, and salad bar; children's menu), and fine dining at The Perfect Wife, Wilburton Inn, and Ye Olde Tavern.

In the Londonderry area: Frog's Leap Inn, Garden Café, Jake's Café, Mill Tavern, Noodle Room (pasta), Three Clock Inn, and Swiss Inn (German, Swiss, Fondue and Raclette) are all good choices while you'll find great Italian at the Red Fox in Bondville.

Accommodations

The bedbase is 8,000 in the region. Inns, motels, ski lodges, B & B's, and condos offer something for every budget or need but accommodations right at mountain are limited so reserve early for holidays/weekends.

Bromley Village Lodging: 800-865-4786; 824-5458.
Bromley Sun Lodge: 800-722-2159.
Manchester and Mountains Chamber of Commerce: 362-2100.
Londonderry Chamber of Commerce: 824-8178.

Après-ski/Nightlife

The Wild Boar Tavern at Bromley offers live music and après-ski fun on Saturdays and holidays. Johnny Seesaw's has live music on Saturdays. In Bondville, The Red Fox Inn offers live music and dancing on weekends, Open Mike sessions on Thursdays, and folk music with "the meal deal" on Sundays.

Summer/Fall

Bromley's Thrill Zone Fun Park features: 456' Big Splash water slide, triple-track Alpine Slide, 100' Zip Line, DevalKarts, Trampoline Things, climbing wall, miniature golf, Pig Dog's Fun Park for little kids with Volcano Peak, Bumper Boats, Inflatable Play Space. There's great hiking on Bromley's trails and magnificent 360-degree views from the Summit. The Annual Bromley Antiques Show takes place during Foliage season along with chairlift rides.

DevalKarts are a big hit with kids. BMSA

Our Bromley Adventure

Date:

Weather:

Companions:

Where Stayed:

Visit Highlights:

Our Discoveries:

50 Burke

The Gap, Burke's five-acre terrain park, features a variety of jumps, hits, and rails.

Burke has two entrances, one for the lower mountain and one for the upper area.

Chapter Five

Burke Mountain
Vermont's Undiscovered Gem

Located in East Burke in the heart of the wild and beautiful Northeast Kingdom, Burke Mountain is one of Vermont's *undiscovered* jewels. It is a mid-sized ski area by modern standards (140 acres of trails), but Burke skis big because there are so many glades (110 acres worth as of 2005), wide cruisers, old-style New England trails, long top-to-bottom runs, and a 2,000-foot vertical.

Burke boasts some legendary terrain and some of the country's best competitors have sharpened their skills here. That's not too surprising as the area is home to Burke Mountain Academy (BMA), a private ski academy and powerhouse that has graduated 39 Olympians and 78 National Team members.

But Burke isn't just for the most accomplished skier or rider. Intermediate trails proliferate on the upper mountain, and there's a big lower mountain novice area where first-timers can learn on gentle terrain and beginners and novices can improve their skills on several long, easy trails. There's even a glade for lower-level tree skiing on the lower mountain.

With two base lodges, childcare, children's programs, ski school, ski, rental and repair shops, and slopeside housing, Burke offers all the services that modern day skiers and riders expect. It has a loyal following among locals, but as one of Vermont's northernmost mountains (it's not located along the spine of the Green Mountain Range but is off by itself to the East) and one that's less well advertised, it's often missed by those who live in metropolitan areas.

That's a shame because this is a mountain that is well worth discovering! There are seldom any lift lines and you won't find skiers or boarders whizzing by in droves even on weekends or holidays! You will find great skiing, lots of long runs, and plenty of challenge for all ability levels. And the views are truly breathtaking. Plus, Burke is very easy to get to from major highways since it's just seven miles from I-91 and just a few miles further to I-93.

To top it all off, Burke is also an affordable area, one where big mountain adventures and family fun can be enjoyed inexpensively. The ski-and-stay deals at nearby hotels and many lodges make getting away to Burke for a weekend or ski week quite enticing. (See Steals and Deals section.)

The Mountain

Burke is a large, broad-shouldered mountain that is extremely steep on its eastern and southern sides but is perfect for ski trails on its northern and northeastern flanks. The trails are interesting, with lots of consistent pitch, sidehills, and undulations. Mountain Operations Manager Ford Hubbard believes in meticulous snow grooming (a Burke strength), but he doesn't believe "in bulldozing every trail flat," preferring "to follow their natural contours."

So most of Burke skis classic New England style, including the wider "open slopes" that advanced skiers and experts enjoy cruising with big, glorious GS turns.

The views from the 3,267-foot summit and various trails are magnificent. On a clear day, you can see out over a valley patchwork of villages, forests and fields to dramatic Willoughby Gap, where Mt. Hor and Mt. Pisgah dive down to meet glacial Lake Willoughby. You can also see Mount Mansfield, Jay Peak, Owl's Head (Canada) and the Presidentials of nearby New Hampshire.

Burke's layout features an Upper Mountain for intermediate through super expert and a trail-and-lift connected Lower Mountain for beginners and novices. Each area has a lodge and its own parking. Burke is particularly suited to snowboarding as it has a consistent vertical that seldom requires walking despite long runs—an exception is the flat runout on East Bowl which skiers can schuss. Burke excels in the glades department with more wooded terrain opening every year—currently 110 acres worth!

Beginner/Novice ●

Among Burke's strengths is its novice terrain with a double chair and several three-quarter-mile-long trails that gently descend 600 vertical feet on the Lower Mountain. Dashney Mile, Binney Lane, High Meadows Pass, and Bunker Hill offer lengthy, wide runs that are perfect for developing turning and stopping skills. A lower level intermediate would do well to warm up on these trails before trying the Upper Mountain.

There is also a 1,000-foot learning slope with J-Bar tucked off to one side so first-timers have a safe and less stressful learning environment. A children's park with mini-terrain features, creature cutouts, and trees to ski around (Carter Country) completes the picture and makes it a well thought-out and fun area. The full-service Sherburne Base Lodge—childcare facilities, rental and repair shops, ski shop, cafeteria, lounge, and ski school desk—is located at the base of the slopes and double chair. Condos dot the hillsides and base area.

Intermediate ■

Although blues predominate on the Upper Mountain, they range from the easy but narrow switchback toll road (doable for advanced novices who don't mind narrow) now known to skiers as Deer Run (since a deer bumped into a skier) to challenging like Dipper (26 percent gradient) to very challenging like Willoughby (average 30 percent gradient) and Little Dipper (38 percent). Lower Warren's Way, Lower Doug's Drop, and Upper and Lower Bear Den offer some especially delightful cruising terrain. Many of the nineteen blues sport natural terrain contours on wide open trails for swooping GS turns.

One of the most delightful and unusual runs, East Bowl (■) dips and dives around the backside (eastern flank) of the mountain and goes through a natural snow bowl area with glades and lots of steep *off piste* tree skiing. The 2.25-mile East Bowl trail includes a "tuck-and-bomb" stretch with thrilling hairpin turns. It's a different, not-to-be-missed experience with some great views of the White Mountains.

Willoughby (■) is another standout, appropriately named after the expansive view one gets of Willoughby Gap and Lake Willoughby from various vantages on the trail. Ultra wide and consistently steep, Willoughby boasts lots of undulations and double fall lines for a mile-plus workout that sets the heart to beating faster. It's a famous favorite for good reason—it's one of the best trails in skierdom for beauty and exhilaration—and attracts lots of advanced skiers.

Since the Willoughby Quad serves the Upper Mountain with a 1,600-foot vertical for every run, intermediates will find plenty of challenge and big mountain skiing to keep them busy, happy, and advancing in ability level.

Advanced/Expert ♦ ♦♦

In addition to the Willoughby Quad which goes to the summit, there's a fast Mountain Poma that goes up about three-fourths of the way for direct access to the race training hill Warren's Way (♦) and several other diamonds. Upper Warren's Way averages a 42 percent gradient and is ultra wide and straight down. Lew's Leap (44 percent) and Upper Doug's Drop (50 percent) crank up the challenge with narrow, twisting runs that demand expert ability.

Double diamonds include the Fox's Folly bump run (ungroomed) and several glades, including Throbulator, Caveman, Birches, the Jungle, and Dixiland. The Birches and Jungle are located on the steep south side while Throbulator and Caveman are over toward the East Bowl. They have lots of cliffs and jumps and vary with open and tight trees.

Glade skiing is big at Burke and exciting to watch—lots of cliff jumpers here. Burke's glade skiers and riders are such an avid bunch that they climb the mountain in fall and brush out their favorite tree areas. These volunteers have been known to find glades not on the map, so woodland seekers might do well

Glades skiing and riding is infectious fun at Burke Mountain. KL

to ask a local for advice—get lucky and you might find your own little bit of paradise a year or two before it gets named on the trail map. New for the 2004 season were the Sasquatch, Y-Knot, Little Chief (all ♦) and Dixiland (♦♦) glades which doubled Burke's tree skiing to 110 acres.

Mining Community Recreation

Mountain recreation at Burke dates back to 1860 when Lt. Joseph Seaver Hall of East Burke cut a trail to the mountain's summit and erected a cabin there. Picnickers and hikers used the trail to climb to the mountaintop which was a popular pastime in Vermont in the late 1800s. In 1904, E. A. Darling bought 4,000 acres on the mountain and after the entire mountain forest burned in a spectacular fire, he had a fire lookout tower built at the peak and built a camp and a picnic area, which became very popular with local people.

The Darling family deeded 1,747 acres to the State in 1933 (for Darling State Park). Due to the popularity of the summit and the trend at the time to use mountains for recreation, State Forester Perry Merrill assigned a contingent of the CCC to build an auto road to the top, as well as many campsites, a new fire tower, caretaker houses, and ski trails so the area could be used for recreation year round.

Skiing and snowshoeing quickly became popular, and the first downhill race was held on the Toll Road (now Deer Run) in 1937, followed by intercollegiate races on the first trails, Bear Den and Wilderness, in ensuing years. The mountain was recognized as a natural one for skiing, but despite various groups trying to get a commercial venture started, nothing came of it until 1953, when a group of thirteen local citizens formed Ski Burke Mountain, Inc.

They leased land on the upper mountain from the State, bought another 80 acres, and ferried skiers up to the trails in a Tucker Sno-Cat in 1954-55. In 1955, they completed a base shelter and parking lot and installed a Pomalift to the summit and a rope tow for a novice area. Due to scarce natural snow, the area didn't officially open as a lift-served area until February 12, 1956.

Burke Mountain Recreation, Inc. (BMR), led by one of the members of the original group, purchased the assets of the corporation in 1964. They replaced the rope tow with a T-Bar, added more trails, installed a second Pomalift, and put in a double chairlift to the top in 1966. They also implemented a master plan, developed by a consultant who specialized in ski area residential planning, and began real estate development with the construction of a few homes and condominiums.

In 1976 the owners instituted another master plan with a first phase including snowmaking on 25 acres of the upper mountain. They also acquired 2,400 acres of land for a village and beginner area with a second base lodge, chairlift, and J-Bar. This land was part of the former Sherburne farm for which the chairlift and base lodge on the lower mountain are named. The original "base lodge" then became known as the Mid-Mountain Lodge and the total skiable vertical increased to 2,000 feet.

The Burke Mountain Academy was founded in 1970 as the first full-time U.S. ski academy and was located in remodeled farmhouses on a lower northeastern flank of the mountain. It soon became known as a high school that specialized in training ski racers. BMA founder and former headmaster/coach Warren Witherell was a pioneer in ski boot fitting (canting) and one of the first to popularize the carved turn and make it a mainstay in modern race training.

Among the 100-plus BMA graduates to go on to National or Olympic teams was Diann Roffe-Steinrotter, who grew up in Burke and became the first woman to win the Gold in Giant Slalom at the World Alpine Ski Championships. She also won the Silver in GS at the French Olympics in 1992 and took home the Gold in GS in the 1994 Olympics. Another graduate Julie Parisien was the 1993 World Championship Silver Medalist.

The Burke Ski Touring Center (now privately owned) was developed by the mountain and an extensive trail network was built with 32 miles of trails in the 1970s. Also in the 1970s, the ski area made a trade with the State, acquiring the campground and giving the State land on the southern end of Lake Willoughby in exchange.

Beginning in 1986, three successive new owners made major improvements to the mountain—the quad to the summit in 1989, more snowmaking, water, etcetera—but each ended in bankruptcy (the late 1980s and early 1990s were difficult times during which the lingering affects of a recession and poor natural snow years caused several Vermont areas to close or change ownership).

To keep Burke alive (and prevent it from being liquidated), Burke Mountain Academy (BMA) purchased the ski area in October 2000 through its subsidiary Burke 2000 L.L.C. Originally its intention was to look for a new owner, but that changed and its mission now is to have the area operate as a break-even venture. With a show of support from the BMA family, community members, season-pass purchasers, the school program for kids (42 schools, 1800 students participated in 2003 for 10,000 visits), and the skiing/riding public, Burke has been able to stay open and entered its fifth year of operations under its new owner for the 2004-05 season.

The story of a community and a ski academy banding together to preserve and support the hometown mountain—one of its most precious recreational assets and economic resources—is unique in Vermont ski history. With the Burke Mountain Operating Company headed by seasoned veterans Dick Andross, general manager (formerly GM at Cannon and Loon), and Ford Hubbard, mountain operations manager (a former Sno-Engineering consultant who worked on and designed ski areas all over the world), Burke is in good hands and continues to offer a wonderful, "big mountain" experience. And they don't mind me telling you that you are "invited to discover Burke."

Impressions

"One of the prettiest mountains I've ever met."

That was my first reaction to Burke as I rode the Quad on a crisp March afternoon. It had been minus 25 during the night but had warmed up to the low teens by the time I arrived and got out with Wayne Brown as my guide.

To my delight, he shared that view and didn't think the word "pretty" inappropriate for this challenging mountain.

The chair ride itself was delightful, first running along rows of spruce trees, then opening up with views of Warren's Way and racers running gates, and then skimming along snow-laden spruce tops toward the summit. At the top, you exit into a unique forest clearing with picnic tables in the snow. (This is the parking area for the Toll Road which is still used in summer.) Giant spruce surround the clearing with trails darting off in various directions.

Wayne, a consummate skier and veteran ski instructor who knows his stuff, took me on a delightful tour, stopping to point out the views. From the top of Willoughby, we looked out onto Willoughby Gap, an amazing sight that more resembled a Swiss scene than Vermont. When we skied East Bowl, we encountered dramatic views of the Presidentials in the White Mountains.

East Bowl itself was skiing like it used to be—a long, winding trail that ended with a flat section. Thanks to Wayne's warning, I gathered speed and tucked for the runout. Imagine my surprise when I found myself having to make some hairpin turns while going lickety split!

My favorites were Willoughby and the Dippers. They were wide and consistently pitched, so I had to watch myself and really control my speed as I encountered double fall lines. Romps on Deer Run, an easy blue, and Bear Den, a more challenging blue, were particularly enjoyable for the scenic feeling of skiing a narrow trail tucked in the trees.

Graceful Telemarker Sean Wallace is a fun sight in his Captain America cape. KL

We put a lot of miles on, but when Wayne left to go vote (it was Town Meeting Day), I took a few more runs because I couldn't resist getting to know the mountain better. I don't think I could ever get my fill of Willoughby, Wilderness, Carriage Road, or those headwalls on FIS-sanctioned Big Dipper. These are all great trails that allow you to run a different line every time.

After a good night's rest in a convenient, comfortable mountainside condo, I met with Dick Andross and Ford Hubbard the next morning. Both are real mountain men (over 50 years of ski expertise between them) who know how to create a good mountain experience. I left my meeting with a better understanding of why Burke appeals to better skiers and a suggestion from Dick to "hook up with a ski patrolman and go do the glades."

I don't normally do trees, but I was willing to see them and photograph some skiers in them. That's how I got my personal tour of the ski patrol hut at the top. I had to meet Mike Tatoyien there, and in the process, I was invited to sample the soup cooking on the woodstove.

The ambiance in this rustic room exuded passion—for home-cooked food, the outdoors, and the camaraderie of patrollers. When Mike asked if anyone wanted to ski the glades, two patrolmen on their day off instantly volunteered.

Mike, Chris Scott, and Jeremiah Jonaitus skied the Birches, and I watched from below as they wove in and out of the trees, disappearing one second and reappearing the next, snow flying and big grins spreading on frosted faces.

Next thing I know, I am walking down into Throbulator, where Jeremiah jumps off a cliff as I click away and my stomach does flip flops.

The glades were beautiful, exciting—the cliffs a little unbelievable. The patrollers made skiing them look so easy that I almost took them up on the offer

Jeremiah in flight in Throbulator. KL

to go into Marshland. Marshland, they told me, is the easiest glade with trails on either side so you can bail out if you get tired or unnerved. I could handle it, they assured me.

I met them at a halfway point, but before I could ski the rest with them, they arrived, blurting out, "That was tough!!"

The snow had gotten heavier and stickier and made it work!

Saved by their admission, I skipped Marshland but getting into the spirit of things, I caught myself thinking, "maybe next time." And catching myself thinking that, I could see why Dick Andross had suggested I meet Mike.

Before I watched these tree skiers, I used to think glades are only for the strong and foolhardy; now I have a better appreciation for the beauty of a controlled, rhythmic descent. I also see what the fuss is all about and how trees make for infectious good fun. But you're still never going to catch me jumping off twelve-foot rock cliffs!

After my glades tour, I had just one thing left on my agenda—Warren's. It was snowing big wet flakes when I got to the top. I am not game for narrow steeps, but I am turned on by historic and wide. Upper Warren's was both. Skiing it was nothing less than thrilling while Lower Warren's (■) was relief!

On my final run, I waltzed down Binne Lane, enjoying the sight of beginners and tiny tots and the fun things in Carter Country and thinking someday I could bring grandkids here. As I joined the throngs of kids heading to their school buses in the parking lot, I noticed the happy faces and wondered whose were the bigger grins—the guys in the glades, the school kids, or my own at discovering another Vermont gem.

Good to Know

Burke Mountain is located in East Burke, just 7 miles from I-91, Exit 23 (Route 5 to 114 to E. Burke to Burke Mountain Road). It is about 3 hours from Springfield and Boston, 3.5 from Hartford, 5.5 from NYC, and 2 from Montreal. (Also, very close to intersection of I-91 and I-93 in NH.)

There are two entrances to Burke Mountain; the first, Sherburne Farm Access Road, leads to the main (lower mountain) Sherburne Base Lodge and the condos. If you have first-timers or beginners, park here.

For intermediates and above, you can take the Mid-Burke Access Road, and park at the Mid-Burke Lodge. (Novices can also ski down to the Lower Mountain from Mid-Burke.)

Burke seldom has liftlines. At peak times (certain weekends or holidays), there *may be* a 5-minute wait. Due to so much terrain and not that many people, the trails never feel crowded. If you question that, do the math: 140 acres of trails for most of us plus 110 acres of glades for the purists. With 65,000 visits for an entire season, it's no wonder the trails aren't crowded.

New for 2005: Glades for the rest of us. Lower level/introductory glade on Lower Mountain (unnamed at press time) suitable for intermediates/novices.

You can watch future Olympians train while riding the Quad or while taking a rest on Warren's. You can also *feel like an Olympian* on Upper Warren's.

Burke's Pond Skimming and Big Air contests in late March are major events; a Mountain Dew Vertical Challenge was added for 2005 season. Check Burke's Website for more events and special festivities throughout the season.

BMA remains a leading mountain school. They teach the spirit of community within the school and foster the ideals of competition on the hill. They combine a focus on character and academics with a fitness and physical conditioning model. You can learn more through their video or at www.Burkemtnacademy.org.

There are condos and homes that can be rented but *not enough* to meet demand for holidays so it's necessary to reserve them *well in advance* (a year or more for school vacation weeks).

The Village of East Burke has a market, great country store, gas station, sports shop, restaurants, and several inns. It's real Vermont—as in charming, unpretentious, and been there a long time.

Burke is close to Lyndon State College, which sits high on a hill with views of the trails. It's a nice campus and worthy of a visit if you have a college-bound teen who likes to ski (check out www.vtcollege.org).

Steals and Deals

Lift ticket prices are among the lowest in Vermont; midweek is a steal.

Ski packages that combine a discounted mountain ticket with discounted accommodations at participating inns/hotels offer some *great bargains* if you don't mind a short (5-20 minute) drive to the area. Check out the Website.

The Village Inn in East Burke offers a midweek (Sunday - Friday) ski/stay package that includes 1 lift ticket, full breakfast and 1 night stay for $59.95 pp (plus tax). Visit www.burkevermont.com for other nearby properties that offer 2-person/2-ticket/1-night stay-and-play special package rates.

Twenty minutes away in "St. J" (local speak for St.Johnsbury), the new Comfort Inn (indoor pool, hot tub, sauna, exercise room, video arcade) right at Exit 20 on I-91 offers a ski package that includes one night for two, lift tickets for two, and breakfast for two for $149.99 ($169.99 holidays). At the Holiday Motel and Yankee Traveler Motel, the 2-person 1-night stay/2 tickets deal is $99.99 ($129.99 holidays) and at the Fairbanks Inn (continental breakfast), $149.99 ($169.99 holidays). *These are total prices (plus tax), not per person.*

Phone numbers are **area code 802** unless otherwise noted.

Handy Info

Website: www.skiburke.com
Email: info@skiburke.com
General information: 626-3322
Snow report: 626-1390; 888-burkevt.
Hours: 9 to 4 daily.
Tickets 2005 season: Adults $32 midweek/$47 weekends/holidays; Youth (13-17)/Senior (65+) $26/$37; Juniors (6-12) $21/$33; Five and under ski free.

Quick Stats

Season: November to early April, average 135 days.
Annual average snowfall: 250 inches.
Snowmaking capability: 75 percent; 105 acres.
Lifts: 4; 1 quad, 1 double, 2 surface (1 J-Bar and 1 Pomalift).
Uphill lift capacity: 3,500 per hour.
Trails: 44; 250 acres including glades; longest, East Bowl 2.25 miles.
Glades: 10 glades encompassing 110 acres, all ability levels.
Bumps: Fox's Folly, Ledges, Doug's Drop, Wilderness, Borderline.
Vertical Drop: Summit to lower base village: 2,000'
Upper Mountain: 1,600'
Lower Mountain: 600'

Ski School 626-1374

Reservations suggested for busy weekends/holidays. The Burke Coaching Center, located in the Sherburne Base Lodge, offers a variety of clinics and programs, ranging from learn-to-ski or snowboard to advanced glade skiing. Group or private lessons are available. Guided Glade Tours (2 hour with tips), Mom and Dad program, and glade skiing are among other options.

Children's Programs

Cub Den Daycare: 6 months to 6 years, weekends & holidays (626-1371).
"Burkie" Bear Cubs: 3-5, lesson & daycare, full or half day, reservations suggested.
"Burkie" Bear Chasers: ages 4-12; mornings, ski with coach.
Bear Shredders: ages 6-12; half or full day, riding with a coach.
Mountain Rangers: ages 10-14, 2-hour upper mountain cruising lesson.
Beginner Skier/Snowboarder Special; ages 6-12, lesson, rentals, ticket for $45.
Burkie Explorers: 4-14 season program, weekends 9:30-12 noon.
Burkie Junior Race Program; season-long program for ages 7-14.

Other Things to Do

Burke X-C Center (535-7722) offers 80 km trails (65 km groomed, 55 tracked, 15 backcountry). Rentals (snowshoes too) and instruction are available.
Snowshoe rentals also available at E. Burke Sports (626-3215).
Snowmobiling on VAST trails; machine rentals in St. J.
X-C skiing and snowshoeing on the Kingdom Trails system.
Visit Bailey's and Burke Country Store in East Burke. This century-old country store has a carved Indian outside and an assortment of everything inside. You'll find clothing, food, practical items, furnishings, and gifts on two floors. There is a deli section, extensive wine room, handcrafted Vermont items from pottery to woodenware, and even a children's section.
Check out Aldrich's General Store in West Burke.
Lyndon: Fenton Chester Ice Arena (626-9361) indoor skating rink.
St. J: Fairbanks Museum and Planetarium (748-2372); The St. Johnsbury Athenaeum and Art Gallery (748- 8291); the NEK Artisans Guild cooperative shop; Catamount Film & Arts Company (748-2600); Gold Crown Bowling Alley (748-9511); movies at 3-plex Star Theatre (728-9511); and wonderful shopping in downtown St. J's interesting boutiques and stores.
Cabot: visit the Cabot Creamery Visitor's Center (800-881-6334) for cheese factory tours and tastings of Cabot products and specialty foods.

Dining Out

River Garden Café (lunch, dinner, Sunday brunch), The Pub Outback, The Old Cutter Inn, The Inn at Mountain View Farm in East Burke and Shelly's Restaurant (by Cole's Filling Station) in West Burke are good nearby choices.

In Lyndonville: Miss Lyndonville Diner, F.Scott's Restaurant, Juniper's at the Wildflower Inn (casual dining), Café Sweet Basil (dinner Wed.-Sat.), Vinny's Restaurant, House of Pizza, Hi-Boy, Subway, and MacDonalds.

In St. Johnsbury: Black Bear Tavern and Grille (generous portions), Elements (new), Cucina di Gerardo (Italian), Surf and Sirloin (popular), Hilltopper, Kham's (Thai), Anthony's Diner, House of Pizza, AJA Pizzeria, Cindy's Pasta Shop, Pizza Hut, KFC, Taco Bell, and Subway. St. Jay Diner for breakfast and lunch.

Accommodations

There are studio and 1, 2, or 3 bedroom condos at Burke, and most are ski-in/ski-out. Within the region, there's a good range of accommodations from historic inns and charming B & B's to modern hotels and motels, some with indoor pools. (Also, see Steals and Deals and check www.skiburke.com for other ski-and-stay packages and updates.)

Burke Area Chamber of Commerce: 626-4124 (burkevermont.com).
Burke Vacation Rentals: 888-327-2850; 626-1161.
Mountainside Property Rentals: 626-3548.
Lyndonville Area Chamber of Commerce: 626-9696.
Northeast Kingdom Chamber (in St. J): 748-3678 or 800-639-6379.

Après-ski/Nightlife

The Bear's Den Lounge at Mid-Burke Lodge is open 7 days, noon to closing with fireplace, billiards, music, televised sports events; Burkie's Bar at the Sherburne Base Lodge has live music, après-ski parties Fridays through Sundays and holidays, noon to closing.

The Pub Outback offers live music on weekends and Shelley's has entertainment Thursdays through Saturdays. In Lyndonville, The Packing House Lounge offers DJ or live music on Fridays, Saturdays, and Wednesdays. In Sutton, country music at Max's Dance Hall.

Summer/Fall

Drive, hike or mountain bike to the summit of Burke Mountain and enjoy a picnic and stunning views. The Burke Mountain Campground is open from May to October (626-1390). Mountain biking, hiking, tennis, and swimming at the mountain. The region abounds with golf courses, trails for hiking and mountain biking, and lakes for swimming and fishing.

Burke is a great base from which to explore the Northeast Kingdom and some of Vermont's outstanding attractions, from Lake Willoughby to the 100-mile Kingdom Trail System (626-0737). Festivals and special events throughout summer and fall..

Our Burke Mountain Adventure

Date:

Weather:

Companions:

Where Stayed:

Visit Highlights:

Our Discoveries:

64 Jay Peak

Jay Peak offers skiing on two different peaks (soon to be three). Stateside area is to left and Tramside to right.

Chapter Six

Jay Peak Resort
Adventures with International Flavor

Jay Peak is a mountain for dedicated skiers and riders. This is the place to come for a few days or a week of serious outdoor activity and a great place to learn a snowsport or to improve through lessons and special clinics.

Jay is famous for its tree skiing, face chutes, plentiful steeps, and deep snows. The mountain advertises the most tree an*d off piste* terrain in eastern North America, averages 355 inches of snow annually (35 powder days a year), and received a record 571 inches of snow in the 2000-01 season.

But 3,968-foot Jay Peak is not just for experts and powder hounds. The area also focuses on beginners, from 'never-ever' to solid novice and low intermediate with its dedicated Beginner Zone, an 80-acre complex with new beginner-friendly lifts, more snowmaking, and novice-rated glades.

Today, you can take a child or adult 'never-ever' to Jay and enroll them in ski school (teens have the Mountain Adventure Program) knowing they will have a fun introduction to skiing or riding. Or you can visit with a group or family and know that lower-level abilities will have lots of their own special terrain to enjoy. Or you can take your hip adult son and his old schussboomer grandfather and have fun cruising long and glorious blues and a nice variety of diamonds together.

If you haven't been to Jay in awhile, you probably won't recognize the resort. (And if you've never been there, you're in for a unique experience as Jay boasts Vermont's only aerial Tram lift.) The original Tram cabins were replaced with modern cars when the entire system was refurbished in 2002. A highspeed quad, the Flyer, was installed parallel to the Tram, and the old Metro T-Bar was replaced by the Metro Quad, which makes it easier for everyone to get up the hill, especially new skiers and riders.

The spectacular glade system has grown into one of the largest in the East and North America. Today, there is an all-terrain ski policy with Jay the first Vermont area to offer this *off-piste* (off-trail) option. In addition to being allowed to ski all the acreage within Jay's borders, it is also possible to get into some serious backcountry terrain. (See Appendix D, page 302.)

There are also modern condo and townhouse accommodations—most are ski-on/ski-off and there's even a village of homes with a lift that runs through it, serving a nice beginner hill. The result of the changes is a modern destination resort, an area that gets better with age. And the excitement is building with a new golf course and expansion plans for additional skiing in the West Bowl. These plans include a new village with more housing and indoor recreation for a four-season resort that will offer more things to do year-round, non-skiers included.

Jay's Right Stuff

For true experts, extreme skiers, and powder lovers, it's Jay's glades, woods, and deep snows that provide the right stuff. With high energy levels and the ability to make tight turns, 'tree huggers' focus on their line, becoming one with the mountain in a very controlled rhythmic dance.

As they do so, "they are traveling three times slower than folks on the trails," notes Jay President Bill Stenger. So while they are dancing with trees, many trails often seem empty—even on weekends. That's the secret to how Jay spreads out the people and how the varied terrain on two interconnected peaks contributes to everyone's fun.

But the delight of playing in the woods isn't restricted to adventurous, physically-fit sport types. Intermediates can sample the peacefulness and beauty of the woods at Kokomo, where narrowish trails meander in different directions among thin stands of trees, allowing a choose-your-own snake line and a taste of the fun that comes from weaving among snow-laden trees. Bushwacker and Moon Walk Woods similarly offer acres of trees for novices in the Beginner Zone section of the mountain.

Such gladed (tree) explorations add a new dimension to skiing and make Jay a mountain of snow adventures and sensory experiences. Jay is about challenge, nature, and seeing things from a different perspective—like a rainbow in the clouds caused by a reflection of the sun. Or *hearing* the cold as your skis squeak beneath you.

Or getting a taste of International as you listen to French Canadians or the German-inflected English spoken by Austrian instructors like Dietrick. He's one of the few remaining Austrians at Jay, a living reminder of the influence of Walter Foeger, who was brought to America to help run the area in 1956.

A Little Jay History

Skiers were having fun on Jay Peak long before the mountain was developed as a ski area. During skiing's first growth period in the 1930s, ski clubs were formed from Philadelphia to Boston and skiers arrived in Vermont by snow train. By 1940, almost every Vermont town had a winter sports club or outing club and rope tows and ski jumps were built throughout the state. People from towns near Jay Peak formed the Jay Peak Outing Club and promoted winter sports with a ski jump, downhill races and winter carnivals.

The development of Jay Peak as a bona fide ski mountain was the brainchild of Harold Haynes, the first president of Jay Peak, and a group of businessmen and avid skiers in North Troy. They, like their counterparts at Burke, Okemo, and Smugglers, were concerned about a flagging economy and saw hope in the new ski trend and leasing land from the state for a ski area. Touting skiing's economic potential, they banded together to start a mountain enterprise by incorporating in January 1955, selling stock at $10 a share, and hiring Walter Foeger, a prominent Austrian racer and instructor, as their first "ski pro."

When he arrived at Jay in late 1956, Foeger was disappointed to find one rough-cut slope, but he fell in love with the mountain's potential and went to work. When the area began operations in January 1957, there was one slope, one trail (the Sweetheart which Foeger cut in a week with help from volunteers) and a platter lift.

As head of the ski school and general manager from his second season on, Foeger put Jay on the map with his well-cut trails and his innovative but controversial Natur Teknik "system" for teaching parallel skiing (on the long skis of the day using "hop turns") from the first lesson. It worked well for many and brought Jay lots of skiers. [The method was also franchised at Okemo and at Camelback, PA.] Foeger also pioneered the use of television cameras to "video" skiers and expanded the area with more lifts and trails.

Jay was sold to Weyerhauser Properties, a subsidiary of the giant lumber company which owned the land abutting the state forest, in 1966. With their considerable resources, Jay saw significant expansion with a new base lodge, the 60-passenger aerial tramway and Sky Haus, the Hotel Jay, and more trails. Having accomplished his dream of a tram and building Jay into a major ski area (and an economic resource for the region), Foeger, who had had a parting of the ways with his new boss, returned to his homeland after twelve years of leading Jay as a true ski pioneer. He left an indelible mark on Eastern skiing.

In 1978 Weyerhauser sold to Mont Saint-Sauveur International, a Canadian company which also owns and operates six other ski areas and a water park in the Laurentians north of Montreal. In 1985 they hired Bill Stenger to lead Jay's efforts to become a year-round destination. A Master Plan was developed, approvals acquired, and construction of residential housing and mountain expansion were undertaken with expenditures of over $34 million to date on new lifts, the replacement of the tram cars, snowmaking, grooming, trails, condos, central sewage infrastructure and utilities.

The plans also included an 18-hole golf course, which was started in 2003 and is slated for play in 2006. Another part of the plan calls for expansion to West Bowl, a 250-acre sunny area with magnificent glades, intermediate terrain, and a 1,400-foot vertical. Three lifts, 9 trails, 8 glades, and a West Bowl Base Village with residential housing will be built in phases. Construction is expected to begin in spring 2005 or 2006, Stenger said.

Under the Tram. JPR

Another important part of Jay's history has been the development of the Glades System. Seeing the joy of those skiing between trails, Stenger consulted (the late) Sel Hannah, a legendary trail designer, who advised a 6-to-8-foot trim radius, no cutting of healthy trees, and a regeneration focus. The first glades were ready in 1987 and the system has grown to what is recognized as the best in North America.

When Jay Peak Resort is complete (sometime in the next 10 years), it will encompass a ski resort with 3 mountain areas, 100 trails, 450 acres of skiable terrain and another 250 acres of *off-piste*. Plus it will offer the 200 acres of outback terrain that backcountry aficionados now enjoy. As the Jay Peak residential Village grows, indoor recreation and additional shopping opportunities and restaurants will round out the project.

The Mountain

For the 2005 season, Jay Peak offers 76 trails, chutes, and glades on two interconnected mountains referred to as Stateside and Tramside. From various vantages along the broad mountaintop, you can see four states (NY, NH, ME, and VT) and Canada, the Green Mountains, the Adirondacks, the Whites, and the Presidential Range of New Hampshire.

Advanced/Expert ♦ ♦♦

Below the Tram, Jay has spruce-laden rocky terrain that beckons to chute and cliff seekers—the expert's expert who is part-mountain goat (of 'kid' age, strength, and daring). The Face Chutes (70 percent gradient) are the stuff 'extreme' skiers crave. Green Beret and River Quai are known as Jay's two hairiest trails because they are very narrow and steep. The two steepest glades are Valhalla and Staircase (52 percent gradient) and the longest is Everglade at 1.25 miles. There are over 100 acres of *off-piste* woods to explore within Jay's boundaries. Out of bounds is the Dip, a rolling wooded stash to skiers' right of the Jet Triple. Another popular out-of-bounds trip is to 'skin' to Big Jay, a peak behind Jay, then ski down to Route 242 for pre-arranged rides back to the area.

> **A note of caution**: Jay's out-of-bound trails lead *away from* Jay Peak base areas and only experts who know what they are doing should head into the backcountry. Getting lost on Big Jay is easy to do and spending the night on the mountain is not recommended. (Guided tours are available.)

For mere mortals who enjoy challenging trails, the Jet Triple at Stateside serves several black diamond trails and glades. The Jet (♦) beneath the lift is queasy straight down steep but very wide and mercifully forgiving on packed powder (hairier than hell on ice). It's intermediate on its lower section as is the U.N. (■), which is narrow and parallels it. The top of UN (♦) is an invigorating bump steep. The wide Haynes Trail (used for races and named after founder Harold Haynes), narrow Kitzbuehl, and gladed Timbuktu, Kitz Woods, and Hells Woods (all diamonds) similarly offer soulful steeps.

There are more diamonds off the Bonaventure Quad with Can Am a 150-foot-wide bump hill under the lift and Deliverance one of several challenging glades. The Beaver Pond Glade, Beyond Beaver Pond, Everglade, and Staircase are all wooded steeps accessed off the Flyer Express Quad.

Intermediate ■

To explore Jay's eastern side off the Tram, you can take Northway and follow it around the back of the mountain to Ullr's Dream (■), an advanced intermediate trail for most of its 3 miles. Ullr's starts with wide steep sections, then narrows and winds around the mountain before becoming a flat schuss to the Tram. The variations make it a popular trail.

You can also access Ullr's from the Flyer Express Quad. Ullr's to Kokomo (■), an

Jon Lorentz on Ullr's Dream. Glades entrance lower left.

easy glade, is a great option—kind of like the Beach Boys song; starts out in a funky groove and ends up fun and soothing (and avoids a longer runout).

Other blues off the Flyer include Poma Line, Alligator Alley, Upper Goat Run, Lower Exhibition, and Northway. Northway to Angel's Wiggle and Northway to Upper and Lower Goat to Rabbit are both long blue cruises to the Bonaventure or Jet chairs which are on Stateside.

You can also take the Tram and follow the Vermonter (■) trail to Stateside. With views to a snow-capped Mount Mansfield to the southwest, it is a stunning run along the mountain's edge that gets progressively more challenging. Following it to Angel's Wiggle provides a long run to the two Stateside chairs. Off the Bonaventure, you can catch Northway to a number of delightful blue cruisers like Angel's Wiggle, Paradise Meadows, and Hell's Crossing. Off the Jet Chair, Montrealer provides a picture perfect cruise to Northway or Angel's Wiggle and more blissful lower-mountain blues.

Lower intermediates would do well to warm up on Interstate and the many novice trails off the Interstate Quad and then stick with blues like Montrealer, Northway, and Angel's Wiggle.

Beginner/Novice ●

The Beginner Terrain Zone (●) offers dedicated 'never-ever,' novice, and lower intermediate terrain. There are four lifts, 80 acres of easy trails, slopes, and glades, a fenced-in learning area, and an indoor learning center.

View of Vermonter and Tram from Montrealer. Note sign in deep snow—the reason the Face Chutes below the Tram opened early on January 27, 2003. KL

Interstate is the popular beginner slope because it's mega wide, but Harmony Lane and Deer Run are also gentle greens. Perry Merrill Avenue to Queen's Highway provides a long green cruise back to the chair. Perry Merrill to Raccoon Run (●) under the Village Chair or to Chalet Meadows (●) a novice slope served by a T-Bar at Stateside are other good options.

Jay does not have novice or beginner terrain off the Tram or upper-mountain chairs, but it is possible to ride the Tram back down so anyone can enjoy the view and lunch at the top.

Terrain Parks

Jay has four terrain parks designed and built on the idea of "Progressive Accessibility." Jay recommends "getting the basics down in the beginner and intermediate parks and then taking your riding to the next level, one-step at a time."

The Grom Park is a freestyle zone set up for entry-level riders and for warm-up hits. Located on the right-hand side of Interstate and accessed directly off the Metro Quad, the Grom Park is a breeding ground for jibbers of the future and is great for early season warm-up sessions. The Rail Garden, located next to the Moving Carpet on Tramside, includes jibables (smaller versions of the rails in The Park) that can be easily reconfigured to create your own line.

The two more advanced parks are located on Stateside below the Bonaventure Chair. The Progression Park (which is transformed into a Boarder Cross for a day mid-season) is located on the trail to rider's left of Lower Can Am. It's the hot spot for dialing in new moves before going big in The Park. The Park is Jay's expert park and includes big hits, table tops, rails, boxes, and other features.

Resort Experience

Our trip to Jay Peak provided a sensory experience of the first order. It began with a scenic ride up Route 100, "the skiers' highway," and picked up intrigue as we left Morrisville and Route 100 at Eden for the wilderness of northern Vermont on Route 118 and the mountainous approach from Montgomery Center (Route 242) to Jay Peak. You can also arrive by Route 100 and 101 to 242 West. Either way, this section of northern Vermont is predominantly flat and desolate with some hills and occasional farms for scenic value, and then suddenly you climb up into the mountains with Jay a sight that makes the heart beat faster—especially if you happen to approach from the Troy side and see the Tram leaning out into space. That's a good image, because as a ski mountain, Jay is certainly out there!

Just seven miles from the Canadian border, coming upon Jay for the first time is like traveling to another country. When you enter the base village at twilight, you find the Austrian-styled, white stucco, wood trimmed buildings and Hotel Jay outlined in twinkling white lights. They issue a greeting of "welcome, you found us" as you enter what can best be described as a small Alpine hamlet.

The Hotel Jay is 50 feet from the Tram Haus (base lodge) and Austria Haus (offices, lounge, dining hall) and 200 feet from a little general store (soda and chips to milk and eggs). The hotel offers a convenient and comfortable place to stay and has wonderful food.

The bilingual welcome sign and Jay Tram as seen from the Hotel Jay in summer. KL

January 15, 2003 dawned bright and cold, minus four, our waiter said, adding his car wouldn't start. The summit would be colder due to the wind and high elevation.

Seizing an opportunity to test out high-tech ski socks, I headed over to the ski shop with son Jonathan. We both ended up with Hot Chilly's, and yes, they did the job.

I asked Jon, a 26-year-old jazz musician, physically-fit grad student, to take a ski lesson. I wanted to test the advice I had passed on in articles that "advanced skiers can benefit from instruction that gets them to the best terrain and helps them improve their skiing." As a fifty-plus woman, I could attest to such advice but would a young, single male?

Knowing my more macho son would really hate being asked to do this, I figured it would be a good test. He would be honest with me as he hadn't skied much during his NYU years and taking a lesson was the last thing he'd want to do on our short two-day trip. Since he hadn't had lessons on shaped skis, I figured this would be helpful to him at best and boring at worst (if they kept to easy terrain or overdid the technique part).

The guys in the rental shop took good care of Jon, fitting him with cool Head Monster demo skis, and that was the last I saw of him as he departed to meet his instructor with a very pleased grin on his face.

Two hours later, the first thing he said to me was, "Thanks, Mom, that was great!!" Relief, then envy flooded through me as he recounted his exciting adventure.

His friendly young ski instructor Chris acted as a tour guide as well as a teacher. Maybe " hip adventure coach" would be the most appropriate way to describe him. I suspect Chris is either a passionate outdoorsman or he sized Jon up and decided to give him the full Jay—probably both.

The cold Summit scene after departing the Tram. KL

First thing Chris did was take Jon up the Tram and hike him up the rock staircase to the ice and snow encrusted pinnacle above the Tram. On the way, he said, "We'll check each other for frostbite occasionally," the only allowance he would make to the wind and cold that day. They took in the magnificent 360-degree view and then hightailed it back to their skis, mixing a fast-paced mountain exploration with pointers on shaped skis and how to use them.

They skied the entire area and even took the Flyer, braving the ridge winds at the top. The word is that people call this speedy chair "the Freezer," because on a very cold, windy day the ride can be frigid. As Chris skied Jon "all over," he gave him some instruction on how to work the shaped skis Jon was new to as well as an introduction to the glades and bumps—where to hit the bumps, how to pick a line and turn on top.

Jon's response was to give his emphatic approval to recommending instruction for expert and advanced skiers. "I never would have skied the woods if I hadn't been in that lesson," he told me. He was duly impressed, explaining how difficult glades are because they "require more energy and control and the ability to deal with moguls," but at the same time proud of having survived the experience! And, he was more than pleased with how much mileage they had put on their boards. Plus, he got to some of the best terrain and was able to introduce me to The Jet after we met up again.

While Jon was off with Chris, my Dad and I were guided around the mountain in a more deliberate and cerebral way by a young PR person. I was eager to have "an official tour" that would give me a sample of everything, including the beginner area and a glance at some sections of the mountain that I would never ski myself.

We started with a warm-up run on Interstate, off the new (2003) Metro Quad and then took Perry Merrill over to the Stateside area and inspected the novice glades on the way. A ride up the Bonaventure Quad provided a panoramic

Riding the Bonaventure chair at Stateside. The Sky Haus which houses the top terminal for the Jay Tram looms out into space off in the distance (top left). KL

perspective on Tramside as well as the Stateside triple chair area to our left. It also gave us a bird's-eye opportunity to watch people below on bump trails and in the glades. Dad observed that Jay is unique in that the lift rides give you glorious views of the mountain itself *and* you also get amazing views of the region from every part of the mountain.

Next we hit the Tram. It is thrilling to be up so high, but because it is such a gentle ride my apprehension quickly subsided. (In my first winter visit a year earlier, I had never ridden it, sticking to the fast Flyer that never had more than a four-minute wait even though it was a busy Saturday in March.)

"Much nicer than the trams at Snowbird and Jackson Hole," Dad commented. When I asked what he meant, he reinforced the notion of gentle, noting the seamless takeoffs and landings. No jolts on the ride either.

The winds at the summit area were bone chilling, but the views were worth it. We hit Ullr's and Kokomo, my personal favorites which I usually ski off the Flyer, and took the Tram again to explore Jay's other side.

Part way down Vermonter, we pulled up at the top of Green Beret to peer over. It's heart-stoppingly steep, and I was quick to shift my gaze to the more peaceful view of Lake Memphramagog.

We stayed on nice, wide, blue cruising trails and rode the Jet Triple, but not having time to do The Jet, we took a long ski back to the Tram base over a meandering trail that passes by the condos and takes in views of the terrain park, glades, and bump trails.

After meeting up with Jon, who had skied The Jet with Chris and assured me it was well groomed packed powder, the two of us headed back to Stateside. It was a tad scary looking straight down the steep Jet trail from the top, but what a hoot to ski! I felt myself skiing better as I sprang into a waltz of turns that energized me. As I began to get my nerve and ski legs back, I discovered what Jay enthusiasts already know—it's exhilarating to meet a challenge.

Unique at Jay

Vermont's only Tram whisks you to the 3,968-foot summit where you can hike up a short rocky trail to the very pinnacle in summer and experience a top-of-the-world sensation. Only the hardy (and crazy) do it in boots in winter.

Perched at the very northern tip of the Green Mountains, Jay's summit is a high-elevation land mass that storm systems hit as they move from the northwest toward Vermont. This mountain range forces the air masses upward, creating condensation, thickening clouds, and localized snowfall. Known as orographic lift, this phenomenon causes what is known as *The Jay Cloud*. The Jay Cloud is responsible for an average of 35 powder days a season.

Jay Peak Resort boasts Vermont's largest glades system for all ability levels and offers backcountry instruction and guided tours of The Dip. Check these options out at the Adventure Center or on Jay's Website.

Good to Know

Jay Peak is located off Route 242 in Jay, about 70 miles northeast of Burlington International Airport and 17 miles west of downtown Newport; 230 miles (3.5 hours) from Boston; 250 miles (4 hours) from Hartford; 371 miles, (6.5 hours) from NYC; and 150 miles (3 hours) from Rutland, Vermont.

President Bill Stenger is one of the fun things about Jay. Attend a ski week and you will have a rousing good time at the Welcome Party when he leads the Skol song in his Norseman getup. Or you might see him greeting guests by the ticket booth in the morning or at the end of the day. He sets the friendly tone for the area because he truly loves what he is doing and you can hear it in his voice and see it in his smile.

There is a free, 2-hour mountain tour led by a Jay Ambassador. Tours start at 9:30 and 1:30 Mondays through Fridays at the Tour sign in front of the Tram and are for skiers and riders of all abilities.

Sample the Stateside area early in the day to catch the sun on the Jet Triple and its challenging trails.

Rumor has it that there's a natural halfpipe in Canyonland. The best glades for riders are Canyonland and Vertigo.

Beginners: don't miss the Village Chair and Raccoon Run.

Parents: check out the ski school programs for kids. If you want to introduce your toddler to snow yourself, you can use the moving carpet in the learning area.

There's a slopeside Clubhouse for children with supervision for kids enrolled in various programs so parents can enjoy a worry-free day on the slopes.

Teens: the Adventure Center offers options to try snowboarding, skiing, snow blading, Telemark skiing, snowshoeing, backcountry adventure clinics, and terrain park clinics.

At peak busy times, if it's *really cold*, head for the Flyer as not many will, so there won't be a wait. If you are warmly and properly dressed with neck gaiter (2 works for me), goggles, and helmet or hat, you can survive just fine. (If *really* windy, just cover your head with your mitts—it's part of the sport!)

The Tram Haus is a full-service base lodge (at the base of the Tram) with fireplace, cafeteria, lounge, etcetera. There's also food service at the Sky Haus at the top of the Tram. The Stateside Lodge has a cafeteria and ski shop as well as parking.

Weekly events include the Monday Night Welcome Party, snow cat rides, dairy and maple farm tours, sleigh rides, torchlight parades and sometimes fireworks. Special events like magic and puppet shows are planned for holiday weeks like Christmas and President's Week. Check the Website for listings of events and competitions.

Hotel Jay packages include dinner and full breakfast. Veal, chicken, duck, shrimp, and steak are among the evening entrees, chocolate mousse or mousse cake among the desserts. The breakfast buffet with hot dish service (eggs, omelettes, French toast, pancakes) is quick, easy, and fortifying.

This 1970s vintage hotel is not fancy, but it's comfortable, convenient, affordable and has a more bona fide rustic skier ambiance than luxury hotels. However, take advantage of the hotel specials soon, because it is slated to be torn down to make way for a larger, more modern facility in the future.

Bill Stenger (center) introduces the Skol song.

Ski writers get into the Skol toast in the International Room where they enjoyed a great banquet. KL

Steals and Deals

Visit Jay's Website or call for details on these and other savings.

Jubilee Fridays: Complete a short form online and get an email coupon good for every non-holiday Friday from December 24 to April 1 for one $40 Adult lift ticket and one $30 Junior lift ticket.

Purchase a Jay Peak Passport for $25 and adults pay $40 and Juniors $30 the first four times they ski/ride at Jay Peak and the fifth visit is free.

Bring a first-time, 'never-ever' skier or rider (age 10 & up) to Jay, purchase a Learn-to-Ski/Ride Package for $45 (includes rental equipment, a group lesson, & Beginner Zone ticket) and you get a free lift ticket for the same day.

College Fridays: with ID, $25 for non-holiday Fridays, starting 1/9/05.

Jay has a $37 Vermont/Clinton County, NY. adult resident, any-day rate (ID/driver's license required); $32 for Juniors (7-17 with ID).

Stay at the Hotel Jay (sauna, Jacuzzi, Lounge, dining room) or a Jay condo during non-holiday weeks, and you get free midweek group lessons for each paying adult and complimentary daycare for kids ages 2 to 7. Children 14 and under in parent's room or a condo, ski and stay free (meals extra), and there are also special teen (ages 15-18) rates.

Phone numbers below are **area code 802** unless otherwise noted.

Handy Info

Website: www.jaypeakresort.com
Email: info@jaypeakresort.com
General information: 988-2611, 800-451-4449
Snow report: 988-9601
Lift Hours: 9-4 midweek; 8:30-4 weekends.
Tickets 2005 season: Adults $56 (midweek, weekends/holidays); College students (valid ID) $30; Juniors (7-17 with ID) $42; Kids 6 & under $6; Seniors (65+) $12; Sunday morning Adult $38/Jr. $33; Sunday afternoon Adult $32/Jr. $28.
Beginner Zone ticket: Adults, $20; Juniors, $10.

Quick Stats

Season: November to April, average 156 days.
Average annual snowfall: 355+ inches.
Snowmaking capability: 80 percent; 308 acres.
Lifts: 8; 60-passenger Tram, 3 quads (1 express), 1 triple, 1 double, 2 surface (1 carpet, 1 T-Bar).
Uphill lift capacity: 12,175 rides per hour.

Jay Peak

Trails: 76, 385 acres of trails and glades; 50+ miles; plus 100+ acres *off-piste*; longest trail: Ullr's Dream, 3 miles.
Glades: 21; for all abilitiy levels, ranging from easy Bushwacker and Kokomo to challenging diamonds like Valhalla, Timbuktu, Vertigo.
Bumps: UN, Kitzbuehel, Can Am.
Parks: 4 parks, entry level to advanced at Tramside and Stateside.
Grooming: 4 groomers.
Vertical Drop:
    Jay Summit to Tram base: 2,153'
    Flyer Quad area: 1,614'
    Stateside Jet Triple area: 1,165'
    Bonaventure area: 1,366'
    Stateside to Tramside: 1,200'

Jay Peak Snowsports School   988-2611 x 2186

Privates, group lessons for skiing or riding. Learn-to-Ski/Ride package (ages 10 & up) includes a 2-hour group lesson, ski or snowboard rentals, and a Beginner Zone lift ticket. Glade skiing clinics; terrain park clinics; guided backcountry tours. Burton Method Center for snowboard instruction.

Children's Programs   988-2611 x 2214

Infant care: for under age 2, reservations required 988-2611 x 8265.
Daycare Nursery: ages 2-7; free for on-property lodging guests.
Kinderski: learning program for ages 3-5, morning or afternoon sessions on snow and indoor ski ramp. Lunch option.
Explorers: learn to ski for ages 5-10, half or full-day.
Mini Learn to Ride: snowboard instruction for ages 5-6.
Mini Riders: learn to ride for ages 7-10, half or full-day.
Mountain Adventures: ages 10-18 with options, including lessons, X-C, snow skates, apprenticing with an instructor. Half or full-day.

Other Things to Do

Massage Therapy: various massage therapies, from deep therapeutic to relaxing Swedish massage. Call to make reservations, 988-2611.
Telemark with instruction, rentals available at mountain.
Cross-country skiing and snowshoeing are offered at nearby Hazen's Notch Association (326-4799) which has 64 km of X-C trails, including some snowshoe-only trails. Rentals and instruction are available.
Snowmobiling: rentals and tours available through Jay Village Inn (988-2306). Extensive VAST trail system allows touring to your heart's content.
Also, après-ski Snow Cat rides, Welcome Party, and Ski Week activities.

For non-skiers: scenic Tram ride and lunch at the top with friends.

Visit the Jay Country Store (a few minutes east in the Village of Jay) for souvenirs, Vermont products, folk art, and wine selection.

Montgomery: quaint shops, antiques, soda fountain at Trout River Traders.

Rustler's Ranch (988-9833) in N. Troy for trail rides, lessons, sleigh rides.

Visit Couture's Dairy and Maple Farm in North Troy (744-2733) for tours of the farm and maple facilities.

Phil and Karen's (744-9928) in Westfield for sleigh rides, hayrides.

Travel to: Newport for dining, shopping, and more (Bogner Outlet); Burlington, Vermont's largest city (home to three colleges) for cultural opportunities, dining, and shopping; Mansonville or Knowlton in the Eastern Townships of Canada for dining, strolling, and exploring another culture.

Dining Out

Alpine Room in the Hotel Jay offers "all-you-can-eat breakfast buffet" and delectable candlelight dinners. The International Room is open for lunch on weekends and is a great option with various lunch specials (sometimes a buffet) with wait service. Special dinners in this room are wonderful and fun.

Montgomery Center: the Belfry for rustic atmosphere, good food, micro brews; Inn On Trout River offers Lemoine's Restaurant (fine dining) and Hobo's Café (pub menu). Trout River Traders (breakfast, lunch, homemade food); Bernie's Restaurant and Pub (chef-owned) serves breakfast, lunch and dinner; and Montgomery Pizza and Sub Shop for calzones, pizza, and subs.

Montgomery Village: The Black Lantern Inn, for candlelight dinner at a restored stagecoach stop on National Historic Register, menu varies.

North Troy: Village Inn and Restaurant (good food in restored inn).

Troy: The 101 Restaurant, for breakfast, lunch or dinner.

Newport: Lago Trattoria, acclaimed northern Italian; variety of eateries from pizzerias to gourmet restaurants to fast food.

Quebec: Owl's Bread Bakery and Restaurant in Mansonville.

Accommodations

The bedbase is 2,000 in the region. At the mountain there are pillows for 1,500+, including hotel, condos, and townhomes, most with ski-on/ski-off access. Several small communities near Jay Peak offer lodgings from B & B to motels, ski lodges to homes for rent, including the towns of Jay, Montgomery Center, Montgomery, Troy and North Troy (within 5 to 15 minute drive).

The city of Newport (the region's largest community at 12,000 people) offers a range of affordable lodgings. The Eastern Townships of Canada, a collection of small communities of English or French heritage offer very affordable lodgings and excellent cuisine due to favorable exchange rates.

For assistance with selecting or making reservations, call:
Hotel Jay: 800-451-4449; 988-9601.
Jay Peak Area Association: 800-882-7460.
Jay Reservations: 800-451-4449; 988-2611.

Après-ski/Nightlife

In the base lodge, the Golden Eagle Lounge downstairs and International Bar, upstairs along with the Lounge in the Hotel Jay are popular slopeside meeting spots with frequent entertainment or theme parties. Après-Ski Party Tramside, Fridays 4-7 p.m. featuring the Frick & Frack Show (DJs with Attitude).

In Jay: Squiddie's Pub at The Lodge hosts live bands; the Jay Village Inn offers a cozy pub.

In Knowlton, Quebec, the Knowlton Pub is a lively après-ski location; nightly from 4 to 9 p.m.

Summer/Fall

The Tram ride is spectacular and an easy way to gain altitude. You meet people from all over the world on the ride. The Long Trail passes over the mountain so you can wander a bit and talk to trekkers or hike down to Route 242 if you have pre-arranged transportation back to the resort. Jay also offers: hiking on its trails; trout fishing in the Jay Branch Brook; large outdoor heated pool, tennis courts, and golf course (2006) with many other courses within in a 20-mile radius. Also, hiking at Hazen's Notch Association trails (no fee).

Explore lakes, rivers, Troy, Montgomery, Canada, and Newport (the "Little City on the Lake"). Lake Memphremagog is a 33-mile-long jewel that extends from Newport 28 miles into Canada. Scenic boat tours leave from the downtown Newport dock daily. The City of Newport offers dining, theaters, shopping, and year-round activities.

Long Trail hikers and their Black Labs take a break on Jay Peak. One of the brother-sister Labs carries a pack. KL

Our Jay Peak Adventure

Date:

Weather:

Companions:

Where Stayed:

Visit Highlights:

Our Discoveries:

82 Killington

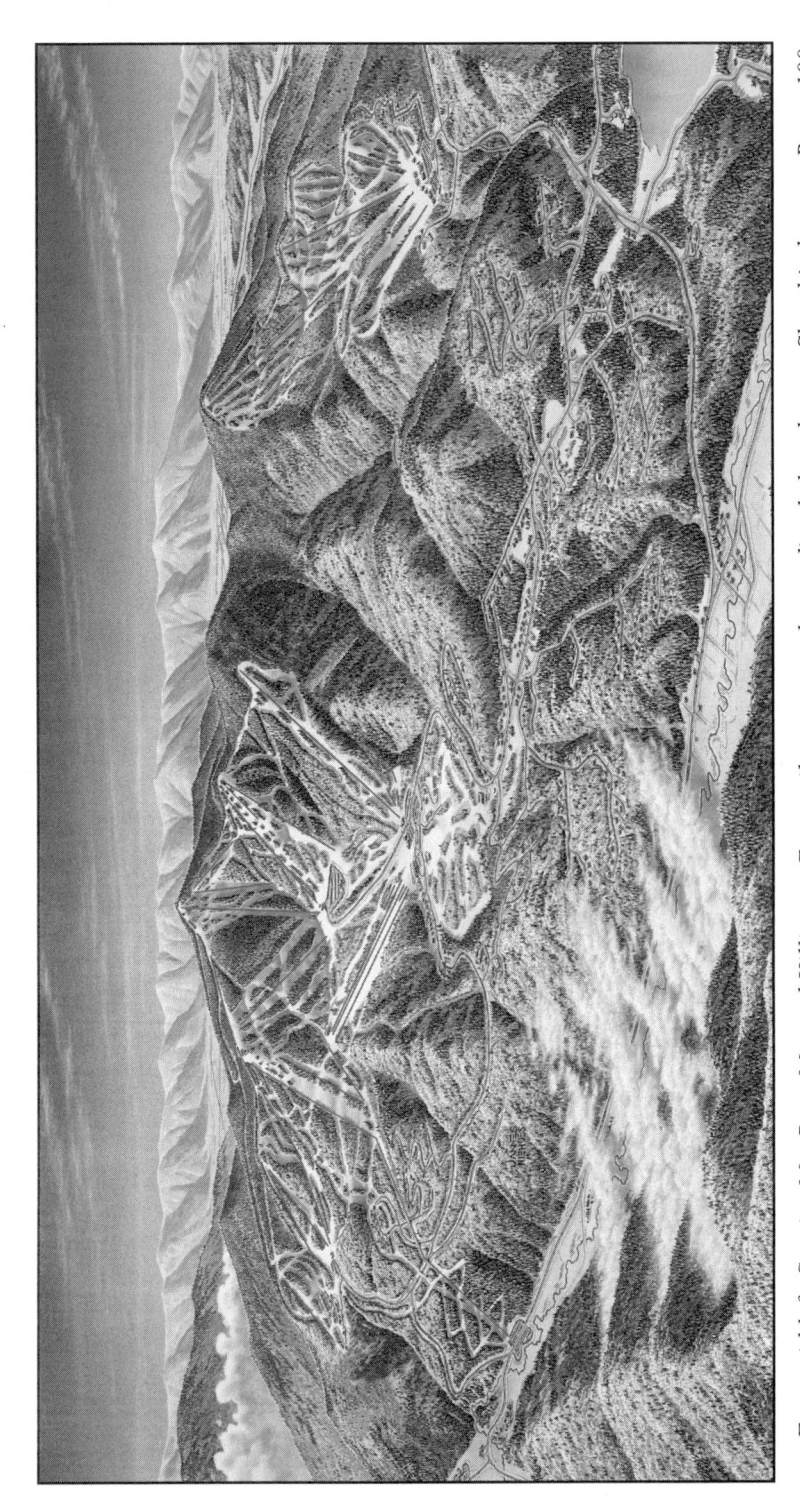

From mid left: Sunrise Mt., Bear Mt., and Killington East trails next to and extending below them to Skyeship base on Route 100. Skye Peak has two of its faces showing and is to left of Killington Peak (highest peak), then Snowdon and Rams Head. Snowshed slopes are lower center to left with the Killington Golf Course below in the "basin." Pico Ski Area is to far right. There are plans to connect the two areas with lifts and trails. Killington Peak is the highest point reached by a ski lift in Vermont and is accessible by all ability levels.

Chapter Seven

Killington
Adventures in World-Class Skiing

The Killington Ski and Summer Resort is not only the East's largest ski area, it's also a world-renowned one that has a colorful history to match its pioneering achievements in the ski industry.

In a word, Killington is about variety. It offers tree skiing for those who enjoy trails the way nature makes them, bumps for the would-be Weinbrechts of the world, ridiculous steeps for thrill seekers, and terrain parks and pipes for tricksters and freeriders. For the rest of us, there are wonderful gentle greens, a mother lode of diamonds, and blues in all hues.

Like all great mountains, Killington has something for everyone. It just happens to have more of it.

And that includes the magnificent mountain vistas and scenery that make a wintry day outdoors a very special experience. It's a world-class experience, heralded by the highest lift-served skiing in Vermont and the Northeast for *all* ability levels. Novices and intermediates can enjoy the mountaintop and a 3,050 foot vertical, one of the greatest in America for green and blue trails.

Killington is part of a *massif*, a series of many high peaks that spread out for miles. These mountains not only create their own weather system, but also are topographically different from each other, creating a huge diversity of terrain and more fun for skiers and riders. Killington has six contiguous mountain skiing areas with all of them skiable by all ability levels.

There's also a neighboring seventh mountain (included on a Killington lift ticket) at 3,967-foot Pico, an area with its own distinct personality and amalgam of trails that was acquired by Killington's corporate parent in 1996. (Pico also has its own lower-priced lift ticket; see Pico Chapter, page 191.) Plans for an interconnect have met with delays, but chances are very good that by the time Killington turns fifty in 2008, there will be trails and lifts that join pioneer Killington with historic Pico, making for a winter-and-summer resort complex of about 5,060 acres (10 square miles) and 8 mountain areas.

For 2005, the combined Killington/Pico resort boasts 1,209 skiable acres that encompass tree skiing (for all ability levels) and 200 trails—trails that are narrow, wide, twisting, straight, moguled up or machine-groomed smooth.

There are bruisers, cruisers, steep and deep, and gentle to the point of flat. The trails total 90 miles and snowmaking covers 61 of those miles, 846 acres worth for the 2005 ski season. There are natural-snow only trails and some trails that don't (or rarely) get groomed like the natural steeps of Royal Flush and Flume or Vertigo (upper) and Conclusion.

Points of Distinction

Killington has a well-deserved reputation as a pioneering ski area with one of the longest ski seasons in the nation, stretching to eight months many years. It boasts state-of-the-art technology featuring: an up-to-date lift system, including two heated, 8-passenger gondolas and six express quads; North America's most extensive snowmaking system with 1,200 land guns and 650 tower guns; and a grooming fleet of 17 machines with high-tech implements.

There is an innovative ski school that has evolved into the Perfect Turn Clinics so more 'never-evers' get their starts here and more advanced skiers become unbelievably good mountain goats.

The distinctions go on: steepest bump trail (Outer Limits); longest beginner slope (Snowshed), longest beginner trail (Juggernaut); longest novice trails (Great Eastern, Great Northern); outrageous steeps (Devil's Fiddle, Ovation); and the greatest vertical in Vermont. Additionally, Killington owns the number-one nightspot in skierdom, the famous Wobbly Barn. The five-mile Killington Road also sports abundant après-ski, from sushi bar to steakhouse, cozy piano lounge to classic hot spots with live rock.

As an area that celebrates winter and snow with serious and joyous dedication, Killington attracts skiers from throughout the world, numbering 20,000 international visitors a year! If this means it can be crowded at times (and it can be on peak weekends and holidays as most areas are), it also translates to a taste of cosmopolitan and the excitement of meeting people from Macedonia to the United Kingdom, from France to Down Under. It should be noted, however, that although lines may *look* long, you can move through them rather quickly thanks to a modern, high-capacity lift system that is also one of the largest in the country.

The K-1 Express Gondola accesses Killington Peak at the 4,215-foot level, the highest elevation reached by an aerial lift in Vermont. (Hikers can go up a tad higher and catch a few more vertical on Cat Walk.) The pinnacle is 4,241 feet above sea level, Vermont's second highest summit (and an easy one to access in summer thanks to the K-1 or a hike on one of the trails).

Killington also has the state's highest base-area elevations: 2,100 to 2,200 feet at Snowshed's three lifts; 2,200 feet at Rams Head and Bear Mountain; 2,500 feet at Snowdon and Killington Peak (base lodge area). This is significant for the amount of snow that falls. The huge Green Mountain massif which

The glorious headwall on Cascade beneath the K-1 Gondola. KR

includes all the various peaks of Killington and Pico causes air masses from the West to rise up and dump *big snows* on the other side. The higher elevations also mean temperatures stay colder and snow lasts longer, whether from the sky or a snow gun. Colder temperatures help Killington extend the ski season with earlier openings and later closings, aided of course by a gargantuan snowmaking system, for the longest ski season in the East for 42 years.

The high elevation of Killington Peak also affords a 3,050-foot vertical descent to the Skyeship Gondola Base on U.S. Route 4. A five-mile easy Great Eastern meanders across several mountain areas, ending at the Skyeship base. There's also a blue route, making for long, fun runs for kids and adults who want to test their stamina or just cruise through some very pretty scenery and ski through a tunnel or two.

Because Killington's six mountains are connected by lifts and trails that novices can handle, skiers of all ability levels can go to the tops of all the various mountains, enjoy the various lift rides and views, and ski to the next area. That's a rare feature that makes Killington one of the most accessible mountains in the United States and the world!

Trail designers also remembered to challenge the experts. The steeps at Killington are truly steep and among the toughest in Vermont. There are sections of trails that go up to 45 degrees or 100 percent gradient, but they are short pitches so Killington rates their trails for overall or average pitch.

In the major trails category (long, top-to-bottom runs), Ovation takes the pitch honors with 60 percent overall gradient (31 degrees). Devil's Fiddle is

59 percent overall although there are sections on the face part, notably "the Cliff," that hit 65 to 100 percent. Outer Limits has a 51 percent gradient (27.5 degrees) with much steeper sections at the top; Superstar has an average 50 percent gradient (26.5 degrees) but has several steeper sections on it. These are some of the major long trails with consistent pitch for their overall lengths.

Other trails like Cascade, Royal Flush, and East Fall have as steep or steeper pitches in places, but they are not as consistently steep overall for as long. Cascade's left fork section boasts a 56 percent gradient (29 degrees) while East Fall has a 600-foot stretch at 50 percent and Royal Flush has a similar section. Downdraft and Big Dipper (tree skiing) have average 53 percent gradients (28 degrees) for 800 feet. (See the Glossary in Appendix B, pages 294-295, for an explanation of gradients and further information on steeps.)

Where History and Mountains Meld

Because area-founder Preston Leete Smith envisioned offering a better ski experience, Killington pioneered many advances that made learning to ski easier and more fun. The Snowshed and Bear Mountain areas were just two of those advances that took skiing to new levels. The Killington Ski School was another. It turned 'never evers' into skiers so successfully in the 1960s that it fueled the growth of the sport and furthered expansion of the area. Because Killington was predicated on providing a better experience, it has been a work in progress for almost 50 years. Whether it's new trail signage, terrain parks and Superpipe on Bear Mountain, and more tree skiing areas (all new for 2005), or creating a special place for families or renaming an area to avoid confusion (The Glades became North Ridge in 2005), Killington continues to grow better with age.

Snowshed Area ●

One of the first advances was Snowshed, which is located on the lower section of Skye Peak. The idea behind Snowshed was to provide gentle terrain (6-15 percent gradient) long enough that skiers could practice and get the feel of gliding and turning on snow so they would progress faster and have more fun. But when Pres Smith ordered the first Snowshed chairlift from the French Pomagalski lift company in 1961, he received a call telling him, "Zer must be some meesestake." They had never built a chairlift for such a flat hill. [That could be why so many of us learned on Pomalifts, rope tows, and T-Bars in the 1950s and 1960s.]

Not only did the chair manufacturer shake his head, so did some of Smith's own staff. They considered a separate beginner area with a three-quarter-mile long trail to be "tremendously risky because it had never been done before in the ski industry" and they "weren't sure it would fly." But Smith, seeing the

Snowshed slope and trails are to left of center, Rams Head to far right. A skier underpass connects the two areas for a logical progression for beginners. Skye Peak is above Snowshed and Killington Peak is center with Snowdon to its right. KR

phenomenal growth of the sport in the 1950s, was interested in catering to beginners and new skiers in a separate learning area that the ski school could also use for its beginner classes.

The original, narrow Snowshed trail (under the lift) and Yodeler proved so popular that a second chair, third trail, and snowmaking were added in 1963. With increasing business, Snowshed was eventually widened to its present width to accommodate more skiers and a third chair was added.

Today, one of those chairs is a detachable quad that makes loading easier. There is also a gentle Pomalift for beginners with a short practice slope. There are three trails (off to skier's left) which tend to get less traffic and fewer hotshots bombing them. One is the idyllic Yodeler, another the return trail from Killington called Idler (reached via Highlander from Snowshed) and the other the Learn to Ski trail. All are long trails that are great for learners.

For the 2005 season, the popular Beach Terrain Park was relocated to Bear Mountain so Snowshed is once again a dedicated, ultra-wide beginner slope.

Rams Head Mountain ■ ●

Rams Head was built in 1962 and offered a 6,600-foot chairlift to the top of Killington's then most northern peak (elevation 3,610 feet), giving the area 1.25-mile-long trails for intermediates. The chair offered a nice sunny ride in spring but a cold one in winter, especially at the very peak where blasts of arctic winds could occasionally stop you in your tracks.

When Les Otten bought S-K-I Limited, the parent company of Killington, in 1996, he replaced the Rams Head lift with a 5,499-foot highspeed detachable quad that ended below the peak. This was in keeping with his vision of creating a family-friendly skiing area at Rams Head and transforming the lodge into a Family Center.

Today, Rams Head is the place where tiny tots have their very own dedicated learning hill with two handle tows and two Magic Carpets near the Family Center/base lodge.

Rams Head also offers good learning trails for adults, and makes a logical progression after a first day at Snowshed. Seeing an 82-year-old lady moving down Header on her third day on skis was proof of that! If you can turn and stop, this area, which has a 1,073-foot vertical rise, offers some very nice terrain and is often less crowded than Snowshed.

Kids in Snowplay Park. KR

If you exit the Rams Head Express Quad to the right, and ski off just a tad, you can see Mount Washington and the Presidential Range in New Hampshire on a clear day. This puts you on Swirl (■), a delightful, wide trail with consistent pitch on its top section. It melds with Criss Cross (■) and becomes a gentle schuss to lower Header. Swirl may be left ungroomed after a snowfall, in which case it becomes a snowfield for purists.

Header (■) runs top to bottom under the chair. It has some steady pitch at the top, levels out and then drops again so it is really a mix of blue and green that strong novices can progress on—or avoid the steeper sections by taking Criss Cross (■) which winds back and forth before becoming Easy Street (■), a trail and terrain park for kids only (adults must be accompanied by a child). At this juncture, adults can also take Header and exit it at Dipsy Doodle (■) to avoid a short dropoff section. This area caters to developing skiers and riders.

Rams Head also has a mile-long tree-skiing area called Squeeze Play (■), and End Zone (●) is an easy tree-skiing area for little ones on the lower mountain. The Timberline Terrain Park (■) to skier's right of the lift was lengthened for 2005 and a quarter pipe was added among other upgrades. Designed for low to upper intermediate skiers and riders, Timberline Park is for those who want to ease into a park with small- to medium-sized jumps, table tops, and rails. There's also a beginner, "kids-only Terrain Park on Easy Street (■).

Snowdon Mountain ♦♦   ♦   ■   ●

Moving from the top of Rams Head over to Snowdon Mountain is a fun trip via Caper (●), which begins gently but steepens (its wide here) before runout on the valley section where the two mountains intersect. It's a nice cruise to Snowdon and kids often find side hills into the woods, which make it an exciting trip for them. Snowdon has three lifts and is a good sized area.

There are lots of options and a variety of terrain from

Miniriders start as young as age four. KR

Snowdon's 3,592-foot summit. The Snowdon Quad gives direct access to: two higher-level blues, Chute and Bunny Buster; two diamonds—a more advanced tree-skiing area known as Low Rider (♦ with direct fall line and trees tend to be a little tight), and North Star (♦), an original natural snow slope that's been missed by many but makes for great bump practice; and a classic green called Frolic that will take you to Vagabond, a natural-snow blue, or to Caper for a long run back to the lift (or to Timberline or Criss Cross for a run to Rams Head). Chop Chop, Patsy's, and The Throne are the new-for-2005 tree skiing/riding areas on Snowdon; all are rated single diamonds.

The Snowdon Triple chair serves Conclusion (♦♦) and challenging single diamonds Highline, Interceptor, Racer's Edge, and Royal Flush. Novices can take Killink (●) or Mouse (●) to Great Northern, which meanders across the mountain and leads to either the triple or quad chairs.

Snowdon Mountain is steeper than Rams Head and makes for a good progression; try it early or late in the day to avoid sharing it with lots of people. There's also an Upper Snowdon Pomalift which lets you run several trails with Upper Bunny Buster an excellent wide true blue you can practice on. You can ski back to Rams Head via the last section of Great Northern (●).

Killington Peak ♦♦ ♦ ■ ●

Killington Peak has several faces and four different skiing areas: North Ridge, formerly known as The Glades (♦■), The Canyon (♦♦), Main Face (♦♦), and South Ridge (♦■●).

North Ridge is a high-elevation area on Killington's northeastern shoulder. (To avoid confusion with the new meaning of "glades," the names of the lift and its trails were changed for 2005.) To access this area, you take the Snowdon Triple to Killink (●) to the North Ridge chair or the K-1 Gondola and Great

90 Killington

Killington Peak (elevation 4,241') is the second highest peak in Vermont and boasts the highest lift-served skiing with the K-1 Gondola alighting at the 4,215' level. This gives Killington the greatest vertical in New England. KR

Northern (●) to the three trails. Reason to Lower East Fall (formerly East Glade) is a wide, challenging blue on the steeper side. Rime is a straight-down under the chair blue with consistent pitch. Ridge Run (old West Glade) is a mix of natural snow, winding narrow top (♦), easy middle, and blue finish.

The mini terrain park on Reason is typically the first to open in the East and stays open until the Timberline and other terrain parks open each season.

Experts can access the **Canyon Quad area** from the base of the North Ridge Chair via Lower East Fall (♦) or from the top of the K-1 Gondola via Downdraft (♦♦). In addition to these two trails, this quad serves Double Dipper (♦♦) and the tree-skiing Big Dipper (♦♦). The Canyon Quad offers a very challenging 1,193-foot vertical on its trails as well as access to the Racer's Edge (♦) and a section of Royal Flush (♦). Or ski past the lift to the Killington Base area and the K-1 Express Gondola on a blue runout.

Main Face. From the K-1 Gondola (1,641 vertical drop), advanced and experts can play on tough Killington Peak trails like Escapade, Flume (old-fashioned narrow with double fall lines), Downdraft, and Cascade, all very challenging and ♦♦ for the most part with varying widths, some with double fall lines, some with bumps, and most with a short blue runout on Spillway to the base.

Novices can ski from Killington Peak across the main face via Great Northern (●) to lower Ridge Run (●) and onward to Snowdon and the K-1 base if capable and experienced, but Great Eastern (●) is an easier route on another flank due to less crossing of expert trails. (*Rank beginners really do not belong on this peak on*

A Telemarker enjoys on-top-of-the-world terrain. KR

weekends and holidays!) Intermediates will do well with any of the easier routes or blues but should avoid the diamonds. Killington's diamonds should be left to advanced skiers/riders and experts!

South Ridge. Connector trails (●) from the tops of the North Ridge Chair or K-1 Gondola lead to Killington Peak's southern face known as South Ridge. [There's the rhyme and reason to renaming the treeless Glades area the North Ridge area—just don't go over the ridge to never-never land or you're in big trouble.] This sunny side of Killington Peak is as friendly and forgiving as the eastern main face is steep and tough. Even if the chair is closed (which can happen midweek), you can still ski this area and return to Bear, Needle's Eye, or Snowshed.

To access the South Ridge area from North Ridge, you take High Traverse (●) to the top of the area. This necessitates careful crossing of the Downdraft, Cascade and Escapade trails which can be tricky at busy times, but it's certainly doable. Just stop and look up the trails to be sure you have clear passage—descending skiers have the right of way but waiting for them gives you a chance to survey the awesome terrain (♦♦) above and below you.

Or, from the K-1 Gondola unloading area, the Blue Heaven (■) trail is an old fashioned, narrow jaunt that picks up speed to South Ridge while Great Eastern (●) affords an easier, winding route for novices. The top terminal of the South Ridge Triple lets you know you have arrived at an outpost of unusual skiing. The Triple is a triangular lift that ascends one way (with a corner jog that lightly jolts riders) and descends by another route. There's lots of good terrain to explore here, and it's apt to be less crowded at peak times so check it out.

South Ridge offers Pipe Dream (● upper), wide open and surreal in its top-of-the-world expansiveness to Great Eastern (●) to Wanderer (●) for a heavenly route to the lift. Solitude (●) to Sassafras (●) offers a classic, natural snow, narrow, *ultra-gentle* meander to the South Ridge Triple. The chair also serves Upper Jug (■) to Escape (●) to Lower Pipe Dream (■), a neat run with variety and a wide, steep finish that is very challenging when moguled up.

Several interesting diamonds worth finding include lower Jug, Jug Handle, Breakaway, and Roundabout. They offer a diversity of skiing on natural snow, some with trees and others as narrow lanes through the woods.

From the base of South Ridge, you can access Falls Brook (●) for a run that follows a ravine between two mountains to the base of Bear Mountain. This route is more difficult than picking up Juggernaut (●) from the Solitude (●) trail but is doable by strong novices or aspiring intermediates. Better skiers can cruise it and will find some interesting turns, dips, bridges, and lovely scenery—look up to your left as you ski it!

Skiers/riders will find a number of terrain parks and glades at Bear Mountain. KR

Sunrise Mountain ●

Juggernaut (●) allows a peak at and connector via Juggernaut Too (●) to the Sunrise Mountain (top elevation 2,456 feet) trails of Bear View (●) and Sun Dog (●). They are fairly flat so intermediates and better do well to avoid this area unless staying in Sunrise Village condos or homes, some of which are ski-on, ski-off and others a short walk to the slopes. (You can also catch Sun Dog from the Falls Brook trail.)

The Sunrise Village chair has a 434-foot vertical rise, which makes it a nice beginner area, and there is a restaurant at the base of the lift for trailside dining at Max's Place. From the top of the lift, Bear View to Falls Brook leads to the exciting Bear Mountain base area.

[If you remember the Northeast Passage area, Sunrise used to be part of that area. At that time trails continued below the base of today's Sunrise chair and ran to the NEP Base Lodge, extending Killington's vertical to 3,175 feet and giving the area the nation's longest trail with the 10-mile Juggernaut. The chair was shortened in 1999 and the NEP base lodge now serves a snowmobiling operation that uses the former ski trails there. The 7-mile Juggernaut trail now ends at the Skyeship base.]

Bear Mountain ♦♦ ♦ ■ ●

The opening of Bear Mountain in December 1979 was one of the most exciting highlights of Killington's expansion over the years. It wasn't until 1978 that Smith thought it was feasible to develop the steep and rugged terrain for skiing. Many on his staff were skeptical, but due to advances in snowmaking and grooming technology, he thought it would be possible to cover the steep terrain with machine-made snow and then groom it with winch cats to provide dependable skiing. Once again, he was right!

Bear Mountain proved very popular and today has three chairlifts, two of which come out at the top of Bear and give access to all the trails and a third that connects to neighboring Skye Peak but also gives access to Bear trails but from a higher point.

The Devils Fiddle Quad (1,086 vertical) serves Outer Limits (♦♦) and Devils Fiddle (♦♦), a very steep, wide corkscrew trail that is known for "the cliff." (It's fun to look up at Devil's Fiddle, when traversing the last 1000 feet from Falls Brook to the Bear chair, and count the number of upright bodies.) The DF quad operates Fridays, Saturdays, Sundays and holidays, but the trail is accessible by the Bear Quad as well. For 2005, snowmaking was beefed up on Devil's Fiddle.

The Bear Mountain Quad travels up the side of the infamous, and awesome, Outer Limits. This is the chair that is the most fun to ride because you can watch people in the bumps. Some are thrashing, some are crashing, and a few are so smooth that it is amazing to behold them "dancing with bumps," a graceful tango to be sure.

Killington sports a full schedule of annual events, including the Annual Mogul Challenge on Outer Limits. KR

Outer Limits (♦♦) covers 1,200 vertical feet in a half mile and is the steepest mogul slope in the East. It is renowned for the Annual Bear Mountain Mogul Challenge as well as for being the training ground for Olympians like Donna Weinbrecht, Chuck Martin, Hannah Hardaway, and Evan Dybvig among other top mogul competitors.

Pipe action moves to Bear Mountain for 2005 and will have its own rope tow. KR

Exiting to the right off the Bear Quad, there's a choice of Wildfire (♦), a curvaceous trail that can be bumped up and truly tough at its mid section although rather nice cruiser at its top. However, things have changed for 2005 so look for terrain parks here now, too. Other upper level blues include: Bear Trap, Bear Claw, Grizzly, and Dream Maker. They ski easy at their tops but get progressively harder and have steep sections like Viper Pit on Bear Claw and the last pitch on Dream Maker. *Many of these blues on Bear used to be labeled diamonds* so be *forewarned that they are of a much greater difficulty than blues elsewhere at Killington.* Lower level or timid intermediates should avoid them. However, the Falls Brook trail off the back side of Bear is a long fun run that lower intermediates can handle.

The truly adventurous will enjoy the new terrain parks, Superpipe with 18 foot walls (near the junction of Grizzly and Dream Maker and complete with its own rope tow), and three new (♦♦) tree skiing/riding areas known as Centerpiece, Devil's Den, and Growler at Bear Mountain (all new for 2005).

The adventurous non-expert (advanced) skier or rider might enjoy taking Space Walk (■) from Wildfire to the bottom section of Outer Limits. It's fun for kids of all ages to say they've "skied Outer Limits"—bragging rights and exaggeration are part of the sport!

Dream Maker is a great but under-utilized trail you can get to from the top of the Skye Peak Quad (loads at the base of Bear) via Upper Skyeburst (■) or Upper Dream Maker (♦). The latter has constant pitch and is a nice wide slalom or GS hill when groomed but is grueling tough when bumped up. The blue section of Dream Maker offers nice cruising with the lower section featuring a short steep that is mean when bumped up in spring—good practice for the lower Outer Limits. You can also access the lower half of Dream Maker from the Bear Quad by taking the Great Eastern/aka Snowshed Crossover to Dream Maker, which is an aptly named, wide way to heaven.

Skye Peak ♦♦ ♦ ■ ●

Skye Peak (elevation 3,800 feet) has three flanks, whose runs terminate at different mountain areas: Bear Mountain, Needle's Eye, and Superstar areas. The southeastern face served by the Skye Peak Quad offers easier greens like Four Way to Frost Line heading south to Great Eastern; Skyeburst, an upper-level blue under the chair; and Dream Maker (♦■). For a route with real variety, take the Skye Peak Quad, exit left onto Skyeburst and follow to the crossover to Dream Maker, and catch Snowshed Crossover to Cruise Control. This section of Cruise Control (■) is a gloriously wide, joyous schuss to the Stage Two Skyeship Gondola and the Needles' Eye Express Quad, which is located here as well.

The eastern flank of Skye Peak is served by the Stage Two Skyeship Gondola (1,342-foot vertical rise) and by the Needle's Eye Express Quad (941-foot vertical). Some of the interesting upper level trails they serve include Cruise Control (■), Panic Button (♦), Thimble (♦), Needle's Eye (♦■ with bumps on one side, groomed on the other, and 35 percent gradient), Needle's Eye Liftline tree skiing (♦♦), and Vertigo (♦♦ ■). This is another area worth discovering with some occasional gnarly spots for the adventurer, but it also has the easy-green Skye Walker trail that leads to Great Eastern for a gentle and very scenic cross-country cruise. (*If new to Skye Peak, do study the map, as the top is a maze of trail starts that can be confusing to the uninitiated.*)

Skye's northeastern face is served by the Superstar Express Quad (1,199-foot vertical) and features: Julio (♦♦) a tree-skiing area; Ovation (♦♦) and Superstar (♦), both wide straight-down, bodacious steeps; Skye Hawk (♦), a wide, steep shortcut; Skye Lark (■♦), a classic that gets progressively harder and has a steep diamond finish; and Bittersweet (♦■), a black-and-blue wide cruiser that can delight or terrify depending on conditions and the size of any bumps.

Superstar has a very steep Headwall at the top and then

The Superstar snowmaking blizzard results in whales that guarantee late season skiing, often into May and June. KR

eases up to a nice diamond but gets a bit tricky with the whales of snow that snowmakers create as the season progresses, building up to 25-foot heights so as to create a glacier for late spring skiing. New additions for 2005 are the tree areas Nowhere, Skyebits, and Somewhere, all diamonds.

From Skye Peak's upper trails, it is possible to hook up with the High Road traverse and ski to the top of Snowshed or to the base of Needles Eye. From the last part of Bittersweet it is possible to pick up Yodeler and ski down to Snowshed, and from the bottom of Skye Peak one can ski over to the Killington Base Lodge and the K-1 Gondola. Again, a map is handy for the uninitiated!

A Vision for the Future

So who could have thought up such a vast and intricate variety of trails, a veritable ski circus on the order of what you find in Europe? And what lies ahead?

Killington's colorful history began with Preston Leete Smith and the man who convinced him to check out the then remote mountain that nobody would develop. Some said it was too steep and others not steep enough!

Smith had been bitten by the ski bug as a teenager and studied agricultural science in college. He joined the New Haven and Waterbury (CT) Ski Clubs as a young man and met Walt Schoenknecht, who was president of the New Haven club and founder of Mohawk, the first bona fide area Smith visited in his high school years.

Preston Leete Smith has received many awards for a lifetime of contributions to the ski industry and was inducted into the Ski Hall of Fame in October 2000. KR

After college, Smith skied as much as he could afford. When he married (the late) Suzanne Hahn in 1954, they honeymooned at Stowe. It was on that trip that he decided that there had to be a better way—the Single Chair had long waits and the trails were narrow and too crowded, he thought.

For Smith that meant finding a mountain. He thought he had found one when he discovered that Ascutney was for sale. However, Forests and Parks Commissioner Perry H. Merrill had always wanted to see Killington developed for skiing since gaining 3,000 acres of "Killington lands" for the State in 1945. He had it surveyed by State Forester Charlie Lord and highway engineer Abner Coleman, who pronounced the mountain fit for skiing, but Merrill couldn't persuade anyone to develop a ski area there. Until he met Smith, that is.

Smith camped out on the mountain in winter, measured snow depths, and skied other areas, finally becoming convinced that Killington had "all the practical considerations of elevation, weather, [nearby] lodging and transportation."

He also determined that "of all the places around Vermont and New Hampshire, this place really had potential."

He returned to see Merrill, who said the State would lease the mountain to him and build a road in to Killington Basin. Merrill, who had sensed in Smith the dreamer and entrepreneur that would be needed to develop this mountain, told Smith, "We'll go to the Legislature and sell them on the idea of recreation for Vermont. It's going to be like Europe!"

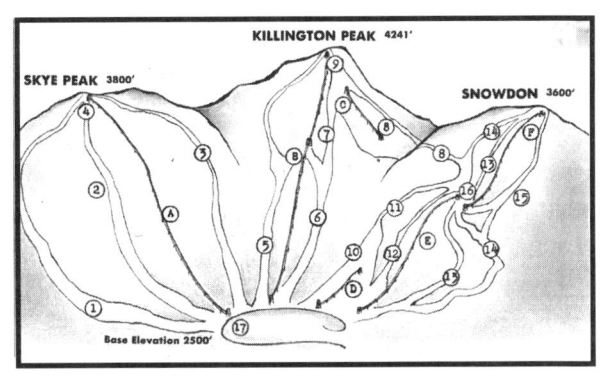

The original vision of Killington Basin as found on the first brochure. Due to the necessity of overcoming challenges of wind, weather and steeps, Skye Peak did not actually get a lift until 1987 (a detachable quad)!

That was May 1955 and it took three years before the road got built. During that time, Smith found financial backing by forming the Sherburne Corporation and selling shares of stock at $250 each. With a shoestring start, Killington opened for business on December 13, 1958 with two Pomalifts operating on Snowdon, a CCC Hut for a base lodge, a renovated chicken coop for a ticket booth, and an 8-seat outhouse. By the end of January, the Glades and Novice Pomalifts were installed and operating, and by President's Weekend, the area had been discovered.

In 1959, the Killington chairlift was built, beginning operations the third week of March 1960 but bringing in significant revenues for summer rides to the summit, the highest point reached by aerial lift in the East [until a North Carolina mountain reached a higher point in 1970]. In 1961, Killington skied until May 8 and Snowshed was built, followed by Rams Head in 1962.

The rest, as they say, is history. Killington continued to expand and grew to the largest area in the East and one of the most successful ski businesses in the country. But that was not all Killington accomplished.

The area developed many innovations, including the ticket wicket (the wire wicket used to attach tickets to skiers' clothing), factual snow reports, and a new way to teach skiing. The experiment to use short skis to teach beginners to ski parallel from the start was the brainchild of SKI magazine. Although three ski areas ran trials using a progression of short, medium and long skis, only Killington saw the potential and embraced what was to become the Graduated Length Method, GLM. The innovative ski instruction made Killington the place to learn during the 1960s when thousands went through its ski weeks, and the method itself revolutionized ski instruction.

In 1968, the area began building the 3.5-mile Killington Gondola, a unique three-stage lift that could operate as independent sections or as one continuous lift. It was the longest lift in the world and first gondola to hold four passengers when built (replaced by the two-stage, 8-passenger heated Skyeship in 1994).

Each year, more innovations and programs were introduced, and Killington made major efforts to expand its summer business in 1972. By 1983 the area had become a six-mountain ski area with year-round business and the parent company, the Sherburne Corporation, also owned Mount Snow which it purchased in 1977 (it had already sold Sunday River to Les Otten, who had worked at Killington before becoming GM at Sunday River).

In 1985, the Sherburne Corporation was restructured, becoming S-K-I Limited, which acquired Goldmine in California in 1988 and later Waterville Valley in New Hampshire. Pico suggested a merger but that fell through.

Then in 1996, Les Otten made an offer to purchase S-K-I at $18 a share, and in June the stockholders approved the deal. Otten formed the American Skiing Company (ASC) and under his leadership, Killington: built the K-1 Express Gondola (fulfilling Smith's initial dream for the peak) and the Killington Grand Hotel and Conference Center; replaced some existing chairlifts with highspeed quads; transformed the old Rams Head base lodge into the Rams Head Family Center; began the development of today's snowmaking system with access to 600 million gallons of water from a nearby reservoir; and acquired neighboring Pico, saving it from oblivion as owners there had run into financial trouble.

ASC eventually experienced financial difficulties of its own, having overextended with purchases of Heavenly Valley, Steamboat, and the Canyons and the construction of several hotels while simultaneously running into

The Killington Grand debuted in 2000 and will be a part of the new Killington Village Center. The hotel has an outdoor heated pool and is a beautiful facility. KR

several difficult-weather seasons and the stock-market "bubble burst." Otten restructured ASC with new financial partners but left the company in 2002. Although he is no longer CEO, plans to connect Killington and Pico remain, and once accomplished will create the East's ultimate mountain resort, fulfilling a Smith vision that dates back to 1964 (when he almost bought Pico).

As of 2004, progress was being made on plans developed during Otten's tenure for the Killington Village with Killington having conveyed several parcels of land to the SP Land Company, LLC (ASC/Killington has a 25 percent stake in this company) which will develop the village phase of Killington's continuing expansion. Skiers and Killington vacationers can look forward to exciting developments with more mountain lodging and village amenities like shops and restaurants being built in the next ten years. Infrastructure (earth) work is anticipated to begin in 2005 and construction of buildings in 2006, according to VP Carl Spangler, and chances are skiers will also enjoy interconnect skiing with Pico before the village is done. There is no exact timetable as variables like the economy and market demand are factors that come into play, but the plans are alive and well, Spangler said.

Up Front and Personal

I've skied Killington since discovering the mountain with a bus load of high school students from Scotch Plains, NJ in 1970. Since then—especially after moving to Vermont in 1978—I've gotten to know Killington on a more intimate level. My store of memories runneth over—from conquering Escapade, Flume, and Cascade to experiencing elementary school kids loving the original 3.5-mile Killington Gondola.

My sisters and I discovered the joy of trailside flirtation one fine spring day when two dashing dudes skied over and taught us to squirt wine from a goatskin flask.

Our boys learned bravery sitting on a stalled South Ridge chair one stormy New Year's Day, and I conquered another challenge when I helped a fear-clutched Junior Program student get down the Viper Pit on Bear Claw.

I remember the noisy bus rides home with local elementary school kids who had sugared up on Toblerones after their Junior Program lessons. To keep the decibel level down, I developed a Killington Trivia Quiz, based on the trail map which was good for a 40-minute ride and our collective sanity.

I treasure the many interviews I did with the pioneers who developed Killington over the years, men and women who transformed a wilderness into a vibrant and fun mountain resort. Every winter I enjoy the warm camaraderie of greeting friends on the mountain and making new ones.

I've got a poster above my computer that reads, "I've Skied Outer Limits."

Outer Limits is a work of art. KR

Truth is, I've only done the lower portion. I could get down it but I couldn't ski it well, so I leave it to the hotshots and enjoy watching them from the lift.

On the other hand, I have explored a lot of Killington's terrain, including trails that most people never find: Frolic, North Star, Flume, Vagabond, Jug, Jughandle, Breakaway, Roundabout, Solitude—even the Juggernaut when it was a ten-miler that ended at the former base of Northeast Passage. It was a secluded marathon cruise in nature and a long 10-mile tuck!

One area I had never tackled was the Canyon Quad. After my "ski chase" in 2003, I took my nephew to Killington on a sunshiny April Sunday and after skiing all over, he said, "Let's do East Fall." The steep dropoff entrance to the trail had always intimidated me, but he assured me there was "another way in" and added his dad had skied it with him, an obvious set-up since we both know I've skied more.

Well, the access was okay, but then there in front of us was a steep, moguled-up slope with people all over it. To say that Geoff looked at me sheepishly is an understatement. He was probably worried about what I might like to do to him, but I had a more immediate concern—get down it in one piece without making a fool of myself. I managed, but it was not a pretty sight. I was so relieved to see the bottom that I fell over after I had stopped to survey the runout!

To be honest, East Fall (renamed Lower East Fall in 2005) wouldn't be that bad without the big moguls of heavy spring snow. If groomed, it would be a sweet steep on a midweek day; if icy, forget it! As it was, I'm glad I took the plunge and had the opportunity to ride the Canyon chair and see the terrain from that vantage (and even happier that I lived to tell about it).

For me, the lessons of life can be found on these trails: learn a skill, practice it so you achieve a sense of mastery and pride (especially good things for children and aging adults), and share it with others for added joy—but above all play in the snow and have fun so you never forget the wonders of nature and winter. Part of the fun is to improve and for me that includes facing fears of formidable terrain.

The great thing about Killington is it really does offer "something for everyone." That means a lot of skiers and snowboarders get their own unique opportunities to meet the mountains' challenges, while making their own special mountain memories.

Mountain views are stunning at Killington. KR

Good To Know

Killington is just off Routes 4 and 100 in Killington, about 14 miles from Rutland, 30 miles from I-89 and I-91; about 3 hours from Boston and Hartford, and 5 from NYC.

Free Meet-the-Mountains Tours are given Mondays through Saturdays and meet at 9:45 in front of the Snowshed Base Lodge. The two-hour guided tour uses easier terrain (or terrain suited to the group) and is *highly recommended for anyone unfamiliar with Killington or needing a refresher.*

Use a trail map and pay attention to the trail signs because people who don't always wonder how they end up where they do. New trails signs for 2005.

Repeat: Killington is a good place to ski with a trail map and a buddy. Those who study the trail map, use the map, and read the signs don't get lost. This is *not* a good mountain to try potluck unless you are a very accomplished expert or know the area well and have a good sense of direction.

If you are "directionally challenged," the Meet the Mountains Tour is a great way to get to know the resort without getting lost. People like to criticize Killington, saying it's confusing because it's so big. I say study the trail map, take the tour, and you won't have any problem getting around. *This is a world-class mountain* so don't expect small unless you ski one section of it and skip the others. It's like skiing in Europe—you wouldn't do that without a map!

See the back of the Trail Map for weekly activities, places to eat, tips for skiing and riding, the Snow Guarantee, and more.

Killington Ambassadors (designation is on their jackets) are out and about to answer questions so ask away, whether for best place to eat or best conditions that day or for best trails to ski for your ability level. Or ask the folks you meet on the lift or in the lodge. You can learn some neat stuff that way!

Warm-up favorites: Rams Head and Snowdon trails. Seniors, who are consummate skiers and riders, tell me they enjoy parking at the Skyeship and warming up on Great Eastern or the blues back to the Skyeship.

Kids love Killington East and the Great Eastern and the Skyeship Gondola. Skyewalker and Cruise Control are two cruising favorites you can get to from the top of Skye Peak. They also enjoy Squeeze Play at Rams Head.

Bear Mountain is warmer in really cold weather because it is lower in elevation and is protected from prevailing westerly winds; it also gets the morning and early afternoon sun.

When taking friends on a tour, treat them to the scenic beauty of Falls Brook, a long meandering ravine trail with some interesting turns, a runout over a bridge, and astounding views of Bear Mountain above you.

The Bear Mountain Quad is great for instant "oohs and aahs" as you view the mogul bashers on Outer Limits. Novices can take the Falls Brook trail to it and off it and can ski back to Needles Eye via Great Eastern or Snowshed via the Snowshed Crossover.

The Snowshed Crossover is closed on some busy weekends and holidays to reduce cross traffic on key trails, but skiers can get to Snowshed via the Northbrook Quad which loads at the Needle's Eye base (take Great Eastern to Northbrook Crossover). There's a 401-foot vertical run on High Road (■) to Northbrook Trail (●) back to the Northbrook Quad for great quickie warm-ups or practice. It can have delightful snow and no one on it! Nice in the spring!

Park in the Vale lot (aside Great Northern) on the Rams Head part of the mountain, and you can ski to and from your car by hopping on what is now the last section of Great Northern (formerly the Vale trail) to Rams Head.

Another convenient place to park is next to the Snowdon Triple at the far end of the Killington lot. This necessitates getting a lift ticket first or skiing down to Rams Head or Snowshed to get a ticket, but anyone with a season's pass or multi-day ticket might find this a great place to park.

If you're an early bird, the Skyeship Lot is another place where you can ski back to your car or close to it. This lot also avoids the congestion on Killington Road at peak times so consider it if you don't need services at the main mountain like childcare.

Anarchy (♦♦) is a new (2005) tree area near Julio on Killington Peak.

The Killington Medical Clinic (422-6125) is located at Rams Head and offers emergency medical treatment for illnesses and injuries by qualified doctors and nurses.

The Killington Mountain School, established in 1974, is a private school that provides a quality educational experience for a select group of athletes interested in and committed to alpine racing or freestyle or snowboarding competition. An approved secondary school for grades 7-12, KMS offers a 5-month indoor education session to complement the outdoor training and competition season. Their new home is the (former) Red Rob Inn.

Killington has many special events, starting in October and running through June 1. Call 422-1700 for details or check the Website.

Aerial shows and fireworks are just a few of the special events throughout the winter. KR

Steals and Deals

Check the Website and sign up for The Drift, Killington's E-newsletter that offers exclusive deals to subscribers before they are announced to the general public; check on the advance purchase of mEtickets (savings up to $20/day at all ASC resorts) or E-tickets. Consult Website or call for info on these deals:

Ski Free with the Bring-a-Friend Program. Pre-register a 'never-ever' 13 years or older for a Learn-to-Ski or Ride lesson *72 hours in advance on the Website* and you receive a one-day free ticket for bringing them to the sport.

Killington Edge Card: free card entitles holder to free day of skiing after purchasing six days. Good at any ASC area and carries over for 3 seasons.

Free Adult Group Lesson: Purchase a 4-or-more day lift ticket and receive a free adult group lesson for the first afternoon of your stay.

Kids 12 and under Ski Free when parents pre-purchase a 5-or-more day lift ticket. One child per adult.

VT, NH, Quebec Days: residents ski for half price on selected dates (non-holiday Wednesdays) with proof of residency and cash only.

Summer is the time to check for upcoming season-pass deals. The All-for-One ASC season passes are good at all ASC resorts in VT, NH, ME. Bronze (14 blackout dates) Pass was $379, Gold (no restrictions) was $699, and college $199 until October 25, 2004. If you missed this in 2004, check out the Website in future summers or call the area! Buying early to save is the new trend!!

Phone numbers are **area code 802** unless otherwise noted.

Handy Info

Website: www.killington.com
Email: info@killington.com
General information: 422-6200
Snow report: 422-3261 (also Website daily).
Hours: 9-4 midweek; 8-4 weekends/ holidays. This applies to key lifts with other lifts operating dependent on weather and schedules.
Tickets: 2005 season: Adults: $67 midweek, weekends/$72 holidays; Juniors (ages 6-12)/Seniors (ages 65 +) $43/$43; Young Adult (13-18) $54/$54; Child 5 and under skis free when accompanied by a parent. **These tickets include skiing at Pico.** Best value is multi-day tickets.

Quick Stats (includes Pico terrain and lifts)

Season: October/November – May/June; average 210 days.
Average annual snowfall: 250 inches.
Snowmaking capability: 70 percent; 846 acres.
Lifts: 33; 2 heated gondolas (Stage-1 and Stage-2 Skyeship and K-1); 12 quads, including 6 Express; 6 triples, 4 doubles, 8 surface (2 Magic Carpets, 3 Pomas, 2 handle-tows, 1 rope tow).
Uphill lift capacity: 52,361 rides per hour.
Skiable terrain: 200 trails, 1209 acres; 90 miles; longest trail: Juggernaut 6.2 miles.
Glades: 16 tree-skiing/riding areas (137 acres); for all ability levels.
Bumps: Outer Limits, skier's right on Needle's Eye, Upper Dream Maker, Vertigo, lower Superstar, Upper Ridge Run, East Fall.
Parks/Pipe: 5 parks (1 early season, 1 late, 3 regular); 1 Superpipe, 1 quarterpipe.
Grooming: 17 groomers; Zaugg Pipecutter for new Superpipe.
Vertical Drop:
        Killington Peak to Skyeship base: 3,050'
        Killington Peak to K-1 base: 1,642'
        Killington Peak to Bear base: 2,115'
        Skye Peak to Skyeship base: 2,520'
        Skye Peak Superstar area: 1,199'
        Bear Mountain: 1,184'
        Snowdon: 1,114'
        Rams Head: 1,073'

Perfect Turn Ski and Snowboard Programs   800-923-9444

Learn-to-Ski-or-Ride programs feature the Guaranteed Learning Method. This unique approach includes its own Discovery Center where participants get skis, learn how to dress and use their equipment through video and pro instruction before heading out for specialized learning terrain. Reservations for the 4-hour program are required.

Perfect Turn pros offer adult clinics that utilize a coaching technique that is based on several principles, including identifying and building from student strengths and skills and promoting fun in a stress-free environment.

Group lessons and private coaching are also available. There are many specialty clinics, including: mogul camps. Women's Turn, Annual School for Instructors (learn to be a ski or ride instructor), racing, and more.

Children's programs   reservations 800-923-9444

The Child Care Center is located at the Rams Head Family Center.

Friendly Penquin Nursery and Daycare: 6 weeks to 6 years; indoor and outdoor activities and snacks.

First Tracks: introduction to snow and skis for ages 2-3 and play activities.

Ministars/Lowriders: Perfect Kids program for ages 4-6; full-day program or afternoon half-day.

Superstars: full or afternoon half-day sessions for ages 7-12.

Snowzone Teen Program: clinics for ages 13-18; skiing, snow-boarding, and ski boarding; full day or afternoon sessions.

Children's programs are very popular at Killington where kids can be introduced to skiing and snowboarding at special learning areas just for kids on Rams Head Mountain. KR

Other Things to Do

Family Ski Week activities, every week mid-December through March. Activities include welcome parties, ice skating, a chance to win a ride on a grooming vehicle, sleigh rides, etcetera.

The Adventure Park at the Killington Golf Course/ Clubhouse offers tubing, snowshoeing, pizza parlor, and an arcade. There are four tubing lanes with lights for night action.

Ice skating is a fun activity at the Grist Mill Pond.

Nordic skiing at: Mountain Meadows X-C Center (800-221-0598) in Killington, 57 km machine tracked; Mountain Top Inn X-C in Chittenden (800-445-2100) 80 km machine tracked.

Killington Snowmobile Tours (422-2121) offers guided tours from Northeast Passage. Tours customized by ability levels (children must be at least 4 years to ride).

Worth checking out: Spa Treatments at Killington's Grand Hotel (for hotel guests only, reservations required: 422-5001) for massage, facials, wraps.

Sleigh rides are offered at the Cortina Inn (773-3333) in Mendon and at the Mountain Top Inn (483-2311) in Chittenden. Snowshoeing at Mountain Top and at Hawk Resort (672-3811) in Plymouth. Ice skating at Grist Mill Pond.

Arctic Paws Dog Sled Tours (786-8028) are offered at the Mountain Meadows Lodge.

The 5-mile Killington Road and nearby city of Rutland abound with shops, restaurants, things to do from movies to concerts. The Paramount Theatre in Rutland and nearby colleges offer shows, concerts. Check Website and local newspapers: the *Mountain Times* (free resort paper) or *Rutland Daily Herald.*

Dining Out

There are more than 100 dining establishments to choose from in the region, and many are award-winning. In Killington, check out:

Hemingway's, a unique experience with superb cuisine and wine list; one of two 4-star restaurants in Vermont and winner of many awards; Birch Ridge Inn, intimate, gourmet, American and Continental Styles; Claude's, chef-owned classic and a favorite; the Grist Mill, great food, ambiance; and the dining rooms at Mrs. Brady's, Grey Bonnet Inn, Summit Lodge, Inn at Long Trail, Inn at Six Mountains, and Sante Fe Steakhouse at Mountain Inn for a variety of fine dining experiences and settings that exude ambiance and originality.

The Pasta Pot, Peppino's, Powderhounds, and Sushi Yoshi (Asian, Hibachi Steakhouse, Chinese cocktails) extend your choices with pizzazz and flavor.

Charity's 1887 Saloon and Restaurant, the Back Behind Saloon, and Casey's Caboose are popular Killington classics known for après-ski, great atmosphere, and good food. (Part of the fun at Casey's is eating in a 150-year-old caboose and plow car; a train runs on a ceiling track and whistles.)

In nearby Mendon, don't miss: Zola's Grille at the Cortina Inn (inventive cuisine blending northern Italian, French bistro, and Mediterranean styles); the Countryman's Pleasure for authentic Austrian/German fare, exquisite dining in a restored farmhouse; or the Vermont Inn and the Red Clover Inn for charming country inn atmosphere with New England and Continental cuisines.

In Rutland, Royal's 121 Hearthside, Three Tomatoes, Sirloin Saloon, and South Station are popular standouts; wide range of more good eateries from Mexican to Chinese and natural food; cozy bistro with piano bar at Tapas.

The Corners Inn in nearby Bridgewater Corners and the River Tavern at Hawk in Plymouth are also great choices for fine meals and libations.

Accommodations

There's a vast range of accommodations from mountainside at the Grand Summit Hotel and the condominiums at Killington Village, Sunrise Village, and Pico Village Square to quaint or luxurious B & B's, inns, lodges, and motels, many along Killington Road. The bedbase is 10,000 in Killington, 18,000 in region (Rutland to Woodstock).

There are bargains to be had (non-holiday) mid-week (some with kids stay free) and an array of price points to make weekends/holidays as reasonable or as high-end luxurious as you like. Check the Website or call for more info.

Killington Resort Village Lodging: 750 units; 877-4-KTIMES
Killington Central Reservations: (8-9 daily) 422-1330; 800-621-MTNS.
Pico Ski and Stay Packages: 866-667-PICO
Killington Chamber of Commerce: 773-4181

Après-ski/Nightlife

Mahogany Ridge Pub in the Killington Base Lodge, the bar at Snowshed, the Wobbly Barn (a living legend with a whole lot of shakin' going on); Pickle Barrel, Night Spot/Outback are among the classics where food, libations, and

The historic Wobbly Barn is one of skierdom's all-time top après-ski and nightlife hot spots. KR

loud music are found. They rock the road and are responsible for Killington's top ratings for après-ski and nightlife. Also the Grist Mill, Casey's Caboose, Charity's, the Saint's Pub at the Summit Lodge, Theodore's Tavern at the Cortina Inn, the Back Behind, and McGrath's Irish Pub are historic watering holes for après-ski/good food. There are many quieter lounges at various inns, and most area restaurants also feature lively après-ski fun.

Summer/Fall

Summer offers mountain hiking and biking on a large trail network, golf on the scenic Killington Mountain Golf Course and also at the Green Mountain National Course in town (and there's another 270 holes at scenic courses within a half-hour drive), plus tennis, swimming, fishing, and lots of activities at the Adventure Centers at Killington and Pico, including: mini golf, rock-wall climbing, water slides, Alpine Sliding, bungee jumping, and in-line skating at the Skateboard Park.

The summer waterslides are very popular with families at Killington. KR

All ages can enjoy the K-1 Gondola rides to the summit lodge for stunning views of five states and Canada on a clear day. Don't miss the Summit Nature Trail for a short hike to the 4,241-foot pinnacle for an extraordinary mountaintop experience. Bring your camera!

Also, scenic chairlift rides at Pico. Plus, explore the Long and Appalachian Trails which cross over the sides of Killington and Pico. There's a great short trip up Deer Leap behind the Inn at Long Trail (at the top of Sherburne Pass on U.S. Route 4) with views of Pico.

Annual summer events abound, Renaissance Festival, Mountain Wine Festival, Brewfest, mountain bike races, craft fairs, concerts, and other activities. Check the Website or call 422-1700 for more information.

Autumn brings foliage rides in both Gondolas, more events, and early skiing on high elevation trails when the temperatures drop—often in October! The annual Columbus Day Weekend Ski Swap and Sale is a ritual and fun event.

There's lots more to do in the region with shopping, antiquing, and attractions from Rutland to Woodstock and beyond.

See Pico Chapter for more winter and summer info.

Our Killington Adventure

Date:

Weather:

Companions:

Where Stayed:

Visit Highlights:

Our Discoveries:

110 Mad River

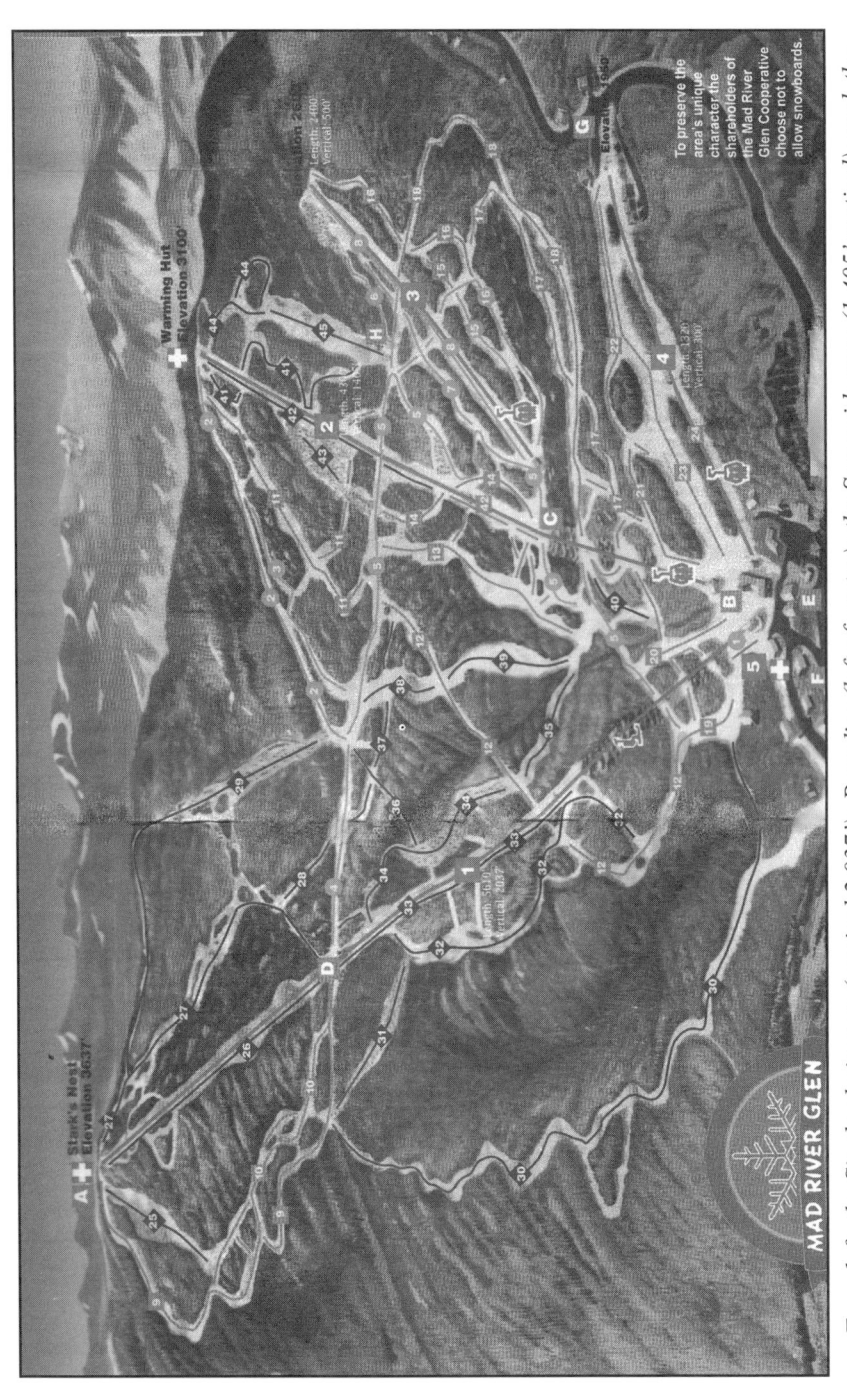

From left: the Single chair area (vertical 2,037'); Paradise (left of center); the Sunnyside area (1,405' vertical); and the Birdland area (500' vertical). The Practice Slope is to lower right. A short handle tow is to left of the single.

Chapter Eight

Mad River Glen
A Classic Maverick

Mad River Glen is a storybook ski area, a Vermont classic. But not in the way that might be expected. Like the Mad River which flows north rather than south, Mad River Glen doesn't conform to the usual expectations.

In fact, it's really not your usual ski area. It doesn't even have your usual family, partnership, or corporate owner. Mad River is owned by skiers, a co-operative venture that makes it unique in U.S. ski history. Mad River doesn't allow snowboarding, which makes it unique in Vermont.

This is in keeping with its tradition because Mad River has been something of a maverick since its founding. It exerts its independence the way Vermont does, in your face but at the same time with substance and conviction.

This is a ski area—not a resort—that began to promote itself with a "Mad River Glen Ski It If You Can" bumper sticker in 1984, a quirky but clever way of saying that General Stark Mountain doesn't cater to or coddle anyone; it challenges all. It turned out to be a successful attention getter that dared skiers to discover its unique brand of challenge.

Part of the dare lies in the conditions. You won't find every trail groomed to corduroy, and you won't find perfect packed powder put down for every run. Nor will you find one trail like the other. There's a different philosophy at work here—one of keeping it simple with legendary terrain, respect for Mother Nature, and fostering a sense of community.

The mountain *skis* like a red badge of courage. The trails off the Single chair on 3,637-foot Stark peak are for mountain goats, macho men, bump revelers—those who seek a Paradise of the fifth dimension (bumps, trees, cliffs, steeps, waterfalls, and a heavenly stash of private powder). When they encounter ice, they don't complain because they know how to fly off it or over it.

But that's not to say that novices and intermediates won't have fun at Mad River. Advanced skiers and solid intermediates can wend their way off the peak on the great blue Antelope trail and live to brag about a nice long run. In fact, there's a diversity of terrain that affords great blues on the lower mountain off the mid-station exit on the Single and at the Sunnyside area as well as greens at Birdland. And since they do groom the greens and blues when there is snow, the challenge is manageable for the non-expert; however, they don't groom when base depths are marginal so as to preserve the natural cover.

History

Throughout its history, Mad River Glen has been owned and managed by people with a singular vision for the mountain. That is the legacy of its founder Roland Palmedo who owned the mountain from 1948 to 1972. Palmedo was one of the original investors at Stowe and a founder of the National Ski Patrol. But when he returned from World War II, he felt Stowe had become "too commercialized" and went scouting for another mountain to develop.

He selected General Stark Mountain in Fayston. He liked the fact that it had snow in April, challenging terrain with constant vertical, and could be privately owned (not on state or national forest land) as this would allow its owner/operator total control.

Palmedo bought over 800 acres from the Ward Lumber Company and set about having a chairlift built in the fall of 1947. However, by Thanksgiving three to four feet of snow had fallen, causing construction to come to a halt. The chair was finished the following year with a formal debut on December 11, 1948; dedication ceremonies featured the Governor of Vermont and Miss Vermont. But since there was little snow that December, ski operations didn't actually begin until January 28, 1949.

The first few seasons were lean snow years but with the return of real Vermont winters, Mad River enjoyed the ski boom that ensued in the 1950s and 1960s. Palmedo, working to achieve his vision of a "winter community," hired ski instructors, initiated a volunteer ski patrol, hosted races, and sold lots for private homes and ski lodges to help pay for it all.

The area thrived in the 1950s and 1960s with the first North American Kandahar race held at Mad River in 1956. The Practice Slope started with a rope tow in 1950 and got a T-Bar in 1958 (replaced by a double chair in 1972). In addition to the T-Bar, the Sunnyside Double was built in 1961, the ski shop, nursery, and ski patrol hut were all added and the Base Box (base lodge) was expanded several times. In 1967, the Birdland Double was added, creating a wonderland of terrain for novices and intermediates.

Palmedo sold to Switt Swett and Truxton Pratt in 1972. When her husband died in 1975, Betsy Pratt continued to operate the area in keeping with Palmedo's vision. She was one of three women to single-handedly own and operate a major ski area in Vermont (the other two were at Pico). With her own streak of independence, she fended off industry changes and added only a modicum of snowmaking.

When a safety problem with snowboarders riding the historic Single Chair caused her to ban riders from that lift, a confrontation ensued that changed her mind about allowing snowboarding anywhere at the area. That snowboarding ban continues under present ownership, making the area one of four in North America that do not allow riding.

Unique Ownership

Pratt sold to the Mad River Cooperative, a group of loyal skiers who now number 1,991 members, in December 1995. They adopted a mission to:

> preserve and protect the forests and mountain ecosystem of General Stark Mountain in order to provide skiing and other recreational access and to maintain the unique character of the area for present and future generations.

With conservative management, the Co-op has paid off the mortgage, replaced the Sunnyside Double with a new double in 1998, and overhauled the original Single (the only diesel-powered single chair in operation in the U.S. today)—all deliberate moves to limit traffic on the mountain. "Low skier density is one of the key elements of Mad River's unique ski experience," notes General Manager Jamey Wimble.

That means there might be a wait for the chair of 20 minutes or more at peak times (on four Saturdays, holidays, and Telemark Festival day, according to Marketing Director Eric Friedman), but the skiers who choose to ski Mad River take that as a *quid pro quo* for preserving the character of its classic New England trails and having the mountain to themselves.

One Co-op member and former instructor proudly explained that, "Most of the trails are narrow by today's standards, but members like them that way." Since they do not make snow on them, it's important to limit the numbers of skiers so as not to use up the snow, he said by way of explanation and approving of the old-fashioned single and double chairlifts.

He added that, "Snowboarding tends to push the snow around and is not viewed as compatible to the mountain's natural snow trails." Since over two-thirds of the members agree that snowboarding would change the character of the mountain (and some say "the shape of the bumps"), the ban remains in effect. (The Co-op votes on this periodically—no predictions of change, though.)

Cooperative members may own one to four shares of stock but have only one vote each. Six in-staters sit on the board and three are from out of state. Shares sell for $1,750 and may be purchased outright or on an installment basis; they come with a commitment to make a minimum purchase (tickets, passes, or other products) each year. The concept is to keep the area the way it is and still make it economically feasible to continue operations.

The Co-op has replaced the old snowcats with two modern groomers (purchased used from another area); added two movable snowmaking cannons; put in a handle tow for beginners at Callie's Corner; and made various other upgrades while adding naturalist programs and a variety of kids ski programs. As a result, Mad River has carved a successful niche for itself among skiers who appreciate its sense of community as well as its rugged individualism. Those skiers also revere the considerable challenge of the mountain itself.

The Mountain

Mad River offers 45 marked trails (about 120 acres) but allows the entire 800 acres to be skied with the *off-piste* proviso to ski the woods in threesomes, before 3 p.m., and enter only from open trails. The only terrain within the area's boundaries where skiers are not allowed are the marked "regeneration zones" where trees are being grown.

Most of Mad River's black diamonds are accessed via the mile-plus long Single chair, which gives a 2,037-foot vertical for every run and superb views from the 3,637-foot summit—Lake Champlain and the Adirondacks to the west, the Greens, Camel's Hump, and Worcester Range to the east. On a clear day, you can also see all the way to the Whites and Presidentials (NH).

Contrary to popular rumor, Mad River does make some snow, but it is mostly on low-elevation terrain like the Race Hill (where high school and college racers train) or lower sections where skiers funnel into the lifts. Interestingly, with an annual average of 250 inches of natural snow, Mad River often skis into April, evidence that the low-density approach works and Mother Nature still rules.

Advanced/Expert ♦ ♦♦

The challenge for advanced skiers and experts comes partly from the pitch and undulations of the terrain and partly from the natural snow conditions. At Mad River, diamonds are left ungroomed so they invariably "bump up." And, the bumps grow large and more plentiful over the course of a winter. There are exceptions: Upper Canyon and Grand Canyon get groomed once or twice a season, and Catamount Bowl might get groomed once. These diamonds are for serious skiers who know what they are doing; others do well to stick to the blues and greens.

Paradise, Chute, Fall Line, and Lift Line are among Mad River's famous black diamonds. They are trails with steeps, bumps, and in some cases trees that glisten with rime ice and whisper "ski us if you can." Paradise, an ultra steep glade with a 1,000-foot vertical, was originally cut by homeowners at the mountain and has obtained mythic status as the upper mountain's greatest challenge. Fall Line is a steep bump run with beautiful views of Camel's Hump. It twists and turns its way down the mountain and around tree lines, offering a variety of challenging lines to choose from.

Lift Line descends straight down the mountain under the Single from the midstation and with its bumps, cliffs, boulders, stumps, and other natural obstacles is the site of the annual Unconventional Terrain Competition. Lots of good viewing from the chair!

When it comes to bump runs, Mad River has more than its share. Grand Canyon is one of the widest and is especially nice in the spring, when it gets lots of snow and soft moguls. Lynx is a lovely bumped-up birch glade that drops steeply from mid-mountain; it feeds in to Beaver, a more open mogul run.

There are also a few diamonds off the Sunnyside Chair, including Gazelle Glades, Panther, Partridge, and the famous Slalom Hill—once a race course but now an ultra-wide, steep mogul field.

Intermediate ■

The intermediate and easy trails are groomed regularly and often boast packed powder conditions. Some blues, like the uppermost section of Quacky,

The famous Single Chair, midstation, and base area with the Base Box Lodge. MRG

are allowed to bump up, but for the most part they are bump free, or if they have bumps they will be on one side of the trail only and not as large as those on the diamonds.

The Upper Antelope (■) to Catamount (■) run off the Single from the summit is a delightful romp (narrow by today's standards) back to Broadway (●), which leads to a host of possibilities, including great cruising blues like Porcupine and Bunny. [The other option of Upper Antelope to Lower Antelope (♦) provides a steeper, mostly narrow 3.5-mile run to the Single.]

The Sunnyside Double serves a second peak with a 3,100-foot elevation. This area offers long runs with a 1,405-foot vertical and a wide variety of blues and greens. Quacky (■), a Mad River favorite, is a naturally undulating run that leads to Porcupine (■) while Fox (●) and Vixen (●) provide scenic routes to yet more greens and blues. The Practice Slope chair serves several shorter blue trails on the lower mountain, including the Practice Slope where you can watch racers training in the gates. Ski a few runs of your own here, and you soon find yourself skiing more rhythmically to the *gates* in your mind.

Novice/Beginner ●

Birdland is the separate novice/low-intermediate area with a group of trails that meander through the woods and a wide cruising trail under the 2,400-foot-long Birdland Double, which only operates on weekends and holidays. Birdland trails are accessible midweek from the Sunnyside chair and from the mid-station on the Single. Novices need to know where they are going in order to get to Birdland since it is located a third of the way up the mountain—consult the trail map! The Birdland trails have names like Loon, Duck, Snail, Robin, Periwinkle, and Wren. They are as serendipitous as their names. Beginners and low-end novices need to be careful to take Easy Way (●) back to the base rather than the more difficult blues that spill down from this location.

In recent years, Mad River has sought to take some of the edge off the "ski it if you can" dare. They've improved their family-friendly image with a section of terrain for 'never-evers' known as Callie's Corner. This area is located at the base off to the side of the Single and has its own handle tow.

Experiences of the Mad River Kind

I first skied Mad River when I took the Scotch Plains-Fanwood Ski Club to the area for a weekend in the early 1970s. We stayed at a nearby rustic lodge with a huge circular fireplace. At that time, I had 48 kids under my wing, but I was so young and happy to get kids skiing that I was undaunted by the responsibility. They were good kids who loved skiing as much as I did and were fun to be with so they were really a great group to work with.

The mountain was another story though. It was a cold (make that frigid) January weekend. The better skiers just needed a trail map, but I had to get the novices up the Sunnyside chair and take them on the easy trails over to Birdland, which required attention to where we were going.

Despite my "standard speech" just before departing the bus—ski in control; fall before you hit a tree; if you are tired, take a rest; and meet at the base at four—one very good skier broke his ankle. They had a clinic right in the base lodge and set it there, so I didn't have to make a hospital run—something I appreciated as I had the others to look out for.

I took a private lesson, and when we skied on ice with poles out front, hopping in the old manner, I took a fall that left me with the biggest thigh bruise I ever got. I remember being grateful to have the excuse of checking up on my chickadees at Birdland and schussing this tamer area with them. It was a memorable trip despite never getting up the Single to the summit.

On my 2003 visit, I was given a tour of the entire mountain and this time got to the summit. Riding the Single was a quiet, contemplative experience. The view was wonderful and our run down Antelope was lovely, a pleasant but not scary challenge. We stopped occasionally and ventured over to bumped-up black diamond terrain where I photographed my guide taking a few turns. Then we hiked out and explored the long interesting trails at the Sunnyside Double that are more to my liking and my knees' style.

Later, I hooked up with Henri de Marne, a former instructor and graceful skier. We skied the Sunnyside and Birdland trails as he told me more about the area and Co-op. I could hear the love and pride in his voice, and as we skied I could understand why that passion for this area is so heartfelt among Mad River's loyal skiers.

Back at the office, my husband's associate beamed when I mentioned my Mad River trip. He lapsed into a rapture, describing Paradise, the hike to it, the tough terrain, the choose-your-own-route glades, and waterfalls. It's an all-time favorite among his patroller friends and enjoys a cult-like following among steep and deep fans.

Flying off the Waterfalls. MRG

Good to Know

Mad River Glen is located on Route 17 off Route 100 in Waitsfield. It's about 3.5 hours from Boston and Hartford, and 6 hours from NYC.

Free tours are given at 10 a.m. and 1 p.m. on weekends and holidays.

The Ski Patrol has revived the No-Stop, No-Fall Run competition started by Roland Palmedo. There are 3 routes so all ability levels can participate: Gold (Fall Line to Grand Canyon), Silver (Catamount to Porcupine), and Bronze (Fox to Easy Way). The contest takes place each Monday throughout the season with registration at the Ski School desk until noon for the 1 p.m. event.

Mad River's Triple Crown consists of three annual events: Mogul Challenge, Unconventional Terrain competition, and Vertical Challenge (check Mad River's Website for dates).

An Annual Valley Winter Carnival is held in January with special events.

There's an adventurous snowshoe trail that links Mad River Glen's snowshoe trail network to the Long Trail and the summit of Stark Mountain.

The Base Box is an historic base lodge that offers the usual services but still retains the rusticity of the old lodges. (It also has a room for brown baggers.)

The parking lot is across Route 17 which can be busy so it's important to keep an eye on little ones and to "look both ways when crossing."

Steals and Deals

Act foolish and ski two for the price of one on April Fools Day.

On the last Tuesday in January, they celebrate Mad River's Anniversary (of the area's opening) by rolling back ticket prices to $3.50 !! Hooky anyone?

Ski for $1: buy a 2-day ticket and the third day is $1, non-holidays only.

The Mad Card is $99 (*sold only until 12/15/04*) and includes: 3 transferable day tickets good any time during the 2004-2005 ski season; $7 off additional midweek tickets and $5 off weekend/holiday tickets; includes free Season Passes for all holder's kids who are ages 12 and under (as of 1/1/05) when you purchase your Mad Card and sign up your children before an *October 15 deadline*; 10% off Ski School Clinics (season-long programs excluded); 10% off Alpine & Telemark Rentals & Demos.

Free season pass for Juniors 12 and under with purchase of adult season pass by 10/15/04 (or with purchase of Mad Card by 10/15/04).

Adult Midweek Season Pass; $310 ($270 before 10/15/04).

College Season Pass: $230 ($199 before 10/15/04). Valid every day.

Ski-and-Stay-the-Valley packages include tickets for both Sugarbush and Mad River when you make reservations for 3-night or more stays on weekends (2 nights midweek); package also includes a ticket for Ole's X-C Center.

Check the Website for weekly coupon specials and deals. Check in summer for annual early-bird specials on season passes and Mad Cards.

Shareholders in the Co-op receive special rates on season passes and day tickets. Shareholders who own four shares can also take advantage of special transferable packages. The Cooperative decides future benefits to ownership. Shares are still for sale; call the area for more information.

Reminder: If you are a snowboarder only, Mad River won't let you buy a ticket or on its trails. (If you are on the *Great Vermont Ski Chase*, simply send in a picture of you and your board in place of a Mad River ticket.) If you're with a family, hop next door to the 'Bush' or try cross-country skiing.

Phone numbers are **area code 802** unless otherwise noted.

Handy Info

Website: www.madriverglen.com
Email: info@madriverglen.com
General information: 496-3551
Snow report: 496-3551
Hours: 9-4 midweek; 8:30-4 weekends.

Tickets 2005: Adults $50 daily; Juniors (ages 6 - high school)/Seniors (65-69) $37; half day, $42 Adults/$29 Juniors/Seniors (includes midweek mornings or afternoons; afternoons weekends and holidays. Seniors 70+ ski free five days per season (shareholders 70+ ski free all season). Children 5 and under ski free with an adult.

Quick Stats

Season: mid-December to April, average 105 days.
Average annual snowfall: 250 inches.
Snowmaking capability: 5 percent; 4 - 6 acres.
Lifts: 5, 1 single, 3 double, 1 surface (handle-tow).
Uphill lift capacity: 3,000 per hour.
Trails: 45; 120 acres; longest 3.5 miles. *Off-piste* 800 acres.
Glades: Paradise, Gazelle, Birch, Upper, Lower Glades, Lynx.
Bumps: Slalom Hill, most of the diamonds.
Grooming vehicles: 2 groomers.
Vertical Drop: Stark Summit to base area: 2,037'
Top of Sunnyside to base area: 1,405'
Birdland area: 500'
Practice Slope: 300'

Ski School   496-3551

Mad River's Ski School offers Alpine and Telemark instruction. Learn-to-ski/Telemark package is $55 for 2-hour lesson, beginner lift ticket, and equipment. Group and privates available.

Children's Programs   496-3551

Mad River offers weekend programs, reservations recommended.
Cricket Club Nursery: childcare for ages 6 weeks to 18 months.
Rockin' Robins 1st Timers, ages 4-12, introduction to skiing.
Chipmunks: 4-7 years for experienced kids able to ride lifts
Panthers: ages 7 and up, skiing with friends in a supervised environment.
Freestyle Team: ages 7 and up, weekends 9:30-2:30.
Development Team; ages 7 +; explore freestyle/racing; improve skills.
Telemark Team: ages 7 +; new program for kids who enjoy Telemark.

Other Things to Do

Snowshoe treks are offered at the mountain with wildlife, ecology, and family treks among the options. Winter nature hikes and educational sessions.

Nordic skiing at: Blueberry Lake X-C Ski Center (33 km, groomed, rentals, 496-6687); Ole's X-C Center (50 km, snowshoe tours, 496-3430).

Sleigh rides, hayrides at Lareau Farm, skating at the Skatium.

Shopping in Waitsfield, Warren; Artisans' Gallery (over 100 artists represented); Warren Country Store; craft, specialty, and antique shops.
Attractions: Cold Hollow Cider, Ben & Jerry's in Waterbury.
Don't miss the Vermont Ski Museum in Stowe (call for hours, 253-2616).
Visit www.madriver.com for Valley events or more information.

Dining Out

The Mad River Valley has been described as a "gastronomical mecca." Although there are no fast food franchises (no traffic lights either), there is a good diversity of eateries—some of which feature takeout or full meals to go, some three meals a day. In addition to some inns or lodges that have dining rooms, you'll find good eats at: John Egan's Big World Pub and Grill (great food, ambiance), American Flat Bread (funky fun, very popular, line to get in), the Blue Tooth (true après-ski), Chez Henri (fine French dining, authentic bistro ambiance, wine list), Common Man (restored barn, European dining), 1824 House Inn (fine dining), The Tucker Hill Inn (fine dining), Warren House (European food, ambiance), Easy Street Café ("the best breakfasts by far"), Purple Moon (casual, pub fare), Millbrook Inn & Restaurant (cuisine of India & America), The Den (American), Hyde Away Inn and Restaurant (locals' hangout, popular après-ski spot), Jay's (New York Style), Michael's To Go (fine dining take-out), Pitcher Inn (gourmet), Valley Pizzeria, Pepper's (another "best breakfasts" vote), The Spotted Cow (casual, fine dining), Bon Giorno's (great pizza), Mad Mexican, and Paradise Deli (lunch, catering, and deli; "awesome and authentic Philly Cheesesteak").

Accommodations

A bedbase of 6,600 in the Valley offers a wide range of lodgings, from rustic to luxurious, B&B to townhouse. Some chalets are rentable at the slopes.
Mad River Lodging info: 496-3551.

Après-ski/Nightlife

Visit General Stark's Pub at the mountain and the Hyde Away for après-ski fun. For nightlife try: The Den for food, bar scene; Purple Moon Pub for live music, food, games; and Tracks, a speak-easy type of lounge beneath the Pitcher Inn. Visit The Eclipse for movies, live music (bands, folk, jazz), café, film festivals, and other special events and The Valley Players Theater for music and live theater.

Summer/Fall

You can hike, mountain bike, or rent a site for your event/tent.
Annual Green and Gold Weekend in fall; also chair rides for superb foliage views from the summit (and on the ride down).

Our Mad River Adventure

Date:

Weather:

Companions:

Where Stayed:

Visit Highlights:

Our Discoveries:

122   Magic

Magic Mountain features "old-fashioned" skiing on legendary terrain with a small Alpine village nestled at its base. Double and triple chairs translate to "affordable" lift tickets. The area also offers a terrain park and tubing under lights.

Chapter Nine

Magic Mountain
Affordable, Old-Fashioned Fun

Magic Mountain in southern Vermont provides a unique opportunity to enjoy old-fashioned affordable skiing and riding. The area sports a small village of Swiss-styled lodges and inns within walking distance of the lifts, a community of chalets tucked into the woods nearby, and several trailside condominiums. Together, they form a mountain-based community that resembles a small Swiss hamlet.

That was the influence of (the late) Hans Thorner who opened Magic for the winter of 1960-61 with a goal to create a small destination resort. He named the ski area he built on the steep north face of Glebe Mountain after the utopian vision in Thomas Mann's novel *The Magic Mountain.* Thorner's vision was to create a community where the mountain experience would provide a common bond and work its spell on those who dwelled there.

He did admirably well, creating a community of vacation homes and a mountain experience that appealed to the best skiers as well as to families. That was not an easy feat because Magic is not a mountain you can easily conquer. But with his talented ski school, he had skiers whooshing down the 1,650-foot vertical on all kinds of terrain—wide slopes to classic New England trails, beginner to expert, including some of the most difficult double diamonds in Vermont.

Today, double-diamonds like Master Magician and The Twilight Zone test the mettle of purists and extreme fans; the diamonds challenge experts; and the blues dare intermediates to get better. Novice runs like the 1.5-mile Magic Carpet trail and lower mountain beginner slopes provide a gentle and wide contrast to the gnarly stuff and make Magic family friendly.

Magic also has a terrain park and offers snow tubing and greatly expanded snowmaking capability. Double and triple chairs go to the top and handle tows serve the tubing park and the first-timer learning slope. A mid-mountain double chair called the Phoenix was planned for the 2005 season to serve intermediate and novice trails on the lower half of the mountain as well as a new expert trail beneath it. The emphasis on being a family-friendly, affordable, fun area has worked well for the area's owners, who revived Magic for the 1997-98 season and are still making improvements in a slow-but-steady fashion.

History

For those who enjoy the hand cut trails at Magic, much of the thanks goes to Neil McKenzie of Chester, who cut the original trails in 1960 for Hans Thorner. Thorner, who was born in Switzerland in 1908, was a Swiss-certified instructor (1934) who taught in the famous Franconia Notch area in New Hampshire and worked in and produced ski films before starting Magic Mountain.

After a search for a good mountain that would accommodate a residential and a commercial village at its base, Thorner purchased 640 acres on Glebe Mountain and opened Magic on December 26, 1960 with a 2,000-foot T-Bar and two open slopes. He added a chair to the top and five trails for the third season. He also imported Swiss instructors for his famous ski school.

Thorner designed Magic to offer a residential community with accommodations in lodges at the slopes and sold land in the base area to potential lodge owners. Dostal's Resort Lodge was the first to be built in 1961 and is still operating as a 50-room inn. The Blue Gentian was built in 1962 and is operated as a 13-room lodge that caters to groups and skiers. Thorner converted a gas station at the corner of Route 11 and the Magic Access Road to the Swiss Inn, which he operated for many years. The large Inn at Magic rounded out the cluster of base-area accommodations in the early years. (As of fall 2004, the Inn at Magic was to be purchased by Magic Mountain and reopened for the 2004-05 ski season.)

Thorner started Magic Mountain by selling stock. Anyone who bought $3,000 worth could purchase a half acre lot for $600 and was entitled to a lifetime of free skiing, with children under 18 receiving the same privilege. He required a Swiss building motif for the private homes for many years. Eighty homes were eventually built, and Thorner later sold a parking lot below the Red lift on which a cluster of 17 condo units were built in 1982.

In 1985, Thorner sold his controlling interest in the mountain to Tower Development, a group of New York businessmen headed by Simon Oren and Isaac Davidov. The partnership improved snowmaking, cut 11 new trails, purchased Timber Ridge (a formerly private area with 23 trails and almost 400 acres on Magic's backside) in 1986, and built a ridgeline trail to connect the two areas. They also formed two separate companies to operate Magic and Bromley, which they purchased in 1987 from Stratton when Bostonians Joe O'Donnell and Bob Palandjian joined their partnership as part the deal to purchase Bromley. They also sold land to developers who put up the 56-unit ski-on/ski-off condo complex called Trailside at Magic in 1987.

By the time they closed Magic in June 1991 after some very difficult seasons, O'Donnell and Palandjian were the sole owners, and over the ensuing years they sold off some of the assets like two of the four chairlifts and the Timberside area. New owners Glebe Mountain Ski Associates (principals Michael Boraski and William Zizus of Pennsylvania and 25 investors) purchased the area in 1995. They contracted with Joseph Aichholz, who had considerable ski area experience in Pennsylvania (he also made snow for all the Nordic events for the 1980 Olympics in Lake Placid), to manage the area for them. He put together an operations team headed by his son Gary (general manager) and Stacey Crooks (mountain manager) and guided the redevelopment operation.

Although the owners and management had hoped to open for the 1996-97 season, various problems, including water and permit issues and a lack of money (to deal with a newly discovered oil leak) delayed the renovations and upgrades necessary for operating the ski area. With $2 million invested in extensive repairs and improvements to lifts, trails, snowmaking system, and grooming equipment and the base lodge completely renovated, Magic returned to the Vermont ski scene with top-to-bottom skiing on December 29, 1997. Magic also boasted a new lift-served tubing area, something Joseph Aichholz had great success with at his small Blue Marsh Ski Area near Reading, PA.

The first start-up season was shortened by an unusual March thaw and proved financially difficult. As a result, the owners reorganized with some new players and with an influx of new capital formed the Old Fashioned Skiing Company to operate Magic for the 1998-99 season. Their intent was to continue to operate an affordable family area and to make improvements as financially feasible. Many people who believed in the area were happy to help out by volunteering for the Courtesy Patrol or other work, and there was good community support in general as Southern Vermont skiers returned to Magic's challenging slopes.

Despite some difficult seasons, Magic continues to operate every winter and makes progress with upgrades to the lifts, trails, facilities and programs. With some additional investor and owner changes, Magic is now headed by the Magic Group, LLC.

This company hopes to have a mid-mountain double chair running for the 2005 season and signed an agreement to purchase the (defunct) Inn at Magic Mountain. GM Gary Aichholz said plans are to renovate the inn and operate it as a hotel with suites, hopefully opening for Christmas 2004. He said plans also include installing a beginner chairlift for the bunny slope, perhaps as early as 2005-06."It will be another step in Magic's continued revival," he said, adding that, "Soon the mountain will be back to the way it was originally, and people really will be able to ski the *legendary* Magic Mountain."

The approach to mountain revival at Magic in recent years has been to avoid expensive highspeed quads, heated gondolas, and fancy condo-hotels. Management makes no bones about not competing with larger resort-oriented ski businesses and has been careful not to over extend itself by doing too much too fast. There is a thrifty approach to snowmaking as well, using it judiciously but still making annual upgrades to the system. The goal is to offer a particular product—in Magic lingo, "a true renaissance of the old-fashioned New England ski area experience at a price that is affordable."

One of the benefits to being "old-fashioned" is that the chairlifts can ride low among the trees and remain open even on high-wind days. Additionally, because the lifts don't deposit as many people on the mountain as highspeeds do, the trails can be left the way they were cut forty-plus years ago; there is no need to make them ultra wide avenues, Aichholz said. The protection afforded by trees means less exposure to the wind for the skiers on the trails and less wind scouring of the snow, which translates to less need to make tons of snow.

The view from the Red chair inclludes the village below and a patchwork of Southern Vermont farms, hills, ski areas, and villages. KL

But old-fashioned does not mean the area does not make any snow at all. There is a modern snowmaking system and a good supply of water, Aichholz said. Grooming plays a roll as well with three grooming vehicles to do the job. "These are modern necessities to assure operations in all kinds of weather or temperatures and snowmaking capability is now up to 87 percent of the mountain. The terrain that isn't covered with snowmaking is the ultra steep stuff with cliffs," Aichholz noted.

Stressing that a conservative approach has allowed the area to be "debt free" in its seventh season, Aichholz called it a key to "continuing to operate" through the inevitable ups and downs of the ski business. It also allows the area to offer a lower-priced lift ticket, he noted. The addition of the tubing park with its own handle tow and lights for night action allows the area to extend operations on Saturdays and holidays to evening hours to please families with an additional fun thing to do, he added.

The Mountain

Magic is a skier's mountain with some funky, quixotic trail names. Broomstick, Carumba, Hocus Pocus, Sorcerer, Slide of Hans, Lucifer, and Master Magician are some of the more Disneyesque names that Thorner decided on after his utopian ones didn't catch on. It's *what's in those names* that makes the difference though. The area's 34 trails (130 skiable acres including two glades) pack a lot of punch and ski more like a rugged Alp than a nicely rounded, southern Vermont hill. In addition, there is *off-piste* skiing on another 100-plus acres for those who like their snow and trees as nature made them, natural and on the wild side.

While not having a huge number of trails, Magic does sport a good diversity and makes full use of the mountain's natural contours. You'll find everything from wide groomed trails to narrow chutes riddled with moguls. There are headwalls, ravines, saddles, switchbacks that twist back and forth across the fall line, and bodacious *off piste* stuff.

No two trails are quite alike, and you often find changes in pitch that surprise you and contribute to an uncanny ability to make you ski better. As skiers/riders master one trail or slope, there is another trail (or even a side of the same trail as in the case of Wand) that takes the challenge up a notch. That progression of difficulty fosters improvement—no resting on one's laurels here.

Beginner/Novice ●

There is a small beginner area with a handle tow for first timers at the lower part of Video Boulevard (●). The new Phoenix mid-mountain lift will afford a natural progression to the gentle lower Magic Carpet (●) for a three-quarter mile run back to the lift—a good opportunity to practice wedge turns and get the feel of skis or boards before taking Magic Carpet from the top.

Other "mid-mountain" options include Wand, which is green on one side of the trail and blue on the other, to other lovely lower mountain greens such as Kinderspiel, Carumba, Showoff, and lower Video Boulevard.

Taking Magic Carpet (●) off the top gives a nice long, 1.5-mile run that can be negotiated by novices with the ability to make good turns and stop (not for first-timers or the timid). For those better skiers new to Magic Mountain, it makes a great warm-up run.

Intermediate ■

The 5,300-foot double chair takes intermediates to the mountaintop where there is a choice of true blues to skier's right and the 1.75 mile Wizard to the left. Wizard is an old-fashioned ridgeline trail that passes by double diamonds as it winds its way down the mountain, affording the opportunity to take a peek at such wonders as Master Magician or Slide of Hans.

On the other side of the chairlift, Whiteout (■) to Up Your Sleeve (■) offers good challenge as do Trick (■) and Wand (■●). Trick is an interesting trail accessed from Whiteout and/or Magic Carpet (●). It offers spectacular views as well as a nice wide consistently pitched section before it narrows.

A snowboarder heads down Trick. KL

It also offers good viewing of the folks coming down two double-diamond glades.

From the new Phoenix lift, lower intermediates can warm up on Magic Carpet (●), and proceed to blues like Wand to Mystery (narrow and more challenging) or Wand to Showoff (■●), wide and playful.

Advanced/Expert ♦ ♦♦

Master Magician has the steepest terrain at the top and with 40-45 degree pitch, it's a 320-foot stretch of dropoff that leads into the 3,075-foot long Heart of Magician (♦), a more traditional expert run that is usually a mogul field and has a nice pine glades on its right. Slide of Hans (♦♦) is a widish drop that gets relief with the classic black diamond Sorcerer.

Upper Talisman (♦) plays host to race competitions. It starts narrow, widens but drops steeply. Lower Talisman (♦) is 100-foot wide, advanced to expert terrain with bailouts on skiers left and moguls and steep drops on the right. For aspiring experts, Broomstick (♦) to Heart of Magician (♦) to Lower Magician (■) offers a nice blend of groomed steep, followed by progressively easier terrain.

For true experts who don't mind an audience, there are two double diamonds under the chairs, Red Line under the Red double, Black Line off the top under the Black Triple, and then Lucifer, a wide steep that is home to extreme competitions. To skiers right of the chairs are Twilight Zone (♦♦), a glade with 10-foot drop-offs, navigable trees, and consistent pitch for its 1,550-foot duration and Goniff's Glade, another double diamond that is truly steep.

Magic 101

The view from the summit was magnificent on the clear but cold January day I first skied this area. A typical Vermont scene was laid out below, providing a

Time-elapsed images show skier making his own trail from just before the intersection of Wizard and Slide of Hans. MM

patchwork of villages, farms, ski areas, and mountain ranges.

The skiing was challenging, and I was amazed to find myself working hard to handle some blue trails that were in no way easy cruisers. On the other hand, I liked the way the trails were cut, the classic New England twists and turns. I found Magic to be more difficult on top and then progressively easier toward the bottom—a nice combo of work and relaxation.

Although it was midweek, there were a few families out and several more snowboarders enjoying what looked like impossible steeps as they came bounding down the Twilight Zone and Goniff Glades. My impression was that the steeps were *really* steep here with lots of dropoffs.

A trailside testimonial from a Telemarker, who had just descended a cliff section, verified this. He reported, "I'm working my legs at Magic on my day off because skiing here is sport like it used to be . . . not active entertainment," a comment I would hear again and again.

After a guided tour, I did some more exploring on my own and found some nice wide cruising terrain on Showoff and Video Boulevard which led me to the opinion that Magic has good variety, not just narrow trails. I only had time for one side of the mountain and since it was early in the season, that was just as well because my legs were tired and from my experience the blues and Upper Trick were about all I could handle at that point.

In the base lodge I met some loyal Magic homeowners who told me how happy they were to have "Magic back." They related how the community had come together to support the mountain. As with Burke and Bolton, I could see that local involvement and pride are key factors to a mountain's revival and continued success. Once again, I sojourned home with a feeling that skiers and riders will rally round a good mountain experience and that it makes skiing a more interesting and fun sport to have unique places like Magic to explore.

Good to Know

Magic Mountain is located just off Route 11 in Londonderry; about 1.5 hours from Albany, 2 from Hartford, 2.5 from Boston, and 4.5 from NYC.

During the week, you'll find this area is your very own private mountain, but on weekends and holidays you will share it with loyal fans and find some lively après-ski in the base lodge which has live music at busy times. Lift lines when there are some tend to be short and most of the time, non-existent.

The greens, blues, and blacks ski more like those of northern Vermont than their southern sisters—they're tougher because this is a steeper mountain.

Magic attracts adventurous skiers, riders, and Telemarkers who prefer *off-piste*. They find their own private stashes after a storm and when asked what part of the mountain they ski, they never point to the trails but rather their own lines in the woods. Except for closed-off areas (dangerous sections marked by ropes), Magic offers *off-piste* skiing within the ski area's boundaries. This is good news for skiers and riders who like uncrowded trails.

Magic Carpet and Wizard shouldn't be missed for a sample of old-fashioned fun; they are wind-protected due to old-growth trees.

All of Magic's trails get the afternoon sun and with good protection from the trees on the lift rides, you might find this north-facing mountain a warmer one than you would expect and one that can operate when winds would normally close chairlifts that are more exposed. That's why people flock to the area on windy days as well as powder days, Aichholz said.

Weekly races, big air competitions, and other special events vary during the season—check the Website.

Steals and Deals

Magic has a number of "Value Days," including $20 lift tickets on Tuesdays; $5 off on Wednesdays with a canned food donation; state appreciation days, and other specials. For Ski and Save packages, check the Website or call. Stay in local lodging and receive $5 off a non-holiday lift ticket. See brochure, call, or visit the Website for names of participating properties.

Phone numbers are **area code 802** unless otherwise noted.

Handy Info

Website: www.magicmtn.com
Email: info@magicmtn
General information: 824-5645; 888-678-7624
Snow report: 824-5645; 888-678-7624
Hours: 8:30-4 seven days a week.
Tickets 2005 season: Adults, $36 midweek, $46 weekends/holidays; Teens (ages 13-17), military, and college students, $30/$40; Juniors (7-12) $26/$36; Seniors (65-69) $15/$20; Seniors 70+ & Kids six and under (with an adult) ski free.

Quick Stats

Season: mid-December to early April.
Average annual snowfall: 160 inches.
Snowmaking capability: 87 percent; 113 acres.
Lifts: 4; 1 triple, 1 double (plus 1 anticipated), 2 handle tows.
Uphill lift capacity: 3,000 per hour.
Trails: 34; 130 acres; 12 miles; longest: 1.75 mile Wizard.
Glades: 2 double diamond; plus 100 acres *off-piste* trees.
Bumps: Lower Talisman, Sorcerer, Lucifer.
Parks: Hocus Pocus terrain park with rails, tabletops, jumps. Ala Kazaam Tubing Park opposite the base lodge.
Vertical Drop: 1,650'

Ski School   824-5645   888-678-7624

Magic offers group and private lessons that come with a satisfaction guarantee. If not completely satisfied, they will provide another lesson at no cost. Two-hour group lessons offered at 10 and 1; privates: 1 or 2 hour, half, or full day. A first-timer ski or snowboard package includes lesson, rental equipment, and lift ticket for the beginner lift.

Children's Programs   824-5645

Weekends and holidays only, reservations required.
Little Dragons: ages 4-6, learn to ski/indoor play; 2-hour morning or afternoon sessions.
Camp Magic: ages 7-12, full day rentals, lunch, instruction.

Other Things to Do

Ala Kazaam Tubing Park: $7.50 for 1 hour, $25 for 4 hours, $30 all day. Tubing hours are 8:30 a.m. to 8 p.m. on Saturdays/holidays; 8:30-4 p.m. Sundays; opens midweek for groups by reservation.

The Viking X-C Center in Londonderry (824-3933) offers 40 km of trails, 30 km machine tracked, over rolling gentle terrain and longer loops through the woodlands. Wild Wings Ski Touring Center (824-6793) in Peru offers Classic X-C skiing on 25 km of machine-tracked, wooded terrain.

Shopping in Londonderry, Weston, Chester, and Manchester with country stores, boutiques, bookstores, art galleries, antiques and craft shops, museums, and outlets. See more to do in the region under Bromley and Stratton.

Dining Out

At the Magic Village, there's Dostal's and the Blue Gentian, and also in Londonderry, the Mill Tavern, Frog's Leap Inn, Garden Café, Jake's Café, Three Clock Inn, Grandma Frisbee's (lunch, dinner), the American Grill, and Swiss Inn (German, Swiss, Fondue and Raclette) for a wide range of choices.

In nearby Jamaica, the Inn at Three Mountains is an historic, beautifully restored inn with fine dining.

Also, the Red Fox Inn (Italian) and The Outback (fine dining and sports bar) in Bondville; Johnny Seesaw's in Peru; and the Old Town Farm Inn (Japanese dining by reservations), and Raspberries and Thyme in Chester.

Accommodations

In the Magic Village, Dostal's Resort Lodge (824-6700), The Blue Gentian Lodge (824-5908), and Inn at Magic (824-5645) offer walk to the slopes convenience. There is a bedbase of 8,000 in the region and a wide range of accommodations can be found in Londonderry, Weston, Chester, Jamaica, and Manchester. Some trailside condos and nearby chalets can be rented.

For more information, call the ski area (824-6700); Londonderry Chamber of Commerce (824-8278); Chester Chamber of Commerce (875-2939); or the Manchester Chamber of Commerce (362-2100).

Après-ski/Nightlife

The Magic base lodge is the scene of live music and fun after skiing on Saturdays/holidays. In Bondville, The Red Fox Inn (297-2488) offers live music and dancing on weekends, Open Mike sessions on Thursdays, and folk music with "the meal deal" on Sundays.

Summer/Fall

Mountain hiking on the trails and occasional activities weekends in fall.

Our Magic Mountain Adventure

Date:

Weather:

Companions:

Where Stayed:

Visit Highlights:

Our Discoveries:

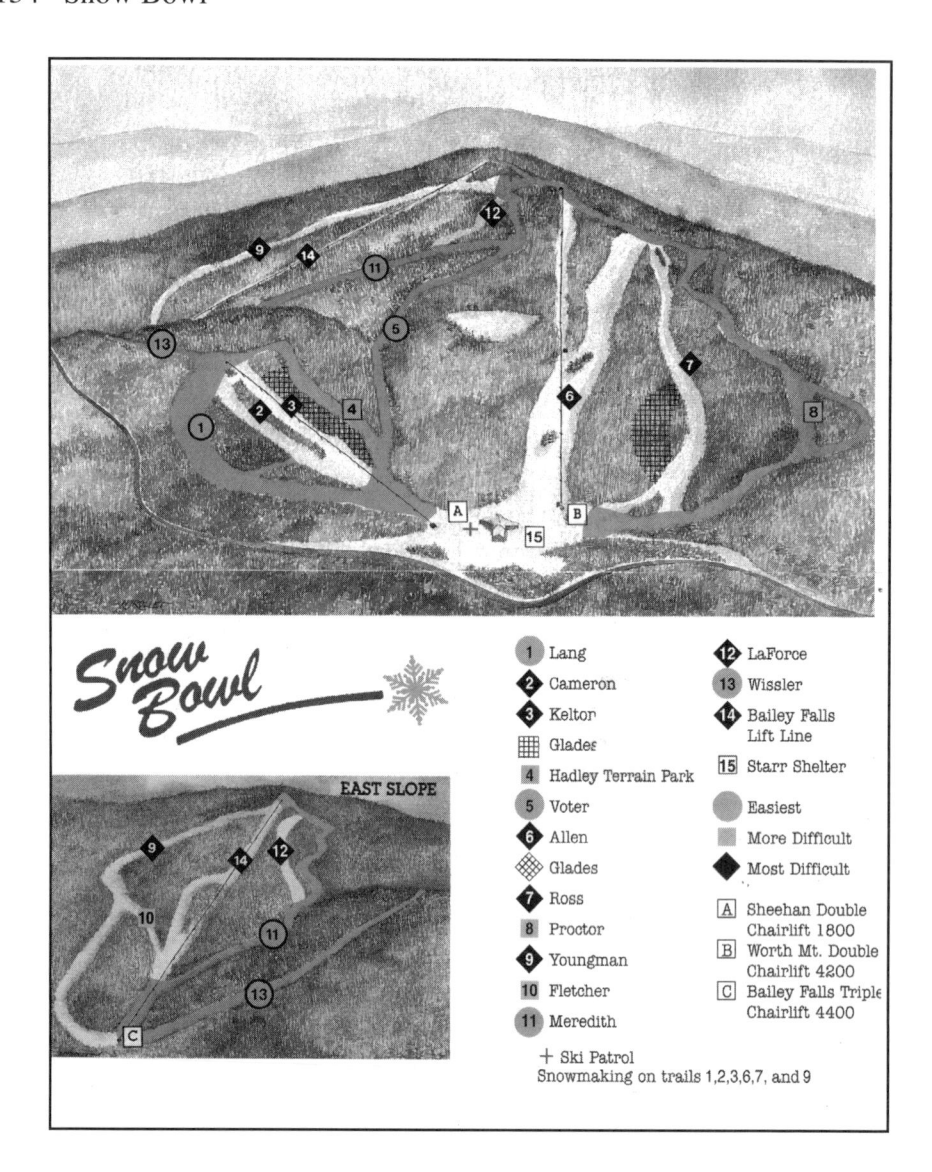

134 Snow Bowl

Snow Bowl

EAST SLOPE

1. Lang
2. Cameron
3. Keltor
   Glades
4. Hadley Terrain Park
5. Voter
6. Allen
   Glades
7. Ross
8. Proctor
9. Youngman
10. Fletcher
11. Meredith
12. LaForce
13. Wissler
14. Bailey Falls Lift Line
15. Starr Shelter

Easiest
More Difficult
Most Difficult

A Sheehan Double Chairlift 1800
B Worth Mt. Double Chairlift 4200
C Bailey Falls Triple Chairlift 4400

+ Ski Patrol
Snowmaking on trails 1, 2, 3, 6, 7, and 9

HOME OF THE PANTHER SKI TEAM
MIDDLEBURY COLLEGE SNOW BOWL

Chapter Ten

Middlebury College Snow Bowl
Convivial, Collegiate Community Hub

Middlebury College Snow Bowl is one of those secrets that just begs to be shared. Located midway between Routes 7 and 100 on the scenic Middlebury Gap Road (Route 125) in Hancock, most of the world simply doesn't know it exists. Yet, it is a wonderful ski area where youthful exuberance belies the mountain's age and stature as one of Vermont's oldest and most historic ski hills. That exuberance arises from an exciting mountain experience where the drama of racing is played out in juxtaposition to old-fashioned lessons for children and the simple enjoyment of recreational skiers and families who call the Snow Bowl their winter home.

They are indeed the lucky ones, for this area, which is open to the public, exudes the best in old-time Vermont skiing.

The approach out of East Middlebury is scenic as you climb out of the valley and up into the Green Mountains, twisting and turning as you follow the Middlebury River until you reach the Bread Loaf Campus—home to the Rikert Ski Touring Center, which is also owned by Middlebury College—and two miles later, the Snow Bowl.

Tucked off to one side of the road, the Snow Bowl is a magical blend of history and modern skiing. On a bright, sunny Winter Carnival day in February 2003, we arrived to the sounds of an announcer on the loudspeaker and the sight of colorful, spandex-clad racers milling about the base lodge.

Inside, the Starr Lodge was bustling as skiers booted up and families readied youngsters for the slopes. We noticed a multitude of ski team plaques lining the walls, evidence of serious competitions and coaching, and instead of a bar, there was a library—all signs that this is no ordinary place.

In fact, the Snow Bowl was a particularly pleasant mountain to explore that vacation week as more families and racers created a sense of expectation, something we shared as we got our tickets and eagerly headed for the slopes.

As I was soon to discover, this is a mountain that appeals to all ages and provides a thrilling training ground for aspiring skiers, boarders, and competitors. Much to our great joy, we found that despite the busy early morning scene in the crowded base lodge, Snow Bowl is big and spreads people out so well that we had most of the mountain and the lifts to ourselves!

Early morning of race day at Snow Bowl looking up the lower Allen. KL

Worth Mountain

Snow Bowl features 110 acres of "open terrain" which is made up of 15 trails and 3 glades on Worth Mountain. The trails offer challenge for all abilities and include a dedicated ski-school trail. There is also a free climbing area so beginners can be introduced to the sport the way it used to be—a climb rewarded by a run. Two doubles and a triple chairlift serve the three mountain areas—each distinctive and connected to the others via easy trails. Snowmaking covers about 40 percent of the terrain, and trails are groomed regularly.

The 2,750-foot summit affords mountain views in all directions. From various vantages on the trails you can see the Adirondacks, Lake Champlain, Pico Peak, and the Breadloaf section of the Green Mountains. The feeling of skiing here is one of being in the wilderness—there are no condos, just the trees and mountains and occasionally a glimpse of Middlebury fifteen miles to the west or of the base lodge as you approach the bottom of Worth Mountain.

The Main Face ♦ ■ ●

The seven-minute ride on the Worth chair moves over a section of the Allen Slope, darts through forest and over a plateau where there's a high mountain pond (used for snowmaking), and then ascends sharp rock cliffs to the top. This upper reach is where 35- and 55-meter ski jumps used to be located.

The summit gives access to the Bailey Falls area via a short "20-pace" climb to the top of the eastern face of Worth Mountain. It also leads to Voter (●), an easy meandering run to the Sheehan Chair area; and to the main face runs—the famous and historic Allen, Ross, and Proctor trails.

The steepest terrain is the extra wide and precipitous Allen Slope (♦) which has an average 30-degree pitch and is 45 degrees at its steepest sections (which are not too long). Allen is a top-to-bottom run that makes it easy to get the sensation of being a racer. The dropoffs get the adrenaline pumping, but the width and some bowl type contours let you swoop to your heart's content, while providing the forgiveness that counteracts the intimidation of the steeps. Islands of trees on its ultra wide lower half add variety. It's terrain you can take many times without following the same line or getting bored. Not surprisingly, the Allen has been the scene of many GS races.

The Ross (♦) is a classic racing trail and boasts the same 30-degree pitch as Allen and also has sections that reach 45 degrees. The Proctor Trail (■) is a delightful, long romp with a few easy side loops, and winds through some pretty terrain. The runout takes you by the bottom of the Ross on the return to the chair. (A combination of the uppermost Ross, middle Proctor, and now defunct Worth Mountain trail served many years as the downhill race trail and was the site of a classic race between Gordie Eaton of Middlebury College and Buddy Werner of Denver University in the 1961 NCAA Championships. Eaton won.)

There is a Glade (♦) between the tops of the Proctor and Ross trails and another Glade (♦) off the Ross trail from about midpoint down. The upper glade is more open with less pitch and the lower is very tight and steep.

Sheehan Chair Area ● ■ ♦

On the east side of the bowl is the area served by the Sheehan Double Chair, named in honor of coach "Bobo" Sheehan who was the first Middlebury alum to coach an Olympics. This area has beginner to more difficult runs, intermediate glades, and a park.

The ultra wide Lang (●) sports a few small jumps and is a gentle beginner slope. The Kelton (♦) under the lift is narrow with a few steep pitches at the top but is really a nice blue the rest of the way. The Hadley offers blue cruising and terrain park features. There's a long glade between it and Kelton. Cameron (♦) rounds out the choices here and is also on the narrow side. From the top of the lift, you can go over the backside of this low elevation peak by following the Wissler (●) trail, a scenic meandering cruise to Bailey Falls.

Bailey Falls ♦ ■ ●

The Bailey Falls Triple Chair, which is 4,400 feet long, serves the longest runs and a 1,100-foot vertical. The Lift Line (♦) and Youngman (♦) runs have good pitch. Youngman has a cross–the-mountain-trail approach that comes out onto a wide section with steep bumps and an equally nice groomed side. It's a swinging cruiser at the bottom. The Lift Line (♦) and LaForce (♦) trails are definite diamonds with good challenge for advanced skiers but are not ultra expert. The short Fletcher (■) and longer Meredith (●), a classic green with turns and runout with rolls, dips and dives to the chair, round out the trails at this peaceful and serene outpost.

Impressions

What's particularly nice about Bailey Falls is that there is nothing at the base except the lift shack and the attendant. It was sunny and bright and a perfect oasis of peace and beauty the day we skied there.

Lift Line looking down to base of Bailey Falls. Note the chairs during a holiday week! KL

It was almost our own private mountain. It should not be missed.

While riding the Bailey and Worth chairlifts, my nephew eyed the woods and commented on all the terrain potential for glades. I checked with General Manager Peter Mackey and learned that there are plans to create more glades, which should make tree fanatics very happy.

On our visit, we skied right onto the chairs for every run except at the Sheehan Double which had lots of families and little kids since it was vacation week. Still, it only took us four to five minutes to load the chair each time and the runs down were uncrowded due to a choice of trails.

I noticed and was impressed by the ability of the "old-fashioned chairs" (detachables are not likely here) to handle the people and the ability of the trail network to disperse us. Discovering Snow Bowl led to the question, "Why have I never skied here before?" The answer probably lies in the fact that there isn't a lot of marketing so we just don't see advertisements and out of sight is out of mind. Consider yourself told and invited to sample a unique treat.

How It All Came About

Long before the first ski tow made its debut on Farmer Gilbert's pasture in Woodstock in 1934, Vermonter and student Fred Harris formed the Dartmouth Outing Club (January 10, 1910) to promote winter sports at colleges. With that impetus the Winter Carnival got its start at Dartmouth College in 1911, and several colleges followed with their own outing clubs and carnivals.

In 1916 Middlebury College students formed an Outing Club and ski and snowshoe teams were organized. *Scribner's Magazine* gave its stamp of approval to college skiing in 1917, extolling the efforts of Middlebury and Dartmouth and giving a big boost to collegiate skiing's popularity.

World War I caused a lag before Middlebury held Vermont's first collegiate Winter Carnival in 1920—the first being a kind of track meet on skis and snowshoes with separate men's and women's events near the school.

In 1921 Middlebury College became one of the charter members of the Intercollegiate Ski Association and participated in intercollegiate events. Its purpose was "the promotion of interest in intercollegiate ski running and the adoption of uniform rules at ski meets."

In 1924 a ski jump was built on Chipman Hill, a small hill across town from the main campus, and in 1931 the Mountain Club was formed to replace the earlier Outing Club, which had faded in 1925. In 1933, a Winter Sports Team was organized, and in 1934 the first trails were cut at the Snow Bowl, making it one of the oldest ski areas in Vermont. At this point, skiers were climbing up for long runs down the mountain as it lacked a tow.

The first meet at Middlebury under the auspices of the Mountain Club was held as part of the 1934 Winter Carnival at Chipman Hill. A new 30-meter ski jump and downhill course were established on Chipman Hill in 1935 with that area still a focus of efforts by the Middlebury Winter Sports Club, an organization of townspeople and college faculty and students that built and operated Chipman Hill and added a tow and lights there by 1941.

With winter recreation recommended as a way to counter the effects of the Depression, skiing was embraced in Vermont during the thirties and forties. The snow trains had followed the collegiate interest and brought skiers to hills throughout the state, starting in 1931. And following the installation of the first rope tow in Woodstock in January 1934, tows began to spring up on cow pastures and mountainsides all over Vermont from 1935 onward.

In 1936 a CCC contingent from Rochester spent more than a thousand hours clearing a new trail at Bread Loaf (as Snow Bowl was originally called in deference to the college's Bread Loaf campus being there) to be known as the Widows Clearing Ski Trail. That was also the year that skiing became "a minor sport in the women's college."

Most skiing events except jumping moved from Chipman Hill to Bread Loaf in 1937, and the following year, members of the Middlebury Winter Sports Club banded together to build a "ski center" with a log cabin warming shelter, beginner's area with 750-foot rope tow, 15-meter ski jump, and a steep downhill racing trail on Worth Mountain. While the Snow Bowl officially debuted in 1939, it wasn't until the end of January 1940 that the rope tow was actually installed and operating.

The Starr Shelter before 2004 renovations. MCSB

Since that first 1939-40 season, the college has always operated the Snow Bowl on the 760 acres on which the the ski area sits—land bequeathed to the college by Joseph Battell along with the Breadloaf property. (The college deeded the rest of the thousands of acres Battell gave them to the Green Mountain National Forest.)

The log cabin which served as the original ski shelter (as base lodges were called in the early days) still stands and has been determined to be the oldest base lodge in the country. It was put back into use for the 2003-04 winter by the Middlebury Ski Club and is now used for their programs.

By 1941, the three runs included the 1.5 mile Burnt Hill Run, the mile-plus long Worth Trail, and the Lake Pleiad Trail with sharp curves and steep grades for advanced skiers. After World War II, Rutlander Joe Jones served as coach for the ski team and then as general manager of the Snow Bowl. He helped to design the area's expansion, including a 1,300-foot long rope tow for the new 1,500-foot Allen Slope and a 55-meter jump.

Jones recalls that the attention of the Press to the Women's Team, which was formed in 1939, "put the Snow Bowl on the map." Becky Fraser who grew up skiing in Woodstock, captained the '45 and '46 Women's Team, and competed in the 1948 Olympics at St. Moritz. That was also the year the Middlebury Men won the National Championships at Sun Valley.

In 1954 the first Pomalift was installed on Worth Mountain. It was a metal overhead cable that had a pole with a disc that the rider straddled to be pulled uphill and was invented by Jean Pomagalski of France.

More Pomas followed in the 1960s, along with a 35-meter jump in 1968. The Worth Double Chair was added in 1969 and its Pomalift went to the new Bailey Falls area. Snow Bowl has since replaced the Pomas with a double chairlift at the Sheehan area and a triple chair at the Bailey Falls area in 1988.

Today, the big wooden ski jumps and original beginners' area are gone, but the trails, glades, and free "climbing hill" still appeal to members of surrounding communities and to collegiate skiers and riders, many of whom staff the Ski Patrol. Loyal local residents support the Junior Program, with lessons for school kids a big part of the scene at Snow Bowl. There are lessons for adults as well as children; and snowboarding and Telemarking are also popular. There is rarely a lift wait.

For the 2004-05 season, Snow Bowl is sporting a newly renovated and larger base lodge. Due to generous donations, the Starr Shelter is growing to 10,890 square feet. Overcrowding will be gone, but the nice thing is the renovations and addition are in keeping with the lodge's character while upgrading its service delivery and increasing seating.

Racing

With Middlebury College an Eastern and National skiing powerhouse, it seems appropriate to include mention of some of the firsts or highlights that the college lists to its credit.

- 1923 First team captain, Cyril Shelvey '23
- 1937 First ski coach, Richard Hubbard '36
- 1939 Women's ski team formed; Men win Middlebury Carnival
- 1948 First female Olympian, Becky Fraser Cremer '46
- 1948 Men win National Championships
- 1952 First male Olympic medalist, Guttorm Berge '53
- 1952 First male Olympians, Verne Goodwin '53, Tom Jacobs '51
- 1956 First Olympic coach, Robert Sheehan '44
- 1960 First female Olympic medalist, Penny Pitou '60
- 1968 First U.S. win at Holmenkollen, John Bower '63
- 1972 First 3-time Olympian, Peter Lahdenpera '59
- 1976 Women win National Championships
- 1983 First 4-time All-American, Leslie Leete Smith '83

Olympian Doug Lewis was one of many to get a start at the Snow Bowl, with racing and training there from age three through his Jr. High years. Nate Sims '93 was a professional Alpine snowboarder for a few years after graduating from Middlebury and was on the Cross M team.

The Bowl has hosted four NCAA Championships (1961, 1973, 1988, and 2001). The 1961 Meet was won by Denver by 9 points over Middlebury and featured Buddy Werner and Chuck Ferries from Denver, and Nordic stars John Bower from Dartmouth, and Bob Gray from Colorado. Werner won the slalom, was second in the downhill, and fifth in jumping. [Buddy Werner was one of America's bright stars when he was killed in an avalanche in Europe in 1964.]

Good to Know

Middlebury College Snow Bowl is on Route 125 about twenty minutes from either Vermont Route 7 or 100; about 4 hours from Boston and Hartford, and 5.5 hours from NYC.

Many of the trails are named for professors who helped give birth to the area and/or contributed to its maintenance over the years. The Starr Shelter (base lodge) is named for Neil Starr, son of its benefactor C.V. Starr who was integral in the development of Stowe. The Kelton trail is named in honor of longtime general manager Howard Kelton, who was the first paid patrolman at the Snow Bowl in 1958 and held positions of co-director of the ski school, racing director, and general manager for many years before retiring from his ski duties in 1995.

This is a great place to ski during a holiday week or on a weekend if you want to avoid crowds. I asked if they ever get real lift lines and the answer was rarely and then usually only five or so minutes.

You won't find lodging at the slopes. There are some inns on Route 125, but the most variety of accommodations is going to be found in nearby Middlebury. The trade-off is that this is as pristine a ski area as you will find!

Snow Bowl sports state-of-the-art grooming, a full-service rental shop, professionally staffed ski school, a renowned racing program, and good, inexpensive food.

Snow Bowl also has the most affordable lift ticket in Vermont. There are very reasonable season passes, including a Middlebury College student or faculty member pass; a midweek season pass for adults; and lots of packages. Check the Website or call for details.

Winter Carnival Race Feb. 21, 2003.   KL

Phone numbers are **area code 802** unless otherwise noted.

Handy Info

Website: www.middlebury.edu/~snowbowl
Email: info@snowbowl@middlebury.edu
General information: 388-4356
Snow report: 388-4356
Hours: 9-4 midweek; 8:30-4 weekends.
Tickets 2005 season: Adults $28 midweek, $35 weekends/holidays; Students (ages 6 - college) $23/$28; Children under 6 $7/$7; Seniors (ages 62-69) $23/$28; 70+ ski free.

Quick Stats

Season: December to early April, average 115 days.
Average annual snowfall: 150 inches.
Snowmaking capability: 40 percent; 40 acres, all lift areas.
Lifts: 3; 1 triple, 2 double.
Uphill lift capacity: 3,400 rides per hour.
Trails: 15; 110 acres; longest 1.5 miles.
Glades: 3: 1 intermediate, 2 advanced.
Bumps: Youngman and LaForce.
Vertical Drop:
    Worth Mountain: 1,050'
    Bailey Falls area: 1,100'

Ski School 388-4356

Snow Bowl's Ski School offers ski, snowboard, and Telemark instruction. Group and private lessons/clinics are available along with recreational racing instruction for all ages, Women's Clinics, and Wednesday Morning adult lessons. Learn-to-Ski/Telemark package includes 2-hour lesson, beginner lift ticket, and equipment. A Wednesday Morning series offers 10 clinics (90 minutes each) for adults, beginner to expert. Call or check Website for details.

Children's Programs 388-4356

Childcare: not available at the mountain.
Junior ski program for local school children.
Ski school lessons for children in snowboarding or skiing.
Winter Series program: weekend instruction for 6 weeks with one-hour
    Alpine ski or snowboard clinics (ages 6 and older, beginner to expert).

Other Things to Do

X-C and Snowshoeing: Rikert Touring Center (443-2744). Situated two miles west of Snow Bowl on the Bread Loaf campus and bordering the Green Mountain National Forest and the Robert Frost Homestead, the Carroll and Jane Rikert Touring Center offers 42 km of varied and scenic trails for X-C skiers and snowshoers. Rentals, repairs, and waxing rooms are available at the Center's Ski Shop along with snacks and a cozy wood stove to warm up by. Group or private X-C lessons are available. The Blueberry Hill X-C Center (247-6735) in nearby Goshen offers 60 km of moderate and challenging terrain, rentals, and lessons.

Shopping, sightseeing in Middlebury with collections of shops at the Star Mill, the Marble Works, and the historic downtown area. Attractions include: Frog Hollow Vermont State Craft Center, Sheldon Museum of VT History, Vermont Folklife Center, and Middlebury College Center for the Arts. Don't miss Otter Creek Brewing (micro-brewery tours, 800-473-0727); Maple Landmark Woodcraft (viewing windows, 800-421-4223); Vermont Soapworks (see how it's made, 388-4302); or the Vermont Book Shop.

Dining Out

Middlebury has excellent restaurants, including: Blue Hen Kitchen, Dog Team Tavern, Fire and Ice, Green Peppers, Middlebury Inn, Mister Up's, Neil & Otto's Pizza, Panda House, Rosie's, Roland's Place, Storm Café, Taste of India, Tully & Marie's (New American /Asian and Mexican influences), the Swift House, and Two Brothers Tavern. In Goshen: Blueberry Hill. In Hancock at the Junction of Routes 100 and 125, the Hancock Hotel welcomes skiers.

Accommodations

The Chipman Inn and historic Waybury Inn on Route 125 are the closest lodgings. Accommodations can be found along Routes 7 and 100 and in Middlebury, where there are many to choose from, including the gracious Middlebury Inn, the Swift House, and new Courtyard by Marriott Hotel with indoor pool, exercise room. Addison Chamber of Commerce: 388-7951.

Après-ski/Nightlife

The Waybury Inn for cozy pub and warm fire. The Two Brothers Tavern offers live music (388-0002) or check calendar of events in the Addison Independent newspaper or www.addisonindependent.com or www.midvermont.com.

Summer/Fall

You can hike on trails at the Snow Bowl or play golf at the Ralph Myhre 18-hole golf course at Middlebury College. (The college also offers the famous and prestigious Bread Loaf School for English in summer.)

Our Snow Bowl Adventure

Date:

Weather:

Companions:

Where Stayed:

Visit Highlights:

Our Discoveries:

146 Mount Snow

Mount Snow and Haystack comprise a sprawling resort with almost 800 acres of skiable terrain. Mount Snow (above) features a main mountain with several faces. It is a very popular year-round resort and is the legacy of founder Walter Schoenknecht, who had visions of providing a grand ski and summer resort long before the year-round destination-ski resort trend caught on. Below is Haystack, a good sized mountain in its own right with diverse terrain and some gnarly runs at the Witches area (skiing area to left of main mountain). Mount Snow acquired Haystack in 1994.

Chapter Eleven

Mount Snow and Haystack
Fit, Fun, and Fabulous at Fifty

In 1961, a *Boston Globe* article proclaimed Mount Snow to be "the world's largest ski area."

To a young girl used to skiing at southern New England areas with T-Bars, Pomalifts, and rope tows, Mount Snow *was* not only the *biggest,* it was also *the best and most fun.*

Being from West Hartford, Connecticut, we often skied Mohawk Mountain in Cornwall, a fairly good sized hill (750-foot vertical) for a non-mountainous state. Mohawk had been founded by (the late) Walter R. Schoenknecht in 1947. When we skied there in the late 1950s, it had seven rope tows, a T-Bar, and lots of nice skiing, but the tows were tiring and sometimes scary.

Walt's second ski area, Mount Snow, pampered us with chairlifts and long easy trails so it quickly became our favorite. And the favorite of thousands of other people who were discovering Walt's flair for making a ski area more than just downhill sliding.

Walt didn't just put in lots of lifts and trails, he created a resort experience on a grand scale. It was like nothing that existed at the time, and every year he added something a little more outlandish.

The outdoor heated pool (first in the East in 1958) and sun deck for tanning were followed by indoor ice rink, fish tank and tropical plants in the base lodge. The 13-acre manmade Snow Lake and Snow Lake Lodge were followed by the Snow Lake Geyser and air cars. Walt's creativity extended to the mountain where he installed chairlifts of his own design and the world's first ski-on gondola. These were just some of his visionary ideas that he touted to the world.

Fortunately, the Nuclear Regulatory Commission didn't go for his idea to detonate an A-bomb to create more vertical on the backside of the mountain! Nevertheless, the tall lanky, somewhat quirky and flamboyant former Marine and the full-bodied 3,580-foot mountain beauty that came to be known as Mount Snow made a dashing story. Although Mount Snow isn't the tallest or toughest mountain in Vermont, it quickly became, and remains, one of the state's and country's most popular ski resorts.

A Mountain of Dreams

In October 1949, Walt Schoenknecht hopped a barbed-wire fence and climbed to the summit of a snow-covered Vermont mountain called Mount Pisgah. (Mount Pisgah was the mountain ridge east of Jordan from which Moses first saw the promised land). Walt must have known his Bible well for years later he would describe his October epiphany this way:

> I looked down at the snow at my feet. I looked out over that broad and beautiful valley falling away below me. And most of all I looked into the future. And there, just waiting for me, I saw the ski resort of my dreams: it would be the largest in the world, it would be second to none, it would be absolutely fabulous.

In 1950 Walt purchased land on the lower part of the mountain from farmer Reuben Snow and began gathering financial backers, cutting trails, and building lifts. He opened Mount Snow on December 12, 1954 with two chairlifts, two rope tows, seven trails and a base lodge. The trails and lifts extended about halfway up the mountain.

He entered into lease agreements with the U.S. Forest Service, which oversees the Green Mountain National Forest upon which the upper mountain is located, and reached the top with lifts and trails two years later. He added a summit lodge and another base lodge at the Sundance area and more lifts and trails in quick succession.

By the time the *Boston Globe* story described Mount Snow as the world's largest ski area, it had grown to 35 trails, 8 lifts and 3 lodges, which was indeed a lot for 1961. A lift ticket cost $6.50. That was a lot then, too.

It turns out that Walt's boast about being "the largest ski area in the world" actually referred to the fact that Mount Snow handled the "highest volume of skiers per hour." Anyone who skied there in the 1950s and 1960s would not doubt that—those skiers often walked on your skis in the long, weekend lift lines but thanks to Walt's special chairlifts, the lines and people moved along fairly fast. Walt got out and tried to keep an eye on things and sometimes handed out cookies while you waited so you really didn't mind too much.

You even ignored the grease that dripped from his innovative chairlifts. He designed his own lifts to get higher capacity at less cost and used "I" beams and conveyor belt rollers and a chain-link drive that required constant grease—they were noisy but they were a lot easier than rope tows! And he tried to prevent the grease from dripping on you by adding tin roofs.

Skiers flocked to Mount Snow because it was big, fun, and close by. The skiing was great, and he kept the area open as long as it had snow. He accommodated skiers even if it was Good Friday in April with bare spots and rocks to step over. In those days, you didn't complain, either. You were just glad to go skiing at a place as extraordinary as Mount Snow.

Walt was a true pioneer and visionary who wanted to make skiing accessible to everyone, not just for the well-to-do or outdoors-oriented, physically fit types. He didn't just want a weekend area; he wanted to spread people out on his mountain all week long and offered the first ski-vacation packages with après-ski activities. He built the Snow Lake Lodge with Japanese dream pools and waterfall and, influenced by Disney, added six-passenger Jetson-styled aircars to transport guests from the hotel to the Main Base Lodge.

That got a lot of attention, but it was the *Fountain Mountain* that garnered the most publicity. Walt's playful Geyser in the middle of Snow Lake sprayed water 350 feet up in the air. On a day when the wind blew the wrong way, skiers returned to their cars to find windshields caked with ice. In summer, they could ski down the glacier that had formed at the fountain's base.

Mount Snow founder Walter Schoenknecht was one of the great all-time visionaries in Vermont skiing. He was also the first to implement a true resort concept. MSR

Walt's ski-on gondolas were a colorful addition that skiers appreciated along with the plentiful and wide slopes and a trail and lift system that grew and grew. How could anyone not like trails like Ego Alley and Exhibition? Or Deer Run and Long John? Mount Snow was a funky family haven and a happening singles resort at the same time—a highly successful Disneyland East—and the crowds loved it.

Flash forward. Today, the area that was an innovative, frills-laden early ski resort continues to be about fun. Although the outdoor pool by the base lodge was filled in by new owners long ago and the aircar dismantled, there's an even bigger heated outdoor pool at a slopeside hotel, which is an even grander vision than Walt's Snow Lake Lodge—and one where you can fall out of bed and hop on a Summit Express lift faster than you could ride the air car to the mountain!

Mount Snow is now the masterpiece that its founder had envisioned and has grown to a year-round destination resort several times its original size (thanks to adding Carinthia and Haystack). Mount Snow/Haystack offers a mega-mountain experience with every conceivable type of trail *and* carries on in the colorful, fun tradition that was Walt's with progressive terrain parks, a Superpipe, and all manner of special events. As a winter playground, Mount Snow continues to be about BIG, bold, and beautiful.

But for all the changes and flourishes, there is still a gentle side with special touches—like the theme weeks for families, the beginner areas that pamper, and the quaint Covered Bridge carpet lift for the Mixing Bowl. Best of all, Mount Snow retains a *Vermont* feel. There is a nicely scaled base area (with add-ons in the unpretentious Vermont manner) that allows you to still see the mountain above. The condos are mostly off-mountain and nearby; with the exception of the Grand Summit Hotel, slopeside units tend to be tucked into the landscape and not in your face. This all makes for a mountain focus that is a pleasing blend of historic ski area and modern ski resort, a place where the trails come first and everything else is a fun amenity to the mountain.

The "Fabulous" Mountain

Mount Snow and neighboring Haystack feature 145 trails, 23 lifts, 48 miles of trails, and 771 acres of skiable terrain (including 145 acres of hand-cleared glades), making it the second largest ski resort in Vermont in terms of skiable acreage. Mount Snow has a broad-summit with three friendly faces and one ferocious one. The summit elevation is 3,580 feet, and the mountain offers a 1,700-foot vertical. The four interconnected skiing areas (102 trails) at Mount Snow offer the proverbial something for everyone.

The Main Face boasts a tremendous variety of trails as well as ultra-wide slopes for novices and intermediates (with learning terrain for beginners on its lower sections). The Sunbrook area is high up on the southern side of the mountain and features 2 lifts and 12 trails of glorious sun-drenched mostly blue terrain. The Carinthia area is a southeastern satellite, reached by trails (or by vehicle). It features Mount Snow's biggest terrain park and trails for all abilities. The steep North Face is for advanced and expert level adventurers.

Born as a nice family area, Haystack is a separate ski area that also offers terrain for all ability levels, a 1,160-foot vertical, an impressive, modern base lodge, and a residential village near the trails. (The condos and homes were built by the mountain's earlier owners to be ski-on/ski-off on novice terrain near the lower base lodge. Currently this terrain is not being used, which is why the mountain's vertical decreased from 1,400 feet to 1,160 in recent years.)

Haystack is located three miles south of Mount Snow and auto transportation is necessary between the two areas. The two mountains are connected, however, by a 2.5-mile Ridge Trail that is a challenging mountaintop run for cross-country skiers or snowshoers. Haystack has been operating only on weekends and holidays in recent years, but it is a ski area that deserves to be explored, especially since it is less crowded and features lots of classically cut trails.

Mount Snow

Main Face ♦ ■ ●

The main mountain area or "main face" of Mount Snow has 12 lifts that access a variety of green and blue terrain and a couple of diamonds. There are several beginner/novice areas, starting with the learning terrain at the Launch Pad area and graduating to the Beaver and Cooper's Junction extra wide slopes. Mount Snow excels at offering long novice runs, with the 2.5-mile Long John (●) and Deer Run (●) two historic favorites off the Summit Express or Sundance lifts.

Intermediates will find a true haven at this area because it boasts a large variety of low to upper level blue trails and wide, open slopes. Snowdance, Exhibition, Ridge Run, and South Bowl are long and ultra wide blues, offering consistently pitched slopes that also feature some double fall lines. Standard and Snowdance, which start out narrow, are popular wide cruisers. There are narrow blues that twist and turn like Uncles and One More Time, and narrowish, fall-line runs like Upper Ledge, Upper Choke, and Upper Canyon. Overbrook is a nice "snake" through the woods.

The Main Face at Mount Snow features many ultra-wide blues and greens, a small village, and a hotel.
MSR

The Main Face also offers several black-diamond rated glades. Yard Sale (♦) is a short but challenging run on the lower third of the mountain within view of the lift.

The Un Blanco Gulch terrain park, on the Main Face, is for intermediates; and The Grommet on Cooper's Junction caters to the 12 and under set (anyone older must be accompanied by a child).

North Face ♦ ♦♦

Trails at the secluded North Face are steep. This is *not* a good place for intermediates or novices, but if one wants to show them the area (or heads there by mistake), it is possible to take the River Run (■) trail to the North Face Triple and connect with easier terrain on the Main Face or at Sunbrook from the summit area.

Mount Snow has some gnarly steeps, including glades, at the North Face area. MSR

The North Face boasts excellent fall-line skiing and riding. It has two triple chairs, 15 trails, and glades to challenge experts at Epiphany (♦), The Plunge (♦♦), and The Trials (♦). With no buildings, it's a great "outpost area."

Ripcord (♦♦) has a 37-degree pitch and although wide, it is made tougher by big bumps. Jaws (♦) is a classic natural trail (no snowmaking) and usually has bumps. With its consistent pitch, Plummet (♦) is renowned as "a favorite fast steep." Free Fall (♦) is another fast steep. Fallen Timbers (♦) is a scenic cruiser with its twist-and-turn, multi-pitched undulating terrain and views of Somerset Reservoir, one of Vermont's most spectacular wilderness areas. Olympic, Challenger, and PDF (all ♦) round out the top-to-bottom choices for some 1,000-feet of vertical, heart-pumping action for every run.

Sunbrook ■

The Sunbrook area is one of Mount Snow's best-kept secrets. Because it's located away from the Main mountain (it's on a south-facing flank), many don't discover its great long top-to-bottom blues.

The bump skiers are the exception. They know about Beartrap, a signature bump run and show-offs' alley under the Beartrap lift (a fast double). This is "the happening place" with music blaring from 900-watt speakers on weekends and holidays and bump contests in spring.

The other trails at Sunbrook are undulating, scenic runs to the 4,410-foot-long Sunbrook Quad. Most are lined with birch trees and are very pretty, and some have views of Haystack. Thanks Walt is the all-time favorite, a nicely pitched run to the Quad, which rarely has a wait.

Tree lovers also have an upper-mountain glade known as the Dark Side of the Moon (♦) in the Sunbrook area.

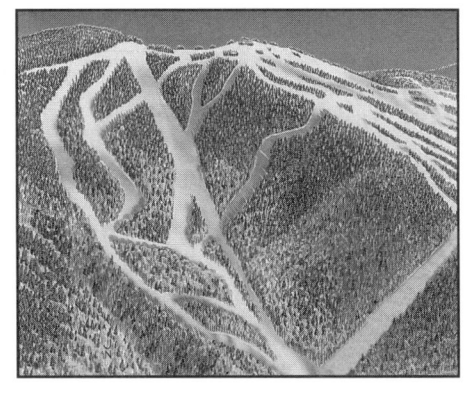

Sunbrook is a "best-kept" blue secret on the sunny southern face. Beartrap is the wide slope to the right.

Carinthia ♦♦ ♦ ■ ●

The 20-trail, 3-lift Carinthia area is famous for its snowboard and freestyle terrain. The Inferno Terrain Park (♦♦) is Mount Snow's biggest (10.8 acres) and most technical freestyle park with extremely large hits, tabletops, and rails. The Gut is a 400-foot Superpipe with 18-foot walls on the Inferno's lower section. Built to competition specifications, the Gut hosts many amateur and professional competitions, and, because it is within walking distance of the Carinthia Base Lodge, it gets a good audience to applaud the action.

The Palmer Ridercross on the El Diablo (♦) Terrain Park features a four-way start gate, colorful banners, and race gates, which give it the feel and look of a real boardercross race.

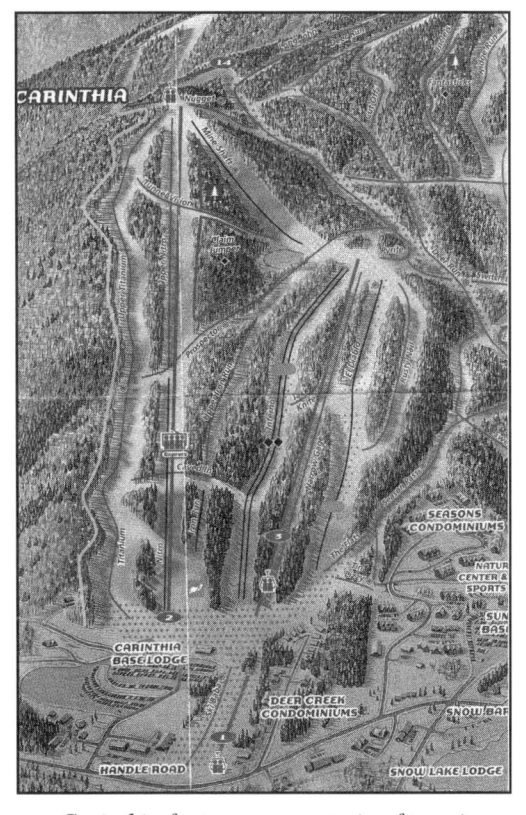

Carinthia features a great mix of terrain and a famous terrain park.

Another best-kept secret is the 5,029-foot Nitro Express Lift and the trails it serves. Titanium (■) is a long, consistently pitched, top-to-bottom run that can please better skiers for its challenge to stamina and line picking. Mine Shaft (♦) is steeper and wider but lets up at Prospector (■), which connects to Nitro (♦) for the finish. Also off the top of the Nitro Express, Claim Jumper (♦) offers a sizable glades and Nugget (●) allows novices to connect to six easier trails for a long ride back to Carinthia's base or to the Main Face.

Haystack

Haystack is a delightful mid-sized mountain and is included on a Mount Snow lift ticket, but it also has its own lower-priced lift ticket for Haystack only. With 43 trails and 4 lifts spread out on 125 acres, including 47 acres of glades, Haystack can keep you busy all day.

A handle tow serves a small learning area while the mile-plus Barnstormer Triple ascends to the main peak and the Hayfever Triple goes up about three-fourths of the way. Both give access to trails for all ability levels as well as the Back Draft (♦) and Secret Passage (♦) glades.

Avalanche (♦) to Barnstormer (♦) is a long, under-the-chair run that only eases up for the 100 feet or so. Stumpjumper and Upper Oh No are shorter upper mountain diamonds that connect to Barnstormer or a host of blues.

Jennifer's Run, Rocker, and Last Chance are some of the dynamite blue cruisers with sidehills and lots of turns for a little more excitement.

Novices will find long runs like Flying Dutchman (●), Yellow Birch Lane (●), and Outcast (●) to test their leg strength and practice their turns. These and other greens are accessed off the Hayfever chair.

The Witches area, an upper-mountain peak south of the main summit, features several black diamonds with consistent steep pitches off the Witches Triple Chair. Enchanted Forest (♦) offers steep tree skiing with tight turns. The wide Gandolf provides a steep under the lift for showoffs. Cauldron, Merlin, and Wizard (all ♦) offer more wide cruising with some nice drops, and Warlock Woods completes the diamond picture.

The Witches area also has long trails for novices and intermediates. Spellbinder (■) offers a nice cruise with the option to reconnect with the Witches chair or the

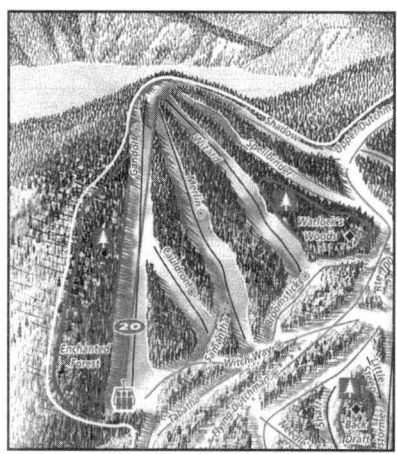

The Witches area at Haystack offers variety and great views.

main mountain. Shadow (●) to Dutchman (●) to Witch Way (●) affords an easy, long green meander from the top of the chair to its base or to Tabatha (●) and Hazel (●) for a sweet return to the lower section of Flying Dutchman (●) and the base area or parking lot.

Innovating and the Realities of the Ski Business

Walt Schoenknecht's entrepreneurial passion for skiing first manifested itself when he was operating Mohawk and experimented with crushed ice for artificial snow in 1949. Working in conjunction with Tey Manufacturing, a Connecticut engineering concern that developed snowmaking guns, he installed what is thought to be the country's first snowmaking system at Mohawk in 1950.

At Mount Snow, Schoenknecht installed the world's first ski-on gondola (1964), which was followed by the geyser in Snow Lake. Modeled after a fountain he had seen in Lake Geneva, Switzerland, it "erupted" 24 hours a day, sending 10,000 gallons of water skyward every minute. As the water fell in winter, it froze into a huge glacier, dubbed "Fountain Mountain," that lasted well into summer and hosted ski-race camps in June. He also had the 18-hole Mount Snow Golf Course built in 1966 (rated a top-five Vermont course by *Golf Digest*) as part of this plan to be a year-round resort.

But time has a way of catching up and paying the bills became harder in the exuberant, over-expanding sixties. Schoenknecht thought that a merger/acquisition with Okuraya-Davos would do the trick, but the 1970-71 ownership change didn't pan out as he had hoped. The 1970s brought the incredibly difficult "no snow, no gas, poor economy years," which were exacerbated by the higher costs of energy, high interest rates, Act 250 constraints, and escalating insurance rates. These events resulted in financial struggles for most Vermont ski areas (with many resulting ownership changes).

The problem for Mount Snow was made worse by the sick condition of its conglomerate owner and the fact that there was no money for Walt to make necessary improvements like more snowmaking and grooming or even to perform proper lift maintenance. Davos mortgaged the area to the hilt, and by 1975 Mount Snow had filed for Chapter 11 Bankruptcy protection.

It was a time when banks did not look kindly on ski areas, seeing them more as "risky ventures" than economic resources for a state struggling to transition from an agricultural base to a modern economy based on many industries. Without the capital to fix its problems, Mount Snow began to deteriorate, and skiers began to stay away. By December 1976, the area was in deep trouble.

The First Wisconsin Bank took over, hired (the late) Dave Rock, a no-nonsense Vermonter to oversee the area for them, and Walt returned to Mohawk. Rock knew the business well, having served as Okemo's GM and a director on

Vintage Mount Snow with the ride-on (skis-on) gondolas and the ultra-wide super trails Walt initiated long before they became popular in the East. Although the area has changed, it remains fit, fabulous, and fun at fifty. MSR

its board. He proved instrumental in getting the Sherburne Corporation, parent company of Killington, to buy the area, often meeting with their officials in his Ludlow kitchen to review operations. He showed them it could be a viable mountain, and they purchased it for $4 million in August 1977.

Chris Diamond, who was an assistant vice president at Killington and part of an acquisitions team that had looked at many ski-areas, was chosen to run Mount Snow. The Killington business approach meant that frills like the air car, geyser, and outdoor pool had to go. They cost money that was needed for snowmaking, grooming, and better maintenance. With almost $1 million in improvements, attention to details, and careful management, Mount Snow recaptured some of its former glory for a profitable 1977-78 season.

The continuous infusions of capital ($26 million in its first decade under new owners); purchase of Carinthia (1986); the development of innovative programs—the Original Golf School (1978), the nation's first Mountain Biking School (1988), and the Mount Snow Academy—and the re-opening of the Snow Barn as a nightclub all helped to restore the mountain's luster.

The efficient business approach that had catapulted Killington into the East's most successful and biggest ski area worked equally well at Mount Snow. By 1988, Mount Snow was the number two area in Vermont and the East and one of the top twenty in the nation, reaping 543,308 skier visits that year.

After a long battle with cancer, Walt Schoenknecht passed away in 1987. Although treated shabbily by the bank that had dismissed him, he was accorded much respect by the Sherburne Corporation and lived to see his beloved mountain attain the success he had dreamed of. Mount Snow paid fitting tribute to this legendary visionary by dedicating one of the most beautiful and popular Sunbrook trails to him, naming it "Thanks Walt."

Mount Snow continued to grow and improve as detachable quads were added and the previously under-developed Sunbrook area was enlarged with a quad, snowmaking, and new trails. Mount Snow continued to innovate, opening Un Blanco Gulch, the first snowboard park in the East in 1992 (the area had opened its trails to snowboarders in 1989), and get bigger, adding Haystack Mountain in 1994.

Haystack, which was launched in 1964 by a group that got overextended in the trying 1970s, actually closed for several years before a second group bought the area in 1982 and attempted to resurrect it by spending millions on upgrades (lifts, golf course, and a new base lodge). They, too, succumbed to financial difficulties at a time when costs for everything from fuel to liability insurance were escalating. Eventually, Mount Snow stepped up to help the area out, first operating under a three-year lease arrangement and then purchasing it outright in 1994.

In 1996, LBO Enterprises purchased S-K-I Limited (formerly the Sherburne Corporation), which was at the time the largest ski-area-only company in the United States. Leslie B. Otten, LBO's founder and CEO, who was something of a self-styled ski entrepreneur in the big, bold manner of Walt himself, then formed the American Skiing Company, which became the largest ski-and-snowboard resort company in North America as it acquired areas in the East and West.

Under his leadership, Mount Snow (and several other New England ASC resorts) introduced the Perfect Turn ® Discovery Center and built the

The Gut provides a training ground for competitors and is host to many amateur and professional competitions. MSR

Grand Summit Resort Hotel and Conference Center, a 197-room, full-service slopeside hotel and conference facility which opened in February 1998. The area also became the site for the Winter-X Games in February 2000, attracting 83,500 spectators over a four-day period, an attendance that surpassed all other previous Winter-X Games combined.

Otten's exuberant acquisition/spending spree came to an end with several poor snow seasons, which, combined with the stock-market bubble burst, found ASC, which had gone public in November 1997, overextended and having to restructure with new partners in 2001. In 2002 Otten bowed out as chairman (he remains on ASC's board and became an owner of the Boston Red Sox).

The vagaries of the ski business being what they are, there is a kind of poetic justice in the events of February 2002, when Mount Snow-sponsored snowboarder Kelly Clark, who grew up skiing and boarding at the area, won the United States' first Gold Medal of the XIX Winter Olympics. By taking first in the Women's Snowboarding Halfpipe Competition, she also won the first Gold Medal in U.S. Olympic Snowboarding history.

If the world hadn't known about Mount Snow before, the excitement generated by Kelly's win certainly changed that as television beamed her story around the world. If there's a heaven for ski-area entrepreneurs, Walt Schoenknecht must have been dancing a jig and boasting in his unabashedly proud papa manner, "absolutely fabulous."

Mount Snow/Haystack Revisited

When I first skied Haystack a few years back, a writer friend was doing an article on carload days so we joined her snowboarding son and his friends at the mountain where we discovered an exceptionally nice base lodge and lots of friendly people.

We thoroughly enjoyed all the trails on a crisp, cold March midweek day with clear blue skies that gave us gorgeous views of the valley and beyond. The guys reported that this was "a cool place to ride" with runs conducive to snowboarding.

Warming up on the main mountain, we discovered trails that are interesting for their sidehills, turns, and mix of widths from wide to narrow. Then we went exploring and made a great discovery in the Witches lift area of the Wizard, Merlin, Gandolf and Cauldron trails. We played there for hours, loving the sun and the wide but steep dropoffs on Merlin, enjoying the hotshots below the chair, and staying away from the Enchanted Forest, which looked impossibly tough from the lift.

The views of the Somerset Reservoir wilderness area are spectacular from North Face trails and the summit year round. MSR

My first revisit to Mount Snow (since college days) occurred in the summer. My husband and I stayed at the Grand Summit and enjoyed the convenient and cool location for exploring the mountain and the valley. We rode the Summit Express chair to the top, walked around the summit on the easy "D" Loop, explored trails I had skied as a child, and peered down the North Face trails I had never skied. We went up into the summit lodge and out onto its upper deck to enjoy the expansive views—range after mountain range of Taconics, Greens, and Adirondacks. We could see north to Killington Peak, east to Mount Monadnock (NH), south to Mount Greylock (MA) as well as the nearby wilderness area of Somerset Reservoir. The valley below and multiple mountain ranges in all directions were absolutely breathtaking. (You get these views in winter, too.)

We walked around the base area, too, enjoying an occasional glimpse of children in day camps or on the mountain-bike track. There were lots of adults and kids out riding on the mountain trails and renting mountain bikes in the hotel's sports shop. We enjoyed exploring Wilmington, going out to dinner, and walking to peaceful Snow Lake in the evenings.

Our stay was a short one, but we did get to enjoy the outdoor pool at the hotel, which was huge, quiet and almost empty until mid-afternoon. Then the seniors and families began to arrive. The golfers came in, the kids arrived from camp, and the ladies from shopping or tennis. The place just buzzed with activity and kids enjoying themselves.

By the time I finally got back to ski my childhood favorite, it was January 2003. I purposely didn't study the map before skiing and put myself into the tracks of Ski Pro Michael Purcell so I could experience the mountain anew. I wanted to *feel* my thirty-five-year hiatus and see what memories would return. It was a skiing experience that was bigger and bolder than the one I remembered. North Face, Sunbrook, and Carinthia simply amazed me.

We skied two easy warm-up runs off the Canyon Express—one of which, Snowdance, seemed comfortably familiar due to its width. Then Mike led me to an idyllic River Run to the North Face, which I had never skied before.

He stopped at an intersection and pointed upward.

"WOW," I gulped.

High above us was Ripcord, a straight-down, steep bump run. Out of four people on it, one was standing, one was in free fall, and two were down. I made a mental note not to try that one and was much relieved to have Mike recommend Fallen Timbers.

North Face is an outpost of pure challenge—nothing but trees, two lifts, and steeps. On the chair ride, I checked out the terrain; I could probably handle four of the nine diamonds (none of the tree skiing).

I followed Mike down Fallen Timbers. Still in the clouds, I found myself picking up speed on double fall lines and having to work some turns to slow down in the fluffy deep powder.

Next, we crossed the summit to another area I had never seen, Sunbrook. It offers lots of meandering blue trails—except for the Beartrap, a bump run for young knees and mogul hounds. Again, no signs of civilization, just a peaceful selection of trails, two lifts, and trees adorned by a now sunny cerulean sky and a few boarders and skiers playing in the bumps.

On to Carinthia, another new experience for me, and an intriguing mix of vintage with its quaint base lodge and modern hip with its parks and pipe. From the chairlift, Mike pointed out a mine entrance and exit. They used to get iron out of these hills, hence trail names like Mine Shaft (♦) and Titanium (■), both great wide cruisers—don't miss them.

Mount Snow is really big, I thought as we did Mine Shaft (nice, mega-wide steep) and hooked up with connector trails to the main mountain and the Summit Express. Mike danced down Exhibition. I followed, enjoying this wide cruiser that was more challenging than it looks. Mike had to leave to go feed his horses, but hating to stop, I managed a few more trails before I realized that I just couldn't do the whole mountain in one day. But thanks to my guided tour, I had met three new faces and renewed one fun acquaintance for a visit that shall live long in my memory book of great ski days.

As I took off my skis, I drank in the scene—people swooshing down the slopes, little kids taking lessons on the learning hill, big kids grabbing their boards and running to catch last runs in the fading daylight.

Turning around, I was in the heart of a charming village with clock tower, Main Base Lodge, and people everywhere. Eschewing pastries, libations, and shopping, I stopped in at the Cape House to view Mount Snow's ski history exhibit. What a great schuss down memory lane! (Don't miss it!)

As I headed for my car, I found myself being wished farewell by no less than three ski pros stationed throughout the village. It wasn't just a "nice touch," it was a warm ending to a great day.

Good To Know

Mount Snow is located on Route 100 in West Dover, 29 miles from I-91; 127 miles (2.5 hours) from Boston; 117 miles (2.25 hours) from Hartford; 68 miles (1.5 hours) from Albany; and 213 miles (4 hours) from NYC.

The Mount Snow Airport is available for small plane access (464-2090).

Mike shared these hints for tackling Mount Snow on weekends or holidays. Start early and board the lifts at 8 a.m. and you can get in a good ten runs before the crowds materialize. Then head for the less popular lifts—take a fixed grip chair without lines versus the Express quads. Try a trail less followed. [Mega areas always have some trails that people don't know about or fail to discover—seek and find, or ask an Ambassador.] Take a lesson. Even if you are an advanced skier, consider a group lesson. The Perfect Turn Pros will lead you to some great terrain, you'll ski a lot, and you'll use the ski-school lift privilege so no wait at the lifts!

The Cape House hosts the Perfect Turn Center, where you can sign up for instruction—a private or group clinic, adult or children's.

Adult Learn-to-Ski/Ride and all children's *programs* are at the Discovery Center. Learn-to-Ski/Snowboard packages for 'never-evers,' race training for youngsters are available. Reservations are strongly suggested for these programs as they often sell out (almost always during weekends/holidays).

The adult learn-to programs are unique. You start in the Discovery Center in a group of 6 [pod]. While you're watching a video that introduces you to the sport and your equipment, your Pro fetches your boots and helps fit you. Your skis or snowboard (correctly sized for you) are all set up and waiting for you. Once outside at the secluded Discovery Area, your Pro will *coach you* in the rudiments. For hot-chocolate breaks or warming up, you revisit the Discovery Center. Back outside, you receive more coaching. The entire process takes about 4 hours (a little less for afternoon sessions).

The lower level of the Discovery Center is for Children with a children's rental shop for those enrolled in programs, a play area, and a meeting area.

The Grand Summit Hotel offers ski-on/ski-off convenience and the amenities of a resort hotel: heated outdoor pool and whirlpool (with entrance from an inside water tunnel); fitness room, yoga classes, a full-service spa (facials, health treatments, nine types of massage), restaurant, pub, deli, sports shop, convenience store, and a beautiful lobby with soaring fireplace. It's a deal midweek!

Events include: Holiday Fireworks Shows, Torchlight Parades, "Big Air" shows and competitions, Snocross Series, Ridercross Series, Mardi Gras and Reggae Festivals, Annual Dummy Downhill, Sink or Swim Pond Skimming, and snowmobile races among many others (check Website or call for updates).

Mount Snow's Adaptive Ski Program makes stand-up or sit-down equipment available for those with physical challenges

Mount Snow is a pioneer of innovative instructional programs for kids. MSR

and provides clinics for visually or hearing impaired and developmentally challenged as well. Manned almost entirely by volunteers in partnership with AbilityPLUS, the 16-year-old program has grown rapidly in the last five years. Reservations are required for clinics (464-1100 x 4699).

As a good citizen, Mount Snow makes snow for the annual Harris Hill Ski Jump competitions in Brattleboro; participates in the Sustainable Slopes initiative; conducts its own Green-Up Day at the area in conjunction with Vermont's Annual Green-Up Day; and makes recycling bins available in every lodge.

The Mount Snow Academy, which includes a winter school term as well as competitions/race training program, is in session from November to March. Kelly Clark started out as a skier at Mount Snow when she was two and got her first snowboard in third grade. She graduated from Mount Snow Academy in spring 2001 and took home Olympic Gold in February 2002. Kelly continues to compete in World Cup, U.S. Open, Winter X Games, and other competitions.

Steals and Deals

Check Mount Snow's Website *in summer* for the best early-bird rates on season passes and all winter long for special bargains or details on deals below. [The All-for-One Season Passes, good at 6 ASC Eastern resorts in various categories ($379 for the Bronze with 14 blackout dates) were tremendous values for early-bird purchases by 10/25/04.]

Mount Snow Edge Card: free card entitles holder to free day of skiing after purchasing six days. Good at any ASC area and carries over for 3 seasons.

A Super Senior (70+) pass is $399 with no exclusions.

Each season, Mount Snow finds good causes to support and rewards participants with free lift tickets. Check the Website for current programs.

A purchase of a Mid-Week Madness Card is $39 and gets a midweek non-holiday ticket for $35 a day all season long.

Vermont residents can enjoy Haystack on Sundays for $30.

There's Superbowl Weekend with special ticket prices, Kids Ski Free packages, Holiday Getaways, Weekend Escapes, Learn 'N Turn, and Ski Free—midweek, non-holiday for those staying at the Grand Hotel or Snow Lake Lodge.

If you need a family vacation, Kids Rule packages (including lifts, lodging) offer three- to five-days of fun activities for families, including free skiing and lessons for kids 12 and under if they are accompanied by their parents.

Consult Mount Snow's Website for details on savings with the advance purchase of the mEticket (savings of up to $20 a day at all ASC resorts) and for other special deals.

All following phone numbers are **area code 802** unless otherwise noted.

Handy Info

Website: www.mountsnow.com
Email: info@mountsnow.com
General information: 800-245-SNOW; 464-3333.
Snow report: 464-2151 and updated daily at Website.
Hours: Mount Snow   9-4 midweek; 8-4 weekends/ holidays.
          Haystack   8-4 weekends/holidays only.

Tickets 2005 season: Adults $59 midweek, $67 weekends/holidays;
Juniors (6-12) & Seniors (65+) $38/$44;
Young Adults (13-18) $50/$57;
Kids 5 and under ski free.
Haystack tickets: Adults $48; Juniors/Seniors $32.

Quick Stats

Season: Mount Snow: mid-November to mid-April; average 150 days.
Haystack: mid-December to mid-March; average 120 days.
Average annual snowfall: 166 inches.
Snowmaking capability: 77 percent; 480 acres.
Lifts: 23; 4 quads, including 3 Express; 10 triples, 4 doubles, 5 surface (3 Magic Carpets, 1 handle tow, 1 rope tow).
Uphill lift capacity: 38,802 rides per hour.
Skiable terrain: 145 trails, 771 acres; 48 miles of trails (excluding glades); longest trail, Deer Run, 2.5 miles.
Glades: 13 ♦; 1 ♦♦; 145 acres. At least one glade at each mountain area.
Bumps: Ripcord, Beartrap, Jaws, Challenger, Free Fall.
Parks/Pipe: 4 parks, 1 Superpipe, the Gut 400' long, 18' high.
Vertical Drop:
Mount Snow main face: 1,700'
North Face: 1,000'
Haystack 1,160'

Perfect Turn Ski and Snowboard Programs   800-889-4411

Learn-to-Ski or Ride programs feature the Guaranteed Learning Method. The unique approach includes its own Discovery Center where participants learn how to dress and use their equipment through video and pro instruction before heading out to specialized learning terrain. Reservations required.

Perfect Turn Pros offer adult clinics that utilize a coaching technique that is based on identifying and building from student strengths and skills and promoting fun in a stress-free environment. The clinics are offered in group-lesson format or in privates and semi-privates (reservations required).

Children's programs   reservations 800-889-4411

Child Care Center: at Main Base Area, 6 weeks to 6 years.
Cub Camp: introductory ski clinic for age 3 enrolled in childcare program.
Snow Camp: Perfect Kids program for ages 4-6; full or half-day.
Mountain Camp/Mountain Riders: full or half-day sessions for 7-14.
Alpine Training Center: for children interested in on-snow training, racing on regular weekend basis December through March.

Other Things to Do

There's a Sno-Cross Track (for snowmobiling) just for kids ages 6-10.

The Tubing Park at the Mixing Bowl operates daily, Friday/Saturday/holiday evenings, mid-December - mid-March, weather permitting.

Nordic skiing and snowshoeing: Hermitage X-C Touring Center (464-3511), 50 km; Timber Creek X-C Ski Area (464-0999) 14 km; White House of Wilmington (464-2135) 60 km. Ice fishing at Harriman Reservoir.

High Country Snowmobile Tours (800-627-7533, 464-2108) offers guided tours from the mountain's base area. Tours customized by ability levels (children must be at least 4 years to ride). Also, in Wilmington: Wheeler Farm snowmobile tours (464-5225) or Sitzmark (464-3384). VAST trails.

Sleigh rides and more at the Adams Farm (464-3762). Don't miss it.

The entire 9-mile-long Mount Snow Valley and Village of Wilmington abound with shops, restaurants, and things to do from movies to concerts.

Worth checking out: Spa Treatments at Grand Hotel (open to public, reservations required; 464-6600 X 6005). Tot Totty: hot oil scalp treatment and massage followed by wildflower wrap, finishing with hand, facial, and foot massage. Or try LaStone therapy, integrated acupuncture or Swedish Massage.

Dining Out

There are more than 60 dining establishments to choose from in the Mount Snow Valley, offering Italian to Chinese, fancy to family fare and a range of prices as well. Many are award winning. Check the brochures, ask for recommendations, or for starters consider:

For fine dining: Le Petit Chef, Two Tannery Road, Gregory's, the White House of Wilmington, and the Doveberry Inn as well as three recipients of the Wine Spectator Grand Award: the Inn at Sawmill Farm, the Hermitage, and the Deerhill Inn.

Locals recommend Fennessey's for good food at reasonable prices; ditto Alonzo's Pasta & Grille; Dot's of Dover for breakfast, lunch or dinner, also at Dot's of Wilmington, and the White House for great brunches, and the Vermont House.

Poncho's Wreck (Mexican, steaks, seafood), the Anchor (surf and turf), the Roadhouse (large portions), and Café Tannery (lighter fare and take-out) are reasonable and good, too.

The Deacon's Den (pizza, burgers, sandwiches), North Star Pizza, First Wok (Chinese), TC's Tavern (good for families), Dover Forge, are popular also.

The Grand Summit Hotel offers: Harriman's Restaurant and Pub (lighter fare), a Deli, and room service. Many other inns and lodges offer dining rooms open to the public, including the Inn at Quail Run and the Red Shutter Inn.

Accommodations

There's a vast range of accommodations from slopeside hotel and condos to condominiums with shuttle service to quaint or luxurious B & B's, inns, lodges, and motels located throughout the valley. Bed base at the mountain is 2,100; 10,000 in the Mount Snow Valley.

There are tremendous bargains midweek (some with kids stay free) and an array of price points to make weekends/holidays reasonable or as high-end as you might like. Check the Website or call:

Mount Snow Vacation Packages: 800-451-4211.
Mount Snow Vacation Services (50 properties): 800-245-7669.
Mount Snow Valley Chamber of Commerce: 464-8092.

Après-ski/Nightlife

Snow Barn, Cuzzins, the Silo, Fennessey's, Dover Bar and Grille, and Deacon's Den are some of the hot spots. Most restaurants and inns have some type of après-ski, whether quiet and cozy or lively with music. The Mo'Jazz Cafe in Wilmington offers live jazz in a speakeasy atmosphere. Don't miss it!

Summer/Fall

In addition to serving as a great base from which to explore a number of towns and attractions, Mount Snow offers: The Original Golf School, Climbing Wall, Fountain Mountain (interactive play pool for children), chair rides to the summit, children's programs (childcare and Outdoor Adventure Camp), paddleboats, Mountain Hiking and Biking Center (clinics to rentals), Bike School, swimming, fitness classes, spa treatments, and self-guided interpretive nature hikes.

There are Wellness packages that focus on doing something nice for your body and soul, Biking packages, Golf School packages, and Foliage packages among others.

Mount Snow's special events include: NORBA Championships, Brewers Festival, Oktoberfest, Rodeos, and more. Plus, there are concerts, garden tours, crafts and arts classes/tours, and festivals throughout the Valley.

The Valley Trail is a unique recreational pathway that runs for 11 miles through the Dover, Wilmington, Mount Snow Resort and Lake Whitingham (Harriman Reservoir) areas. The path is used in season by hikers, bikers, X-C skiers, and snowshoers.

Nearby, there are: horse stables for riding; lakes; North River Winery; Adams Farm; Wheeler Farm; Harriman Reservoir for a cruise, boating, swimming, or walking the recreation trail; museums; Somerset Reservoir for wilderness explorations; and a wealth of antiquing and shopping opportunities.

Our Mount Snow/Haystack Adventure

Date:

Weather:

Companions:

Where Stayed:

Visit Highlights:

Our Discoveries:

168 Okemo

Okemo consists of two mountains and a golf course (lower right). From upper left is South Face (partially hidden), the main mountain, and Solitude. Jackson Gore is the area to the far right. There are several villages with homes and condos.

Chapter 12

Okemo Mountain Resort
State-of-the-Art Excitement

Okemo is an ever-changing, ever-growing, exciting mountain resort that features five express lifts, high-tech snow, and miles of playful mountain terrain—42.5 miles to be exact! The resort boasts a 2,200 -foot vertical, 610 skiable acres, 18 lifts, 115 trails, and is bigger than all but a handful of New England areas; it's the third largest in Vermont.

But Okemo hasn't been just growing bigger, it's been growing better. There are more glades and advanced trails with steeps to keep hot shots happy, including nine double diamonds. The area also has added more beginner 'never-ever' terrain, and has six terrain parks for the young and the restless. And when it comes to convenience for families, Okemo can't be beat for trailside condos and children's programs. In fact, the area boasts the most trailside, ski-on/ski-off accommodations in Vermont or New England.

What's particularly nice is that Okemo's development of three entirely new lift-and-trail complexes (South Face, Solitude, and Jackson Gore) over the past twenty years has taken skier trends and needs into consideration. The 2004 debut of Jackson Gore made this mountain more complete as well as more fashionable with the addition of a luxury hotel with sports center, several restaurants, and heated outdoor pool.

With the new Jackson Gore Village and terrain—and some exciting future plans as well—Okemo continues its winning streak of offering skiers and riders something new and different. The area has steadily reinvested in its facilities, creating a state-of-the-art resort that has grown in popularity. And with its dedication to snowmaking and grooming, it now has one of the longest, dependable ski seasons in the East, operating from early November to late April most years.

By 1996, Okemo had joined the twenty ski areas in the nation that regularly post half a million or more annual skier visits. Today they remain in the top echelon, doing over 600,000 visits annually. That tells you they are doing something right. And yes, that is a lot of people.

The good thing is that they spread those visits out over a long season and a big physical layout that stretches to over two-miles wide so that even on the busiest days, you can find a section of the mountain with lonely trails. (That goes for the height of the Christmas holiday and weekends, too; just search out the outermost places—trails like Dream Weaver or Tuckered Out—or sections of the mountain that don't have the express lifts and therefore are underutilized. Another important factor is that Okemo does a good business midweek so not all those visits occur on weekends. And with the new Jackson Gore entry area and base village, which duplicate all the skier services found at the original Okemo main base area, guest arrivals and departures are also being spread out.

Like any "mega resort," Okemo has a diversity that requires you to seek out its hidden treasures. They include "outpost" areas like South Face and trails like Searle's Way and Fast Lane—places most people miss because they fail to explore the whole enchilada. And this is one big, overflowing enchilada with lots of cruisers to boost the ego!

The Mountains

Okemo Mountain Resort is comprised of two major mountains which are separated by a ravine and brook but are connected by ski trails. Okemo Mountain (elevation 3,344) has three peaks on a broad mountaintop. The tallest peak is at the top of the South Face chair, which is a tad higher than the tops of the nearby Glades Quad and Northstar Express Quad peaks. There are four distinct skiing areas on this mountain: South Ridge, South Face, Solitude and the main mountain trails.

The Jackson Gore Peak to the north has a summit elevation of 2,725 feet. At Jackson Gore, there are two distinct skiing areas: the upper mountain with predominantly advanced to expert trails and glades and some intermediate and novice terrain, and Lower Jackson with novice and beginner trails and a gentle learning area.

After a snow storm, several trails are allowed to remain natural (ungroomed) so adventurous powder hounds should inquire or try Defiance, Searle's Way, Stump Jumper, Challenger, Triplesec, or Fast Lane for steep and deep freshies. There are also a good number of mogul trails that can challenge experts when they get big. Sel's Choice, Nor'easter, The Plunge, and Ledges are almost always bumped up while trails like Punch Line and Upper Limelight vary from groomed cruisers to mighty mogul fields.

Okemo is known for its cruisers, in part due to the abundance of wide trails that invite swooping GS turns and in part due to the grooming which is so good—they do two passes over a trail—that it inflates the ego of any skier. Lower level intermediate cruisers include Catnap and Sprint. Heavens Gate, Sapphire, Tomahawk, and Lower Limelight are among the many many true blues while upper end, challenging trails like Timberline, Screamin' Demon, and Sidewinder give a taste of steeper blue cruising. Defiance, Upper World Cup, Upper Chief, and Exhibtion are among the great diamond cruisers.

Parks and Pipes

Okemo excels in the parks and pipe department with six terrain parks, a superpipe, and a mini halfpipe. Park rangers add to and change the features regularly, but here's an idea of what you can expect to find at each.

The Nor'easter Terrain Park on the main mountain is the grand-daddy of Okemo parks due to its size and constant pitch. It features rails, step-downs, spines, S-turns, tabletops, double tabletops, fun boxes, hips, hip tables, pyramid jumps, and rollers. With staggered takeoffs, all ability levels can enjoy it.

Getting air is a popular Okemo activity.
OMR

The Zone Jib Park is located above the SoBe Superpipe and is accessed from the Black Ridge chair or the Pull, a surface lift. It caters to the hip set with music and rails galore, including rainbows, C's, flat to down, flat stock, and roller coasters. The Superpipe is a ground-excavated 500-foot-long pipe with walls that go up to 22 feet and is the scene of many a colorful competition.

The Blind Faith Boardercross Park at South Face features rollers, bank turns, and table tops. It is a popular place for big-air seekers on weekends (and with a wide bail-out lane to the side makes a great place for skiers who might want to try some of the features without an audience midweek).

The Tomahawk Terrain Park has air features that vary from 20 to 70 feet in length.

Hot Dog Hill is a mini park with miniature-size features, including a mini halfpipe on the main mountain below the Sugar House Lodge.

There is also a Snowskate Park at the Jackson Gore base area with 10 foot rail and air features.

South Ridge ●

Novices have two quads, a 420-foot vertical, and south-facing wide trails and open slopes at the main base area known as South Ridge. The long runs are conducive to mastering turns but don't miss the Kettle Brook trail which offers a meandering route less taken (with a ski tunnel for lots of kid fun).

Also at the base area but off to the other side, beginners have the F-10 Poma area and Fairway to learn on. Tykes in lessons learn at the Galaxy Bowl with carpet and gentle beginner Poma. Due to the 4.5-mile Mountain Road built prior to the ski area's existence, South Ridge chairs angle sideways up the mountain and serve as transportation to the upper mountain chairs as well.

Snow Stars start young. OMR

Main Mountain ♦ ■ ●

Three lifts access various sections of the main mountain. The Sachem Quad which goes two-thirds of the way up, serves a glorious meandering route of Easy Street to Home Stretch to Sachem for a long green with a tunnel and nice scenery. It also serves Lower World Cup and Lower Chief, both wide blue cruisers, and Ledges (♦), heaven with attitude for skiers who crave bumps.

Off the Northstar Express which goes to the summit, Defiance, Upper World Cup, Upper Chief and Fast Lane are long, wide diamonds with lots of undulations, and Searle's Way (♦) is a classic, curving narrow tumble through the woods. All are great trails that invite cruising but get tired or careless and they can turn you into a rolling snowball. This lift also serves the Nor'easter (♦) and its terrain park as well as many classic blues, including: Jolly Green Giant, Timberline, Sapphire (one of Okemo's stellar cruisers, don't miss it), and Upper Tomahawk. The latter trails can also be accessed by the upper mountain Green Ridge quad, which is good to know about as it rarely has a lift wait.

The Black Ridge Triple serves mid-mountain trails, including Sel's Choice (♦) a tough bump trail, Wardance (■), Black

Riding the rails. OMR

Out (■) another bump run, and Lower Arrow (■), all of which provide good practice before the upper mountain (with Lower Arrow the easiest).

On the upper mountain, the Glades Peak Quad serves Okemo's original gladed trails, Double Diamond (♦♦) and Outrage (♦♦) which get bumped up big time by spring and a handful of great diamonds that spill down with consistent pitch and challenge, including Upper Fall Line, Challenger, Triplesec, and Defiance. It also serves Rimrock (■) for a varied and long run back to the chair on an Okemo classic that combines skiing on two mountainsides.

Enjoying the Glades. OMR

The Mountain Road is a main mountain, top-to-bottom novice trail reached from the Glades Peak summit or via Easy Rider from the Northstar Express summit. It's 4.5 miles (Okemo's longest trail) and allows beginners to access the mountaintop.

South Face ♦♦ ♦ ■ ●

South Face has a 4.5 minute express quad, 1,072-foot vertical, mountainous scenery, and a diversity of trails for better skiers. This is an outermost area, where there are no lodges or condos in view and it's apt to be the warmest and sunniest due to its southern exposure. And loneliest area as fewer skiers discover it. [If you are *wildly adventurous*, it's also a short hike from the lift top through the woods to the fire tower where you can climb up ice-encrusted metal steps to imbibe 360-degree views of a wild winter world. This is not a trek for the weak or squeamish or little children, but it is a thrill for a strong, determined view seeker. It's an easy visit in summer/fall when the Mountain Road is open to vehicles; the hike in from the parking area is a short, easy one with far less exertion or danger entailed.]

The trails at South Face blend a bit of classic New England with wider boulevards that offer steep pitches and challenging glades. Dream Weaver (●) is a classic trail that strong, improving novices can handle and intermediates or better delightfully dance down. It starts narrow and twisty but soon widens and has long rolls that are fun to let loose on and finishes with a twisty more narrow run to the lift.

Rimrock and Off the Rim are the only blues here. Rimrock is accessed by the easy Sun Dog (●) and is a solid blue with two options. One is to stay on it and enjoy the ultra wide but steeper descent to Cat Nap (■) back to the lift. Cat Nap is a narrow flat so it helps to know when it is coming up so you can schuss the right-hand turn in a racer tuck and glide to the chair. When you get good at this, it's a fun run. The other option is Rimrock to Off the Rim, a wide cruiser that meets up with Dream Weaver for an easy finish.

The advanced (♦) trails of Stump Jumper, Punch Line, Wild Thing, and Blind Faith offer challenges from rolls to bumps to cruising freedom. The top of Upper Wild Thing is a short jaunt to Rimrock from which you can peel off to the other diamonds. But stay on Wild Thing and you encounter a narrow, double fall-line goat path under the lift with enough rocks to keep energetic, strong legs happy and hopping—ditto for the double-diamond glades Loose Spruce and Forrest Bump.

Stump Jumper is a delightful trail that rolls with steep dropoffs and runouts. Due to its width, it's a pleasant diamond, but you can really gain speed on it. Punch Line is one over and sometimes is bumped up big time and at others it's a groomed cruiser. Wild Thing from its mid-point is a fun under-the-lift, consistently-pitched trail that is great for wide or tight turns. Blind Faith is a popular boardercross park but with a bailout lane on the side—a wonderful midweek cruiser with good steeps.

Solitude ♦ ■ ●

The Solitude area features a 1,115-foot vertical for every run on the upper mountain (519-foot vertical on the lower section), a nice mix of terrain, and a residential village along with first-class dining at The Gables restaurant in the Solitude Lodge. This skiing area can be reached from the main mountain via the Northstar Express and Sunburst (●) trail or via the Black Ridge Triple and Ridge Runner (■) to Screamin' Demon. It can also be accessed from the top of Jackson Gore via Sunset Strip to a short jog on Mountain Road, which connects with all the upper Solitude trails at midpoint.

The Upper Solitude area features an express quad and a long novice root in Coleman Brook to Mountain Road to

The base area at Solitude with the Lodge and Gables Restaurant left and lift to right. KL

Village Run for an easy route back to the lift. Heaven's Gate, Screamin' Demon, Lower Exhibition, and Sidewinder provide challenging blues with occasional steeps for pushing the envelope. Upper Exhibition is the only diamond but by taking a blue, one can access The Plunge (♦) which offers a challenging bump run for young knees before easing up on the runout back to the lift.

Beginners have several long runs on lower Solitude where the Morning Star Triple serves gentle novice and lower intermediate trails for easy cruising. Green trails also serve the Solitude Village residential units and Southern Crossing (●) connects this area to the base area of Jackson Gore.

Jackson Gore ● ■ ♦ ♦♦

The lower section of this mountain (vertical 400 feet) features the village, the Jackson Gore learning area (for all ages) which is served by the 400-foot Stargazer carpet, and a beginner trail served by an express quad. Ski school and children's programs are offered at this area also, and there's a first-timer carpet just for little ones at their own special learning slope.

Upper Jackson Gore (1260-foot vertical) is served by another express quad. Off the top, Tuckered Out (● but not suitable for rank beginners) provides a challenging, long roller-coaster ride for strong novices/aspiring intermediates that winds and bends as it dips down to connectors to the upper chair and to the lower mountain. Sunset Strip (●) to Mountain Road (●) provides a long route to the base of Okemo Mountain that is suitable for beginners who can turn and stop.

Intermediates might want to warm up on Tuckered Out before tackling Blue Moon (■) and Lower Limelight (■), which are accessed by a lovely cruise on Sunset Strip before reaching these consistently pitched trails to the lift.

For advanced skiers and riders, Upper Limelight (which is very tough when bumped up), Vortex and Quantum Leap (a 4,100-foot-long trail with 1,260 feet of vertical) are diamonds that provide good challenge with some major steeps on the upper section of Quantum Leap that reach 50 percent (gradient). Two double diamond glades Supernova (a 3,200-foot glade off Limelight) and Black Hole (1,550 feet long, off Tuckered Out) add further challenge, and skiers and riders can look forward to more trails at this area in the future. Also on the drawing board is a gondola that would connect the base of Jackson Gore with the Okemo Mountain summit.

Resort News

The debut of the Jackson Gore base and village area for the 2003-04 season was a watershed for Okemo. With two highspeed quads and a separate learning hill, this complex combines convenience with comfort and excitement.

The new base area village at Jackson Gore in March 2004.

Most spectacular is the new village. It is a horseshoe-shaped complex with 117 residential units (hotel rooms, studios, and one to three bedroom units) and all the usual skier services you find in a base lodge—childcare, ski shop, rentals, demos, lessons, rest rooms, restaurants, and cocktail lounges—plus amenities like swimming pools and fitness center.

The boot-friendly restaurants break the usual tradition of a base-lodge cafeteria with three concept-centered eateries. They include the full-service Coleman Brook Tavern for breakfast, lunch and dinner. This is an eclectic, colorful place with overstuffed chairs and couches and Shaker-style booths for eating. The food goes up a notch as it's prepared under the direction of an executive chef, and best of all, this restaurant is open to the public, not just the hotel's guests. Plus there's a nice lounge area called Coleman's.

The Round House is a 390-seat food court that features: Starbucks for coffee and pastries; the Grill for burgers; the Deli for salads and sandwiches; a pizza station; a hot foods/daily special station; and a dual beverage station with kid-friendly low counters for youngsters. A soaring stone fireplace, windowed walls, high ceilings and wood beams lend a rustic but elegant look, and the brushed chrome chairs with fabric seats and round tables make the Round House a bright and cheery place to congregate and eat.

The Vermont Pizza Company restaurant, a 280-seat pub and lounge features wood-fired pizzas, homemade soups, chili, and a full-service bar with micro brews. There's a fireplace and this second-floor eatery (located above the Round House) stays open later in the evening (until 9 p.m. on Fridays) so arriving guests won't go to bed hungry.

Six years in the making (due to a lengthy, $5-million permit process), Jackson Gore is a testament to perseverance and vision. Despite the expense and length of time, owners Tim and Diane Mueller never considered giving up. Diane Mueller, who is a runner, likened the process to the grueling challenge of marathons. "You expect to hit some rough going at times," she said, adding that they always approach their projects "with a positive attitude."

Still, she admitted that there were some real frustrations, and at the opening ceremonies for the upper section of Jackson Gore in December 2002, Tim Mueller repeated (then) Vermont Gubernatorial Candidate Con Hogan's observation that "the Allies got through Normandy in less time than Okemo got through the permit process."

Their can-do attitude and willingness to work through the permit process and with some vocal opponents have earned the Muellers the respect and admiration of their community and of their ski-industry peers as well as a degree of success that is unique among Eastern family-owned ski areas. It's a track record that quintupled Okemo skier visits from their first season in 1982 to a record 604,000 for the 2002-03 season, their twenty-first year.

That track record also includes leasing Mount Sunapee from the State of New Hampshire, investing over $10 million in upgrades and improvements there and more than doubling skier visits to a record 272,000, making this day-destination area the number-two ski area in New Hampshire. It's a record that also includes the purchase of Crested Butte in Colorado in March 2004, a purchase that residents there welcomed for their faith in the Muellers' ability to help that resort achieve its potential.

The Okemo Difference

The (late) ski writer and author I. William Berry, when asked what he thought about Okemo in 1990, said that while it was one of his favorite mountains, he wondered if it had a future because he thought the intermediates would get better and go on to other areas.

When I returned three months after my December 2002 visits with my two twenty-something hot-shot sons, I noticed that they ate up this mountain—it was big and challenging enough to make them happy and what with the latest demo skis, they were in seventh heaven on Okemo's black diamonds.

At the time they were from New York City and had been able to ski very little so their perspective was one of precious little time and a keen appreciation to be able to get outdoors on a mountain again. The critic of the two, a bright know-it-all (who really does) but lovable son, had this to say about Okemo: "They do everything right here."

Asked to explain, he went beyond the terrain, lifts, grooming, and convenient trailside housing to mention—are you ready—"clean restrooms where everything works, rubber mats at the entry to the rental shop, and helpful, friendly people at rentals, the demo center, and the Sugar House Grill."

Two years later, my sister who hadn't skied for some 25 years went to Okemo's Jackson Gore with me and commented on "how helpful and friendly the people at rentals were" and how nice and helpful her instructor was.

Therein lies the answer not only to the conundrum that Berry had posed but also to Okemo's amazing success. Okemo is about service as well as high-tech snowmaking, lifts, and adding tougher trails. And skiers of all abilities appreciate that along with the ease of ski-on/ski-off housing.

This is a mountain where the leaders teach their staff to care about their guests. Owner Diane Mueller explains to all workers what skiers and riders and families have to go through just to get to the slopes. All are cognizant of the packing, journey in all kinds of weather, unpacking of gear, getting tickets, and if staying over, efforts to get settled in, then get fed and out on the slopes early the next day. Staff are taught to appreciate the nuances of the *work* and expense it takes to get to the snow so that they are able to treat skiers courteously and with patience and helpfulness. And to perform their jobs with cheerful effort so that whether it's a clean restroom or loading a lift, a fitting of boots and skis, or a quick edge and hot wax, skiers and riders are made to feel that they are *welcomed guests*.

Learning about bindings. KL

That is a potent philosophy that has earned Okemo visitor appreciation and loyalty. Combined with the ever-changing and improving mountain experience, the corduroy and express lifts, Okemo is rewarded with a steady customer base that gives the resort high marks for "jumping through hoops" for their guests.

History

Like many Vermont ski areas started in the 1950s, Okemo began on a shoestring—even children invested $10 in a share of stock to help get it going. Founded by Ludlow businessmen and skiers to benefit the local economy and run by a board of directors, Okemo's early leaders thought big from the get-go with a goal of becoming "a major family ski center."

To accomplish that, they started with inexpensive, fast Pomalifts. In addition to the lower Yellow Poma for the beginner area, the Upper "Red" was over a mile long, making it the longest Poma in the country when Okemo officially opened on February 1, 1956. They also chose to offer Natur Teknik, a method that taught parallel skiing from day one on long skis. Later, the directors embraced GLM, teaching parallel on three graduated lengths of skis. Okemo was among the first areas to envision slopeside vacation homes, starting its own Alpine Village in 1961. Snowmaking and chairlifts were installed in the sixties as the mountain added more trails and built a state-of-the-art base lodge, making the area an increasingly popular one. Early on, *Barron's* financial magazine singled out Okemo for being "profitable in a risky business."

But although Okemo grew to 175,000 skier visits in a good year, it also suffered from the challenging no-snow, no-gas, recession years in the 1970s and early 1980s. After extending snowmaking to the summit, the area found itself unable to replace the Pomas with chairlifts due to a lack of funding when the banks pulled back on granting loans to "risky" businesses. Knowing its "Pomalift image" (6 Pomas, 3 doubles) threatened its future at a time when skiers expected the ease and comfort of riding on chairlifts, the board of directors recommended finding an owner who could invest in the area's future. To go from a shareholder-owned ski area to a private one was seen by the majority of shareholders as a necessary sacrifice in order to move the mountain forward and to meet its potential.

Tim and Diane Mueller, who were operating a vacation resort in the Virgin Islands, were looking for a resort business in the states when Okemo came to their attention. They became majority owners in 1982 and began replacing the aging Pomas with triple and quad chairs. They expanded and upgraded the snowmaking and grooming systems; enlarged the base lodge several times; added a welcome center; built three new mountain lodges and a 70-million-gallon water storage pond; and added more trails and brand new mountain areas—Solitude Peak (1987), South Face (1994), Jackson Gore upper (2002), and Jackson Gore Village and lower mountain (2003). They also arranged for the construction of trailside condominiums and homes on the private land that

Okemo's base features a skier drop-off area and a small village with clock tower and welcome center to its right. Above are the main base lodge with condos to left and above right. The South Ridge novice slopes and quads are the wide open trails above the lodge and upper mountain trails appear off to the left. OMR

Okemo owned (much of the mountain is on state lease land but not all), greatly increasing the number of ski-on/ski-off units and boosting the mountain's popularity with families. They also added a number of trails and glades for experts.

In 1997, the Muellers bought the nearby 9-hole Fox Run Golf Course which they reconstructed into the 18-hole Okemo Valley Golf Club and Okemo Valley Nordic Center. The 2004 purchase of the Windham Hill Golf Club in nearby Chester will offer even more summer options for Okemo's guests as they improve it to another 18-hole course (renamed after its historical name, Tater Hill). Both of the golf courses as well as the master plan for Jackson Gore are part of ongoing efforts to become an active year-round vacation resort.

The Muellers. OMR

The Muellers' commitment to offering a top-quality ski experience and consummate customer service, along with their successful track record, has led to numerous awards for Okemo and also to their being awarded the lease to operate Mount Sunapee in nearby New Hampshire in 1998. They have successfully improved and enlarged that area as well. In March 2004, they purchased Crested Butte in Colorado. (The resort has 85 trails spread over 1,058 acres with 14 lifts and is known for some of the best extreme skiing in the world.) Together, the three mountains represent over 1.2 million skier visits a year.

The Muellers never imagined that Okemo would grow to one of the largest and most successful resorts in the East. But combine an entrepreneurial spirit and an astute recognition of Okemo's potential with a hands-on management style and a "team approach" to the ski business and you have Okemo today. It is a success story that brought the area to the "major family-center" envisioned by its founders in 1955.

The future holds more year-round activity with additional facilities at Jackson Gore to include a conference center and recreational center, with plans to add tennis, a 9-hole golf course and still leave lots of open spaces for hiking, picnics, cross-country skiing, snowshoeing, and other outdoor activity.

Mountain Joy

I had the pleasure of some "first tracks" on the new Quantum Leap (liftline) trail, which is now Okemo's steepest major trail, at the December 6, 2002 debut of (upper) Jackson Gore. Stopping to take some photographs gave me a chance to catch my breath, survey the trail, and take in the view. Outside of Double Diamond and Outrage (both gladed trails with steep sections), this trail provides the steepest and most challenging terrain at Okemo but for longer stretches (50 percent gradient) than the other two.

In full view of the chair above, skiers have reason to ski well here—or try to. Not all skiers and snowboarders were handling the trail with ease or grace, a sign that the mountain can still rule despite the nice carpet of snow that Okemo's snow-makers had laid down.

Upper Limelight and Vortex provided additional black-diamond steeps while the Sunset Strip to Blue Moon to Lower Limelight route was a delightful, long cruise that started easy and then ratcheted up to true blue.

Okemo is top ranked for its parks and pipe. OMR

After skiing these Jackson trails, I made tracks to the opposite end of the mountain. Time: forty minutes to ski and ride four express quads to get to the top of South Face—an experience that showed me just how big this area has become!

South Face is one of my favorite areas. It has a fast lift, great views, and a good variety of terrain. I enjoy Dream Weaver for its classic New England top section, wide running middle, and twist and shout finish—great for warming up. Stump Jumper, Wild Thing, Blind Faith, and Punch Line are among my "workout" trails where I wear myself out with slalom or GS turns. I've never experienced a lift wait at this area, which I relish for its 'outpost' feel.

On a return weekend trip to Okemo, I took two lessons for black-diamond skiing. They were so student oriented that I actually gained some confidence along with improving my skills, not a bad idea for the beginning of the season and adjusting to my new shaped skis. (I had used demos and rental shaped skis for three years before changing over. My thighs loved the decision!)

While riding the chair, we were asked what we hoped to get out of our lesson. What a change from lessons in the 1960s when it was a demonstration and drill approach. Today, the instructor involves you in the learning process in such a positive way that you're not embarrassed or fearful. From my perspective, that

Anita Duch learns to use the carpet, gets a review of proper stance, and makes a few turns for her instructor.
KL

really is "cutting edge" and a great reason to go to, or return to, ski school. You not only ski better, you feel better, gain confidence, and have more fun.

Or put another way, if you are a woman, you no longer have to "freeze" at the sight of bumps, steeps, trees, or ice. You can "flail" big time, like the guys.

I'd better explain that. In the early 1990s, at a Women's Ski Spree week at Okemo, we had in a psychology-on-skis session where we "gals" learned that we tend to freeze when faced with things that strike fear in our hearts—icy patches, moguls, steeps, whatever.

To counteract that tendency, we practiced "flailing" with arms and bodies doing exaggerated motions and paying no attention to "good form" as we skied over a not-so-perfect (i.e., icy) or not-so-easy section.

The point was that we could handle what we thought we couldn't (what was fearful), and we learned we didn't have to be the weaker demure sex—it was okay to "go for it" like guys do. We learned we would not get hurt or suffer embarrassment from a failure to ski well or gracefully. We weren't doing cliffs or challenges out of our ability range, but we did learn to comfortably handle those that were well within our skill levels.

Comfort levels have a lot to do with nerve, and the more comfortable you are with the mountain and your abilities, the more nerve you have and the less you are apt to freeze up for fear of what's in front of you. The less you freeze, the more skillfully, and joyfully, you meet the mountain's challenges.

While that helps one to get better and keep on improving the more you ski, the changes in skis themselves sent some of us back to learning all over again. Fast forward to December 2002. After my two lessons, I left the mountain with a sense of being able to get better at something as I grow older. I had learned to use my shaped skis correctly and in a way that was helping me to eliminate my 40-plus years of ingrained up-and-down movement. Thanks to my feet working better, I was neither freezing nor flailing (nor experiencing the old thigh fatigue) but learning to handle black diamond challenges better.

The proof of what lessons and new skis can do for a person was driven home to me the day I took my sister to Jackson Gore in March 2004. She had skied in her youth and early twenties but dropped out although she did continue to do some Nordic skiing. I had re-introduced her to the sport in a three-hour session at nearby Bear Creek, and she had had so much fun that she was game to try skiing again.

I had worked hard to keep her in her comfort zone so she would have a good time, but not being a professional ski instructor, I wasn't really sure how to take her to the next level of carved parallel turns. I suggested ski school at Okemo and although nervous, she agreed. Two hours later I was amazed to see her carving parallel turns. (I was also a little envious as she had ditched the up-and-down body movement it took me years to get rid of.) While she enjoyed the new lifts and skis, it was her glowing praise for her instructor that made me realize just how wonderful progress is.

With her comment, "It's just too bad it took me so long to try skiing again," I knew I had a convert and new ski buddy. But I also realized just how far skiing has come—not just in the realm of high-tech lifts, snow, and skis, but in the personal dimension with instructors who can dip into their 'bag of tricks' and magically transform fearful persons into gung-ho skiers who can't wait to get to the mountaintops!

Good to Know

Okemo is located just off Route 103 in Ludlow, VT. It's about 3 hours from Boston or Hartford, 5 from NYC.

Okemo's free Resort Shuttle serves their slopeside properties, base areas, Nordic Center, and outer parking lots which are used on weekends and holidays. There is also a Village Shuttle which serves Ludlow and the mountain.

Okemo's friendly Ambassadors are out and about to answer your questions. They also give free Guided Mountain Tours anytime from 9 a.m. until 2 p.m.

on weekends and holiday weeks. You'll find them at the Mountain Information Booth next to the Sugar House Lodge (yellow and blue flags wave out front).

The Second Entry to Jackson Gore is north of the Okemo base entry. You can park for the day (a van takes you from your car to the slopes) or a stay at the hotel (underground parking) and access the other mountain areas from its lifts. With a future gondola planned from the Inn to the Okemo summit, the excitement at Jackson Gore is just beginning!

Okemo offers season-long Alpine competition/training programs for ages 7-18 in racing, freestyle, and snowboarding.

For recreational racers, try NASTAR at the Mountain Dew Race Arena under the Black Ridge Triple Chair.

The Okemo Mountain School for students in grades 7-12 offers a combination of winter athletic on-mountain training and classroom education for serious competitors. It has its own facility to house and educate students in Ludlow.

The Gables Restaurant at the Solitude Day Lodge offers exceptional lunches. Also, check out the barbecue lunches at Smoky's Jo's Grille at the Sugar House or the sandwiches at The Sitting Bull (in the main base lodge)—big enough for two if you have a fifty-plus or lady-like appetite.

The focus on families includes childcare options, the Introduction to Snow for tiny tots, lots of convenient on-mountain housing, and a Kids Night Out.

Kids' Night Out is offered on Saturdays from 6 to 10 p.m. for ages 6 months to 12 years at the Jackson Gore Day Care Center; reservations required (228-1780). Check the Website or call for details.

Every morning the first hour of lift operation (9:00 to 10:00 a.m. midweek; 8-9 a.m. weekends/holidays) is free so Okemo skiers and riders can "check out" the snow conditions before they purchase a lift ticket.

Events galore from festivals, fireworks, and pipe events to Mountain Dew Challenge with giveaways and annual Ski Ball. Check Website or call.

Purchase a three-day or longer lift ticket or lodging/ticket package and you can ski one day at Mount Sunapee Resort (NH) or Stratton Mountain (VT).

You can get lift tickets the night before and be ready to hit the slopes and make first tracks! You can also arrange rentals and lessons ahead of time. Check the Website or call for times and places.

Steals and Deals

Okemo has a number of specials and packages for the budget conscious. Check the Website or call for details. Following are some examples.

Early Winter Weekend Warm-up: lifts and lodging from $63.95 pp/day.

Discover Skiing/Riding Midweek: packages with lifts, lessons, equipment and lodging from $78.25 pp/day.

Midweek Family Values, Weekend Mini-vacations, March Midweek Madness Getaways, and Spring Weekends also offer savings.

Special Okemo Appreciation Days: $39 lift tickets offered on selected dates. Midweek Super Pass: a non-holiday (nh) adult season pass good at Okemo/Mount Sunapee is $359 (Super Seniors $209) or Okemo/Stratton $379.

Okemo Flex Card: purchase the card [adults, $94; young adults (13-18)/Seniors (65-69), $84; Juniors (7-12)/Super Seniors (70+), $74] and save 50% midweek (nh) tickets, 25 % off weekends/holidays. Card is honored at Mount Sunapee as well and also applies to Appreciation Days and has an early/late season bonus of 50% off every day.

VT/NH Resident Specials: Sunday afternoons (nh) for $21; selected all-day Wednesdays, $39 with proof of residency.

College Card: full- or part-time students purchase this card (cost of one day of skiing) and ski that day free. Future days save 50% midweek (nh), $10 off weekends/holidays. Also good at Mount Sunapee and Bretton Woods.

College Season Pass: full-time students no restriction pass good at Okemo/Sunapee or Okemo/Stratton (ages 18-25 only): $399 ($299 if purchased by 12/03/04).

Eight-packs: 8 days for the cost of 7 with option to use one or two tickets each day and may share with family or friends.

All phone numbers are **area code 802** unless otherwise noted.

Handy Info

Website: www.okemo.com
Email: info@okemo.com
General information: 228-4041
Snow report: 228-5222
Hours: 9 to 4 midweek; 8 to 4 weekends and holiday periods.
Tickets 2005 season: Adults $61 midweek, $67 weekends/holidays. Young Adults (13-18)/Seniors (65-69) $52/$57; Juniors (7-12)/Super Seniors (70+) $40/$44. Kids 6 and under ski free.

Quick Stats

Season: early November to mid/late April, average 170 days.
Average annual snowfall: 200 inches.
Snowmaking capability: 95 percent; 570 acres.
Lifts: 18: 9 quads (5 express), 3 triples, 6 surface (3 carpets, 3 Pomas).
Uphill lift capacity: 32,250 rides per hour.
Trails: 115 trails; 610 acres; 42.5 miles; longest trail 4.5 miles.
Glades: 8: Double Diamond, Outrage, Forrest Bump, Loose Spruce, Supernova, Black Hole, The Narrows, Whistler.
Bumps: Sel's Choice, Ledges, The Plunge, Blackout, Nor'easter.

Parks/Pipes: 6 terrain parks; 1 Superpipe; 1 mini halfpipe.
Grooming fleet: 12 Bombardiers, Zaugg pipe monster.
Vertical Drop:
> Okemo Peak to Okemo base: 2,053'
> Northstar Express area: 1,673'
> Northeast Summit to Jackson Gore base: 2,200'
> Jackson Gore: 1,660'

The Cutting Edge Learning Center 228-1780

Okemo offers many lessons options from privates to group classes, one lesson to multi-day, and new workshops. Specialty programs include Telemark Privates, Women's Ski Spree, First Tracks, Double Tracks, Adaptive lessons, and a host of upper level clinics: bumps, black diamonds, parallel turns, shaped skis, or park and pipe.

Kids' programs are popular at Okemo. OMR

Children's Programs

Reservations for children's programs are recommended midweek and are required for weekends/holidays (228-1780).
> Penguin Playground Day Care: 6 months to 6 years full or half day; with a Mini Stars (ages 3-4) one-hour on snow option. Reservations required.
> Snow Stars: ages 4 –7, on-snow learn-to-ski program.
> Snow Star Riders: ages 5-7 snowboarding program.
> Young Mountain Explorers/ Riders: ages 7-14, full day or single lesson.
> Racing Program for ages 7 - 18 (weekends, holidays).
> Parent and Tot: one-hour lesson for parents skiing with young children.

Other Things to Do

Nordic skiing and snowshoeing at Okemo Valley Golf Club/ Nordic Center (228-1396), which offers 20 km of skating lanes that wind their way along pristine meadows and glades. Also, 10 km of dedicated snowshoe trails venture through open meadows and glades. The trail network is groomed daily.

The Indoor Golf Academy offers swing stations, computerized golf simulator, practice putting green and golf instruction year round.

Snowshoe rentals are also available at the Okemo Express Rental Shop; guided tours are offered several times a season on Okemo Mountain.

Ice skating at Dorsey Park in Ludlow.

Vermont Snowmobiles Tours (228-1396; 800-286-6360) offer guided tours 7 days a week from 5-8:30 p.m. (from the main Okemo base area).

Explore Mount Sunapee for a day; just an hour's drive away.

Shopping in Ludlow, Weston, Rutland (Diamond Run Mall), Manchester (outlets galore), Woodstock, and Bridgewater Mill Mall.

Visit the Long Trail Brewery (Route 4 in Bridgewater), the Green Mountain Sugar House (Route 100N in Ludlow), Singleton's Country Store (Route 131) and Black River Produce (Route 103) both in Cavendish for some unique experiences/shopping. Ludlow offers a wide variety of specialty shops and boutiques—cooking, crafts, pottery, antiques, fine furnishings and furniture, clothing, and an art gallery among them.

Dining Out

There's an excellent array of eateries from quick and easy to family to gourmet within a ten-mile radius of Okemo. The Gables at the Solitude Lodge offers breakfast, lunch and dinner. At Jackson Gore, Coleman's Tavern provides full-service dining also as does Willie Dunn's Grille at the Nordic Center.

In Ludlow, DJ's (rustic decor, excellent food); Wicked Good Pizza (and subs); Baba Java (home-cooked meals); Pot Belly Pub (a skier favorite); Sam's Steak House (and seafood); and Harry's (Indonesian) offer something for every taste and budget. Also some inns offer dinners to house guests and to the public. The Black River Brewing Company in Proctorsville and Charaktors in Ludlow offer dining and entertainment.

The Castle (upscale dining) in Proctorsville, the Echo Lake Inn (historic country inn) in Tyson; and the River Tavern at Hawk in Plymouth feature gourmet meals in beautiful settings.

Accommodations

Slopeside lodgings are an Okemo strong point. You can choose from a mountain home, condo, hotel room or studio to 3-bedroom suite at the Jackson Gore Inn. Some condos and the hotel have sports centers with swimming.

There's also a wide range of accommodations from quaint B & B's to motel to luxurious inns in Ludlow and other nearby towns; total bedbase of over 10,000 within a ten-mile radius.

Okemo Mountin Lodging handles off-mountain properties as well mountain-resort properties. 800-786-5366; 228-5571.

Après-ski fun at the Sitting Bull Lounge. KL

Other rental agencies: Strictly Rentals (800-776-5149), Slopeside Condos (228-8999); Trails End (888-872-4544); CyberRentals (228-7158); Okemo Mountain Vacation Center (800-829-8205); Snow Town Lodging (228-7660) represent other properties.

Après-ski/Nightlife

The Sitting Bull and Coleman Brook Tavern offer après-ski with live entertainment on weekends and holidays. The Loft Tavern at the main base area is also a jumping place for après-ski and night-time action. Willie Dunn's Grille, Pot Belly Pub, and the Black River Brewing Company are among other happening locations. Charaktors offers dining in a nightclub format with live entertainment.

Summer/Fall

Okemo offers a cool location from which to enjoy the fresh mountain air and activities like hiking, mountain biking, tennis, and golf as well as a home base for visiting Vermont's many attractions or using one of the pools/fitness centers some condo complexes and the hotel offer.

The Okemo Valley Golf Club offers an 18-hole course, a clubhouse, an indoor learning center, and an adjacent outdoor learning center. It's a highlands links styled course that has gotten rave reviews for its play and avant garde teaching center that uses the PowerLINK 3-D System.

The Mountain Road is a free auto road (it's the Mountain Road ski trail) with some scenic pull-offs/lookouts and leads to a small parking area on the summit. From there a short hike takes you to the Fire Tower where you can climb up and enjoy 360-degree views. You can also hike on Okemo's trails.

Check out Buttermilk Falls for a summer hike, picnic or swim. Also, the West Hill Dam Recreation area. The Healdville hiking trail ascends Okemo from the Mount Holly side on the west for another spectacular foliage hike. The mountain offers chairlift rides during foliage season. The region abounds with special events, concerts, crafts fairs, flea markets, and attractions—Fletcher Farm Craft School, Black River Academy Museum, Calvin Coolidge Homestead, Weston Playhouse, and more nearby

Call the Okemo Valley Chamber office (228-5830) for information and free guidebook.

Our Okemo Adventure

Date:

Weather:

Companions:

Where Stayed:

Visit Highlights:

Our Discoveries:

Kurt Belden (right) tries to catch brother Kent in dual pro race for a car. P

From left to right: Little Pico, Pike and main face, Golden Express area, Outpost area, Triple area, and Bonanza beginner hill on lower right.

Chapter Thirteen

Pico Mountain
An Updated Classic

Vermont's third oldest ski area and one of the first thirty in North America, Pico is a mountain where a sense of community and the joy of skiing prevail. Since its opening in 1937, skiers of all ages have found Pico to be a fun and challenging mountain, one imbued with a sense of family commitment to skiing "as a way of life."

Pico's founders and owners led the mountain in this direction with the result that throughout Pico's long history, skiers and families got together and had fun pursuing their common passion. They patrolled the slopes, assisted injured skiers, taught kids to run gates, cheered on racers, and showed school children how to ski on Sunday afternoons. In fact, it was that same spirit of participation that led to the founding of the Otter Ski Patrol, the nation's oldest and longest continuing volunteer ski patrol.

The competitive spirit was also alive at Pico from its earliest days. As a training ground for racers, Pico provided early support for Alpine competition, helping to promote racing both in Vermont and nationally. This began with the area's founders and assistance from the Otter Ski Club (OSC), formed in 1938, and continued with its successor Pico Ski Club and the area's later owners.

Founded as "a working club" to foster fun and fellowship and to promote skiing, the Pico Ski Club held races for members and facilitated a large Junior Program, which supported the development and training of young racers and taught local school children how to ski. The competitions program sent several skiers to the Olympics, including Andrea Mead Lawrence, the first and only American to win two Golds in one winter Olympics.

Support from the increasing numbers of families and members of the Otter Ski Patrol also engendered a mountain rapport and camaraderie that filtered through to all Pico programs, from ski school to special events. This spirit earned the area the nickname of "the friendly mountain" as well as a large, loyal following of local and out-of-state skiers.

Over the years, Pico kept up with developments in skiing, adding modern amenities like snowmaking, higher capacity triple chairlifts, and eventually fast quads. It even developed a small resort village and activities for summer fun. But what differentiated the area, and still does, is that it grew slowly and carefully and retained its special character by remaining mid-sized.

Of course, that is the hardest size for a ski area to be if it wants to offer the amenities that larger areas can afford to offer—by virtue of spreading the costs of upgrades like snowmaking and highspeed detachable quads among more ticket sales. As can be seen by the number of areas that changed hands in the 1970s, 1980s, and 1990s, that challenge was a major one, and it finally caught up with Pico in 1996 when it had to be rescued by Killington's owner.

Now as the seventh mountain at Killington, Pico remains a self-contained mountain in its own right, with the full range of services that guests have always enjoyed (ski school, Junior programs, races, special events, retail, rental and repair shops, food service, and lower-priced lift tickets and passes). But it's also become a "bonus" mountain for Killington skiers as it is included on the Killington lift ticket and most American Skiing Company (ASC) passes.

Despite passing from family ownership to a corporate parent in its sixtieth year (1996), the camaraderie of the skiing experience continues to flourish at Pico. As the new owner, ASC has been careful to retain the mountain's character and focus as "the friendly mountain." So what you find at Pico today is largely what skiers found in the many decades since its founding—a classic but updated mountain with the social activities attendant to skiing and racing as a way of life. The "resort movement" hasn't spoiled Pico, but it has made it more convenient to ski and stay there.

The Mountain

Looming above U.S. Route 4 nine miles east of Rutland, Pico is a dramatic, tall, and broad mountain with 50 trails, 6 lifts, including 2 Express quads, a 1,967-foot vertical, and a good diversity of terrain on 214 skiable acres. The 360-degree views from the summit are stunning. What is particularly convenient is that all trails lead back to one base, which is served by a large three-story lodge with fieldstone fireplaces that are still used.

Advanced/Expert ♦

Pico's black diamond terrain can be found on several mountain areas, including Little Pico, the Outpost, and the (upper sections of) trails spilling off the main summit before they give way to blues about halfway to the Summit Chair. Upper Giant Killer (♦) is probably the toughest trail at Pico. It is narrow and steep at the top for a sustained length that requires commitment to ski it well. It broadens out some and eventually lets up at Lower Giant Killer (■) for a swinging cruise to Fool's Gold (■) back to the chair.

The historic, half-mile A Slope off the top of the Little Pico Triple, is similarly steep (♦, 38 percent gradient) at its top but not for as long as Giant Killer and being wider makes it more forgiving before it cruises out as blue, mega-wide terrain. B Slope (♦) is not quite as steep but has consistent pitch for its entire

Skier on Upper Giant Killer. Pike is the trail in center of photo. DH

length; it is wide and undulating with dips and bowls and offers "the rock" for a neat jump finish for advanced daredevils.

Upper Pike (♦) drops off the Summit under the Quad and is narrow at the entrance but widens out to a width that makes it look easier than it is. With moguls, it is a mine field for experts. With a bailout lane, it's a steep, invigorating dance down the side. When groomed powder, it's fun for less intrepid advanced skiers. Pike eventually lightens up to an ultra wide blue cruiser back to the lift.

Upper KA (♦), named for owner Karl Acker, features narrow twist-and-turn terrain and a wondrous feeling of solitude and beauty. The Summit Glades (♦) constitute a 1.75-mile natural-snow jaunt among trees that are both tight and wide. When this trail gets bumped up with deep snow, it is tough, but it can't be beat for its sparkling quality on a sunny day after a storm. The Summit Glades can be taken to connector trails to the Summit chair or to C-Slope (a narrow schuss through the woods) and Lower Pike for a varied long run to the base (2.5 miles in all).

Two new tree-skiing areas, the Doozie (♦) in the Outpost area and Birch Woods (♦), a stretch of tree skiing and riding between the Birch Glade and Mid-Pike, were added for the 2005 season.

The diamonds off the Outpost Double include: Sidewider, natural snow and wide; Pipeline, a natural snow, under-chair trail with consistent pitch but not much width; Bronco, ultra wide for the dance fandango; and Wrangler, natural snow and GS fun. The four trails are relatively secluded and tend to get less people, which makes them doubly worth discovering. However, this chair usually only runs during weekends and holidays so catch it when you can.

A ski-boarder in the lovely Birch Glade. P

Intermediate ■

The Knomes Knoll Triple chair and its Triple Slope (●), which is super wide and offers many different routes, provide a great hill for lower level intermediates to warm up on. Once the turns are flowing, Sundowner (■) offers a pretty through-the-woods romp on an old-time Pico classic that shouldn't be missed. When in the groove, intermediates can tackle Ace of Clubs (■), a straight-down but wide solid blue with a couple of steep spots that make it good practice for the Upper Mountain and the right place to perfect rhythmic slalom turns.

Off the Golden Express chair, intermediates have several blissful blues to choose from, including Fool's Gold, Lower Pike, Expressway, and Prospector. Some spill into greens on the route back to the chair and others lead to the summit chair. Skiing under this chair provides a great way to meet up with friends.

On the summit, strong intermediates have Forty Niner (■), a trail that is 100- to 150-feet wide and about a mile long with consistent pitch. It was built in 1986, Pico's 49th season, and as predicted, has proved to be one of the area's most popular trails. It has an overall 25-percent gradient (with some steeper sections up top) for a sustained length that makes it challenging while its width makes it forgiving fun for upper level intermediates and a fast track for aspiring racers. Forty Niner can be taken to a choice of connectors that give access to other blues (Lower Sunset 71, Mid KA, Mid Pike, and the Birch Glades as well as other trails to the base) or to Mid Pike and back to the Summit chair. They're all different and should be sampled (a trail map will come in handy).

Mid Pike (■) is one of the sweetest cruisers to ever receive corduroy grooming. Located under the Summit chair, it is a showoff's delight and provides another opportunity to meet up with friends who can look for you from the lift.

Beginner/Novice ●

Pico has a dedicated beginner area with a gentle double chairlift and two slopes (●) known as Bonanza 1 and Bonanza 2. They make it easy to take a small child or adult out for the first time. Bonanza is located to the far right of the base lodge, away from the main traffic so there's no chance of schussboomers intimidating first timers, but you do have a short walk to get there.

The Knomes Knoll Triple Slope (●) and chair next to Bonanza offers a chance to move up to a longer slope with lots of different routes thanks to islands of trees to duck around and in and out of. The Golden Express Chair takes novices to Gold Rush (●), a gentle wide slope, which can be followed to Swinger (●) and then to Triple Slope for a long easy glide back to the chair.

Novices can also take the Little Pico Triple and enjoy a long cruise via Bushwacker to Swinger to lower Triple Slope back to the base. Similarly, they can take the Outpost chair and follow That-A-Way to Gold Rush to Swinger and the Triple Slope to the base. All are rated as green circles.

A History of Family, Community

Pico was the dream of avid skiers Brad and Janet Mead. They installed a rope tow at Framar Farms in nearby Mendon for the 1936-37 winter and traveled to Europe to research developing a "real ski resort." They searched for the "perfect mountain" and chose Pico for its snowbelt location, exposure (north and east), easy access, proximity to a major Vermont city, and ski potential.

Being dreamers and visionaries, they planned for a complex of mountainside homes, a large trail network, an aerial tram to Pico Peak, and resort-styled amenities like swimming pools, ice skating rinks, and tennis. But first they had to get access to the mountain itself.

They convinced Mortimer Proctor to lease the mountain to them and formed Pico Peak, Inc. with their friend Bill Field, owner of the *Rutland Daily Herald*.

Pico debuted with a 1,200-foot rope tow and skiing on the A and B Slopes as well as on C trail on Little Pico on Thanksgiving Day, November 27, 1937. They also had a rough-cut, narrow Sunset Schuss trail from the summit, which required a long hike up from the top of Little Pico to get to it.

In 1938 the Meads added two more rope tows and widened Sunset Schuss, which became a popular 2.5-mile trail

Aerial view of the 2.5-mile Sunset Schuss and Little Pico in 1941. A Slope (expert) is to the left, B Slope (then intermediate) is the wide slope to right, and C Slope (novice) is the narrow trail on the right that wound off the back of Little Pico. The T-Bar went up the center.

The T-Bar installed on Little Pico in 1940 was the first Constam Alpine lift to be installed in America. P

used for recreational skiing as well as downhill racing and the famous Pico Derby.

Although Vermont sported many local hills with rope tows at this time, most were on pastures, not mountains. Of today's major ski areas, just four were operating with tows for the 1938-39 winter—Suicide Six (with a rope tow to its top), Mount Mansfield and Bromley (each with two tows on their lower mountains). Except for Suicide Six, which has a lesser top elevation, all required a hike up to ski down from their respective summits.

In 1940, the Meads, who had been researching lifts in Switzerland, installed a Constam "T-stick" on Little Pico, the first T-Bar and, at the time, the highest capacity lift to be installed in North America. The Meads also brought Swiss ski instructor Karl Acker to America to run Pico's Ski School.

After Brad Mead died in a tragic boating accident in 1942, Janet managed the ski area and kept it operating even during the difficult World War II years when Karl enlisted in the famous 10th Mountain Division. A determined and passionate skier, Janet purchased the entire mountain in 1947 and lowered ticket rates to fight inflation and deal with the competition that was springing up with the expansion of such areas as Big Bromley, Mt. Mansfield (Stowe) and the Middlebury College Snow Bowl as well as the advent of new areas like Mount Ascutney and Mad River Glen.

When Karl Acker returned from the war, he coached the Meads' daughter Andrea who was chosen to attend the first post-war Winter Olympics in St. Moritz, Switzerland in 1948. The 15-year old almost won the downhill but crashed at the very end of the course. (Fellow U.S. Team member Gretchen Fraser won Gold in the slalom, the first American to win an Olympic Gold medal in Alpine skiing).

In the 1952 Olympics, Andrea (who had met and married racer David Lawrence) became the first American to win two Golds (in the giant slalom and slalom events) in one Olympics—a feat not repeated by any American skier since, male or female—and helped to keep Pico in the forefront of skiing history.

Earlier, Pico skier Wendal Cram had been chosen to attend the 1940 Olympics but they were cancelled due to the situation in Europe. However, other skiers who had learned at Pico represented the U.S. at future Olympics, including Suzy (1968) and Rick Chaffee (1968 and 1972) and Harry "Rebel" Ryan (1968). Many others went on to compete at the Eastern, collegiate, and national levels and some to compete on the professional circuit.

In 1954 Karl and June Acker bought Pico and expanded the operation with a T-Bar on Knome's Knoll (now called the Triple Slope). Tragedy struck again when Karl died suddenly from a heart attack in 1958, leaving June to carry on. With these two tragedies, Janet and June became two of the earliest women to own and operate a ski area in the United States. Part of their ability to carry on came from the assistance of a loyal group of skiers, both paid personnel and volunteers from the Otter Ski Patrol and the Pico Ski Club.

Andrea Mead Lawrence, 1950.

June carried out some of Karl's plans with the installation of a chairlift that went halfway up the mountain but couldn't get financing to get a chair to the top. In 1964, she sold to Bruce Belden who headed a group of investors from New Jersey. He had been working at Mount Snow since 1955 and was "just itching" to try his hand at operating his own ski area.

When Belden took over in 1964, Pico had 2 T-Bars, a J-Bar, and a chairlift that served Lower Pike and an 800-foot vertical drop. Recognizing that the key to Pico's future was to get lift-serviced skiing to the top, Belden installed the Summit Double, cut new trails, and built a new base lodge during the busy summer of 1965.

The next year he put in the Bonanza double and in 1969 added the Outpost chair and trails. He eventually replaced the T-Bars with triple chairs (the triple he installed in 1970 was the first triple in the state) and added a Glades chair and an upper mountain Pomalift as well as snowmaking. In 1981, Pico installed an Alpine Slide for summer rides on B Slope. The Golden Express detachable quad was added in 1987.

An astute businessman, Belden was aware of the need for increased snowmaking, which skiers had come to expect, and amenities like fast lifts and convenient trailside villages. The Village Square condominiums and the Pico Sports Village and Sports Center were designed to meet the needs of skiers and keep Pico competitive.

Belden retired after 32 years in the ski business, selling his shares to the company he had headed. The Pico Corporation carried on after a proposed merger with Killington fell through (despite a trial year during which Killington managed Pico with great success). Pico hit some rough sledding in the 1990s and by summer 1996 its future was uncertain.

The slopeside Village at Pico boasts a Sports Center. P

Les Otten came to the rescue when ASC purchased the assets in November 1996, and Killington managers got the area up and running. They also reconfigured the lift system, adding a second detachable, the Summit Express; removed some lifts; and improved snowmaking and grooming. Plans to connect to Killington with trails and lifts were announced and then delayed. ASC Vice President Carl Spangler is optimistic that the inter-connect will happen within the next ten years.

Pico Personal

My association with Pico dates to 1970 when I took a busload of high-school ski clubbers to the area. Two years later my husband and I bought a vacation home nearby and became Pico regulars along with my dad and siblings.

We loved the sense of adventure we always had at Pico, whether negotiating the Summit Glades (long before tree skiing became *de rigeur*), being scared on the old T-Bar (it was a truly *steep* and scary climb after the halfway point), sunning ourselves on Pike, or "mooing" in the woods at the top of the Outpost chair. I can't remember how that got started but I think it was my high-school ski clubbers who began our tradition of taking the narrow paths through the trees and mooing on the dips and twists—just a fun, silly thing to do long before tree skiing became trendy.

During my early reporter years, I covered Pico racing, and I vividly remember being impressed by the Ski Club support for the kids and the palpable camaraderie among club parents. That and interviews with the owners and general manager gave me an impression of Pico as "an extended family," united by the enjoyment of skiing and desire to provide a fun experience for everyone along with serious race-training programs.

On a revisit in March 2003, three generations of my family (grandfather, two mothers, three sons) skied together, exploring and rediscovering the joys of Pico trails and each other. My dad particularly enjoyed watching his grown grandsons ski with their young cousin.

Young Geoffrey reveled in showing off "his home mountain" and my boys who hadn't skied it since they were tykes, thrilled to the tour, the trails, and the vistas as well as being "wowed" by their young cousin.

"What other sport allows you to participate all together like this?" Dad asked as his young "tigers" cruised the trails together.

To be honest, I don't think there is another one.

His joy and that of my sons reminded me of my own discovery of Pico some thirty-plus years earlier. Much had changed during that time, but Pico was still the same friendly and interesting mountain where all ages and abilities can connect in an exhilarating experience. Skiing Forty Niner was living proof of that, although we older folks had a hard time keeping up with our progeny.

Three generations enjoy a day at Pico. From left, Jason and Jon Lorentz, Grandfather Bob Duch, Aunt Bobbie Ballou, and Cousin Geoffrey Ballou. KL

Good To Know

Pico is located nine miles east of Rutland on U.S. Route 4; it's about 3 hours from Boston, 3-plus from Hartford, 2 from Albany, and 5 from NYC.

Pico is a host site for the Vermont Adaptive Ski and Sports program, which is dedicated to providing recreational sports opportunities to people with disabilities. VASS offers ski and snowboard clinics at Pico to adults and children of all ages with any type of disability. Reservations are required. For more information, call the VASS office at 786-4991.

Tele Tuesdays at Pico feature lifts-and-lesson packages and fun races; they are very popular with Telemarkers and would-be Tele skiers.

You can ski Pico on its own lift ticket (not good at Killington) or on a Killington ticket. Plans call for the two areas to be connected by a series of trails and lifts between Rams Head and the top of Pico with some fine intermediate terrain between the two.

A competitor performs a helicopter in front of the Pico Base Lodge. DH

Warm up on the Golden Express early in the day, then move on up to the upper mountain and the Summit Express until you've had your fill or it starts to get crowded (which is on a very few peak holidays and Saturdays during the year). Then head for the Outpost. Don't forget the Triple chair at A Slope—hit this at lunchtime and you'll have it to yourself.

Built for the needs of all skiers, the Pico Base Lodge has a brown bag cafeteria on the ground level which is also the site of the VASS Desk; a full-service cafeteria with Burrito Bar on the second level; and the classic Last Run Lounge on the third. A huge deck overlooks the slopes, providing a place to congregate or catch some warm sunny rays. Across the way and connected by the second level deck is the ski shop with rental and repair shops downstairs. It's a convenient set-up and a fine example of a classic base lodge.

The Pico Resort Hotel and Village Condominiums are located at Pico's base and are ski-on/ski-off. The Pico Sports Center features a 75-foot heated pool, hot tubs, sauna, and exercise room. Free shuttle service to dining, entertainment, and the other six mountains of Killington is available.

Steals and Deals

Pico has affordable lift tickets, ski packages, and specials during the season. As always, call or check the Website for best prices and packages. Multi-day tickets offer good value.

There's a Pico Card ($49 in 2004) that gives discounted lift tickets.

Full-time College Students ski for $29 any day with valid ID.

Pico Etickets lock in savings on tickets, clinics, rentals, and lessons and METickets also save—both are purchased online.

VT, NH, Quebec Days: Residents ski for half price on non-holiday Wednesdays throughout the season with the free Resident Card. Check Website or call for details. Proof of residency is required.

Kids ages 12 and younger ski and ride free the same number of days as their parents when parents pre-purchase (prior to arrival) a 5-day or more lift ticket. Check for details. Kids ages 5 and younger ski/ride free when accompanied by an adult.

Each summer check the early-bird deals on season passes. For 2005, ASC introduced its All-for-One season passes at bargain rates—see Killington chapter—which included Pico. Other early-bird deals included a Full Pico Season Pass for $349 (no blackout dates) for 2005 if purchased by 10/25/04.

Phone numbers below are **area code 802** unless otherwise noted.

Handy Info

Website: www.picomountain.com
Email: info@picomountain.com
General information: 866-667-7426; 866-667-PICO
Snow report: 422-1200 and updated daily at Website.
Hours: 9-4 midweek; 8-4 weekends/ holidays.
Tickets 2005 season: Adults (19-64) $49 daily; Young Adults (13-18) $39 daily; Juniors (6-12) / Seniors(65+) $29 daily; Five & under ski free (with paying adult). Multi-day best value.

Quick Stats

Season: Mid-December through end of March; average 105 days.
Average annual snowfall: 250 inches.
Snowmaking capability: 75 percent; 156 acres.
Lifts: 6; 2 express quads, 2 triples, 2 doubles.
Uphill lift capacity: 10,000 rides per hour.
Trails: 50 trails, 214 acres; 15 miles; longest trail 2.5 miles.
Glades: 4; Summit Glades, Birch Glades, Doozie, Birch Woods.
Bumps: Upper Pike, Summit Glades, Upper Giant Killer.
Parks/Pipe: 1 park at Triple Slope with variable features.
Vertical Drop:
Pico Peak to base: 1,967'

Perfect Turn Ski and Snowboard Programs (888-765-7758)

Group lessons, private coaching, specialty clinics, and Telemark lessons. See Killington chapter for description of Perfect Turn programs.

Children's Programs   reservations 888-765-7758
Childcare: not available at Pico; offered at Rams Head at Killington.
Ministars/Lowriders: Perfect Kids program for ages 4-6; full or half-day.
Superstars: for ages 7-12, full or half-day sessions.
Snowzone Teen Program (13-18): skiing, snowboarding & skiboarding clinics.

Other Things to Do
Check out the Pico Sports Center: Olympic sized swimming pool, fitness equipment, classes. See Killington Chapter for more to do in area.

Dining Out
There are more than 100 dining establishments to choose from in the region. At Pico, Dinky's for soup and sandwiches. Close by on U.S. Route 4: Inn at Long Trail, Zola's Grille at Cortina Inn, Vermont Inn, Red Clover. In Rutland, Countryman's Pleasure, Royal's 121 Hearthside, South Station, Little Harry's, Tapas, Three Tomatoes, the Sirloin Saloon, and the Palms are just a few of the standouts. For more area restaurants see Killington Chapter.

Accommodations
Pico Village Square and Sports Village condos at the mountain.
For Pico Ski and Stay Packages, 866-667-PICO.
See Killington for more options in the region.

Après-ski/Nightlife
Last Run Lounge at Pico, McGraths' Pub at Inn at the Long Trail.

Summer/Fall
The Adventure Center at Pico offers miniature golf, the Alpine Slide, bungee jumping, climbing wall, and chairlift rides. Pico hosts a lively annual Renaissance Festival in August. The Long and Appalachian Trails, which cross over the sides of Killington and Pico, can be explored for a day hike or longer trek. There's also a short hike up Deer Leap behind the Inn at Long Trail with great views of Pico. Proper footwear recommended. See Killington for golf, tennis, and more opportunities in the area.

Our Pico Adventure

Date:

Weather:

Companions:

Where Stayed:

Visit Highlights:

Our Discoveries:

204 Smugglers'

Morse Highlands and Morse Mountain on left with village below and to both sides, Madonna center, and Sterling right.

Chapter Fourteen

Smugglers' Notch Resort
A Family Focus on Outdoor Fun

Smugglers' Notch Resort caters to families with a dedication that surpasses the steepness of the Black Hole, Vermont's only triple diamond. This 'Club Med' of ski resorts takes the hassle out of vacations for parents by working hard to keep kids happy. They do this by offering a variety of indoor and outdoor activities for all ages and interests.

That attention to their needs starts at six weeks—the age they will accept infants for daycare. Smuggs (their own affectionate nickname) built a 5,400-square-foot state-of-the-art childcare center, aptly named Treasures, to accommodate their youngest guests of six weeks to three years. This slopeside facility has radiant heated floors, one-way glass so parents can check up on little ones, and remote access cameras. There's an adjacent 4,000-square-foot outdoor playground for Treasure's adventurous toddlers.

Older kids haven't been forgotten, either. With an abundance of activities (outdoor ice skating, tubing, snowmobile tours, swimming, etcetera), special facilities (two teen centers, FunZone, Video Arcade, basketball court), and activities (parties, bonfires, torchlight parades, fireworks) kids *and teens* are kept busy and happy.

To keep parents happy, there's a pedestrian village with shuttle service (to condos and slopes) that makes a car unnecessary. Evening programs for kids give parents opportunities to dine out or up (on top of Sterling Mountain).

And yes, Smuggs also has skiing and riding for all ability levels and a mountain for each. In fact, you don't have to have young kids to enjoy it—just ask any of the 136 members of the Smugglers' 55+ Club. They'll give you a sense of the fun that trail-minded, young-hearted Seniors find on the mountain and off.

There are numerous instructional programs for children that are geared to get youngsters out on the hill and loving skiing or riding. They do that with special facilities, cute mascots, several dedicated learning hills and programs, and talented staff who enjoy being with children. Teens have their own special coaching in group "camp" sessions with several options, from social/fun mountain exploration to learning the basics of Alpine racing. There's even a Night School for Boarding for skiers wanting to give snowboarding a try.

There's Snow Sport University for adults, so parents get to learn or improve skiing and riding skills, too.

Smuggs' many loyalists tell their friends—and strangers like me while waiting for the shuttle bus—that this is a neat place to visit even if you don't ski.

In addition to the convenience of lots of slopeside accommodations and many village amenities, there are options for adults that include a range of educational and crafts classes (painting, sculpting, stenciling, etcetera), health and fitness opportunities (yoga, facial workshops, massages), as well as a chance to try other sports like snowshoeing and cross-country skiing. Talent night/jam sessions, Karaoke sing-a-longs, and dance parties are other options for adults, but for the truly adventurous (or romantic), there are top-of-the-mountain dinners with moonlit snowshoe tours to cap the day.

A family snowshoe trek is a popular activity. SNR

Put "family resort, activities, and non-skiers" together in one sentence and someone is apt to think, "ah, it must be a whimpy ski hill—can't offer much for advanced skiers and hotshots or rippers who crave park or pipe action."

Wrong. Yes the mountain features a wonderful progression of beginner and novice terrain. And excellent intermediate trails of all persuasions. But it also boasts some distinctive diamonds and some tough double diamonds that have cliffs, chutes, ice walls, waterfalls, and bumps with the best of them. And the Madonna I Summit Lift has one of the top verticals for a single chairlift ride in the state with 2,130 feet of vertical for every run off the chair! Serious skiers and riders will find plenty to challenge them on Madonna and Sterling Mountains, which they will have mostly to themselves during non-holiday weeks—and not find overly crowded on weekends either since the double chairs don't put too many people on the trails at one time!

While the Village boasts all the amenities and modern-day accoutrements of a true destination resort, the mountain experience is traditional New England. There are only a few allowances to modern trends, notably snowboarding, terrain parks, and a Superpipe. There are no highspeed quads or triples. Narrow trails that snake back and forth in the classic New England style abound. While there are snowmaking and grooming capabilities, trails are not manicured into billiard-ball smooth. Smuggs does not overgroom its terrain and will leave some trails with untouched powder after a fresh snowfall, including novice runs—all part of the "traditional" ski experience that Smugglers' takes pride in offering.

A warm friend in the petting zoo. KL

That's why management spent $500,000 to recondition the Madonna I chairlift rather than replace it with a higher capacity lift. They chose to invest in an engineering feat that would enable it to operate during times of high winds by lowering its profile at the top section of the mountain rather than simply replace it. Had they installed a quad or highspeed detachable quad, "That would have meant widening the trails to handle more skier traffic and losing the area's unique character and classic terrain," notes owner Bill Stritzler.

Such dedication to a traditional ski experience is part of Smugglers' appeal, especially for those who crave skiing the way it used to be. Combining that with year-round family activities has made Smugglers' a very successful resort, one that skiers and families consistently vote as the number-one family resort in North America and return to year after year.

A History of Community and Opportunity

Smugglers' Notch Ski Ways on Route 108 in Jeffersonville was started by a group of Cambridge businessmen under the leadership of Dr. Roger Mann. They leased land from the State of Vermont as many small communities were doing in order to create economic opportunity through recreational ski facilities. They opened Smugglers' Notch Ski Ways for weekend skiing with two Pomalifts, which in combination reached to the top of Sterling Mountain, in 1956. (The area was named after the nearby high-elevation pass through which British goods were smuggled in the early 1800s and alcohol in the 1900s during Prohibition.)

Their unique challenge was to compete with a famous neighbor by the name of Stowe. To do that a group of New York investors led by IBM Chairman

Skiers on Morse head back to Smugglers' Notch Resort Village. Three interconnected mountains surround the self-contained Village where all facilities and amenities are within a short stroll of condominium-style lodgings.

Thomas J. Watson, Jr., bought and began improving the area—building a 6,600-foot double chair to Madonna's summit in 1963, putting in more ski trails, replacing Pomas on Sterling with a chairlift, and changing the ski area's name to Madonna Mountain.

Wanting to emulate the European ski village concept as seen at Vail and Aspen, Watson bought acreage at the base of Morse Mountain and asked developer Stanley Snider (of the Sudbury, MA based Stanmar, Inc.) to build a village. Snider began building condominiums in 1967, and Watson created a novice area on neighboring Morse Mountain.

After buying the resort in 1973, Snider continued to add more lifts and trails, implemented summer programs in 1974, and changed the name to The Village at Smugglers' Notch. He also inveigled Bill Stritzler, an AT&T executive and condo owner, to become the resort's managing director in 1987 and sold the area to him in 1996.

Under Stritzler's guidance the area perfected its reputation as a place for year-round family fun. Today, the large self-contained 85-acre slopeside village boasts a FunZone featuring huge inflatables, indoor and outdoor pools, hot tubs, waterslides, a Petting Zoo, a Nordic Center, a country store, restaurants, shops, teen centers, a nursery, and some 560 condominiums that radiate out from the Village Center and up the sides of Morse Mountain. Complimentary slope- and village-shuttle buses operate continuously, making it easy for families or groups to do different things.

The Mountain

Smugglers' has three distinct, ski-trail connected mountains, each with its own special features. Morse and Morse Highlands cater to beginners and novices and have many trailside condos. Sterling is predominantly for intermediates and advanced while Madonna has intermediate trails, advanced, and expert terrain that goes right up to Vermont's only triple-black diamond.

Morse Mountain and Morse Highlands ● ■ ♦

Morse (elevation 2,250') is the novice mountain that rises up out of the Village. It has an ultra-wide gentle learning hill with handle tow called Sir Henry's Learning and Fun Park; a toddler's first-time area with carpet lift; and a special low-to-the-ground, slow-moving double chair, called Mogul Mouse's Magic lift which three- and four-year-olds can ride without an adult! The Village Double Chair goes a tad higher to the 2,250-foot summit and offers options of connector trails to Morse Highlands or Madonna as well as its own set of mostly easy trails to the bottom. There are a few challenging trails at Morse—Upper Morse Liftline (♦), a bump run under the chair; Billy's Beartrap (♦); and Snow Snake and Evaporator, two cruising blues.

Children in Discovery Camp riding Mogul Mouse's Magic lift with Mogul himself. SNR

Morse Highlands provides an adjacent upper-mountain learning area that is home to young ski campers (ages three and up). It has its own double chair, which loads very close to the ground, and a special kid-oriented base lodge with child-sized tables and chairs and a fieldstone fireplace.

Madonna Mountain ■ ♦ ♦♦

The easy Midway (●) trail connects Morse to Madonna, where two chairs serve very challenging terrain. The Madonna I chair goes to the 3,640-foot summit and gives a 2,130-foot vertical drop for every run back to its base—one of the top verticals in the state for a single uphill ride. The Madonna II chair goes about three-fourths up the mountain, which has its own base lodge (cafeteria, lounge, ski shop, information desk, ticket sales). The free shuttle bus drops skiers by the lodge and those driving can park in the lot across the road.

Madonna's summit offers spectacular views of nearby Mount Mansfield and scenic distant views to Mount Washington and the White Mountains of New Hampshire as well as the closer Adirondacks in New York.

There are many blues at Madonna, including two off the summit that should not be missed—Drifter and Chilcoot. They are two of Madonna's original,

View of Madonna (left) and Sterling as seen from the Midway trail. KL

classic trails with stunning views. Drifter is an upper mountain run with a nice snaky New England ski trail feel to it. Chilcoot is wider at the top and longer as it runs right to the bottom of the two chairs.

Blues off the Madonna II lift include Gary B's Northwest Passage, Father Bob's, Ruthie's, Link, and Waterfall, all nice cruisers with interesting scenery and variety.

There's an abundance of double-black diamonds on Madonna, including all of Smuggs' "Fabulous Five" runs, that one instructor described this way:

- ❖ Robin's Run (♦♦) is probably the toughest trail. It is a 1,200-foot gnarly run that twists you down 500 vertical feet via a narrow corridor over cliffs and stumps.
- ❖ The Black Hole (♦♦♦) is a triple-black diamond and is filled with hair-raising steeps, cliffs, and moguls threaded through ungroomed snowy woods. The top 600 feet of this 1,600-foot trail are pitched at a 65-70 percent grade. The vertical drop is 800 feet.
- ❖ Freefall (♦♦) features a 54-percent grade, obstacles, and 620-foot vertical.
- ❖ Doc Dempsey's (♦♦) is a tree run, filled with ungroomed snow, moguls, and chutes with a 600-foot vertical. (It's named after a local skiing legend and St. Alban's physician who visited Smugglers" back when it was Smugglers" Notch Ski-Ways. He also worked in the ski school.)
- ❖ The F.I.S. (♦) is a bump run from top to bottom unless the groomer has worked flatness magic. Otherwise, be prepared for some Volkswagen-sized moguls!

Upper Liftline and Upper F.I.S. are two more of Madonna's double diamonds for experts and Shuttle (♦) is a connector for Sterling.

Sterling Mountain ■ ♦

Sterling Mountain (elevation 3,040') is served by a double chairlift and has a new post-and-beam warming lodge at the top that is light and airy. The runs that predominate are blues—from low to upper level intermediate, narrow to wide, smooth to bumped up. They are interesting and tend to wind their way down the mountain, taking shortcuts through narrow rock passes or offering double fall lines as opposed to being straight boulevards. Sometimes they connect with short black-diamond options that allow a taste of bold and a return to blue relief.

Family skiing in the glades. SNR

Rumrunner (■) is a long, long favorite that comes out at the Madonna base area or you can take Upper Rumrunner and choose from lower mountain trails that stay on Sterling. Another favorite Sterling trail is Black Snake (■). It offers lots of variety—groomed sections that cruise, a double-fall-line steep section with moguls, and a wide-open ending for wanna-be downhill racers. It even has an off-shoot named Snake Bite (♦), a hoot of a trail with a kicker finish. Sterling has several more "doable" single-black diamonds than the hairy stuff on Madonna, including Smugglers' Alley, Bootlegger, Upper Exhibition and parts of Pipeline.

Practice Slope (■) offers a wide open slope with a steep pitched top. There's a lower mountain T-Bar that serves a race training hill, the SnowZone Terrain Park (♦), and the lower section of Practice Slope. The base of Sterling is a short ski to Madonna's base lodge. The Slope Shuttle makes regular stops at all the areas, including Sterling's upper parking lot (which you can ski to and from) so those who don't relish flat schusses home/back to the Village, can catch a ride to wherever they need to go.

Parks/Pipe

Smuggs' terrain parks include: entry-level terrain gardens on Morse and Morse Highlands; the entry/intermediate level Birch Run Park on Sterling; the expert Prohibition Park on Lower F.I.S.; and an expert SnowZone park off the Sterling T-Bar. The 450-foot Olympic-sized Superpipe caters to intermediates and experts at the Playground slope on Madonna.

Glades

Novices can get a taste of easy gladed terrain at Whitetail Glades at Morse Highlands or on the Wanderer Glades at Morse. Intermediates have Enchanted Forest at Morse and Red Fox, Moonshiner's and Three Mountain Glades on Madonna. Advanced skiers have Pirate's Plank, Powder Key, Highlander, and Deer Run Glades on Sterling.

In 2004 Smugglers' added 40 acres of new glades on Madonna which opened more terrain along the natural contours of the mountain for intermediate and expert skiing and riding adventures. With the addition of yet more glades in 2005, the resort's gladed-acreage jumped to 22 percent of overall terrain. Experts also have Doc Dempsey's and lots of woods to explore thanks to an *off-piste* policy. That policy, which is found on the trail map, reads as follows:

> Wooded areas beyond the marked ski area boundary as shown on the trail map are closed to skiing and snowboarding. Woods between open trails are not marked trails, are not patrolled, and have no skier/snowboarder services. If you decide to ski or snowboard inside the ski resort boundary, enter from and exit to an open trail. If you ski or snowboard in these wooded areas, you are solely responsible for yourself. You should be an expert skier or snowboarder and stay in groups of three or more. If you ski or snowboard beyond the ski resort area boundary, Vermont Law provides that you are liable for all expenses for search and rescue services.

Peak Experiences

My first introduction to Smugglers' occurred on an August day when we drove over the Notch and stopped in to take a peek. I was impressed by the size of the village, the number of people, the abundance of activities, and the kids everywhere, doing everything.

There were teens playing basketball, kids and adults on the tennis courts, families in the pools and on the water slides, and the cutest tykes walking with backpacks and holding onto their counselors' hands as they visited the animals in the petting zoo. I saw more people in the hour we walked around than I do in a day in Rutland, Vermont's fourth largest city.

So on my first winter visit, maybe I shouldn't have been surprised when I checked in and was handed a 39-page booklet and asked what I wanted to sign up for. Since I was solo and anxious to taste the resort experience, I chose the evening dinner and snowshoe tour and made my menu selection before dashing off to my noon ski lesson.

I got lucky and missed the first parking area, which is for Madonna Mountain, and ended up at the Sterling lot. This allowed me to park trailside and ski down to the meeting place versus a short walk up from Madonna.

Despite the frigid cold, there were a sizeable number of adults gathered round chatting. As the new kid—the others were lucky ski weekers—I got to describe my ability level and what I was hoping to gain and given the option of joining two different groups. Not knowing the trails, I chose to play it safe with a level 7.

Steve "Punque" Vance the instructor took us up Sterling and down challenging blues to warm us up. Then on to the steep and deep. And narrow.

I promptly fell in deep ungroomed powder on what was essentially flat terrain. Not a bad fall, more of an edge-catch thing. But getting up was tough. I panicked for a second, praying I wouldn't embarrass myself by needing help. Prayer one was mercifully answered.

The trail led to a narrow steepish chute between rocks, something I would normally avoid. But the other two, who were technically less proficient but younger than *moi*, were unphased.

Prayer two, "let me make it down in one piece." I took it slow, tentatively traversing and choosing my spots to turn.

I made it! As we regrouped before a mogully section, I thought I would surely die when I saw the challenge ahead. My body was bone-chilled freezing, I couldn't feel my toes, and my head was praying again. Then a miracle happened.

Punque said something like, "That was good, Karen. You did the right thing. You weren't ready and so you kept going until you found a spot you liked and were ready to turn. That is a good skill to have."

That said, he traverses through this bump terrain, picks an easier spot to make his turn and all the while, he is saying, "I am not ready, I am taking my time, I don't like this place but I like this one, I am ready and I am turning." And he repeated that litany for a second and third traverse.

I don't know if the relief from the permission to be cautious triggered my hot flash or if it was just a happy coincidence, but I had a hot flash that warmed my frozen feet and at the same time I mentally relaxed from the encouragement— both brought me to an inner glow, a comfort zone heretofore unknown to me when in difficult places. (And a realization that hot flashes have their usefulness in a winter as frigid as 2003's record cold.)

I made it through those big moguls, and then a second pointer session got me turning a bit more aggressively, talking to myself when I needed to (I am not ready, I don't like this, I like this, I am ready) and getting over some inner fears of steeps and bumps.

View of Sterling Pond and the dramatic cliffs of the Notch from Drifter.   KL

Psychologically, that was an important watershed for me. It also proved to me that today's instruction is indeed centered on student needs, comfort levels, and enjoyment as well as on technique, a major improvement over the 1960s!

When the lesson was over, Punque escorted me to the Madonna Base Lodge where I was to meet Barbara for part two, a guided tour of the mountains. He not only made me feel more comfortable on the slopes, he made sure that my simple task of meeting up with someone went smoothly, a gesture that was indicative of the helpfulness that I experienced at Smuggs. Everyone was nice, from cafeteria workers to strangers to the shuttle driver and snowshoe guides.

It was a good thing I had a chance to have a personal tour, otherwise I would not have known that some of the bodaciously bad terrain beneath the Madonna I chair is a ski route—hard to call a cliff and ice falls a trail in my book!

Besides pointing out the expert stuff, Barbara filled me in on the area's policy of letting skiers and riders go anywhere within the resort's 1,000 acres, 300 of which are trails and the rest woods. While Smugglers' has a variety of glades, there's a lot more uncleared, *au naturel* woods that allow for a "choose-your-own-adventure" for those who are good enough to handle it.

Our exploration was more mild mannered with runs down Chilcoot, Drifter, and several trails on Sterling. The views were magnificent, but they had some pretty stiff competition in the scenic trails themselves.

Normally, I would have relaxed after such a long day (I left home at 7 a.m.), but this time I skied to my car, hightailed it to the condo where I stashed my gear, and rushed back to Sterling for my third adventure of the day.

A large group of couples and guides had already gathered at the lift for a night-time rendezvous with the mountaintop. After a cold ride up, hot chocolate warmer-upper and brief introduction to the lightweight and easy-to-use snowshoes in the new Top-of-the-Notch Lodge, we took off for a guided tour of Sterling Pond, Vermont's highest mountain lake at an elevation of 3,008 feet above sea level. It was a serene yet adventurous experience.

As darkness fell, we enjoyed a delicious dinner by candlelight back at the lodge before embarking on our moonlit snowshoe tour down the mountain. As we started out, we could see the lights of St. Albans in the distance (you can see to Montreal on a crystal clear night).

The trek down was demanding because you have to hold yourself back on steep sections. But walking by the light of the snow was a new and special experience and it was probably the only time I didn't get forward while descending a mountain! (Hint: ski poles are helpful if you go on this trip.)

By the time we got to the bottom, it was 9 p.m. and I was one tuckered-out, last-person-off-the-mountain adventurer. Back at the condo, I relaxed in a well-deserved whirlpool bath. I still marvel at the memory of driving four hours over snowy roads, taking a ski lesson and a mountain tour, and then snowshoeing down a tough trail in the colder than cold dark of night. It was an exhilarating 14-hour "mountain chase" I shall never forget.

Good to Know

Smugglers' is located 5 miles south of Jeffersonville on Route 108 and is 30 miles east of the Burlington International Airport; the area is 220 miles from Boston, 241 from Hartford, and 291 from NYC.

New for 2004-05: The Mountain Experience Adult Camp, a weekly four-day ski program with lunch daily plus a choice to demo equipment or get a tune/wax. Also, more glades on Sterling steeps near the summit and a section on Madonna that connects with Sterling. The Little Rascals learn-to-ski program was added for two-and-a-half and three-year-olds.

Check the Website for details on the new Club Smugglers' Advantage package which includes a free 2005 season pass.

Smuggs gets 24 feet of snow in an average season. But when they don't get all the snow they need, they make it; with 26-million gallons of water in snowpond reservoirs and recent increases in snowmaking capacity, over 63% of the trails can be blanketed. There is top-to-bottom coverage for all three mountains if Mother Nature doesn't cooperate.

Smugglers' gets away from any unpleasant connotation of "going to ski school" by dubbing their instruction for vacationing children as Kids Camp; for adults it's Snow Sport University, a fitting image for lifelong learning.

Kids will enjoy meeting Mother Nature in her Tepee in the woods or learning about snowmaking at the Family Snowmaking Learning Center.

Smuggs has an evening Study Hall for ages 7-17. It's to help kids keep up with school assignments while on vacation.

Seniors can join the Smugglers' 55+ Club (annual fee $20) for 50% member discount on lift tickets, X-C fees, rentals, lessons; info: 644-8851. Socializing, complimentary coffee and bagels, Alpine/Nordic skiing, and clinics on Wednesday mornings followed by 2 p.m. programs on a diversity of topics. You don't have to be a local to take advantage of this program.

Two of the things that parents rave about are the instructional programs for kids and the separate novice areas at Morse Mountain and Morse Highlands. The terrain gardens help kids learn by doing and having fun.

Kids' Night Out is hosted at Treasures with an evening meal so parents can enjoy an activity just for them, whether dinner out or up on Sterling.

The rental shop has been expanded (doubled in size) and is in its own building along with a retail outlet for equipment, accessories, and ticket sales.

Steals and Deals

Purchase a Bash Badge at $109 ($89 prior to 11/1) and pay just $20 for tickets every day of the season; plus 50% off equipment rentals, group lessons, X-C trail fees, and other discounts. See Website for details.

The new Club Smugglers' Advantage Package includes condo lodging, lift tickets, X-C passes, lessons/camp for all children ages 3-17, Learn-to-Ski lessons for adults, 50% off lessons for adults who ski and ride. The package features an overall reduced daily rate per person plus a *free* Season's Pass for guests vacationing 5 nights or longer (the pass is valid through mid-December 2005 with no restrictions).

Parents get 50% off childcare for ages 6 weeks to 2 years old at Treasures Child Care Center when staying 3 nights or longer on the Club Smugglers' Advantage Package. Valid December 10-18, 2004 and January 2-29, 2005.

Phone numbers are **area code 802** unless otherwise noted.

Handy Info

Website: www.smuggs.com
Email: smuggs@smuggs.com
General Information: 800-451-8752; 644-8851
Snow Report: 800-523-2754

Hours: 9-4 daily for most lifts; Sterling, Village lifts 8:30-4 midweek.
One lift on each mountain opens at 8 a.m. on weekends.
Tickets 2005 Season: Adults $56; Youth (ages 6-18) and
Seniors (65-69), $40; Kids 5 and under and Seniors 70 + ski free.
Half-day. additional day, early/late season, early-bird pass discounts.

Quick Stats

Season: late November to mid April.
Average annual snowfall: 304 inches.
Snowmaking: 63 percent; 189 acres.
Lifts: 8; 6 double chairs, 2 surface (1 handle tow, 1 T-Bar).
Uphill lift capacity: 7,053 per hour.
Trails: 78; 28.4 miles; 300 acres; longest 3 miles; plus all-terrain policy.
Glades: 66 acres; beginner to expert over three mountain areas.
Bumps: F.I.S., mid sections of Upper Liftline, Smugglers' Alley,
Exhibition, plus gladed terrain added in 2004 and 2005.
Parks/Pipe: 3 parks; 450' Superpipe (17' radius).
Grooming: 6 Bombardiers; Pipe Cutter.
Vertical Drop:
Madonna Summit to Village base: 2,610'
Madonna Summit to Base: 2,130'
Sterling Mountain: 1,500'
Morse Mountain: 1,220'

Snow Sport University   800-451-8752

Peter Involdstad directs a staff of 300 professional learning guides. SSU guarantees technique improvement (or a refund of the lesson portion of a person's vacation package).

Group, private, ski, snowboard, Telemark lessons/coaching available.

First-Timer Package: lesson, beginner lift, equipment for 1-day or 3-day.
Specialized Clinics: halfpipe, family tours, terrain tactics, style, racing.

Children's Programs   800-451-8752

Treasure's Nursery: childcare for 6 weeks to 3 years.
Little Rascals on Snow: ages 2.5 – 3; half-day lessons & half-day nursery.
Discovery Dynamos Ski Camp: ages 3-5 all day on and off slope.
Discovery Dynamos Snowboard Camp: all day for ages 4-5.
Adventure Rangers: all-day ski or snowboard camp for ages 6-10.
Notch Squad: all-day ski or snowboard camp for ages 11-14.
Instruction for ages 7-14 in 1.5 hour lessons.
Teen Ski/Snowboard: 1.5-hour mountain exploration for ages 15-17.

Other Things to Do

There are many activities for families to do together: Bingo Blast, Tube Sliding Grand Prix, Showtime Follies family theater, Family Karaoke. Check the Website or call for details or a brochure.

Nordic Ski and Snowshoe Adventure Center; 30 km X-C trails, 20 km snowshoe trails. Snowmobile tours. Dog sled rides. Ice skating.

Sleigh/trail rides: Wildbranch Trail Adventures (888-9233); LaJoie Stables (644-5347).

Classes, sauna, massage. Day-off exploration: Burlington, Vermont's largest city or take the Smuggs' day trip to Montreal.

Worth checking out: Boyden Valley Winery in nearby Cambridge.

Dining Out

In the Village: Hearth and Candle, Green Mountain Deli, Morse Mountain Grille, Riga-Bello's Pizzeria, Ben and Jerry's, Snow's Bistro, Green Peppers Pub. Nearby: Stella Notte, Three Mountain Lodge, Angelina's, and 158 Main (breakfast, lunch, and dinner).

Accommodations 800-451-8752; 644-8851

A good diversity of trailside and base-area condos to choose from, some with family-room sized bathrooms with whirlpools and washers and dryers as well as double sinks; others with outdoor or indoor pools and fitness areas. On-mountain pillows number 2,400 while other accommodations add 150 in motels and inns within a 10-mile radius.

Après-ski/Nightlife

Family activities include bonfires, sledding, marshmallow roasts, Showtime Theater, FunZone, Family Snowshoe Cider Walk, Torchlight Parade and Fireworks Finale. Older teens have Outer Limits Teen Center; teens 13-15 have Teen Alley. Adults have The Mountain Grill, Bootlegger's Lounge, Snowshoe Dinner on Top of the Notch, and nightly entertainment such as Marko the Magician, Talent Night & Jam Session, and It's All About The Comedy.

Summer/Fall

Summer and fall are not an "off season." Smuggs is water park heaven with 8 pools and 4 water slides. There are also: 10 outdoor and 2 indoor tennis courts; golf driving range for practicing; day camps for children; hiking, upper mountain adventures, and family-oriented activities that make Smuggs a most happening summer resort in Vermont and the number-one family destination for U.S. families.

Our Smugglers' Adventure

Date:

Weather:

Companions:

Where Stayed:

Visit Highlights:

Our Discoveries:

220 Stowe

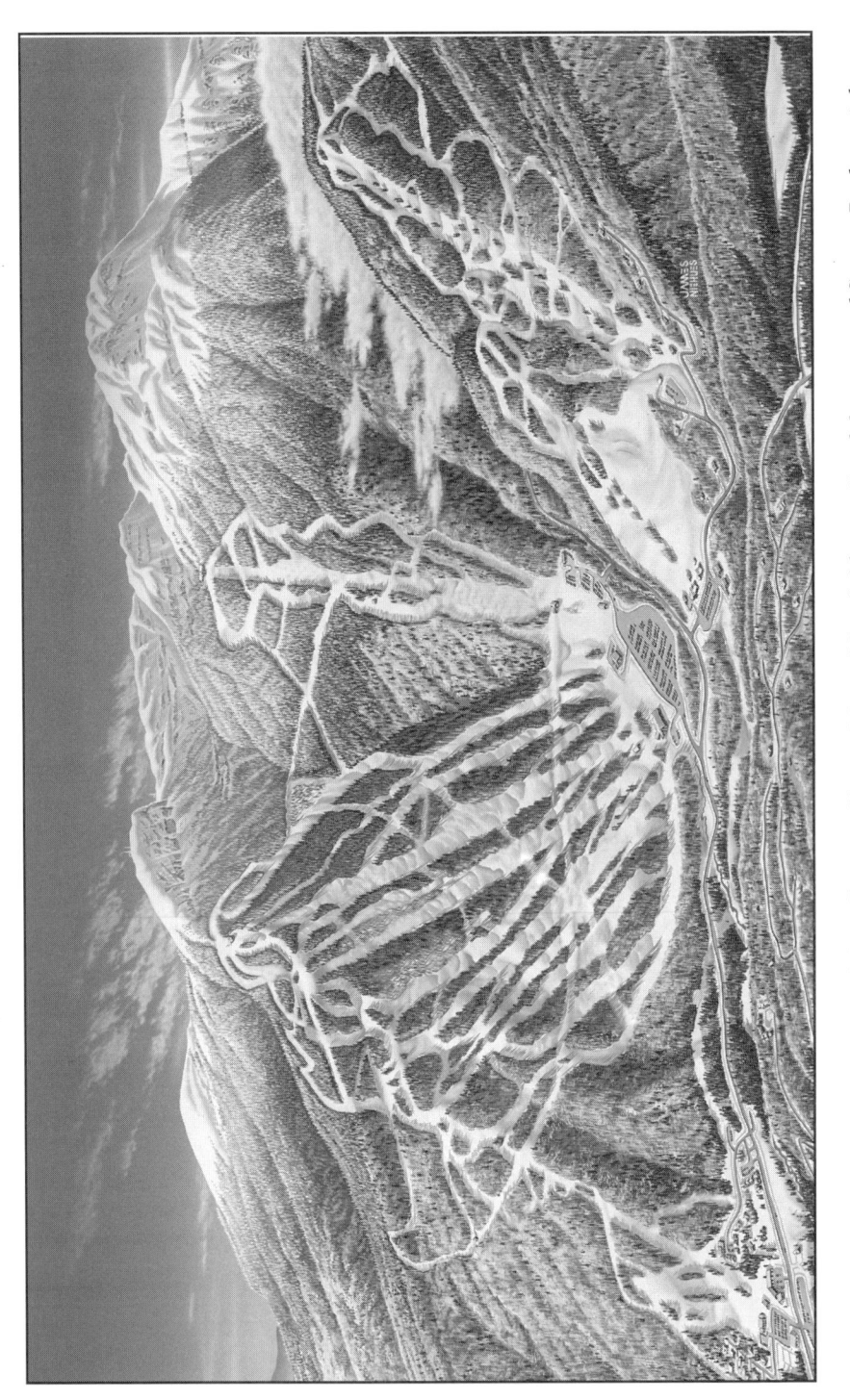

Stowe Mountain Resort, from lower left: Toll House Slopes, Mount Mansfield area, Gondola area, and Spruce Peak on right.

Chapter Fifteen

Stowe Mountain Resort
Ski Classic, Recreational Mecca

As the state's tallest mountain (elevation 4,395 feet at the Chin), Mt. Mansfield has a history of outdoor recreation and adventure that dates back to the early 1800s, long before it became a ski mecca in the 1930s and the centerpiece to the modern Stowe Mountain Resort.

Famous for its profile of a human face in repose (hence the names for the highest points like the Nose and Chin), the Mt. Mansfield massif has a unique two-mile-long ridge that dominates northwestern Vermont. The Nose section constitutes the original skiing area on Mt. Mansfield, which was known as the Nosedive Skiing Area in the early years. Even after a chairlift accessed this area, skiers often hiked up to the very top of the Nose to gain an extra 500 feet of vertical (a practice which led to extending the Nosedive trail to the top of the Nose in 1952). It is still possible to hike this uppermost section, but the arduous climb and ungroomed run are best left to physically fit and accomplished adventurers.

Mt. Mansfield is not a mountain that pampers. Many people like it that way. Despite all the advances in skiing, at this area you still get the sense that the mountain reigns, that its challenge still beckons to the adventurous.

The helicopter flying overhead the morning we arrived was testament to that. An experienced adult skier had gone *off piste* the day before to enjoy untracked tree skiing and had gotten lost. It was one of the coldest nights of the year, so concern and the need for a rescue were understandable. (His rescuers note that he did very little correctly and is lucky to be alive.)

When you see Mansfield up close—the towering craggy rock above the gondola terminal or the forests that flow down its flanks—it's possible to begin to understand the attraction of rugged terrain, the beauty in wilderness and the powerful lure of untracked snow. That combination is making *off piste* and backcountry a major phenomenon in snowsports today.

But it can also prove a fatal attraction for the unprepared, or an expensive ordeal for the lost. Mounting rescues have become a costly and time-consuming operation for Vermont ski areas. When I asked about the *off piste* policy at Stowe, I got this response:

We absolutely do not promote *off piste* skiing at all. We simply patrol and manage the open and designated trails at Stowe Mountain Resort. Mt. Mansfield is on State land, and therefore we cannot stop people from exploring it. However, they should know that this terrain is not patrolled and if they get hurt, they might not be discovered.

Even if Stowe Mountain Resort knows about an off-property accident, our first priority is taking care of guests at the resort. If our resources are tapped out, we contact Stowe Hazardous Terrain for the rescue. The gentleman who required a rescue by fifty people and a helicopter the day you visited will be receiving a significant bill. He also might lose part of his foot to frostbite.

We do not candy-coat the backcountry experience. It is dangerous and every precaution should be taken—from taking supplies in case you become stranded in Arctic conditions to going only with a guide who knows the terrain intimately. *Off piste* necessitates travel in a group of three or more people early in the day and only in good weather.

Therein lies an interesting conundrum: Mansfield's trails are located on State land (the area leases 1400 acres from the State of Vermont) and skiing off the area's trails for powder and solitude is not part of the official Stowe Mountain Resort experience. Yet, *off piste* is highly touted by adventure seekers and part of the attraction for purists who relish turns in the wilderness. [See pages 302-303.] For most of us, however, Stowe Mountain Resort offers plenty of challenge on its great assortment of maintained trails and glades!

The Mountain

Stowe Mountain Resort is comprised of five distinct skiing areas. The "main" Mt. Mansfield area is connected by ski trails to the lower Toll House Slopes and to the Gondola area. The separate Spruce Peak area is made up of Little Spruce and Big Spruce. A free shuttle moves guests among the various areas. An aerial lift is planned to connect Spruce and Mansfield as part of a ten-year revitalization project.

Toll House Slopes ●

Beginners have their own easy greens at the secluded Toll House area with its gentle, 6,375-foot double chairlift and long runs. They include the lower section of the Toll Road, Easy Mile under the chair, and Mountain Glen. A lovely connector trail, Lullaby Lane (●), leads to trails on Mansfield.

Spruce   ● ■ ♦

Across a narrow valley from Mt. Mansfield lie the sunny slopes of Little and Big Spruce Peaks. The trails here provide a progression of difficulty that allows learners to move up to more challenge without being intimidated by the experts who crave the famed "Front Four" on Mansfield.

Little Spruce indulges the learner with wide-open, beautifully groomed terrain on Easy Street (●) and the Meadows (●). The new Adventure trail (●) caters to learners

A lesson on Easy Street on Little Spruce. SMR

with an 8 to 10 percent gradient and single fall line. The Sunny Spruce Express Quad and Triple (new lifts for 2004-05) serve the Little Spruce area as does a Mitey Mite tow. The Stowe Ski and Snowboard School is headquartered here.

Little Spruce also has some intermediate slopes and trails, including the Slalom Hill (■) which is used for racing and the steeper West Run and West Slope, both blues. There are also several connector trails to Big Spruce, which is one of Stowe's *best-kept secrets* (great terrain and no crowds).

The 6,390-foot Big Spruce Double (slated to be replaced by a detachable quad in 2005) serves a 1,550-foot vertical and mile-plus runs from low intermediate on Sterling (■), a scenic cruiser, to advanced intermediate on Smugglers (■), a natural bump trail that dips and winds. Whirlaway (♦) offers a tumbling, natural terrain park that's created by the wind creating waves of natural snow. Main Street (■) is fantastic freeride terrain, boasting a mix of wide and narrow lift-line running with stands of trees to weave through and many routes to take. Several connector trails lead back to Little Spruce.

Gondola Area   ■ ♦

The Gondola Area debuted for the 1968-69 season with a 4-passenger gondola but now sports a highspeed, 8-passenger gondola. Challenging trails spill down from the 3,660-foot top terminal that's located beneath the 4,395-foot Chin. There's a 2,160-foot vertical for every run, which makes this a favorite area with advanced and strong intermediate skiers. "Even experts love to cruise here," a knowledgeable local noted.

Perry Merrill (■) is a classic trail that offers broad-sweeping vistas of the valley below. Gondolier (■) with an average pitch of 20 degrees is a mile-long, under-the-lift, wide cruiser with a wicked (♦♦) waterfall upper section. Chin Clip (♦, ■) is a winding, fun steep known for its bumps—diamond above and blue below but thankfully wide for most of its length. It's a natural-snow trail for the majority of the run so purists and bump skiers love it. Switchback (■) provides a long, traversing cruise.

Skier on Mansfield with the Cliff House and Gondola area in the background. The views are dramatic on Mt. Mansfield. KL

The Cliff (■) trail leads from the Gondola Area to the original skiing section on Mansfield and provides a long "chute" type run through the woods to the Nosedive trail. You enter on the wide section (25-degree pitch) that eases up to blue, providing an opportunity to experience part of an historic trail even if you are not an expert. The Rimrock trail (■ but accessed from the upper Nosedive) provides a return from Mansfield to the Gondola Area as does the lower and easier Crossover (●) trail.

The Gondola Area features night skiing from 5 to 9 p.m. Thursdays through Saturdays on Gondolier and Perry Merrill. The Midway Mini Park is also lit up for skiers, snowboarders, and snowdeckers. Word has it that the groomers do "a superb job of giving night skiers a fully groomed surface that normally lasts for the entire evening."

There's a parking lot and shuttle bus stop at the Gondola base and a Midway Lodge with food service. The Cliff House Restaurant at the top offers a special place to eat lunch (exceptional quality, not standard cafeteria fare) but in a casual atmosphere with divine views of the valley.

Mount Mansfield   ● ■ ♦ ♦♦

From the base of Mt. Mansfield proper, the 6,400-foot FourRunner Quad is a six-minute ride to the top (2,055-foot vertical). The Octagon offers cafeteria food and fantastic views from this 3,614-foot elevation.

Mt. Mansfield is famous for the Front Four: Starr (♦♦), Goat (♦♦), National (♦♦), and Liftline (♦). They are among the oldest and most demanding trails in the East with overall pitches of 30 to 37 degrees. Starr and Goat are narrow, natural (not groomed) moguled steeps (pitches of 20-36 degrees on Goat and 21 to 37 degrees on Starr) that demand precision. National is a combination of bumps and groomed with an overall pitch of 30 degrees; it hosts the bump contests in spring. Liftline often offers both a mogul side and a groomed side. Of the four, it's the most "forgiving" with pitches from 11-35 degrees.

One of the most famous trails in ski history, Nosedive (♦, ■) got a nose job in 1965 when the seven sharp turns were reduced to three S-turns; still it's a challenging (15-33 degree pitch) 2-miler that's technical on top and a blue cruiser below. Bypass (♦♦) off its top is a steep chute riddled with rock ledges and spruce trees. Nosedive Glades (♦♦) offer a nice section of rolling terrain among well-spaced trees below the intersection with Rim Rock.

Mansfield's "blues" are long, and boast twists, turns, varying widths, and some steeps. Lord (■) is a top-to-bottom historic classic that has been widened over the years. It gives access to Standard, Gulch, and North Slope—all great blues. Gulch is rarely groomed these days, making it an in-your-face bump trail. Hayride (♦, ■) is a thriller with steeps at the top and relief toward the bottom. It was widened and homologated for FIS sanctioned races in 2002.

The Mountain Triple and Lookout Double chairlifts on Mansfield also serve the latter trails as well as Hackett's Highway (♦♦) and Lookout (♦♦), and give access to Tyro, which hosts a terrain park (♦♦). One veteran described Hackett's Highway as "exactly how I remember skiing in the early 1950s—rocks, stumps, streams, logs, brush—everything that made skiing wicked fun! Today's skiers who want the 1940s,' 50s' and even 60s' experience should try this trail. Highly recommended for history buffs."

The Toll Road (●) is a 3.7-mile novice trail that drops 2,360 vertical feet if you ski it to its base at Toll House. Although it is an easy trail, it offers a scenic meander through the woods and is worth taking just to enjoy the history of it and to catch a glimpse of the Chapel in the Woods where services are held on Sundays in winter.

Parks/Pipe ♦♦ ♦ ■

Beginning tricksters have the Midway Mini Park, which is located on Gondolier near the Midway Lodge. It has small features (jumps, jibs, and rails) and a surface lift; demonstrations are often held here with easy viewing from the lodge. The Terrain Park on Tyro features big table tops, quarter pipes, hip hits, gap jumps, rail slides for expert skiers and snowboarders. A 400-foot halfpipe with 17-foot walls is located on Lower North Slope and is a popular

Action in the park. SMR

area for freeriders of snowboard and skier persuasions. There's also a terrain park on Spruce with features that change from year to year.

A Celebrated History

Long before Stowe became known as a winter paradise, Mt. Mansfield was known as a summer destination. People first began climbing up for the exercise and views in the early 1800s (from the western Underhill side). By 1850, the first hotel in the Village of Stowe, the Mansfield House (now part of the Green Mountain Inn), was accommodating tourists who wanted to climb the mountain.

Thanks to the advent of the railroad which dropped off mountaineers and sightseers in nearby Waterbury, the Village of Stowe became a destination for those who sought the respite of cool Vermont summers and mountaintop experiences. By 1858 there was a rough road up Mt. Mansfield from the Stowe side to the Summit House, a rustic hotel built by Stowe attorney William H. Bingham, that was operating on a plateau below the Nose.

This was the era of American Romanticism and the extolling of sunsets and sunrises as seen from high places along with the benefits of "pure, healing air." Bingham sensed a golden opportunity and with a group of investors formed the Mount Mansfield Hotel Company in 1859. His goal was to make Stowe a summer destination that would "rival the White Mountains and seacoast resorts."

To convert the town of Stowe into a vacation paradise, the company built the lavish, 200-room Mansfield Hotel on Main Street. When it opened in June 1864, people flocked to it and soon a 100-room Annex was added along with a bowling alley and a pond for bathing and boating. (This hotel burned down in 1889). Since a major part of the hotel's attraction was the scenic trip up to the Summit House, the hotel company re-constructed five miles of the old carriage road and then collected a toll near the top of what became known as the Toll Road. They also expanded the Summit House.

A man of foresight, Bingham took pains to protect his investments. He arranged to preserve the wilderness of the summit by deeding 400 acres of the Mansfield ridgeline to the University of Vermont (for $1,000) with the stipulation that it only be used for scientific purposes. He also arranged a leaseback of 20 acres on which his Summit House was located for one cent a year for "as long as grass grows and water runs."

The Summit House proved so popular a summer retreat that it turned out to be the state's longest-lived summit hotel, thanks in part to improvements to the Toll Road in 1922 that made ascent by auto easier. It operated seasonally for 101 years, giving guests access to stunning views and mountain exploration of such wonders as the Lake of the Clouds, the Rock of Terror, the Cave of the

Winds, Wall Street, and the Needle's Eye. It ceased to be a hotel in the fall of 1958 and was razed in 1964.

Today, hikers (including those on the Long Trail which passes over the mountain) and those who drive up the Toll Road or ride up the gondola and venture out on what has been called the "ridgepole of Vermont" can still access these natural wonders and taste the adventure that first put Stowe on the map.

The second event to secure the town and mountain's places in history was the advent of winter sports and skiing. In the early 1900s, local boys tried skiing on homemade boards but soon gave up as they lacked the ability to turn. When some Scandinavians moved into town in 1912 and used their wooden skis for winter transportation, local interest was renewed, and the newcomers were soon making skis for others and teaching them how to use them.

Although "skiing" had largely consisted of jumping and cross-country until this time, Alpine skiing was beginning to have a following in the college clubs that were being formed. The arrival of Austrian and Swiss instructors in New Hampshire in the 1920s furthered the interest in "downhill running" and slalom skiing. Soon Vermont towns were forming Outing Clubs and Winter Sports Clubs and holding winter carnivals. Stowe was one of them.

The first known skiing descent down the Toll Road occurred in 1914 (by a Dartmouth College librarian). In 1921, Stowe held its first Winter Carnival with ski dashes, ski jumping, and toboggan and snowshoe races. By the 1930s, skiers were climbing up Mt. Mansfield on skins to ski down. The advent of the first Boston snow trains in 1931 made New Hampshire and Brattleboro, Vermont hills popular, and by 1935 the overnight "Skimeister" trains from New York City and Connecticut were reaching Waterbury, where Vermont Transit buses transferred skiers to Stowe.

In 1933, the Mt. Mansfield Ski Club (MMSC) was organized and counted among its members Abner Coleman and Charles Lord who had tramped the mountain and laid out trails which they hoped might be cut one day. That year a contingent of CCC men began to cut ski trails on the mountain at the direction of State Forester Perry Merrill. The Bruce was cut in 1933 and the Nosedive and (old) Chin Clip followed in 1934-35, joining the Toll Road and the old logging paths as the ski area's original ski trails. Trails named after Perry Merrill (1937), Charlie Lord (1939), and the "S-53" CCC contingent from the Camel's Hump Camp in Duxbury that built the trail (1940) followed.

In 1933 Roland Palmedo and the Amateur Ski Club of New York decided Stowe would be a good place to ski, and the MMSC helped owners of the Ranch Camp (a lumber company lodge for loggers) fix it up into winter accommodations for skiers. [Much of the original, early pre-Nosedive skiing in Stowe was done in the hills above Ranch Camp. Today, Nordic and *off piste* adventurers still explore the old trail network that was largely developed by lumbermen who found it easier to get around on skis in winter.]

Early years at the Octagon at the top of Mt. Mansfield. VSM

In 1933, a long hike up the mountain was still required for a ski down, but Mt. Mansfield acquired a good following nonetheless. From the beginning, Mansfield was preferred among the elite corps of proficient skiers who skied at the Nosedive area, but, as noted, it also provided a training ground for beginners on its gentle Toll House slopes.

A 1,000-foot rope tow was installed at the Toll House in 1936, but it didn't begin operating until February 7, 1937 due to a lack of snow. Austrian Sepp Ruschp was hired by the MMSC to teach skiing at the three-trail Toll House area for the 1936-37 season. A day ticket cost fifty cents and a season pass was five dollars!

The next year a 2,500-foot rope tow was in operation for a new Practice Slope on lower Mansfield, and in 1939 a log State Shelter was built by the CCC. On December 9, 1940, the Single Chair (funds provided by Palmedo and others) debuted as the longest (6,330 feet) chairlift in the world, outdistancing the Sun Valley chair (first in the U.S.A. in 1936) and one at Gunstock, NH (built 1938). The Octagon warm-up hut was also erected near the upper terminal.

A 4,000-foot T-Bar and four trails (Tyro, Standard, Gulch, and North Slope) followed for the lower Mansfield slopes in 1946-47, due to an investment by C.V. Starr, and a new company was formed to operate this lift. Starr was an avid skier and the founder of American International Group (AIG), the insurance and financial services conglomerate that owns Stowe Mountain Resort today.

With the various lodges, ski schools, and lifts owned by different companies and the MMSC organizing the paid ski patrol, there was a need for a central owner and from 1949 to 1950 the old hotel company bought out the others and renamed itself the Mt. Mansfield Company, Inc. (with C.V. Starr as the first president and Sepp Ruschp succeeding him). The company developed the "sunny slopes" at Spruce Peak for the winter of 1949-50 on some of the 3,000 (private) acres that it acquired from the Burt Lumber Company.

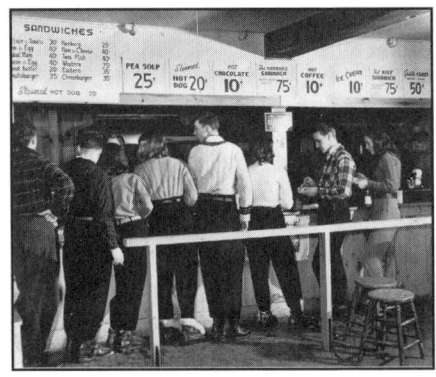

An early cafeteria scene. VSM

During these formative years, the Winter Carnival was resumed in 1933; the MMSC formed the nation's first ski patrol in 1934 (first as a volunteer and then as a paid patrol in 1940-41) which gave birth to the National Ski Patrol System (1938); famous races were held (the Stowe Derby, the 1937 Eastern Championships, the 1938 National Women's Downhill Championship, and The Sugar Slalom to name a few); and the area became the training ground for a number of ski racers who would go on to Eastern and National titles.

Sepp Ruschp first taught skiing at the Toll House slopes in 1936-37. VSM

Marilyn Shaw was one of the first homegrown skiers to bring fame to Stowe, winning the Women's National Combined Championship and the Harriman Cup at Sun Valley in 1940 at the age of 15. She went on to win other titles and was named to the 1940 U.S. Olympic Team. Billy Kidd, who grew up in Stowe, went on to win the Olympic Silver in Slalom in 1964, the first American male to medal. Many others won Eastern and national titles and Stowe continues to serve as a training ground for Vermont competitors and as home to the UVM Ski Team.

During Sepp Ruschp's long association with the mountain (42 years with 25 of them as president and general manager of the Mt. Mansfield Company), Stowe became known as the Ski Capital of the East and was famous for its challenging skiing as well as the Sepp Ruschp Ski School. Many improvements occurred during these years, including the replacing of rope tows with T-Bars and later with chairlifts, the addition of the Mansfield Double Chair next to the Single, development and expansion of Spruce Peak (including the addition of snowmaking in 1967 and more chairlifts), and construction of the first gondola at the Chin area.

Although Stowe enjoyed great prestige as a leading ski center for many years and made big strides in becoming a year-round destination resort, the late 1970s and early 1980s saw a major change in skiing. No longer satisfied with just a good day on the slopes or iffy conditions if it didn't snow, skiers began to demand reliable snow and the convenience of slopeside housing as well as more to do on a ski vacation. The lack of adequate water for snowmaking and enough slopeside accommodations to meet demand put Stowe at a disadvantage as its competitors moved ahead with massive snowmaking projects, destination villages, and more slopeside amenities.

Today, Stowe is remedying these deficits by undertaking a $250-million, 10-year revitalization project. This project encompasses an 18-hole golf course located on 170 acres to the east of Spruce (Stowe's second golf course); slopeside accommodations at Spruce; a resort spa with health and fitness facilities at the new Spruce "Village" area; and a small performing arts center. A town green will serve as a focal point and host summer activities and a winter skating rink. In all, a variety of 400 residential units are planned, including single-family homes, mountain cabins, and condominiums and hotel rooms with fractional ownership .

The mountain projects that are accompanying this development consist of lift and trail changes at Spruce and increased snowmaking coverage throughout the resort thanks to a new 117-million-gallon snowmaking pond (a 40 percent increase in snowmaking capacity for the 2005 season). An aerial connector lift between Spruce and Mt. Mansfield along with new base lodges at Spruce and Mansfield are a few of the others changes that are planned to meet the needs of today's discriminating vacationers.

Stowe Revisited

From the time you leave the busy Village of Stowe and head up the Mountain Road (Route 108), passing inns, lodges, hotels, restaurants, shops, and nightspots, you know you must be heading for something special. Suddenly, six miles later, the development ends as you enter State Forest lands en route to the slopes.

After passing the small but pretty enclave of buildings at Toll House, you enter a type of natural bowl with the rugged massif of Mansfield towering above and forest all around. No condos, no village, just a parking area and the original Mansfield log (base) lodge built by the CCC (since added onto).

Wishing to get reacquainted with Stowe on a frigid January day, we headed for Spruce and took a first run on the sunny Meadows—so perfectly groomed you would swear you could teach Grandma to ski here.

At Big Spruce we took the long, slow, cold chair ride, and were rewarded by gorgeous views that included Smugglers' Notch ski area, a sea of mountain ranges, and the nicest cruise on Sterling—wondrously long and rhythmical on a fresh corduroy surface.

Our "come-uppance" came on Main Street. My old favorite was unpacked powder, a foot and more deep. It was tough turning, but it was also fun to flounder a little and sit back. A taste of big bumps on Smuggler's sent us back to a lower groomed Main Street and a cruise back to the base of Little Spruce. Onward to Mansfield by way of the shuttle bus which dropped us at the Gondola. We enjoyed swooping down Gondolier and Perry Merrill, long runs that brought back fond memories. The run over to Nosedive on the narrow, winding Cliff trail was a definite yodel through the trees. As we came out on Nosedive, we found ourselves opening up on a wide, nicely pitched cruiser. Stopping to catch our breath, we looked at each other and grinned. Nice!

On the chair ride, I told Jon about my first adventures at Stowe, a college break in 1967 when a two-day blizzard dumped on the area and a ski week with my Dad in 1968 when we took E-2 classes. I recalled learning to hold Head Masters on blue ice by angulating in a comma position with one knee tucked behind the other and the thrill of skiing Nosedive.

But much has changed on old Mansfield—the FourRunner Quad is a fast improvement over the old Single we used to freeze on even when buried under two blankets. I recalled a day when the wind almost swung my chair into the tower and the attendant at the top sent me inside, telling me I was starting to get frostbite. It was "before warm-ups, ski suits, Gore Tex, and neck gaiters," I told my disbelieving son. (I had worn a tarpoon cloth parka I had make in Home Ec class over two wool sweaters and deerskin mitts over wool mittens!)

On this cold day in 2003, our ride up took just six minutes, but we elected to go in to the Octagon anyway to have lunch. And reminisce some more. Dad pointed out a single chair on display, and Jon exclaimed, "No way."

"Yes," we told him, racking up our points and thinking him a tad "spoiled" or deficient for never having survived cold, wind-blown rides on a single chair!

Discovering the Web Café was as surreal to me as the chair was an anachronism to Jon. The gallery of artwork depicting the trails got us moving outside.

The summit was more expansive and open than I had remembered it, and despite the wind and cold, we took a few moments to drink in the views and snap photos.

The rediscovery of the Lord trail, a long, classic New England run, was a meaningful thrill. With its 18-31 degree pitches, this is a challenging steep.

Up again, and on to more sensations—the most gripping being looking over the edge of Starr (37 degree top pitch) where a woman had just dropped in and called to her companion, "It gets better after the first few icy turns."

Some things are better left unskied, I murmured as we headed to Sunrise, a blue that was more my idea of bliss. We explored other trails like Ridge View, another scenic blue, and moved on to the most aurally exciting, Hayride.

"Bam, bam, bam!" That was the explosive sound of racers smacking the spring-loaded slalom poles out of the way. I watched, mesmerized by their finesse. Then, emboldened by what I had seen, I tackled the steeps on the gateless side. With pitches of 25, 30, and 35 degrees at various sections, this is a true diamond and I was thankful that it wasn't bumped up that day!

The visual surprise of the day was watching the halfpipe action on North Slope. Snowboarders are amazing enough, but seeing skiers pop two boards above the wall was confounding.

By contrast, following a Telemarker on another run was a sensory treat. Her descent was so graceful and controlled that I found myself wanting to bend a

The pipe on North Slope sees a lot of action from skiers and snowboarders. KL

leg to turn—it was an unconscious thing like my cat's jaw chattering as she watches birds. Now I can understand the graceful allure that has made this "old way" of skiing so popular again.

I understood a lot of things as we left the mountain that day—how times change but a good mountain still lifts your spirit; how it offers a variety of experiences, not just for youthful legs, but for aging ones; and not just for your body, but for your soul, too. The sensory experiences, the skiing, and the memories made the trip special for Dad and me. For Jon, his introduction to Stowe was a taste of a mountain adventure that melds history and the old way with the new and efficient. For all of us, that led to a greater appreciation of our time together and this mountain classic.

Good to Know

Stowe Mountain Resort is about 45 minutes from Burlington International Airport, 4 hours from Boston and Hartford, 6 from NYC.

Stowe Hosts give free tours at 10:30 and 1:30 daily (meet at the FourRunner Quad). The hosts are also available to answer any questions you may have.

Mansfield trails get sun early in the day. Spruce gets sun all day.

Stowe attracts a good number of skiers who appreciate ungroomed trails so the mountain always has trails that are left in their natural state. Some trails are usually that way, like Chin Clip or Whirlaway. Some trails like Lift Line often have bumps on one side and are groomed on the other side. Then there are trails like Lord and Ridgeview that are almost always groomed.

The FourRunner Quad opens at 7:30 a.m. on weekends and holidays. (You might get lucky with the gondola opening before its usual time on a powder day—no guarantees, but it does happen.) Lifts open at 8 a.m midweek which is the earliest in Vermont.

Stowe Mountain Resort recently instituted a program called the Triple A's, which encourages staff and guests to consider Attitude, Awareness and Accountability at the resort. The goal is a safe, respectful and friendly environment for everyone to enjoy.

At the Stowe Toys Demo Center, located next to the FourRunner Quad, you can try snowdecks, boards, Telemark skis, snowshoes, and demo skis.

Slopeside lodging is available at the Inn at the Mountain and Condominiums, which are located at the Toll House area. The Inn has nice accommodations, full-service dining, and lovely views. Check out special midweek package rates. Coming soon, slopeside lodging at Spruce.

The six-mile Mountain Road (Route 108 on the map) is replete with places to stay, eat, and shop, with something for every taste and wallet.

The historic Green Mountain Inn in Stowe Village offers luxurious rooms and suites, many with whirlpool tubs, four poster beds, and fireplaces. There's an indoor pool, fitness area, and two dining rooms (open to the public). Check out the Inn's gallery of vintage photographs for a fun visual history.

The daily Village Shuttle bus takes guests from the village to the mountain with frequent stops along Mountain Road (modest fee).

Events: Stowe Winter Carnival, Torchlight Parades with Fireworks, Stowe Slopeside Series, Pizza and Movie nights, UVM Winter Carnival, Stowe Derby, bump contests, Telemark Festival, and spring celebrations. Check the Website or call for details.

Earn the "Club 48" pin for skiing "the great 48" trails. Check for details at Guest Services.

The Stowe Card offers savings: purchase before Christmas and save 25 percent on lift tickets with the seventh one free. Check this and other savings on the Website.

All phone numbers are **area code 802** unless otherwise noted.

Handy Info

Websites: www.stowe.com   www.ridestowe.com   www.13pitch.com
Email: info@stowe.com
General information: 253-3000; 800-253-4SKI
Snow report: 253-3600
Hours: 8-4 midweek; 7:30-4 weekends/holidays with Mansfield Forerunner Quad guaranteed to open that early and other lifts opening that early based on skiers showing up. Night skiing 5 - 9 p.m. Thursdays through Saturdays at Gondola area.

Tickets 2005 season: Adults $62 midweek/weekends, $64 holidays; Child (6-12) & Seniors (65+) $42/$44. Ages five and under ski free when accompanied by a paid adult. As always, best value is multi-day tickets.

Quick Stats

Season: Mid-November to late April or early May; 160 days.
Average annual snowfall: 333 inches.
Snowmaking capability: 73 percent; 354 acres.
Lifts: 12; 1 express gondola, 2 express quads, 2 triples, 5 doubles, 2 surface.
Uphill lift capacity: 13,966 rides per hour.
Trails: 49; 485 acres; 39 miles; longest trail: 3.7 mile Toll Road.
Glades: 3: Nosedive, Tres Amigos, Lookout.
Bumps: Smugglers, Chin Clip, Starr, Goat, National, Gulch.
Parks/Pipe: 3 terrain parks; 1 halfpipe.
Vertical Drop:
    Toll House Area: 900'
    Mansfield ForeRunner Quad Area: 2,055'
    Mansfield Summit to Toll House base: 2,360'
    Gondola Area: 2,160'
    Little Spruce: 940'
    Big Spruce: 1,550'

Stowe Ski and Snowboard School   800-253-4SKI

Professional instruction with group or private ski or snowboard lessons, available as part of a lift and lesson or lift, lesson, and rentals package or in lesson-only format. Learn-to-Ride program features the Burton Method Center with special equipment designed to help learners hone carving skills. Women in Motion 3-day clinics and Telemark lessons are also available.

Children's Programs   253-3000

Cubs Daycare: 6 weeks to 6 years, full-day program, ski-lesson option for ages 3 and up. Reservations required: 800-253-4SKI or 253-3000.
Children's Adventure Center: for skiers ages 4-12 and riders 7-12; includes lift, lessons, and lunch in full-day program.
Holiday Adventure Camp: for advanced skiers and riders ages 11-14; coaching in bumps, glades, steeps and freestyle terrain, full day.

Other Things to Do

An abundance of X-C trails interconnect to provide a network of 150 km of groomed trails and 100-plus km of backcountry. They are accessible from:

Stowe Mountain Resort Touring Center (253-3688); 35 km groomed, 40 km of backcountry high elevation trails over rolling gentle terrain and longer loops through the woodlands.

Trapp Family Lodge X-C Ski Center (253-5755); 100 km, 55 km tracked.

Edson Hill Touring Center (253-7371); total 50 km, 35 km groomed.

Topnotch Resort (253-8585); 30 km, mostly groomed and tracked.

The Vermont Ski Museum in the Village of Stowe is a repository of Vermont ski history.

Shopping: along Routes 108 and 100 in Stowe, and in nearby Waterbury with country stores, sporting goods stores including Tubbs Snowshoes, boutiques, art galleries, antiques and craft shops, and specialty stores galore.

The Topnotch Resort has an indoor tennis center open to the public; the Jackson Arena offers ice skating; and indoor swimming is available at: the Swimming Hole, the Golden Eagle Resort, Mountaineer Inn, the Stoweflake, The Northern, Topnotch Resort, and the Town & Country Motor Inn.

Horseback riding, sleigh rides, snowmobiling are available. Check with your host, a guide, or stop in at the Stowe Area Association on Main Street. The Stowe Cinema is a modern triplex with first-run films in the village.

Don't miss the Vermont Ski Museum (253-9911) on Main Street next to the Green Mountain Inn in Stowe Village; Cabot Cheese, Champlain Chocolates, Cold Hollow Cider Mill, and Ben & Jerry's in Waterbury.

Dining Out

Seek and ye shall find. The food ranges from burgers to haute cuisine. We've discovered great restaurants on every trip to Stowe. Choose from:

Austrian Tea Room (at Trapp Family Lodge), Blue Moon Café, Cactus Café, Carriage Room at Town & Country Resort, Charlie B's Pub & Restaurant, Colonial Café, Commodores Inn Yacht Club Restaurant, Depot St. Malt Shoppe, Dutch Pancake Café, Emily's at Stowehof Inn, Edson Hill Manor, Fireside Tavern, Foxfire Inn, Gables Inn, Gigi's Deli & Bakery, Gracie's, Grill 108, Hob Knob, Kirtwood's Pub, Matterhorn, McCarthy's, Michael's on the Hill, Miguel's Stowe Away, Morning Star Café, Mr. Pickwick's Pub, Olive's Bistro, Partridge Inn, Pie in the Sky, Pie Casso, Red Basil Thai Cuisine,

Swisspot, the Shed Restaurant & Brewery, SkiMeister Café, Sunset Grill & Tap Room, Trapp Family Lodge (dining room and lounge), Trattoria La Festa, the Whip Bar & Grill in the Green Mountain Inn, and Winfield's Bistro.

Accommodations

Stowe offers every conceivable accommodation from dorm inexpensive to top-of-the-line hotel room or mountain villa, from "infamous" digs to the historic and famous Trapp Family Lodge. There are limited at-the-mountain lodgings (Inn at the Mountain and Condominiums) but that will change with the residential village at Spruce. Along Route 108, there are many lodges and hotels that are resorts unto themselves with spas, health clubs, and other facilities.

Information: 800-247-8693.

Stowe Area Association: 253-7321.

Après-ski/Nightlife

The Shed (historic night spot with its own brewery), Matterhorn, and Rusty Nail (largest music venue and dance scene) are the most lively places for après-ski action. There are others that offer quiet gathering places—many inns and restaurants have pubs or bars, including the Fireside Tavern at the Inn at the Mountain, Miguel's Stowe Away, The Whip Lounge (Green Mountain Inn) among others. There's also The Seed, a brew pub.

Summer/Fall

Stowe is a true resort town that swings in summer and autumn. In addition to the activities in town (concerts, festivals, films and fairs), Stowe Mountain Resort offers scenic hiking trails for wilderness exploration; a Country Club with challenging golf course and golf school; the Alpine Slide at Spruce; and the historic Toll Road. The Toll Road ascends to a Green Mountain Club information lodge, where you can stop in and view the educational exhibits before taking a walk along the Ridgeline Trail. If well prepared, you can trek all the way to the Chin, which overlooks the Gondola Area. Spectacular scenery and great views in all directions make this a once-in-a-lifetime hike not to be missed.

Gondola SkyRides and delectable lunches at the Cliff House Restaurant are offered summer and autumn for a civilized, high-elevation treat.

Tennis, swimming, and a sports/fitness center are available for those staying at the Inn at the Mountain and Condominiums.

Mansfield's ridgeline. SMR

Our Stowe Adventure

Date:

Weather:

Companions:

Where Stayed:

Visit Highlights:

Our Discoveries:

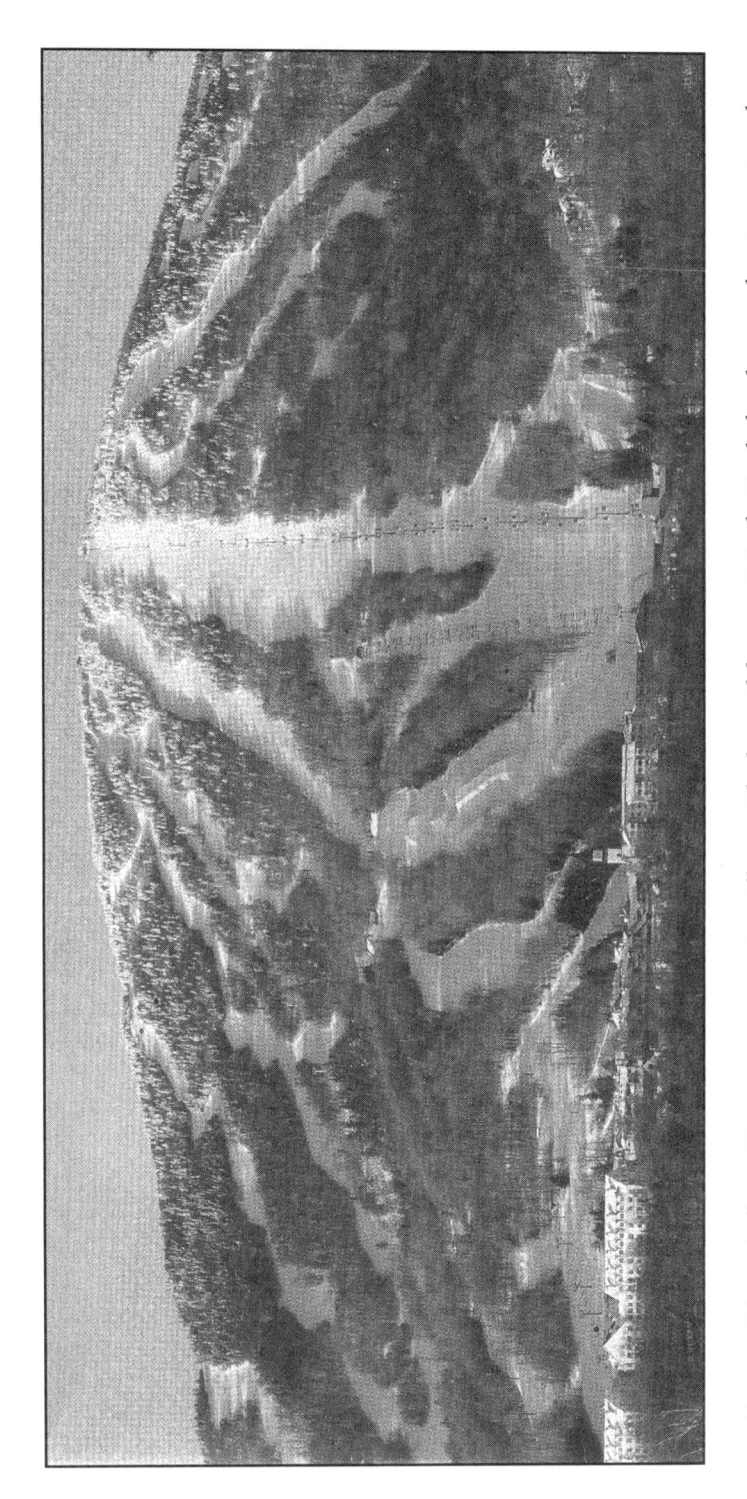

Stratton Mountain Resort features an expansive village at the base of the mountain that includes shops and restaurants and a vast variety of lodging. There's also a wealth of mountainside housing both at the main mountain and at its Sun Bowl area (not shown) as well as a Sports Center and Nordic Center.

Chapter Sixteen

Stratton
Four-Season, Upscale Resort

Stratton Mountain Resort is southern Vermont's most fashionable year-round destination resort. From its large slopeside pedestrian village of shops and restaurants with heated cobblestone walkways to an abundance of modern accommodations, Stratton pampers guests with convenience, luxury, and amenities.

That extends to the mountain where a highspeed, twelve-passenger gondola and four six-passenger express chairs whisk skiers to the trail tops in ease and comfort. The trails themselves pamper—well groomed and snow-covered, they provide a course in how to make skiers look and feel good.

The diversity and challenge satisfy most serious skiers and riders as well as the families whose children are being introduced to snowsports. The slopes are also training terrain for students at the Stratton Mountain School, many of whom have gone on to become world-class racers in Alpine and Nordic events as well as snowboard champions. Snowboarding is *big* here, with parks, pipes and contests to please freeriders of all abilities.

There's much to discover at Stratton, more trails than you can ski in a day and all manner of activities from snowshoe treks, sleigh rides, and cross-country skiing to indoor racquet sports at the Sports Center. Add opportunities for shopping and dining in Stratton Village at the base of the lifts, accommodations for 5,000, and a host of special events each year, and it's clear that this is a winter resort in the true sense of the word.

A tennis program, a 27-hole golf course and golf school, kids camps, and a summer roster of activities and events that extend into autumn also make Stratton a year-round resort. With so much to do in all the seasons, Stratton has become a mountain community unto itself—one that exudes energy, excitement, and a clear penchant for an eclectic mix of outdoor sports, cultural activities, and educational opportunities.

As a recreational community, Stratton sports an array of vacation properties and accommodations, from homes and condominiums to inns and lodges. That is what the area's founders had in mind some forty-plus years ago when they envisioned a place where people would enjoy skiing and other forms of

Scanning passes for the 6-passenger Ursa Express allows direct access to the slopes. SMR

outdoor recreation year-round. Liking the mountain's physical attributes and location near so many metropolitan areas, they determined that it would be the perfect place to build a mountain-resort community, not just another ski area.

The Mountain

Stratton's broad summit is southern Vermont's highest peak at 3,875 feet and affords breathtaking views of a sea of mountain ranges and ski areas. The mountain offers a diversity of trails and slopes and has grown to 583 acres of ski terrain (including 90 acres of glades), 90 trails, 16 lifts, and a computerized snowmaking system that can blanket 90 percent of the mountain. There are six terrain parks, a 420-foot Superpipe, and a 2,003-foot vertical.

One of the most distinctive aspects of this mountain is the lift system. Stratton has Vermont's first-and-only (as of 2004-05) six-passenger chairlifts as well as the only 12-passenger gondola. These highspeed lifts have been strategically placed to create a fast and efficient lift system.

Technology has also been employed to create a highly advanced snowmaking system. A SnowScan system combining radar and GPS is used to map out snow depths on trails and greatly assists in snowmaking and grooming decisions. The results are a manicured mountain that boosts the ego, to say nothing of increasing one's enjoyment of a day on the slopes.

Beginner/Novice ●

Stratton has an abundance of gentle terrain in the 45-acre Learning Park, which features 10 trails, a terrain garden, 3 chairlifts, and 2 carpet lifts for small children. Once beginners have mastered turns and stopping, it's on to the summit for panoramic views and a taste of big mountain skiing on easy greens of Wanderer, East or West Meadow, and Lower Wanderer to the gondola. Or to Drifter Link to the Snow Bowl chair to explore more delightful upper mountain gentle runs. In the Sun Bowl on the other side of the mountain, Churchill Downs to Lower Kidderbrook, and the Lower Middlebrook trails are delightful greens through some very scenic country. There are a group of greens at the Solstice area as well.

Intermediate ■

Black Bear is a long upper mountain blue cruiser accessed from the fast Ursa Express. On the far side of the gondola Get My Drift to Upper and Lower Drifter affords a great cruising blue run with nice GS turning off the Snow Bowl chair; or connect with any of several easy trails back to the gondola. On the Lower Mountain, Yodeler, Betwixt, and Lower Standard provide more cruising off the American Express Quad. Lower Downeaster and Gentle Ben at Solstice and the Sunriser Trail on Sun Bowl all afford long blues of varying terrain. There are many other blues to be discovered that are as much fun as their names—Tink's Link, Beeline, Snow Bowl Alley, and Old Smoothie among them. Intermediate-level skiing is a Stratton strength.

Advanced/Expert ♦ ♦♦

Tamarack, North American, and Polar Bear are diamond cruisers off the upper-mountain Ursa lift. Grizzly Bear (♦♦) ups the ante but Lower Grizzly (■) to Yodeler (■) releases the edges for a smooth schuss to the base.

There you can catch a variety of lifts, including the American Express six-passenger chair or the 12-passenger gondola and continue your westward movement to Upper Standard (♦) to Switchback (♦) to the Snow Bowl lift.

Liftline (♦) and Drifter (■) are great cruisers for advanced skiers and you're likely to see racers (particularly SMS students) training here during the week. World Cup (♦♦) is a steep bump trail in the Snow Bowl area and since it is served by its own chair, you get the feeling of being in a more secluded mountain world (fewer signs of civilization). Upper Spruce (♦♦) to Lower Spruce (♦) makes for a great top to bottom route off the Snow Bowl Quad. Upper Slalom Glade (♦) to Lower Slalom Glade (♦♦) is another option here.

Over at the Sun Bowl, Bear Down (♦♦), Free Fall (♦♦), Upper Kidderbrook (♦), and Upper Middlebrook (♦) all offer a variety of (mostly) upper mountain challenge off the Kidderbrook or Shooting Star chairs.

Glades

For beginners, Daniel's Web (●) and Get Stumped (●) offer a nice intro to tree skiing and riding in the Learning Park.

Emerald Forest (■) and Buckshot (■) at the Snow Bowl area and Eclipse (■) at the Sun Bowl offer wider spaced trees for intermediates.

Cabin Fever (♦) provides a good, steep, tight run through the forest and Dancing Bear (♦) is also accessible off the Snow Bowl Quad. Off the Ursa Express there are a number of double diamond glades, including Shred Wood Forest and Moondance (upper main mountain steeps that hold natural snow) and Free Fall Gully, Kidderbrook Ravine, and Vertigo at the Sun Bowl.

The parks and pipes are very popular at Stratton which has gained a reputation for world-class snowboarding and freeriding. SMR

Parks/Pipe

Stratton's six parks and the pipe are part of Stratton's claim to fame. Legend has it that Jake Burton Carpenter, founder of Burton Snowboards, climbed the trails after the lifts closed so he could try out his prototype snowboards. After he added metal edges to his boards, he talked Stratton into allowing the "radical new sport" of snowboarding on the slopes, making the mountain one of the first to embrace riding when it welcomed snowboards in 1983.

Stratton is home to the U.S. Open Snowboarding Championships, which are held on a superpipe and park built specially for the event on the Sunriser Supertrail at the Sun Bowl. This event attracts some 500-plus top competitors annually. Women compete on the same courses and for the same prize money as the men, making this a truly "equal" Open. Additionally, the Junior Halfpipe Jam showcases the talents of snowboarders ages fifteen and under.

Ross Powers, a graduate of the Stratton Mountain School (SMS), and a two-time Olympian and medalist (one Bronze, one Gold) is one of many top riders who participate in the Open. Powers also runs a Snowboard Camp at Stratton, which is open to anyone.

The Tyrolienne Kids Park (●) has small rollers, spines, mini pipe, and more for beginners to get the feel of contoured terrain. A section of trail is designed for race training and a Snowskate Park is located at the bottom.

The East Meadow Park (●■) has two sections and is located on the west side of the mountain off of Mike's Way and Janeway Junction. The Upper East Meadow Family Park offers a beginner garden/park atmosphere with rollers, S-spines, spines, and bank turns for advanced beginners to get the feel of contoured terrain. The upper section is shaped for a continuous run through rolls and banks. Lower East Meadow is ranked for intermediates and features some rollers and woops all the way to Drifter Link. The Snow Bowl quad serves this park.

East Byrneside Park (♦) has hits, spines, a boardercross course, and a variety of changing features. Suntanner (♦) is the most popular park and features the pro Power Park and Power Superpipe which were designed and built with guidance from Ross Powers. In addition to its Superpipe with 17 to 22 foot walls, the park features a variety of rails, fun boxes, and other jibs. Those wishing to use this park must complete a safety awareness session first.

Bear Bottom (♦♦) is for experts and has large hips, tables, and rails for the most serious skiers and riders. The entrance to this park is at the junction of Bear Bottom and Lower Grizzly.

Genesis of a Successful Resort

In 1959 Bob Wright, a ski instructor from Stowe, convinced Frank Snyder a skier from Greenwich, Connecticut, that 3,875-foot Stratton Mountain would make a great place to ski and should be developed for skiing. The snowbelt location and height were persuasive factors, and when ski-area designer Sel Hannah confirmed that it would be a good mountain for skiing, Snyder began what would become a long association with a group of people who would help make Stratton a reality.

The search for financing was an uphill battle and the original founders who had formed the Stratton Corporation struggled to get the area operating. With no Wall Street firms willing to bankroll a ski area, they ended up doing what others did, they sold shares of stock to investors with incentives of lifetime passes and an opportunity to purchase building lots or chalets at a discount.

The founders also convinced the state legislature to build a four-mile "access road" to the mountain, and they utilized a helicopter to place the towers for the three chairlifts they installed for the first season. This use of a helicopter was a Vermont (and ski-industry) first that enabled the area to open as planned on December 23, 1961 with skiing on ten trails.

Expansion was costly, and there was a constant need to raise money to fund capital improvements, but the leaders persevered and were successful during the 1960s' boom in skiing's popularity. This success was due in large part to their creation of a vacation community. Because Stratton owned land at the base of the mountain (they leased upper mountain acreage from the International

Paper Company for ski trails), they could sell lots for private homes and lodges to be built, thus ensuring a bedbase for skiers and capital for expansion.

The dream was to integrate a village, chalets, lifts, and ski slopes in a planned and logical way—something that the founders thought was necessary and missing at other areas. Their vision was to "build a resort community" rather than add "another drive-in, drive-out day ski area." It was a vision based on the European/Sun Valley/Aspen type of destination resort and foreshadowed the year-round major resort trend that hit Vermont big time in the late 1970s.

While Frank Snyder envisioned a residential village and ski area, another of the founders, Tink Smith, dreamed of building a golf course and a chapel. A Vermonter, Smith owned land on Stratton Mountain, which he sold to the ski corporation so that they could build what they felt was needed—unlike areas located on state "lease land" where ski-area operators were restricted from commercial ventures. The result was that from the very beginning the conceptual plan for Stratton Mountain Resort included a 28-acre lake, an 18-hole golf course, a 20-trail mountain, a base lodge, residential clusters, and a commercial village core.

Although the Stratton Corporation principals would continually look for ways to raise capital (as most areas had to when banks were not keen on ski area loans), they always focused on the vision of a year-round resort community. Some aspects of the plan like the pedestrian village core and the Sun Bowl took far longer to bring to fruition than ever imagined.

The founders also adhered to certain principles, including control of all aspects of Stratton's development. One example of a concern for aesthetics and the environment was the Access Road, which was built with a green belt surrounding it and a 150-foot setback requirement that effectively restricted commercial development along the road. Wanting to preserve the feel of a rural Vermont road, they tucked the housing away on the side roads and followed a plan of high-density development in the Village core.

This early concern with the preservation of the Vermont landscape and the desire for a high-density core coupled with open green spaces was ahead of its time. Ironically, 40 years later, many land planners (and anti-sprawl activists) advocate the same avoidance of strip development and the concept of high-density cluster areas. However, that didn't change the rigors of the Act 250 permitting process and as the mountain grew, Stratton endured its share of anti-growth sentiment. Planners worked through these issues and ultimately were successful, culminating in the largest ski-resort village in the state.

This comprehensive planning approach combined with an emphasis on quality and providing a topnotch experience has resulted in an expensive product, one that primarily appeals to higher-income families. The creation of Stratton's own real estate department ensured that control was maintained over the construction, sales, and management of homes and condominiums. At the same time, this department provided a major revenue source to help offset the increasing costs of ski-area operations.

On a Roll

One part of the original land-use plan called for the construction of four inns in the base area which resulted in the building of the Stratton Mountain Inn, Birkenhaus, the Liftline Lodge, and Hotel Tyrol (all built by private developers from 1961 to 1965). Another part led to the construction of the Chapel of the Snows in 1963 and a small convenience market. Lots were sold to stockholders and others, and soon homes were going up at the rate of twenty or more per year.

Many people caught the Stratton spirit and one early result was the Stratton Arts Festival, which was inaugurated in the autumn of 1963 as an event to promote Vermont art and artists. Another was the formation of the Ski Education Foundation (SEF). Brainchild of Warren Hellman, a chalet owner and Stratton regular who was coaching Junior racers, the SEF gave rise to the Stratton Mountain School, a private school which Hellman founded with Donald Tarinelli in 1970.

This SMS Academic building debuted in 1999 at the new ten-acre SMS Campus. KL

The enthusiasm for the resort got a big boost with the opening of the golf course in 1964. The Arnold Palmer Golf Academy was added in 1969 and was followed by Nordic skiing on the golf course in winter and a skating pond by the Chapel in 1975. The John Newcomb Tennis Center debuted in 1976 with the development of the Sports Center, a big step forward in the quest for year-round recreational-community status.

During this time, more lifts and trails were built on the mountain and snowmaking was added in 1965. Stratton's first venture into vacation housing began with nine village chalets in 1969. Then the first Shatterack condominiums were built in a joint venture with IP Realty in 1976. As the area grew there was a need for more housing, and Stratton went into the real estate development business using its land in the surrounding base area to build convenient trailside condos.

There were also some difficult times, especially in the early 1970s when environmental restrictions and Act 250 were new; they were followed by the poor snow, no gas, weak economy years. As a result of this and other events,

On-going improvements have been part of Stratton's history. Here, heating pipes are being installed under the village walkways in 1999. SMR

expansion to the Sun Bowl area, which was on the agenda since 1965, got postponed for close to twenty years.

Just as Stratton started to move ahead with major capital plans, the 1979 and 1980 "no-snow" seasons dealt another harsh blow. Like many areas at this time, Stratton, found itself facing the need for infusions of cash in order to move forward, but the banks weren't in the lending spirit. That's when Moore and Munger, Inc., the company Snyder worked for, purchased a controlling interest and Stratton became a subsidiary of Moore and Munger in 1981.

Plans for the Sun Bowl ski and lift area proceeded and were followed by the start of the new Stratton Village Lodge condo-hotel and the $50-million commercial Village Center in 1984. The Village Center was seen as increasing the reasons to visit and stay longer—more to do would create the "critical mass" necessary to establishing a year-round resort that could be self-sustaining. The greater usage was also seen as a way of reducing the risk factor in the ski business.

The economics of keeping a ski area going are considerable—maintain, run, and repair machinery and facilities; install the new faster, higher-capacity lifts and snowmaking (and find water sources for it); and purchase state-of-the-art grooming machines. All are expensive and beyond the capability of an operating budget in a poor winter. Yet these are all things that larger numbers of skiers were increasingly expecting.

Having bowed to the suggestion of Stig Albertsson that there would be economies and efficiencies in owning two areas, Stratton had purchased neighboring Bromley in 1979. But the poor snow years led them to sell the area in 1987 so they could concentrate on plans for Stratton. As Stratton moved along with its real estate construction and mountain improvements, the area was sold to Victoria, Ltd., a Japanese sporting goods concern that also purchased Steamboat, and was sold again to Intrawest in 1994.

Intrawest, a former urban real estate company, switched gears and began its resort development business in earnest with the purchase of Stratton (previously having purchased Blackcomb, Tremblant, and Panorama). Intrawest installed the American Express six-passenger lift in 1995 and followed up by unveiling a $250-million Master Plan in 1996.

That ten-year plan included new lifts, more snowmaking and trails, and 1,300 residential units. The construction of a 150-million-gallon snowmaking pond was both a strategic move to ensure a good water supply and an environmental step to ensure that water stream flows, which are low in winter, would be maintained so as to not adversely affect the aquatic environment. In addition, Stratton set aside 1,200 acres for environmental preservation as part of its mitigation to go forward with its build-out plans.

$8 million was invested in snowmaking improvements for the 1996-97 season, including a 150-million-gallon snowmaking pond (above). SMR

Although the vision of the founders has taken 40-plus years to accomplish, it has resulted in Stratton attaining its own unique market niche. By seeking to create a true resort and listening to guests' desires, planners have succeeded in developing a top-of-the-line mountain that appeals to the second-home market. They are purchasing the upscale resort homes and townhouses that fuel real estate profits, which, in turn, enable the area to further improve the mountain and add such amenities as the new Stratton Mountain Club as well as offer the year-round activities that reduce reliance on one season. Concurrently, the continuing construction of condos and townhomes fuels the bedbase, which creates the visitor base needed to sustain year-round operations of so many facilities and activities.

For the homeowners, guests, and day visitors, it means more to do and enjoy in any season, including winter. For Intrawest and Stratton, that means a viable business and a successful resort that continues to employ over 1,000 workers. Becoming a full-fledged, year-round mountain-resort community was not easy, but by realizing this vision, Stratton has created a unique and lively Village with year-round activity.

Stratton Revisited

When we first skied Stratton in the 1970s, it was still predominantly a ski area. When I returned in 1984 to see the commerical village that was going up, I was impressed not only with the models and plans for the village but also with the amount of housing in the area and the size of the mountain itself.

During the 1980s, our family attended several of the annual tennis tournaments hosted at Stratton. It was always an exciting time to see up-and-coming top players like Andre Agassi, Michael Chang, and the top women who played in the Volvo and Acura tournaments. It was also inspiring for our boys, who would always go home revved up to go out and play more tennis.

Visiting Stratton was synonymous with fun and excitement but being busy with three growing boys and the demands of their school days, I seldom got back to ski. So it wasn't until April and December 2002 visits that I really got to know the mountain well again. Both visits were midweek, which was skiing heaven as there were no lift waits, the trails were uncrowded, and I got to see a lot of the area as well as put a lot of mileage on my skis.

What I discovered was a vastly expanded ski area. It wasn't just a bigger mountain that made my visits fun, though. The new Sun Bowl area with its long trails and diversity, the fast express lifts, and excellent snow coverage made the skiing great, but it was the very friendly people that made it memorable. The new six-passenger lifts were a big part of that.

For those of us who remember the days of skiing when the oldest kid in the family or group had to ride alone because the chair only accommodated two or three, the new highspeed lifts that seat six are wonderful! They are also great for meeting people, something I appreciated when skiing alone and invited to join a couple and their friends whom I had met on a chair ride.

Learning that I hadn't skied Stratton in some years, they took me on a whirlwind tour of the mountain, starting with all the trails off the Ursa Express where we had met. Moving to the Gondola, they provided insights on just how user-friendly the resort has become and the great variety of terrain from classic New England trails to wide, top-to-bottom cruising trails like Standard and Liftline.

Then to be sure I really understood 'user-friendly,' they showed me the delightful and scenic schusses on the East and West Meadows. They even designed a route back to my car for me, which is how I came to discover the steeps of Upper Middle Brook, the ease of Churchill Downs and the loveliness of Lower Kidderbrook. It was a spectacular long run that enabled me to experience the expansiveness and beauty of the area.

On a far colder December day, a guide showed a group of ski writers around the mountain and led us to a neat discovery that many miss, the Snow Bowl area. It is almost a secret section of the mountain because so many gravitate to the highspeed lifts that this long chair with its double-diamond gems like World Cup (a steep bump trail), Upper Spruce, and Lower Slalom Glade, its advanced terrain like Liftline and Switchback, and its many blue cruisers are easily missed. The chair also serves several gentle greens so it makes a great lift/trail complex for all ability levels. The combination of Get My Drift and

Drifter trails provided a particularly fun run—wide and scenic at the top, narrower and old fashioned winding and undulating in the lower section.

One of the best runs was skiing the same trail that competitors from the Stratton Mountain School were training on. To watch them in the gates was interesting—you could analyze technique due to being so close, which one of our group did quite capably. It was also exciting at my age to even ski the same trail as those young stud legs with their nerves of steel.

Shaped skis changed the way we ski by making carved turns easier for us (and shaved time off racers' runs). Above, Anne DeWater of Rossignol demonstrates the smooth carve of the super-sidecut ski. SMR

Being a "day tripper" facing a deadline, I headed home after my last run, but I'm looking forward to a return trip for an overnight stay. It'll provide the opportunity to sample resort life and food and maybe do some shopping or try the new Spa. I might even forego the slopes for a day of more discoveries, something my "drop-out" (former skier) husband is sure to appreciate.

Good to Know

Stratton is located off Route 30 in Bondville; it's about 3 hours (140 miles) from Boston, 2.5 hours (120 miles) from Hartford, and 4 hours (235 miles) from NYC. From I-91 (Exit 2), it's about 42 miles via Route 30.

Telemark skis, snowboards, snowblades, and freeride skis are available at the Adventure Center for those hankering for a little variety.

Stratton inaugurated the Vermont Freeskiing Open with Slopestyle and Superpipe competitions at the Sun Bowl in 2003, and the stage was set for an annual repeat because it proved so popular. Check the Website for details.

The Sun Bowl is a great place to start a ski day and take advantage of the early morning sun. After exploring this area, the six-passenger lifts can transport you to trails that lead to the main mountain base or to the summit .

Plan to arrive very early to park in the main village lot at peak times. Once full, you park in one of the outlying lots and use the free shuttle bus to the village. If staying overnight, you can walk or shuttle bus to the slopes.

A good place to park is at the Sun Bowl (be early on weekends and holidays), which has its own base lodge, and two six-passenger chairs for fast lift rides.

Nature lovers and families should check out the wildlife workshops which Stratton hosts each season—presentations by the Vermont Institute of Natural Science include such topics as Bats: Navigators of the Night; The Magnificent Moose; and Bear Facts. (Since 1994, Stratton has permanently protected over 1,200 acres of wildlife habitat, sponsored habitat studies, and won awards for conservation and environmental initiatives while expanding as a ski area.)

The Carlos Otis Clinic is a not-for-profit medical facility staffed by orthopedic surgeons and medical physicians to provide general medicine, minor surgery, orthopedics and advanced life support (297-2300).

Stratton offers a Women's Snowsport Workshop with coaching, video analysis, and afternoon sessions at the Sports Center several times a season. Burton's LTR program is included in 2005. Check the Website for details.

A KidsKamp Center debuted for the 2004 season. The spacious slopeside facility (just below the Learning Park) accommodates the Big and Little Cub programs and has rentals in the same location. Convenient for lunch and cocoa breaks and check-in for Junior instructional programs.

The Stratton Trailblazers, a ski club for the 50+ gang, holds weekly ski clinics, regular social events, and plans trips. They number over 1,000 and welcome "Junior" members. Learn more at www.strattontrailblazers.com.

The Stratton Mountain School is an independent ski academy that is renowned for training competitors in Alpine, Nordic, and snowboarding disciplines. Since its founding in 1971, SMS has graduated 75 students who have become National Team members and 20 who became Olympians, including two-time medalist Ross Powers, Alpine skier Pam Fletcher, and Nordic Skier Kerrin Petty. Today, SMS has its own state-of-the-art campus on ten acres near the Sun Bowl with residence hall, classroom building, and athletic field house.

Steals & Deals

Although Stratton has one of Vermont's most expensive one-day lift ticket for weekends and holidays, it also has a variety of special deals and packages that substantially reduce the price of skiing as does the purchase of multi-day tickets. Check the Website for details and the latest deals or call the area.

Lift & Lodging packages start at $59 pp/d.o. Available Sunday – Thursday, non-holiday (nh) and select weekends.

Stay for Free: Buy a 3-day midweek (nh) lift ticket ($144) and get 2 nights free at the Liftline Lodge (pp/d.o.). Lodging upgrades available.

Ski for Free: Book a 2-night stay starting at $79 pp/d.o. and get 2 free lift tickets each. Available early/late season only.

2005 Stratton/Okemo Super Pass, midweek (nh) season pass: $399.

Stratton/Okemo College Pass, valid every day is $299 by 12/3/04.

With the Stratton Express Card ($95 for 2005), a midweek ticket is $29.50 a day and $19 on non-holiday Thursdays; Sundays are $49, Saturdays, $59; and holidays, $64.

New for 2005 is a Sunday (nh) season pass for $299 and a Sunday through Friday (nh) season pass for $599.

All phone numbers are **area code 802** unless otherwise noted.

Handy Info

Website: www.stratton.com
Email: skistratton@intrawest.com
General information: 297-2200; 800-STRATTON
Snow report: 297-4211
Hours: 8:30 - 4 daily.
Tickets 2005 Season: Adults $59 midweek, $72 weekends/holidays; Juniors (7-12) & Super Seniors (70+) $46/$51; Young Adult (13-17) & Seniors (64-69) $52/$60; Ages 6 and under are $5.

Quick Stats

Season: Mid-November to April, average 150 days.
Average annual snowfall: 180 inches.
Snowmaking capability: 90 percent; 525 acres.
Lifts: 16; 1 twelve-passenger gondola; 4 six-passenger express chairs, 4 quads, 1 triple, 1 double, 5 surface.
Uphill lift capacity: 29,550 rides per hour.
Trails: 90; 600+ (total) acres; longest run 3 miles.
Glades: 100+acres; 8 glades for all abilities from beginner to expert.
Bumps: World Cup.
Parks/Pipes: 5 terrain parks, 1 superpipe, 1 minipipe.
Vertical Drop: Summit to Base (village): 2,003'
Sun Bowl Summit to Base: 1,500'

Snow School   800-Stratton

Private or group lessons for beginner to expert. Both the MagicTrax (ages 7 and up) Learn-to-Ski program on short-cut skis and the Learn-to-Ride program (ages 7 and up) on special Burton boards, include equipment, a.m. and p.m. instruction, and lift ticket for the Learning Park.

Burton Method Center, Junior Method Center, and Learn–to-Ride Instruction for adults and children. Season-long racing and development programs. Ross Powers Snowboard Camp. Women's Snowsport Workshops and LTR.

Children's Programs   800-787-2886

Reservations are required for Childcare; recommended for Little, Big Cub programs.

Childcare: 6 weeks to 4 years, half or full day.
Little Cub: 4-6 years; 1/2 or full day; indoor play and lesson; lunch.
Big Cub: 7-12 years; indoor fun, 2 lessons, and lunch.
MagicTrax: ages 7 and up, ski-to-learn program with 2 lessons.
Learn-to Ride: for ages 7 and up offers the Burton LTR system.
Seasonal programs are available; see Website or call for details.

Other Things to Do

Massage, facials, body treatments, healing therapies at the Spa (297-3339) in Stratton Village.

Kids Night Out: movies, pizza, snow tubing, activities, 5:30-9:30.

Under 21 Club: evening entertainment (movies, games, video premieres).

Adults can enjoy a Snowcat ride to a gourmet dinner at the Mid-Mountain Lodge, Tuesdays, Saturdays 6 to 8:30; reservations required: 800-Stratton.

Stratton Ski Touring Center (297-4114) at the Sun Bowl offers 20 km of tracked and 50 km backcountry skiing. Nordic Center at Stratton Mountain Country Club has beginner terrain. Rentals, instruction, Nordic and moonlight tours are available.

Also, X-C and/or snowshoeing at Hildene in Manchester (362-1788); Viking Ski Touring Center in Londonderry (824-3933); Nordic Inn in Peru (824-6444).

Alpine Snowmobile Tours (297-4454) offer a 3-hour wilderness tour in the Green Mountain National Forest and 1-hour rides on the ski trails at Stratton after the lifts close. Mini-Z snowmobiles for children at the base of Stratton Mountain.

Sleigh rides are given by Belgian brothers Smoky and Bandit from the Sun Bowl Ranch (297-9210) to a campfire in the woods; weekends, holidays. Also by Horses for Hire (297-1468); in Landgrove by Karl Pfister (824-6320); in Londonderry by Taylor Farm (824-5690).

Snow tubing under the lights at mountain. Ice skating on rink at Long Trail House or in Manchester at Riley Rink (362-0150).

Snowshoe guided walks, backcountry tours and moonlight treks to Pearl Buck cottage for hot chocolate by the fireplace. Summit snowshoe tours to historic fire tower with views of four states.

Pool, tennis, racquetball, squash, massage, weight and fitness equipment, steam room, whirlpool, aerobics studio, classes at Sports Center (297-4230).

Shopping: Stratton Village has an array of boutiques and sport shops. Manchester offers 50 outlet stores, restaurants, movie theater, and one of the best independent bookstores in the country, the Northshire Bookstore.

Visit the Northshire Museum and History Center (362-0004) on Route 7A and/or the Southern Vermont Arts Center (362-1405) in Manchester.

Dining Out

There's a good variety of cuisine at Stratton Village, including: Luna (classic; reservations required) at the Stratton Mountain Club; Verdé (fine dining), Mulberry Street (Italian), Mulligan's (casual bistro), and Blue Moon Café.

The following also offer a diversity of dining experiences:

In Bondville: The Red Fox Inn (Italian), The Outback (casual fare).

Jamaica: Three Mountains Inn (fine dining in beautiful restored inn).

Men Who Cook was a popular Stratton Foundation fundraiser. SMR

Manchester: Angel's at the Village Country Inn (inspired New England cuisine), Bistro Henry (Mediterranean, classic and contemporary favorites), Black Swan (fresh fish, game, pasta, homemade desserts), Candeleros (southwestern cantina and grill), Christo's Pizza and Pasta, The Equinox (elegant dining room or Marsh Pub), 4940 Main Street (creative American Bistro), Friendly's, Garlic John's, Laney's (open-kitchen concept with wood fired oven, sports bar, ribs to pizza), Lilac Café (eclectic menu and take out), Mulligan's (burgers to seafood, children's menu), Panda Garden (Chinese), Sirloin Saloon (a popular classic featuring steak, seafood, and salad bar; children's menu), The Perfect Wife, Wilburton Inn, Ye Olde Tavern.

Peru: Johnny Seesaw's (hearty American fare with distinct French accent).

Accommodations

Resort accommodations include cozy lodges, full-service hotels, spacious condominiums, luxurious townhouses. Bedbase is 8,000 in the region. From a room at a quaint B & B to a slopeside penthouse, there is something for every budget and need.

Stratton lodging: 800-Stratton.

Manchester and Mountains Chamber of Commerce: 362-2100.

Londonderry Chamber of Commerce: 824-8178.

Après-Ski/Nightlife

At the mountain, Grizzly's offers après-ski and entertainment on most weekends. Under 21 Club in the Village; Mulligans has après-ski fun and evening action in their Green Door Pub with live entertainment Saturdays

The Red Fox Inn (Bondville) offers live music and dancing on weekends, Open Mike sessions on Thursdays, folk music with "the meal deal" on Sundays. Johnny Seesaw's (Peru) offers live music on Saturdays.

Forty Nine Forty Main Restaurant in Manchester Center: Open Mike, Wednesdays 8 p. m. to closing.

Summer/Fall

Stratton offers golf and golf school, tennis and tennis instruction, kids camps, mountain biking, hiking, horseback riding, swimming, and the facilities of the Stratton Sports Center. There are sightseeing rides to the summit, special events, festivals, and activities like wine tasting dinners, cooking lessons, and the Annual Stratton Arts Festival. More golf in Manchester as well.

Nearby attractions include: the Southern Vermont Art Center, American Museum of Fly Fishing, and Hildene in Manchester; the Southern Vermont Natural History Museum in Marlboro; and the Bennington Museum in Bennington. The Mount Equinox Skyline Drive is a 5.2 mile paved toll road that provides a breathtaking experience and many picnic places with a view.

The 27-hole championship Stratton Golf Course and Golf School are part of summer offerings that also include tennis and other sports. SMR

Our Stratton Adventure

Date:

Weather:

Companions:

Where Stayed:

Visit Highlights:

Our Discoveries:

256 Sugarbush

The topography of each of Sugarbush's six mountain areas is different from the others, making for trails that are distinctive. They constitute some of the most diverse terrain in the East. And with the Sugarbush penchant to honor the New England classic style trails (i.e. following the natural contours of the mountain and not put in the mega-wide "super trails" that are popular today), the trails remain more challenging and interesting. This is particularly true at Castle Rock, earning Sugarbush a reputation as one of the best all-around "natural skiing mountains." However, they do a good job of snowmaking, grooming, and have some wide trails, too.

Chapter Seventeen

Sugarbush
From Glitz and Glam to Soulful Recreation

Sugarbush Mountain Resort in Warren is a favorite of sports-minded outdoors types, but it's also become something of a best-kept secret in Vermont skiing. The latter might have to do with its out-of-the-way, off-the-beaten-path location as well as the passage of time.

Once world famous for its glitz and glamour (and compared to such elite resorts as Sun Valley, Gstaad, and St. Moritz), today the resort is an understated oasis of four-season outdoor recreation, a place where nature is celebrated, not celebrity or status. Its location in the wildly beautiful and idyllic Mad River Valley is part of the area's appeal—quite simply the quintessential Vermont that you see in magazines and postcards.

As you travel north to Warren on Vermont Route 100 ("the skier's highway"), you really do pass white-steepled churches, red barns, and homes with smoke curling out of chimneys. That is when you are not negotiating the beautiful but treacherous Granville Gulf, from whence the Mad River flows north and the White River south.

The run south down Route 100 from I-89 is only a little less scenic, missing as it does the Granville Gulf but making up for it with hillside farms and a dip through the Village of Waitsfield before turning off onto the Sugarbush Access Road, an easy three-mile climb to the ski area.

With an hour-long run up Route 100 (from its intersection with U.S. Route 4 in Killington) or a half-hour sprint from I-89 at Waterbury, Sugarbush *seems* more remote than many Vermont ski resorts. The Route 100 Valley with mountains rising steeply on both sides and hemming in small villages on the valley floor contributes to that feeling. This distinctively different and narrow route reminds one that nature is a force to be reckoned with, one that shaped Vermont's mountains and valleys over 10,000 years ago when the last glaciers retreated.

This section of Route 100 between Routes 4 and I-89 is different from other areas of the state in its ruggedness. Further north the traveling is through flatter more wide open terrain and in central and southern Vermont it is over highways and byways that have more signs of civilization. It seems only natural then that

Sugarbush, a ski area composed of three of the highest peaks in the Green Mountain National Forest, would be a place where nature and the outdoors are celebrated.

That can be seen most obviously in the skiers, snowboarders, and Telemarkers who enjoy the mountains' diverse trails, slopes, and glades. It can be seen in the challenges of Rumble or Paradise, in the smiles of children learning to slide on snow, or in the greetings of old-timers out for a jaunt on Jester.

It can also be witnessed in the hardy adventurers who snowshoe or cross-country ski along the Long Trail which traverses its peaks. And in the eyes of the backcountry enthusiasts who take guided tours in the spectacular 2,000-acre wilderness known as Slide Brook. Traveling on skis, snowboards, or snowshoes, visitors to "the Slide" get an incomparable backcountry experience as guides give them tips on skiing/riding and information on the fauna, flora, ecological zones, and geological history of the area. This enjoyment and celebration of the mountains is a major change from when Sugarbush was young!

Sugarbush Then and Now

That was a time when Sugarbush Valley Ski Area was the home to the *Jet Set*—celebrities like Oleg Cassini, Skitch Henderson, Kim Novak, Armando Orsini, and the Kennedys. It was the fashion-conscious tastes of New York models and others who came "to be seen" (not necessarily to ski) that blurred the area's reputation and led to the moniker "Mascara Mountain."

In reality, Damon and Sarah Gadd and partner Jack Murphy had founded a real mountain, one with character and soul, steep pitches and long runs. With its opening on December 25, 1958, Sugarbush was the first ski area in the state to have an enclosed lift, a 9,300-foot, three-passenger gondola that was the longest single-span lift in the United States. The 2,388-foot vertical was the greatest in Vermont then, and with trails like Organgrinder, the area was known for its challenging skiing.

It was also known for its ski school directors, starting with Peter Estin, who helped attract the more famous patrons to the area's slopes and continuing with Stein Eriksen, a charismatic Olympic racing legend who epitomized grace and elegance on the slopes and excitement in his Moebus flips. The Sugarbush Ski School earned international acclaim under Director Sigi Grottendorfer (1967-1989), and although the *Jet Set* skied there, many became excellent skiers.

Sugarbush sizzled in the sixties as homes went up in the forests below and lodges, inns, and restaurants sprang up along the three-mile access road. Various entrepreneurs put up a golf course, tennis center, condos, and restaurants, forming the nexus of the first ski-area four-season destination village. By the 1970s, serious golfers and skiers were becoming year-round visitors.

Change came when the area was sold to Roy Cohen and his brother Solon in 1977. He expanded the ski area and purchased neighboring Glen Ellen from Harvey Clifford in September 1978, renaming it Sugarbush North.

Clifford had bought Glen Ellen in 1975 from Gina and Brown Van Loon. They, in turn, had purchased the mountain from founder Walter Elliott who opened the area with two chairlifts, a T-bar, and a 2,600-foot vertical in 1963.

Clifford had upgraded or replaced old equipment, extended the snowmaking system, and improved the grooming. Previous to his purchase, Glen Ellen's reputation had been suffering from

View of Mount Ellen, elevation 4,083 and second highest lift-served skiing in the state. SR

the lack of needed improvements, a not uncommon plight among areas in the difficult 1970s. Clifford was turning that around when Cohen came knocking with dreams of offering skiing in the basin between the two areas, shuttle bus service, and one lift ticket for the two mountains.

Although Cohen and his brother Solon succeeded in the buyout, he never was able to add ski trails to connect the two areas. What he did accomplish, however, was to add Vermont's second-highest skiing peak (4,083 feet) and the second-greatest vertical ski descent of 2,600 feet. He also had acquired an area with more snowmaking, lots of long intermediate and expert runs, and a modicum of novice terrain. The main, upper, and Inverness skiing areas were served by four chairlifts and a T-Bar, along with a base lodge and upper mountain lodge.

In 1995, Sugarbush was joined with Mount Ellen via the Slide Brook Express Quad which is the world's longest and fastest highspeed quad, taking 9.5 minutes to get from one area to the other. Slide Brook Basin provides awe-inspiring terrain for cross-country, snowshoe, Telemark, and Alpine guided ski tours.

In 1983, ARA Services purchased Sugarbush as part of a merger with Solon Automated Services (the company owned by Solon Cohen) and replaced the original Sugarbush Gondola with two triple chairs to quadruple lift capacity to South's summit. ARA sold to Claneil Enterprises in 1985. In addition to installing new lifts at Mount Ellen, they entered the resort phase with the purchase of the golf course, tennis center, cross-country ski complex, three restaurants, and the Sugarbush Inn and Country Townhouses, as well as securing management of many condominiums in the Village.

By the mid-1990s, mountain-mogul Leslie B. Otten, who had turned Sunday River in Bethel, Maine, into a huge success, was starting his resort purchasing spree. He entered into a purchase and operating agreement in the fall of 1994 and consummated his purchase of Sugarbush in May 1995. He invested millions in snowmaking, including a 50-million-gallon snowmaking pond, chairlifts, grooming, and the connection of North and South with a ten-minute chair ride—one of the most scenic and thrilling rides in the Northeast.

Otten gave up his development dreams for ski trails in the Slide Brook area in order to secure environmental approvals for a resort hotel at the base of Lincoln Peak. When the planned Grand Summit Hotel which he felt was essential to Sugarbush's revitalization wasn't met with enthusiasm, Otten shifted his attention to the other resorts he had been acquiring in his newly formed American Skiing Company (ASC) group — Attitash Bear Peak in New Hampshire; Killington, Pico, Mount Snow/Haystack in Vermont; Sugarloaf in

Maine; Steamboat in Colorado; Heavenly Valley in Nevada/California, and the Canyons in Utah.

It wasn't so much that he was ignoring 'the Bush' as that it was his philosophy to focus on bringing each area up to speed and to then move on to the next area, so each had its "turn." Sugarbush's turn ended when the hotel was stymied and attention was focused on another acquisition.

That didn't make a lot of people in the valley very happy, and in 2001, dedicated Sugarbush skiers Win Smith and Bob Reimer joined Bob Ackland, (former) GM at Mad River, to form Summit Ventures NE and purchased Sugarbush from ASC. In 2002, after the sudden death of Reimer, a new investor Adam Greshin joined Summit Ventures. Their vision is one of a finely tuned four-season resort for outdoor enthusiasts who appreciate challenging mountains and the pleasures of a natural environment, one where they are welcomed by friendly people who share their interests.

In a way, Sugarbush is returning to its roots—the founders' vision of "a gathering place for outdoor enthusiasts." The difference is the sense of place and community the new owners bring. Perhaps because times have changed and they come from "away" (they are out-of-staters who have lived in the area long enough to be considered "locals"), the owners have an appreciation and respect for Vermont's special environment and thus "no desire to make Sugarbush the Vail of eastern skiing." No pretentious goals, just a desire to let Sugarbush shine in its own natural way and in cooperation with her neighbors, Mad River Glen and the residents of Warren and Waitsfield.

Some of this spirit of cooperation can be seen in the new Ski-the-Valley ticket that gives skiers who stay three or more nights at participating lodging properties a lift ticket that allows them to ski both areas and try cross-country as well. This realizes a dream Cohen had, and it offers up an incredibly diverse bounty of trails and mountain experiences, from old-fashioned ski area to modern mega mountain. (Mad River, however, bans snowboarding, so it's an experience only Alpine or Telemark skiers can know.)

That same spirit incorporates listening to the skiers and correcting the former three-lift ride problem at Mount Ellen. The new owners removed the lower fixed grip quad at the base and put in the Green Mountain Express chair (GMX) to the Glen House and made other changes that enable the area to work better, such as re-instituting ski school at Mount Ellen for the 2004-05 season and adding a progression of terrain parks there. Other improvements included snowmaking system upgrades, new signage, and a new Adventure Learning Center. Sugarbush also appointed "extreme legend" John Egan director of the Sugarbush Ski and Ride School.

Although the new owners are focusing on "fine tuning, the natural environment, and fostering a sense of community and good citizenship," they

John Egan enters Paradise at Lincoln Peak with the long spine of the Green Mountains laid out before him. SR

are not oblivious to what visitors desire today and plans are to add a finishing touch with slopeside accommodations at the base of Lincoln Peak.

The Mountains

Sugarbush is a modern multi-mountain resort that has grown to 17 lifts (5 of them Express quads), 115 trails (54 miles and 468 skiable acres) on two separate, lift-connected mountain complexes, that of Mount Ellen to the North and Lincoln Peak to the South.

The 2,600-foot vertical drop at Mount Ellen and the 2,400-foot vertical at Lincoln Peak are among Vermont's top four and translate into some of Vermont's most diversified terrain and longest New England-styled runs. Skiers can stay on advanced or intermediate trails all the way to the bottom of Mount Ellen with only a short easy schuss of green at the end of the run, making Mount Ellen the biggest consistently challenging vertical for advanced skiers in the state and the second greatest for intermediates. The 2,400-foot vertical at Lincoln Peak also offers consistent pitches for intermediates and advanced skiers for long runs that only let up at the final runout.

Mount Ellen (AKA Sugarbush North) ♦♦ ♦ ■ ●

Mount Ellen's summit is 4,083 feet above sea level, the second highest elevation reached by aerial lift in Vermont. This is significant for the top-to-bottom long runs that are afforded to intermediates and experts who take the in-tandem GMX and Summit Quads to the top—total riding time 13 minutes.

One would expect to encounter a wait at each lift, but the truth is that you don't midweek and even on weekends it's apt to be non-existent or a short five minutes because Mount Ellen is simply a "best kept" secret. Like Pico at Killington and Haystack at Mount Snow, people tend to gravitate to "the big kahuna" and forget about—or fail to sample—the 'big fish' next door. Even on holidays and peak weekends, Mount Ellen often remains uncrowded.

Mount Ellen has both a base lodge and the Glen House, which sits on the upper mountain between the GMX and Summit lifts. The parking area is downhill from the lifts and base lodge, necessitating a hike. However, there is a drop-off area for passengers and equipment, and at peak times there is a jitney to take skiers to the base area.

Mount Ellen doesn't give you a hundred trails, but it does give you a wide variety of long, interesting, and uncrowded terrain that makes it well worth a day's exploration. Additionally, there is a halfpipe and terrain parks, which can be accessed from the GMX Quad and the Sunshine Double. The snow-excavated halfpipe is to the left of the base lodge for easy viewing.

Advanced/Expert ♦ ♦♦

Mount Ellen's summit is a steep and narrow one that affords just three ways down for the first quarter mile and then the ski area boundaries progressively broaden out to encompass more trails and the Inverness section to the north (2,750-foot summit for a 1,265-foot vertical from its lift).

Experts using the Summit Quad can choose from a number of most difficult trails like FIS (♦♦), Black Diamond (♦♦), Exterminator (♦♦), The Cliffs (a ♦ bump trail), and Tumbler (♦). The first two spill off the top like water running straight down and both are deserving of their ♦♦ ratings.

The two-mile FIS is a very wide steep that plummets precipitously at the top and then joins Rim Run (■) for a breather before turning into Lower FIS (a ♦ natural snow trail) for a long narrow cruise to the base with good pitch until a relatively flat runout. The Black Diamond trail under the lift makes bravado necessary—not much bailout room with rocks hemming in the trail—and any mistakes made are in full view of lift riders.

Exterminator and Bravo are reached via a short schuss off the summit on Rim Run or via the Northstar Express lift. Upper Exterminator (♦♦) eases into a single diamond for its lower half. It is longer than Upper FIS but not quite as steep although narrow by comparison. Bravo (♦) is one of the East's true toughies with a 65 percent gradient.

There's also an interesting mélange of black diamonds off the GMX, including South Bound to Lower FIS. Hammerhead is tight and steep and is considered Ellen's hardest by Sugarbush staff. Encore, The Cliffs, and Tumbler offer more options (wide, narrow, bumps, steeps) and meld into Crackerjack another diamond before easing up for the last 1500 feet (●) to the chair.

Intermediate ■

Intermediates have a diversity of blues to choose from and a challenge off the very top on Rim Run (or the scenic, short Panorama go-around alternative to get to Rim Rum, allowing great views to Lake Champlain and the Adirondacks) to Elbow to Cruiser to Straight Shot (●), a famous two-mile run. It's possible to play at the top off the Summit Quad for several hours as Rim Run and Lower Rim Run offer a number of lines to take and other options like Looking Good, Elbow, and Spread Eagle are also fun, true-blue challenges back to this lift.

The racing terrain at Inverness (■), where the competitors of the Green Mountain Valley School train, is sweet cruising and an ultra wide slope that invites the biggest GS turns you can muster. Semi Tough (■) is a narrow, natural snow twister that gets bumped up and makes less-than-daring intermediates feel like novices again. Brambles adds another winding narrow blue.

Off the GMX, Cruiser (■) and Which Way (■) offer good challenge before allowing a rest on the easy Straight Shot to the lift.

Beginner/Novice ●

Mount Ellen also has a base-area beginner hill at the Sunshine Double which serves three easy, wide runs—Riemergasse, Sugar Run, and Graduation. There's a first-timer's handle tow here as well.

Novice terrain on the main mountain is limited to one run off the GMX, Northstar (●) to Straight Shot (●), a nice long route that is designated a slow skiing/riding area and to Walt's Trail (●) at The Inverness Quad, a wonderful meandering, natural snow green back to the chair (named for area founder Walter Elliott).

Lincoln Peak (aka Sugarbush South) ♦♦ ♦ ■ ●

At the Lincoln Peak area, there are five distinct skiing areas due to a cluster of four peaks that form a huge basin that funnels into one, fairly wide base area. There are three lodges: the Gate House at the base area, the Valley House a few hundred yards up the slope, and Allyn's at the top Gadd Peak. What is particularly nice is that the various lift-and-trail complexes all have distinctive terrain and offer a unique feel, from a family atmosphere at the Gate House area to hot-shot, *extreme* heaven at Castlerock. Add the fact that you can get to Mount Ellen via the Slide Brook Express and back again, and this gives Sugarbush some of the most diverse and dramatic terrain in the East.

Most of the trails here are of the New England classic variety. They twist and turn their way down the mountainsides, following the natural contours of the terrain. There are very few of the wide western-styled boulevards although there are a few straight down fall-line trails like Organgrinder.

The Magic Carpet below the Valley House Lodge in the base area provides a handy learning hill with two lodges to retreat to for hot chocolate or lunch. The Bravo Express Quad, which ascends Gadd Peak, is to the right below the Valley House and Gate House Lodge is immediately adjacent but out of the photo. KL

Gatehouse Area ● ■ ♦

At the Gate House area on North Lynx Peak, beginners have their own dedicated learning areas with wide open slope skiing/riding at the First Time beginner poma and at the Village Double chair which serves Easy Rider, the Out to Lunch trail, and the Sugarbear Forest fantasy terrain garden (all ●).

They are all part of the Family Adventureland, a slow skiing/riding zone that goes halfway up North Lynx Peak and offers a nice progression of terrain from the easy aforementioned beginner slopes to the longer greens (Pushover, Sugarbear Road), blues (Sleeper, Hot Shot), and diamonds (Sleeper Chute, Deeper Sleeper, and Waterfall) accessible off the Gatehouse Express Quad.

There's also a Magic Carpet between the Gatehouse Base Lodge and Valley House Lodge for 'never evers' and beginners in the base area.

North Lynx Peak ♦ ■

The top section of North Lynx Peak is a separate area served by a triple lift. There's a great blue cruise on Birch Run and nice diamonds on Morning Star and Sunrise. It's a great off-by-itself area with a six-minute chair ride and an opportunity to make non-stop runs.

Castlerock ♦♦ ♦ ■

The legendary Castlerock is an upper mountain area that can be reached by either the Bravo or Gatehouse Express Quads. Castlerock Peak (Nancy Hanks Peak on the state map) has a summit elevation of 3,812 feet and offers a 1,600-foot vertical for every run on the chair (2,237 foot vertical to Lincoln's base). Castlerock offers narrow steeps for true experts who like natural snow trails and has an upgraded double chair that allows for good skier dispersal on the trails.

Hotshots describe Rumble (♦♦) as "Sugarbush's most difficult trail overall. Rumble keeps you honest. It's too narrow to bring your skis across the fall line for too long. You just have to charge it. For Experts Only!" Upper Lift Line (♦♦) is only a tad wider and requires as much finesse as Rumble. Castlerock (♦) and Middle Earth (♦) are more doable challenges with blue turn-off options (onto Troll Road) for those who tire.

Lincoln Peak ♦♦ ♦ ■

Lincoln Peak boasts a top elevation of 3,975 and a 2,400-foot vertical for long runs via two lift rides, the Super Bravo Express Quad and Heaven's Gate Triple (14-minute total ride time plus a short run on Downspout (■) between the two chairs). Off the summit, Jester (■) is a classic blue, twist-and-turn trail all the way to Gondolier (●) for the last 1500 feet of easy cruise to the lift. Jester also connects with a variety of other blues at mid-mountain to vary one's runs.

Other choices off the top include the historic Organgrinder (♦), a steep straight-down run to Gondolier (●) to the base, and a short jaunt on Jester or Organgrinder to Spillsville (♦) to Lower Ripcord (♦) to the Heaven's Gate Triple. Rip Cord (♦♦) and Paradise (♦♦) are legendary toughies for their upper sections, single diamond lower. Sugarbush staff consider Paradise to be Lincoln's hardest run.

Gadd Peak ♦♦ ♦ ■

Gadd Peak (elevation 3,150 feet; 1,575 vertical) is served by either of two chairlifts, the Valley Double or the Super Bravo Express. It features the most intermediate, advanced, expert, and gladed acreage of any of the areas at South and includes the famous Stein's Run.

Valley House Traverse to Snowball to Racer's Edge is a terrific long, wide open blue cruise and Spring Fling (■) offers ultra wide sailing down to the Race Arena on its lower section. Moonshine (■) gives a taste of narrow and is marked as an Adventure Trail, which means it has trees on it but is not strictly a glade run. Domino, Lower Jester, and Downspout complete the variety of blues with twists, turns, and nice cruising and Murphy's Glade gives intermediates their own tree terrain; all lead back to the Bravo or Valley chairs.

Allyn's Lodge on Gadd Peak (3,150') below Lincoln Peak (3,975') with Jester on left, Organgrinder center, and the famous Ripcord and Paradise to the right. KL

The mile-long Stein's Run (♦♦) begins narrow but progresses to ultra wide as it bumps straight down with an average pitch of 30-35 degrees. Egan's' Woods (♦♦) is tight and steep while Eden (♦) offers a more open glade. Lower Organgrinder, Twist, The Mall, and Lew's Line round out the black gems in this area.

Impressions

I first explored Sugarbush (South) several years ago when my oldest son and I only had five hours, hardly enough to do it justice, but we got a great taste of South with runs off every lift except the beginner area and Castlerock. We thoroughly enjoyed the diversity of our adventure, including heading to Mount Ellen via the Slide Brook Express chair.

That ride was spectacular—and a tad scary. For one thing, there is a section where the lift gets high off the ground. For a second, it was a windy and cold ride. On the other hand, I didn't mind being at Nature's mercy. I like the idea that I have to pay attention and dress for the occasion—that there is a force that has to be reckoned with. To me this is part of the winter mountain experience. Since I was properly attired (including some insulating body fat) and able to cover up on the windy stretch, the frigid cold wasn't a problem for me.

But be forewarned, this is not the place for squeamish or afraid-of-heights folks. If in doubt, try the chair yourself before taking kids or the "uptight" or "nervous" on it. Better to use the free shuttle bus between the two areas than to scare the fun out of anyone. But it would make a fantastic opportunity for a marriage proposal, one you'd never forget!

We discovered some nice runs off the upper Mount Ellen chairs but left before we could explore the rest of the mountain, which I had last skied in the 1980s (we wanted to return via the Slide chair before it closed). Once back at South, we sampled the North Lynx area. Birch Run was a fun challenge for me with some big soft moguls in the setting sun. Morning Star, a nicely pitched diamond, about did me in as I was fast fading.

That night we enjoyed a wonderful stay at Tucker Hill, a restored and updated lodge with individually decorated, gracious rooms. The public places (living room, downstairs lounge, and dining room) exude the warmth and character that come from pine floors, wood furnishings, and fieldstone fireplaces. Our dinners were superb (try the crab cakes) and breakfast in the Greenhouse room was cheery despite the rainy day outside. (Jason recommends Tucker Hill for its romantic charm, noting it has red clay tennis court for summer/fall visits.)

When I returned to take a proper tour with someone from the area in February 2003, I enjoyed discovering miles and miles of interesting terrain, but what made my day extra special was the palpable friendliness. From arrival greetings to skiing with strangers to warm good-bys by Mountain Ambassadors, there was a cheerfulness that bespoke the joy of being in the mountains. Even in the base lodge, we got into discussion with someone who was visiting from out West. Somehow the old reputation had made me expect less, but this was definitely a very friendly place.

We sampled the various areas of Lincoln, and I was really wowed by how long the run on Jester was to the bottom. Skiing again off the Super Bravo lift and taking the traverse to Spring Fling was glorious with a nice run on part of Moonshine giving a taste of glades with wide spaced trees and then some real glades. Gadd Peak has great blues, with Snowball to Racer's Edge a joyful long schuss on some of the widest terrain at South.

A hot chocolate break gave me a chance to see the lodge and watch little kids going off to their classes. There was a nice hum to the whole scene and a warm feeling in the lodge. I particularly liked the original rustic decor and fieldstone fireplace.

Telemarker Jennifer Hewitt on Moonshine. KL

A Sugarbush Terrain Park Ranger floats onto the Jester trail. SR

On our ride to Mount Ellen, my guide told me about the tracks below us and explained more about Slide Brook, including how experts ski from off the North Lynx Peak into the Slide Brook Wilderness Area.

We explored all of Mount Ellen, taking a variety of blues on the upper mountain and then hooked up Rim Run to Elbow to Cruiser, an amazingly long route with a good amount of challenge.

We also visited Inverness. This area is definitely worth a look/see and ski/ride. The training hill is ultra wide but the Semi Tough trail is a hoot and holler for those who might not be proficient on narrow bump trails like *moi*. I found myself flailing and whooping it up just to get down the darn thing.

Before heading back to South, the young men who skied with us at Ellen gave us friendly hugs good-by. It gave me the "glad to share our mountain with you" feeling that a friend had described when talking about "Mount Ellen loyalists."

Back on the North Lynx area at South, we cruised Hot Shot to Waterfall, a nice steep dropoff section, where I actually enjoyed an adrenaline rush rather than fatigue—my day was that good that I felt I was starting to ski better. Or maybe it was the hugs.

I have to go back to try Castlerock, the only area I missed. I'm going to pick a midweek day when they've just had a foot and go ski the easiest trail there just to experience the place. I've listened to enough people wax poetic about this "special place" that I just have to see it. If I can ski it, great—if not, I can always bail on Troll Road and live to tell about a mountain to be reckoned with.

Good to Know

Sugarbush is located 3 miles off Vermont's Route 100 in Warren; about 18 miles from Waterbury (I-89, exit 10 or the Amtrak station); 45 minutes from Burlington International Airport; 3.5 hours (190 miles) from Boston; 3.5 hours (210 miles) from Hartford; and 6 hours (325 miles) from NYC.

New for 2005: Ski School lessons at Mount Ellen; a new affordable Mount Ellen only season pass for 5, 6, or 7 days (rates for all ages) and Mount Ellen-only single day tickets; 40 acres of gladed terrain and progressive parks at Ellen; Blazer groups for kids; Burton Learn to Ride program; and Adventure Programs designed by John and Dan Egan.

Off-site, advanced ticket sales enable the purchaser to go straight to the lifts, saving time and money. Check off-site locations on the Website.

Slide Brook Basin tours (2,000 acres accessed by lift) are available from the Guest Service Center at South. Advance reservations are recommended.

Friendly Ambassadors give free tours daily at 10:30 at both mountains. They also greet people in the parking lots, help out with questions or problems throughout the day, and wish you a fond farewell as you leave at the end of the day. The warm fuzzies are a nice touch.

The Vermont Adaptive Ski and Sports program for people with physical or mental disabilities operates out of Mount Ellen lodge (802-583-4283).

A Courtesy Shuttle (free) operates continuously, 8-4:30 daily, between Lincoln Peak area and Mount Ellen. The Mad Bus (free) runs seven days a week among the 3 ski areas and into town and shopping areas, along Route 100, Route 17 and the Sugarbush Access Road, and to the condos so people can park and ride

Mount Ellen is a great place to ski at peak times.

To beat the traffic when there's 20 inches of new snow and everyone's headed for Lincoln Peak, turn off Route 100 at the Mad Mountain Tavern (Route 17) and head for German Flats Road, the back door to an entire peak of secret stashes at Mount Ellen.

After a big dump of snow, Sugarbush has been known to open Castlerock early.

The Inverness Quad and North Lynx Triple areas offer interesting, out-of-the-way terrain and sunny slopes.

When there are crowds or busy times at South, eat at the Valley House Lodge (nice views) which has a full-service cafeteria that is underutilized because most people converge on the Gatehouse Base Lodge.

Sugarbush has lots of special events, including but not limited to: Annual Castlerock Extreme Challenge; Big Air Events; Presidents' Week festivities; races; spring celebrations including Reggae Fest, pond skimming, triathlons, mogul contests, and Easter activities.

Steals and Deals

New Mount Ellen-only ticket: $45 weekends/midweek; $49 holidays.

Stay-and-Ski-the-Valley packages begin at $69 pp; include Ole's X-C Center, Mad River Glen, and Sugarbush skiing. Call or check Website for details.

SugarCard: purchase for $59 and pay $45 for Midweek ticket, $52 for Weekends and Holidays for this Direct-to-Lift pass (connected to a credit card).

Escape Pass: 12-ticket packs for $660: must be *purchased by December 24 but* can be *reloaded at any time* throughout season (online or at Season Pass office). Cost per day is $55. Use any number of tickets any day (transferable) with no blackout dates.

College All Mountain Pass (all season): $399.

The Midweek non-holiday All Mountain Pass is $524.

The Midweek, non-holiday Mount Ellen-only pass is $374.

The Mount Ellen season pass (no restrictions) is $536.

Visit the Website for up-to-date information, specials, or call.

All phone numbers are **area code 802** unless otherwise noted.

Handy Info

Website: www.Sugarbush.com
Email: info@sugarbush.com
General information: 1-800-53-Sugar; 583-6300.
Snow report: 583-Snow.
Hours: 9 to 4 daily; Super Bravo @ Lincoln Peak: 8 to 4 and Green Mountain Express @ Mt. Ellen: 8 to 4 holidays and weekends.
Tickets 2005 Season: Adults $62 7 days a week; $65 holidays; Juniors (7-12) / Seniors (65+) $40/$42; Young Adult (13-17) $55/$59; Kids age 6 and under ski free.

Quick Stats

Season: November to April, average 160 days.
Average annual snowfall: 262 inches.
Snowmaking capability: 286 acres, 66 percent.
Lifts: 16; 7 quads (5 Express), 2 triples, 4 doubles, 3 surface (2 carpet, 1 handle tow).
Uphill lift capacity: 25,463 per hour.

Trails: 111; 508 acres; 54 miles; longest trail at South: Jester, 2.2 miles; at Mount Ellen: FIS , 2.5 miles.
Glades: 11, Eden, Murphy's, Egan's Woods, Lew's Line, Paradise, etcetera.
Bumps: FIS, Ripcord, Stein's Run, Liftline, Rumble, Castlerock Run.
Parks/Pipe: 9 parks, including progression parks, 1 pipe.
Vertical Drop:
Mount Ellen Summit to base: 2,600'
Lincoln Peak to base: 2,400'
Castlerock area: 1,600'
Gadd Peak area: 1,575'

Sugarbush Ski and Snowboard School 800-53-SUGAR

PSIA-certified instructors offer a variety of lesson options for skiers, Telemarkers, and snowboarders that include: group, private, never-evers, and powder, bumps, and steeps clinics. Adventure programs for all ages.

Women's Ski Discovery Programs are taught by women for women.

Burton Learn-to-Ride Program.

Children's Programs   reservations required

Childcare: Day Care Cubs for kids ages 6 weeks and up. Available at the Valley Daycare Center in Sugarbush Village (583-6717).

Microbears: Daycare and Intro to skiing for 3 year olds, Valley Daycare Center (583-6717).

Mini & Sugarbears meet at Gatehouse Lodge, reservations: 888-651-4827.

Minibears: ages 4-6, ski lessons and play activities, half or full day.

Sugarbears: ages 7-12, ski or ride lessons, full or half day.

Egan's Adventure Blazers; for kids looking to ski steeps, bumps, trees, parks, pipe.

Lewi's Race Blazers: focus on running gates, NASTAR, and how to set a course.

Other Things to Do

Explore Slide Brook on a guided tour; sign-up at Guest Service Center at Lincoln.

Tubbs snowshoe rentals (Guest Service Kiosk at Lincoln). Inquire about a self-guided snowshoe tour at Lincoln Peak.

The Sugarbush Health and Racquet Club at Sugarbush Village offers: Valley Rock Gym, pool,

Snowshoeing in the Mad River Valley. SR

tennis, racquetball, squash, whirlpool, saunas, steam room, massage, free weights, aerobics, and climbing wall. (583-6700).

Alta Day Spa on Main Street in Warren offers massage treatments, facials, body wrap, and beauty salon (496-2582).

Nordic skiing at: Blueberry Lake XC (31K, groomed, rentals, 496-6687); Ole's X-C Center (50 km, full service, snowshoe tours, 496-3430).

Sleigh rides, hayrides at Lareau Farm; skating at the Skatium; shopping in Waitsfield and Warren with many craft, specialty, and antiques shops.

Annual Winter Carnival in January.

For more Valley events or more info, visit www.madriver.com

Nearby attractions: Cold Hollow Cider, Ben & Jerry's in Waterbury.

The indoor climbing wall at the Health and Racquet Club is popular. with families. SR

Dining Out

In Sugarbush Village, historic Chez Henri offers lunch, après-ski, and dinners (fine French dining, authentic bistro ambiance, great wine selection), and the Phoenix Bar and Grill has good food and a lively night scene.

Heading off the mountain, Warren House (European) is a favorite with a good wine list. Further down the road, there's the Sugarbush Inn (fine dining in a gracious restored inn), The Common Man (restored barn, European dining), and The Blue Tooth (true après-ski).

The Mad River Valley offers an array of eateries (some feature takeout/full meals to go, some offer breakfast, lunch, dinner), including: American Flat Bread, Tucker Hill Inn & Restaurant, Easy Street Café, John Egan's Big World Pub and Grill, Millbrook Inn & Restaurant, The Den, Hyde Away Inn, Jay's, Michael's on the Go, The Spotted Cow, BonGiorno's, The Pitcher Inn, Valley Pizzeria, Pete's Eats, and Paradise Deli. Warren Country Store for the best breakfast burritos.

Accommodations   800-53-SUGAR;   800-828-4748

Sugarbush Village is located off to one side of the base of Sugarbush South. If you're a day skier, you could miss ever knowing it's there except for a directional sign. In addition to some 2,200 beds mountainside, there's a bedbase of 4,400 in the Mad River Valley with a diversity of lodgings from funky dorm to ultra fine. (No ski-on/ski-off lodgings at Mount Ellen.)

Après-ski/Nightlife

Chez Henri's Back Room, The Phoenix, Blue Tooth, Sugarbush Inn, the Den, Purple Moon Pub (live music, family-styled with games), and Tracks, a speak-easy type of lounge beneath the Pitcher Inn. The Eclipse for movies, live music (bands, folk, jazz), café, film festivals, and other special events. Valley Players Theater for music and live theater.

Summer/Fall

Sugarbush Village provides a convenient and idyllic location from which to explore on-mountain opportunities and The Mad River Valley via canoe, bike, or glider ride. Fishing to shopping, the region abounds with outdoor activities, special events, craft shows, and festivals.

Sugarbush features the Robert Trent Jones, Sr., 18-hole golf course; it offers beautiful, challenging terrain with long tees, large greens, and a cool mountain setting. The Sugarbush Tennis School helps players of all levels build on strengths and develop new skills and strategies. The indoor and outdoor (seasonal) hard and clay courts are available for guest use at any time.

The Sugarbush Health and Racquet Club has a skilled staff and is a good place to work out, learn a racquet sport, or relax (hot tubs, massage, Yoga).

The mountains offer hiking opportunities and a chance to explore the famous Long Trail, which passes over the various peaks of Sugarbush.

The Lincoln Gap Road is a particularly pretty, mountainous road that climbs over the Green Mountains and offers a spectacular foliage tour. Nearby Moss Glen Falls and Texas Falls Recreation Area offer thrills for all ages.

When the snow melts, the action switches gears to mountain biking, hiking, golf and racquet sports. SR

Our Sugarbush Adventure

Date:

Weather:

Companions:

Where Stayed:

Visit Highlights:

Our Discoveries:

276 Suicide Six

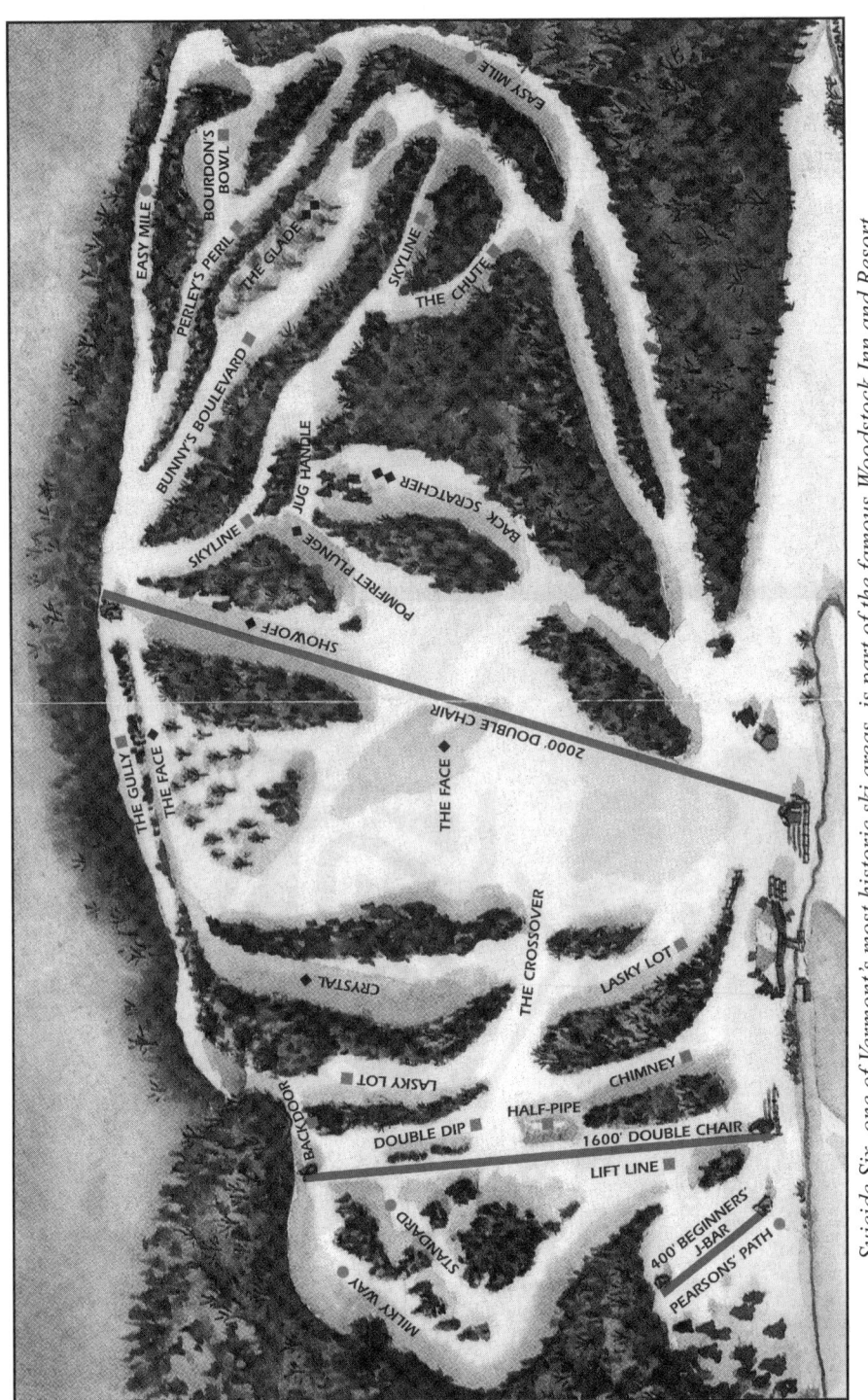

Suicide Six, one of Vermont's most historic ski areas, is part of the famous Woodstock Inn and Resort.

Chapter Eighteen

Suicide Six
Where Laughter Echoes in the Hills

Suicide Six is Vermont's oldest lift-served ski area. Located three miles from the Village of Woodstock, Suicide Six is reminiscent of early skiing when rope tows dotted farmers' pastures and skiers made the stark white hills come alive with the sounds of laughter.

Today, Suicide Six is a more modern ski area, and although it doesn't boast a big vertical, highspeed lifts, or condos, it does feature one joyous melting pot of school children, college students, local residents, racers, families, and vacationers. Together, they create a vibrant winter wonderland, turning a white snowscape into a colorful playground as they enjoy skiing, riding, racing, and jumping in the terrain park.

The excitement at Suicide Six extends from the first thrill of little ones learning to balance in wide wedges to racers honing skills straight down the Face. And it's been that way since 1937 at Suicide Six and since 1935-36 at its backside Gully slope.

Although the original rope tows have given way to chairlifts and snow farming has replaced a reliance on Mother Nature, the atmosphere here is still a warm, friendly one with a genuine sense of community and fun. Suicide Six is a small ski area that has withstood the ups and downs of the ski industry and the lure of bigger is better. Six has been able to survive where others haven't due in large part to the support of its parent company, the Woodstock Inn and Resort.

But the loyalty of locals who enjoy their home hill is also in large measure what makes this area work. It's a winning blend of community members and vacationers skiing a mountain of surprising diversity and having a good time. Success at Suicide Six is also part of the natural evolution of Woodstock's own history as a "cradle of winter sports."

As a "shire town," i.e., site of the Windsor County Courthouse, Woodstock has a long history as a thriving village where trade and commerce flourished and inns catered to guests and summer residents who sought the cool climate as an escape from hot cities. They came with steamer trunks in the 1800s, first arriving by horse and carriage and later by the Woodstock Railway. But while promoted as a summer destination during the era of the mineral springs and mountain recreation, Woodstock was exceptional in that the town also began to promote winter sports in 1892, the first in Vermont to do so.

Woodstock: Cradle of Winter Sports

That was the year the Woodstock Inn opened its doors. Built in the grand Victorian style, the Inn entertained winter guests with cross-country ski treks that started in its yard and ended up at the Country Club. The charm of this New England village and the availability of snowshoeing, ice skating, sleigh riding, and tobogganing soon attracted paying guests in winter. By 1910, the Inn had built a Winter Sports Center, including long toboggan chutes (with uphill transportation supplied by horse-drawn sleighs) and a ski jump where "hot-dog skiers" from Dartmouth College performed somersaults and simultaneous jumps—an early forerunner to freestyle.

The emphasis on winter appealed to members of the famous Appalachian Mountain Club, who arrived by the Woodstock Railway and spent time tramping around the hills on snowshoes "to explore the mountains of New England for scientific and artistic purposes" as their by-laws required of the snowshoe division. Evening treks with torches to light the way and suppers on a moonlit hilltop were romantic and popular pastimes. So was ice skating on Mount Tom or sleighing over endless networks of roads.

Woodstock brothers Leo and Allan Bourdon, who had built a ski jump at the Winter Sports Center, staged jumping matches and exhibitions. They also outfitted a bobsled with skis for runners and became known for their wild flying leaps on "ski-bobs" off the jumps. They became manufacturers of skis, bindings, and sleds that were sold as far away as Abercrombie and Fitch in New York, doing their part to make winter fun and put Woodstock on the map.

As the "ski craze" caught on in the 1930s, the hills in Woodstock and nearby towns were touted by journalists and proponents as the "best open slopes in the East." It didn't matter that these mountains were not as tall as others in Vermont and New Hampshire. Beginners didn't need steep downhill racing trails. In fact, the instructors hired by Woodstock's various inns to teach their guests this new sport preferred nice wide, gentle "open" slopes for their students.

One group of visiting skiers felt there had to be a better way to enjoy the sport than to climb up a hill for every run down. They asked their hosts, Bob and Betty Royce, the owners of the White Cupboard Inn, to look into a tow they had heard about, and they also put up funds to help get one started.

The Royces secured some design information for a rope tow that had begun operating in Shawbridge, Quebec in January 1933 and hired a mechanical engineer David Dodd from Newbury, Vermont to build their "ski-way." It debuted on Clinton Gilbert's farm on January 28, 1934, and thus began the transition in skiing from a sport for the ruggedly fit and well-to-do to a winter pastime for thousands.

Farmer Gilbert asked Wallace "Bunny" Bertram, a Dartmouth College grad, ski instructor, and coach, to set up the tow on his sheep pasture for the 1934-35 winter. Knowing that the first rope had twisted and frequently broke down, Bertram copied the pulley system of a ferris wheel, put an electric motor at the top of the hill, and operated a much-improved device which he named a "ski-tow."

His invention of the "first continually operating ski tow" in the United States deserves credit for popularizing the idea of uphill transportation and spurring the development of "ski centers" all over Vermont.

The first rope tow built for the owners of the White Cupboard Inn on Clinton Gilbert's Farm. WIR

The next season (1935-36) Bertram began his own operation at a nearby location called "The Gully." This was a south-facing expansive meadow with a higher elevation and longer, steeper slope than Gilbert's pasture. Elizabeth Fisk, who had three daughters whom she taught to ski, built a (base) lodge at the Gully and to further encourage the fun of the sport sponsored the Fisk Trophy, which became a famous annual race—now one of the oldest in the country and held on The Face by the Woodstock Ski Runners Club.

Ski history changed again, when in 1937, Bertram put a tow on the other side of the Gully, a 2,000-foot pasture slope that had been designated as "Hill #6" on topographical maps. Its steep "face" with an average gradient of 33 percent (10- to 40-degree pitch over its 2,000 foot length) and 650-foot vertical presented plenty of challenge, and liking the alliteration, Bertram named his area Suicide Six—a name that was also in keeping with dramatic names for skiing's early trails like Nose Dive, Hell's Highway, and The Thunderbolt.

During these formative years in ski history, rope tows sprouted up on hills in the Woodstock area (Mount Tom, Prosper, Gilbert's, and "Bunny's Slopes" had twelve tows by 1941) and throughout the state with some fifty "ski centers" reported by 1941.

Suicide Six

Robert Barron, former president of the Woodstock Inn and Resort, Bunny Bertram, founder of Suicide Six, and Maynard Russell, former manager of SS in 1978. WIR

In the post Depression years, skiing was regarded as a wholesome way for boys and girls, men and women to enjoy the outdoors in winter and was considered good for the morale of Vermonters who had previously had to suffer through a long, cold, dark season. Merchants and development leaders also saw the economic potential in winter and did their part to further the new craze in various towns throughout the state, often promoting their nearby ski areas in their store windows.

One year Bertram livened skiing up even more with his "rocket tow." He set up a rope tow along the top ridge with a hillock at the end and often stepped up the gas to propel skiers 50 mph or more off "the jump."

Bertram was passionate about skiing and greatly enjoyed operating his area and welcoming all ages to his slopes. Sir Arnold Lunn, who developed slalom and was a founding father of the Alpine events in the Olympics, visited Suicide Six and pronounced the wide and steep Face the "best natural slalom training hill" he had ever seen.

Racers came from far and near over the years to train and race at Suicide Six. They included Brooks Dodge, Tommy Corcoran (fourth in the 1960 Olympic Slalom), Bill Beck, Betsy Snite and many Dartmouth greats like Dick Durrance, Ted Hunter, Ed Wells, Charlie McLane, and Jack Tobin. Becky Fraser (Cremer) learned to ski as a youngster at Six and went on to race for the Middlebury College women's team and made the 1948 Olympic Team.

Bertram helped found the Woodstock Ski Runners (one of the oldest and longest continually operating ski-club programs for children in the United States), pioneered Standard races (the forerunner of NASTAR) on The Face, and held the first certification tests for U.S. ski instructors. He installed a Pomalift in 1954 and after twenty-five seasons sold the area to Laurance Rockefeller (1961), making him one of the longest continuing owner/operators of a ski area in Vermont. In 1980, Bertram was elected to the U.S. Ski Hall of Fame in recognition of his many contributions to the sport of skiing.

Suicide Six now operates as a part of the famous Woodstock Inn and Resort and has grown to 23 trails served by 2 chairlifts and a beginner J-Bar. Suicide Six was one of the first ski areas to welcome snowboarders and hosted the first U.S. Snowboarding Open in 1982. Being owned by the Woodstock Inn and Resort provides a unique advantage that has helped this small ski area carve its niche as a family-friendly area and recreational resource. With abundant accommodations available at the Woodstock Inn and other places nearby, there is no need to develop condos or a resort village and the area continues to operate as an old-fashioned ski hill. Additionally, guests of the Woodstock Inn are treated to complimentary skiing midweek, making the area a most unusual amenity to a very historic inn.

The Hill

Suicide Six offers a great variety of trails and slopes on its 100 acres of terrain. There is the mega-wide steep "open" slope on the main face (logically called The Face) as well as the "hidden" terrain of the even wider (but gentler) Gully beyond the summit. There are classic New England type trails, liftline runs, challenging glades, and a small terrain park and halfpipe for snowboarders.

Suicide Six has a quarter-mile-wide, 1,200-foot-tall summit with lovely views to Mount Ascutney to the southeast and in all directions to valleys below and hills beyond. Its broad ridgeline makes it easy for people to congregate at the top and decide whether to ski the front side or wind around to the back where you can still ski all-natural snow on the wondrous Gully.

Six also features a large, full-service base lodge, professional ski instruction for all ages, and state-of-the-art grooming and snowmaking technology, including tower guns. The base lodge, built in the late 1970s, is an architectural marvel with a striking fieldstone fireplace and soaring glass facade that affords dramatic views of the straight-up Face.

Beginner/Novice ●

Beginners have a gentle 400-foot J-Bar and wide open Bunny Slope to learn on. There is a nice progression to the nearby 1,600-Foot Double Chair (its actual name on the trail map), which goes up higher but not quite to the top. It gives access to two smooth trails: Milky Way and Standard.

Novices can also take the 2,000-Foot (summit) Chair and enjoy the Easy Mile trail (●) for a nice, wide meandering run that brings them back to the lift. The Gully, while steeper and rated blue, offers another possible route that advanced novices will find fun and doable because it is so wide.

Intermediate ■

The Lift Line below the 1600 Chair is a straight down blue trail and the Double Dip is an interesting blue that leads to Snowboarder Heaven (■) and

Three skiers on the top of the famous Face. before it plunges down into the valley. WIR

the small halfpipe or back to the lift for great warm-up runs.

The summit chair affords a 650-foot vertical drop for every run with several choices for intermediates from the top. The Gully to Back Door to Laskey Lot and Chimney provides a very interesting long run with lots of terrain variations and scenery changes and is blue all the way.

Skyline (■) is a classic and while narrow, it offers a nicely pitched challenge that skiers can really improve on. Perley's Peril, Bunny's Boulevard, and Chute are wider blues that provide ample variety and nice runs even for advanced skiers on the front side.

Advanced/Expert   ◆

Advanced skiers will find The Face (◆) gives a number of different possible routes and its wide-spaced trees at the top allow for a taste of glades. The overall 33 percent gradient makes The Face a challenging fun run. The Crystal (a nearby trail with similarly steep pitch), Showoff (narrow under the chair, often with bumps), and Pomfret Plunge (short but steep) are all diamonds that can be trickier than they look. The Glade (◆◆) and Back Scratcher (◆◆) take the challenge up a notch, making the area fun for advanced and expert skiers.

Zippiddy Do Dahs

My nephew and I discovered a cheerful playground on our visit on a bright February Friday of Presidents' Week. There were the sounds of birds chirping and a lift attendant was dressed for the occasion in shorts and sandals—one of the few warm afternoons of a record-setting cold Vermont winter (2003).

We started with the gentle green and lower intermediate blue trails off the 1600-Foot Double. They were interesting and boasted a pipe on one of them— "good for families," Geoff commented, noting it wasn't huge.

He couldn't resist trying the J-Bar and pronounced it a "piece of cake." He was worried when he saw the line at the summit chair, but he soon learned that looks can be deceiving as we boarded within six minutes.

While riding the lift up The Face, we became aware of the sounds of giggles and laughter—it came from a hill echo, a unique reverberation of the people on the lift and trails. Spread out below, we saw some wide-tracked snowplowers descending straight down the tough Face. Watching them got us to giggling. More awesome were the graceful experts—some dancing in the bumps, others gliding effortlessly down the slope, and yet others cruising it. They were inspiring for their smoothness, especially given the varying conditions from soft to slick, smooth to bumps.

On another ride up, we found ourselves giggling again, this time at the sight of some plucky skiers trying to negotiate the narrow and steep Showoff. It reminded us of our own sorry run when the bumps proved tough. Our laughter was a nervous acknowledgment that even a small mountain can rule!

Geoffrey Ballou tries out the ski chair at the top of Suicide Six. Good use for old skis! KL

On our tour of the historic Gully (much, much wider than it looks on the map), we discovered a humongous bowl of soft snow that ended at a neat trail called the Back Door. It took us through the dark woods and back to the base area over some interesting terrain (the Crossover) with several choices of cutoffs and trees to duck around.

Geoff found some small jumps at the upper section of the Gully so we went back several times, and I never retraced my tracks as I GS'ed this ultra-wide slope—no wonder Bunny had three tows operating here at one time!

As we skied all over, Geoff discovered the glades (he pronounced them "pretty good" which means they weren't easy) while I enjoyed running Bunny's Boulevard, Skyline, Perley's Peril, and Bourdon's Bowl—all interesting with turns, undulations, sidehills, and varying widths, some with bumps. The Face was challenging, as I knew it would be, but its width made it fun. The only trail we skipped was Back Scratcher—problems on Pomfret and Showoff made us wary so we played it smart and got our fill of The Face instead.

Good to Know

Suicide Six is located on Stage Road about ten minutes north of Woodstock; 2.5 hours from Boston, 3 from Hartford, and 5 from NYC.

There is a display of the history of Suicide Six (and Gilbert's Hill) in the base lodge—a great opportunity to learn more about our fascinating sport. The photos make you appreciate modern equipment and technology.

The base lodge offers good food in the cafeteria, and The Lounge affords slopeside dining with views of The Face. The food here is very good.

Six is home to local school children's learn-to-ski programs with some 300 students from nearby schools participating. They celebrate their season with their own March Carnival with races, scavenger hunts, and special treats.

Woodstock is a quintessential New England town, complete with a covered bridge, working farms you can visit, and lots of opportunity for fun exploration, shopping and great dining.

Steals and Deals

Two-for-One Tuesdays (non-holiday). Buy one ticket and get one free.

Ski Vermont Free Program: Guests staying at the Woodstock Inn, arriving any night Sunday through Thursday, enjoy free midweek skiing at both Suicide Six and the X-C Center. Guests staying over Sunday nights can also ski free on Sundays. Call or check the Website for family packages and other savings.

Phone numbers below are **area code 802** unless otherwise noted.

Handy Info:

Website: www.woodstockinn.com
Email: www.woodstockinn.com
General information: 457-6661
Snow report: 457-6666
Hours: 9-4 daily.
Tickets 2005: Adults $29 midweek, $50 weekends/holidays. Juniors (14 and under)/Seniors (65+) $23/$34. Beginner J-Bar only ticket $7.

Quick Stats

Season: mid-December to late March, average 100 days.
Average annual snowfall: 100 inches.
Snowmaking capability: 50 percent; 50 acres.
Lifts: 3; 2 doubles, 1 J-Bar.
Uphill lift capacity: 3,000 per hour.
Trails; 23; 100 acres; longest 1 mile.
Glades: 2 The Glade (♦♦) and top of The Face.
Bumps: Showoff.
Vertical Drop: 650'

Ski School

Group and private lessons available from professional instructors. Learn-to-Ski-or-Snowboard packages, including clinics for older adults (or any age) learning to snowboard.

Children's Programs

Daycare: not available; but sitter service is available and arranged through the Woodstock Inn concierge for hotel guests.

Children's program for any preschool children midweek, part day.

Other Things to Do

Tubing and sliding on Mount Tom just down the road from Suicide Six.

Cross-country skiing and snowshoeing at the Woodstock Ski Touring Center (457-6674); 60 km of groomed trails utilize a century-old system of carriage roads. Guided tours, lessons, rentals available. Wilderness Trails X-C Center for snowshoeing and X-C (18 km) in nearby Quechee at the Quechee Inn at Marshland Farm. Tobogganing, ice skating, sleigh rides are all available in the Woodstock area.

Work out at the Woodstock Inn's Health and Fitness Center (457-6656). Racquet sports include tennis, paddle tennis, racquetball, and squash. Large pool, Nautilus fitness center with full range of exercise and aerobics equipment. Steamroom, whirlpool, sauna and massage; restaurant.

Woodstock has 3 churches with Revere Bells, Historical Society Museum (457-1822), art galleries, Gillingham's Country Store, and boutiques to explore.

Visit a real working farm year round at the Sugarbush Farm (457-1757).

The Billings Farm and Museum (457-2355) offers a glimpse of a working dairy farm and a farm-life museum. It is open on select winter dates and throughout the summer (fee). This is a "must visit" with a nice museum shop.

Don't miss the Ottauquechee Valley Winery (next to Quechee Gorge) or Long Trail Brewing Company in West Bridgewater.

Nearby, shop at Quechee Gorge for gifts, food, wine and antiques and visit the Antique Mall at Quechee Gorge Village and the Toy and Train Museum (fee)—both educational fun and walks down memory lane for all ages.

More shopping at Old Mill Marketplace in Bridgewater, Village of Quechee, and nearby in White River Junction.

Other nearby attractions include: Vermont Institute of Natural Science and Raptor Center on Route 4 in Quechee (457-1052); Montshire Museum (649-2200), and King Arthur Baker's Store (800-827-6836) in Norwich.

Try a ride in a hot-air balloon. Balloons Over New England (800-788-5562) and Balloons of Vermont (291-4887) operate year round out of Quechee.

Dining Out

There's a great variety of cuisine in Woodstock, including: the main dining room (4 diamonds) or Eagle Café (informal) at the Woodstock Inn, Bentley's Restaurant and Café, Prince and the Pauper, Mangowood in the Lincoln Inn, Dave's Country Kitchen, Maplefields (deli, eat in/take out), Pizza Chef, New

England Steakhouse, The Village Inn, Wild Grass Restaurant, Mountain Creamery, and the Jackson House Inn.

In South Woodstock, the Kedron Valley Inn offers fine dining.

Quechee: Quechee Inn at Marshland Farm (exquisite gourmet dining), Simon Pearce Restaurant, Parker House, Black Angus Café at the Quality Inn, Firestones (wood-fired flatbread pizza to gourmet dinners), Farina Family Diner, Sakura Island (Chinese, Japanese; eat-in/take-out) and Pizza Chef.

Barnard: Inn at Chelsea Farm, Barnard Inn Restaurant, Maple Leaf Inn.

White River Junction: Café Coolidge at the Coolidge Hotel, Como Va (Italian), China Moon (buffet style), and A.J.'s Steakhouse (great salad bar).

Hartland: Skunk Hollow Tavern (casual pub fare and fine dining).

Accommodations

The Woodstock Inn (800-448-7900) is a first-class hotel with award-winning cuisine and an array of fine rooms and suites; amenities include free use of Fitness and Health Center facilities year round. A free shuttle van transports skiers to Suicide Six, the Touring Center, and the Health and Fitness Center.

There are a number of motels, fine B & B's, inns, hotels, and lodges within a 20-mile radius, including towns of Woodstock, Bridgewater, Quechee, Barnard, and White River Jct./Hartford.

Woodstock area Chamber of Commerce: 457-3555; 888-4Woodstock.

Hartford Area Chamber of Commerce: 295-7900; 800-295-5451.

Après-ski/Nightlife

At the Inn, Richardson's Tavern offers cozy cocktails by the fire with entertainment on weekends. Open Mike Night Thursdays at Firestones. Skunk Hollow Tavern features local bands on weekends. Après-ski at many local restaurants. Check local newspapers for concerts, theater, and other events.

Summer/Fall

The Woodstock Inn and Resort offers golf and tennis and all the activities of the Health and Fitness Center plus indoor and outdoor pools. The Woodstock area abounds with hiking trails, and mountain biking is an option on Mt. Tom and on any number of the old carriage roads and trails.

Local attractions include the Billings Farm and Museum and the Marsh–Billings–Rockefeller National Historical Park (only national park to focus on conservation history and the evolving nature of land stewardship).

Woodstock hosts festivals, art exhibits, special events, performances, and walking tours of the village throughout the summer and fall.

Nearby, there are many intriguing places to explore, from Quechee Gorge, Vermont's 'little Grand Canyon' to the Coolidge Homestead and Cheese Factory in historic Plymouth Notch.

Our Suicide Six Adventure

Date:

Weather:

Companions:

Where Stayed:

Visit Highlights:

Our Discoveries:

Appendix A

Essentials To Good Mountain Times

Here's a quick review of some mountain essentials. Experienced skiers, snowboarders, and Telemarkers might want to share this section with people they bring to the sport. Knowing and adhering to Your Responsibility Code makes the outdoor experience more enjoyable for all people through common courtesy and consideration as well as through individual accountability.

Your Responsibility Code

1. Always stay in control and be able to stop or avoid other people or objects.
2. People ahead of you have the right of way. It is your responsibility to avoid them.
3. You must not stop where you obstruct a trail or are not visible from above.
4. Whenever starting downhill or merging onto a trail, look uphill and yield to others.
5. Always use devices to help prevent runaway equipment.
6. Observe all posted signs and warnings. Keep off closed trails and out of closed areas.
7. Prior to using any lift, you must have the knowledge and ability to load, ride, and unload safely.
8. Vermont State Law requires that you give your name to a ski area employee before you leave the vicinity if you are involved in a collision resulting in an injury.

More Tips to help reduce risk and have a more enjoyable experience:

❖ It's a good idea to learn the rudiments of a snowsport, whether riding, skiing or Telemarking from a competent person who is able to impart the safety considerations and responsibilities listed above and help with such things as getting on the lift correctly. Professional ski instruction is so good today that it makes sense to invest a little time and money into the development of skills that will help you to become more competent and enjoy the sport more.

❖ When skiing an area new to you, look at and use a trail map and warm up on a slope or trail that is below your ability level so you can get to know the general type of terrain, its level of difficulty, and conditions at that area.

❖ Ski and ride in areas compatible with your ability. *Never take family members or friends down trails beyond their abilities.*

❖ Ski with a buddy and take a rest when you become tired.

❖ Don't overlook the value of getting into shape, especially if you are sedentary. Leg strengthening and agility exercises along with aerobic activity like walking several times a week will contribute to your enjoyment of the slopes and may help prevent injury. Stretch before you begin skiing or riding.

❖ Be sure your equipment is in good condition and properly tuned; wear appropriate clothing for the weather; and consider the use of a helmet. See Appendix C (page 298) for more information on helmets.

❖ For freestylers and riders who enjoy the challenges of a park or pipe, it's also important to familiarize yourself with the instructions and warnings of any freestyle terrain or pipe prior to use. In addition to Your Responsibility Code, the following are some basics to your safety and enjoyment.

Freestyle Terrain Responsibility

1. All terrain park elements and landings should be inspected prior to use.
2. Wait your turn and let others know when you are dropping in.
3. Have a spotter tell you when the feature and its landing are clear.
4. Never stop within the feature's in-run, takeoff, deck, landing or outrun.
5. Be sure your ability and speed are appropriate for each feature.
6. Perfect your skills on smaller features before attempting larger ones.
7. It is your responsibility to control your body in the air.

Equipment

If you own equipment, remember to check and repair or adjust bindings, edges, and running surfaces (or have done by a ski shop) regularly or at least annually. Update your weight or skill level changes for binding adjustments.

If in the market for new equipment, be sure to describe yourself, the type of trails you ski, and your goals to the shop person. It's okay to say you are timid, aggressive, have physical problems, or want to be a competitor. The more they know about you, the better they can steer you to the equipment that is right for you and your style of skiing or riding.

There's equipment specifically made for women (lower center of gravity and mass than men have), so consider buying or renting a woman's ski.

If you are a beginner, you do not need or want the most expensive skis in the shop (get a good learning ski). Look for the best possible fit in boots because a poor or improper fit will affect your ability to progresss and be comfortable.

Consider last year's models of boots or boards if budget constraints are a factor. You may be able to get great bargains on older models or on stock reductions or sale of demo or rental equipment. Shop the sales and save!

Learn about what's available and what advances might be good for you. The new lighter ski poles are wonderful for those with arthritic hands, for example.

Clothing

If you dress correctly, you can be comfortable on the most frigid of days. Here's a quick *primer* for those who get cold easily or those new to the sport.

High-tech clothing is great and helps keep you warm and dry. The principle is to dress in layers so you can add more when it's very cold or take a layer off when you're too warm. By dressing in layers, it is possible to ski at 36 below zero in comfort! Buy large enough to allow for those layers and movement!

Ski clothing can be expensive, or inexpensive when purchased on sale. It is an investment that can last you many many years with proper care. Look for sales, especially at the end of the season, during the summer, or early fall. (Take a trip to a Vermont ski area during foliage and you can find tremendous ski sales.) Check out the ski magazines for informative articles and inquire about fabrics (waterproof, breathable, wicking action) and features of a garment (vents, hoods, closures, pockets, etcetera) in the ski shops.

Fashion is a form of function and anything goes on the slopes these days, but jeans and sweatshirts will not keep you warm and dry! Ski or snowboarder clothing makes a good gift for holidays and birthdays. One's snowsport wardrobe should contain these basic items:

1. Good long underwear - thermal tops (or t-necks) and bottoms ('longjohns') that wick moisture away from the skin are a must because they will keep you drier and warmer. (Cotton is a 'no-no' because it absorbs moisture.)
2. Insulated ski pants or bibs to wear over thermal long underwear; or shell pants (of waterproof fabric) and fleece pants to wear underneath them.
3. A good insulated parka (jacket) to wear with pants or bibs. A one-piece ski suit is an alternative to jacket and pants/bibs.
4. A good hat or helmet - it's important to cover your head so as not to lose body heat. See Appendix C for helmet information.
5. Waterproof, insulated ski mitts or gloves to keep hands warm and dry.
6. A neck gaiter - a fleece tube that you can pull up over your chin and lower face when it's really cold out; it's less bulky and safer than a scarf.
7. Goggles - eye protection is important; orange lenses are good all-purpose lenses for a range of light conditions (flat to bright).
8. Good ski socks with wicking action to keep your feet dry and toasty.
9. Thin sweaters of wool or blends and/or a fleece pullover or vest. Fleece vests can be worn over a sweater and under a jacket for added warmth.

Optional: hand and foot warmers (small packets that you put inside your mitts or boots). They really work, cost a few dollars, and are well worth it for the coldest days. Heaters for boots are another (more expensive) option.

Appendix B

Glossary

Trail Marking Symbols ● ■ ♦ ♦♦

These symbols are designations of the level of difficulty of the trails, slopes and glades at a ski area. [There are no exact criteria that areas go by to mark their trails although there are some guidelines.] The symbols indicate *the relative difficulty of the terrain at that area only*.

The green circle ● is defined as an easier (or least difficult) trail, the blue square ■ as more difficult, and the black diamond ♦ as most difficult. What is green at one area may be blue at another. It depends on any given mountain's natural contours and steepness (some mountains are rounded and have less steep terrain and others are more straight down and steep) and the goals of the trail designers who work with those contours. Some bulldoze a trail 'flat' with no sidehills while others adhere to the natural contours and allow all the sidehills or double fall lines to challenge the skier or rider.

● A green solid circle indicates gentle terrain that beginners and novices can handle. You might find trails have a gradient of 5 - 25 %. (See page 294 for an explanation of steepness.) A green off the top of a mountain is seldom the same as the green at the base where you learn to ski or ride. Upper mountain greens usually require the ability to stop and turn, which translates to skiing in control and having some experience (like a couple of days to a week on snow). The width of the trail makes a difference—wider is easier.

■ A blue square symbol indicates more or moderate difficulty, more steepness to the trail (probably 20-40% gradient), maybe more undulations and double fall lines. These trails may be green if only looking at steepness but marked blue because they are narrow and winding. Blues indicate that more skill is needed to negotiate them and have a good time. They loosely translate to intermediate ability level (stem turns to parallel skiing). You may see novices making wedge turns (snowplowing in the old lingo) and getting down with some difficulty on a blue trail or an expert gliding down effortlessly in a fast cruise. The latter person is not technically challenged by that trail, but they can still have fun on it! And, if a young kid, the snowplower is probably having fun, too!

♦ A black diamond indicates the most difficult terrain at an area. It is steeper (most likely 40 percent gradient or better) and may have a variety of snow conditions, double fall lines, bumps, glades, tight trees, or be narrow —all demand the exact turning and stopping skills and keen judgment of advanced skiers.

♦♦ A double diamond is for experts only; it's very steep (probably 51-80% gradient) and may also have extreme terrain conditions like rocks, chutes, cliffs, waterfalls, or trees. This terrain is for riders and skiers with expert ability to handle anything and the nerve to do it. Or it may be so narrow that there is no choice of where to turn—you have to commit to ski or ride it.

REMINDER: Because mountains differ, it's best to get to know a mountain by starting on trails below your ability level. Think of it as a wise warm-up and a great way to enjoy the scenery and get your day off to a fun start.

Skier Levels

Today, most ski areas use a number system to designate skier levels for ski school purposes (from one to nine) and they have definitions of skills for each level. However, it is helpful to use the old terminology of beginners, novices, intermediates, advanced and experts to describe ability level when talking about skiing in general. Also, these designations loosely translate to the trail symbols and trail designers take their skills into consideration when developing and laying out a trail.

'Never-Ever' - a first-time skier or snowboarder, as in "day one" on the slopes; ski lingo for first timer.

Beginner - someone out on their second or later day and still learning the basics of straight running, turning, and stopping. Snowboarders are learning to slide in a straight run, stop and turn.

Novice - a skier who can make a basic wedge turn and stop and ski in control (stop when they want to stop and turn where they want to or need to so as to avoid another person or an object). Novices usually have had several days of experience and are off the "bunny" or beginner hill and tackling the area's various green circle trails. Snowboarders are making skidded turns and side slipping with both feet.

Intermediate - skiers are advancing with stem turns (a parallel traverse and wedge turn) and can handle blue squares. Advanced intermediates are making parallel turns and can handle more varied terrain (steeper or with sidehills and moguls) with good control and a variety of speeds.

Intermediate snowboarders - the skills to ride progress from basics of stopping and turning with skidded turns to being able to make rounded and controlled turns in both directions and handle more terrain variations. Advanced intermediates are beginning to make carved turns and vary their speed and turns while still riding in control and can handle steeper terrain.

Advanced skier - someone who can make short and long radius parallel turns; a good advanced skier can handle almost any terrain (not necessarily bump trails, glades, or super steeps if they prefer not to do them) including black diamonds in most snow conditions. They can also carve turns versus skid them. The carved turn uses the dynamics of the new shaped ski to do much of the work that the body and legs used to have to do to make the older, straighter skis turn.

Advanced snowboarders have mastered a variety of turn shapes and speeds, and can carve turns and handle varied terrain in all snow conditions. They may or may not choose to tackle terrain parks and pipes, but they can handle diamonds. Many enjoy getting air in the parks and pipes.

Experts - they can do it all on anything with comfort although they may opt out of bumps, trees, parks and pipes for personal reasons of not being into "adventure" stuff. Experts, whether skier or snowboarder, have excellent skills and judgment along with the ability to handle all terrain (including "the truly steep") and conditions with finesse and grace at a variety of speeds.

Extreme skier or rider - one who likes trees, bumps, chutes, rocks, and cliffs, *the steeper the better (gradients of 80%+)*. Extreme skiers and riders thrill to the challenge of "impossible stuff" and relish the opportunity to go *off piste* or backcountry.

Ski and Snowboard School

There are many different names for what used to be referred to as ski lessons and ski school. Today, the terms coaching and clinics are often used to get away from the old way of learning by lining up and doing drills. There is no comparison with the way skiing is taught today to the 1950s or 1960s. Teaching techniques have changed drastically as boards have changed and improved.

Another difference is that today the *focus is on fun*, and you are asked what you want to accomplish or why you are taking a lesson or clinic. The teacher takes your comfort level into consideration and does not push you to do something that will make you afraid or uncomfortable. They figure out whether you are a cerebral learner (you process information and then do the maneuvers) or if you are someone who learns by doing and needs more trail time and less talk. They also are trained to recognize problems whether psychological or physical and know ways to help you with them (euphemistically called "digging into their bag of tricks"). The magic is that those "tricks" often work! Resulting 'breakthroughs' can be pure heaven!

Usually, a person enrolled in clinics or classes advances fairly quickly, and someone taking a ski week with a daily lesson might go from 'never-ever' to beginner to novice in one week. Lessons or coaching will improve your skills and help you to have more fun more quickly—highly recommended for all ability levels. Even advanced skiers can learn new tricks, like how to handle moguls or trees or carve and have more fun!

Learn-to-ski-or-ride packages combine lesson, equipment rental, and lift ticket for an introduction to skiing or riding. Usually, the package is a good deal (costs less than if you were to rent, take a lesson, and purchase a lift ticket separately) and is the best way to learn to ski or ride. They come in one-day, two-day and multi-day packages at many areas.

Learn-to-ski weeks combine a daily lesson for 5, 6, or 7 days with time to practice what you learned. They often also include activities for après-ski fun and social events. It's a quick way to learn and improve.

Ski packages and ski weeks for experienced skiers are particularly good deals when you can get away midweek and often include après-ski activities.

Steepness: Gradient and Pitch

Gradient is a term used to indicate the steepness of a trail; it's a ratio of the rise (vertical) to the run (horizontal length of trail). Engineers and trail designers work in percentages (ratios of rise to run) which is why we most often see trail steepness expressed in percentages rather than degrees.

Degrees are also used to describe a trail's pitch (the degree of slope or inclination). The pitch of a trail is the angle formed by the trail and run. A trail with a 45° pitch has a 100 % gradient. Not only is that rare at U.S. ski areas, it is so steep that it is hard to stand on it.

Gradient Degrees
20% = 11.3°
30% = 16.7°
40% = 21.8°
50% = 26.5°
60% = 31°
70% = 35°
80% = 38.6°
90% = 42°
100% = 45°

Gradients (percentages) do not exactly correlate to black diamonds or blue squares — those symbols describe a trail's difficulty relative to other trails at that same mountain or skiing area. One resort's blues may be black at another area. Or if a mountain has several skiing areas, a blue at one lift area may be much harder than a blue at another lift area. Furthermore, a trail with a 30% gradient would normally be considered as intermediate in difficulty, but in the trees it becomes tough and may be labeled black diamond; or if the trees are tight and moguls big, double diamond.

Gradients pertain to the overall trail (it's an average), and there may be some much *steeper sections as well as some flatter parts* on that trail. Longer steeps make you work harder (up the pulse rate) than shorter ones, but both can give an adrenaline rush! If narrow, or bumped up, they're twice as hard!! The length of the trail makes a difference—not all steeps are a mile long.

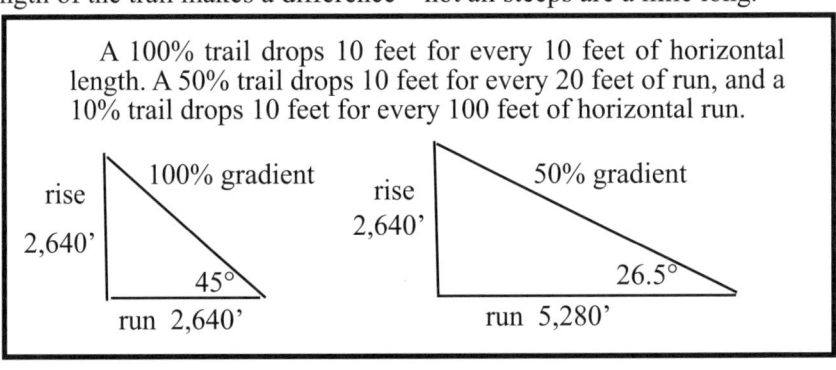

A 100% trail drops 10 feet for every 10 feet of horizontal length. A 50% trail drops 10 feet for every 20 feet of run, and a 10% trail drops 10 feet for every 100 feet of horizontal run.

rise 2,640' 100% gradient 45° run 2,640'

rise 2,640' 50% gradient 26.5° run 5,280'

Skier level	Trail Gradient	Snowboarder level	Trail Gradient
On-snow orientation	0-4%		
First Timers	5-10%	First Time Beg	5-8%
Beginner	9-12%	Beginner	9-12%
Adv. Beginner	13-20%	Novice	13-20%
Novice	Up to 25%	Low Intermediate	Up to 25%
Low Intermediate	Up to 30%	Intermediate	Up to 30%
Intermediate	Up to 40%	Adv. Intermediate	Up to 40%
Adv. Intermediate	Up to 50%	Expert	Up to 50%
Expert	51-80%	Adv. Expert	51-80%
Extreme	Above 80%	Extreme	Above 80%

These specifications are from the Handbook for trail design, courtesy of the SE Group, a planning firm specializing in ski-area design for over 45 years. [Note that snowboarders advance more quickly (steeper learning curve)]. Not all ski areas use these exact specs, but the info gives us an idea of what we ski.

Samples of Vermont's steepest terrain include: Paradise (89%), Chute (83%) at Mad River; Ripcord (70-80%) at Mount Snow; Ovation (60%), Outer Limits (51%), Downdraft and Double Dipper (53%), Superstar (50%) at Killington; Goat (50%), Starr (40%) at Stowe; Freefall (54%), Bootlegger's (46.5%) at Smugglers'; Upper Doug's (50%), the Ledges (43%), UpperWarren's (42%) at Burke; Stein's Run (48%), Ripcord (48%), Rumble (40%), Lift Line (43%) at Sugarbush. Some trails have *steep sections* like Vortex and Quantum Leap at Okemo (50%); Allen Slope at Snow Bowl (100%); top of Devil's Fiddle (60-100%) at Killington; or top of Black Hole (65-70%) at Smugglers.' At Stowe, there are lots of *steep sections*: Nosedive has sections that range in pitch from 15-33°, National from 24-36°, Starr 21-43°, Goat 20-36°, Lookout 21-34°, Hayride 25-35°, Lift Line 11-35°, and Lord 9-31° (see gradient/degree chart).

Fall line

The fall line is the steepest way down from any point on a trail. If you drop a marble, it will roll down the fall line. Sometimes the fall line drops straight down the trail. However, mountains also have sidehills—if you look to your right or left, you may see the hill drop away from you in that direction. If it is dropping sideways *and* also straight ahead, that is referred to as a **double fall line**. Skiing is more difficult when you're dropping two ways as you descend. Some areas grade their terrain, or some of it, to have one fall line. Others follow the natural contours of the mountain, thus creating a trail with more natural undulations and sidehills and therefore much more challenge.

Vertical

A mountain's overall vertical is the difference between the *summit elevation of the top lift* and the *base elevation of the lowest point you can ski to*. At most mountains you don't ski this total overall vertical for every run. Often the expert terrain is on the upper mountain, so experts ski less than the overall or advertised vertical. This holds true for beginners also. Many ski resorts put the vertical for their respective mountain areas (each lift-served area) on their trail maps. Generally, the greater the vertical, the longer the trails. Shorter trails with big verts mean steep stuff and extra-long trails with big verts signal gentle terrain. Many times, the longer the trails, the more lift rides to obtain them.

The chart below lists total verticals for each ski area first and other "big verts" at the specified lift-served skiing next. The number of rides to attain a vertical is given along with ability level of top-to-bottom (TB) trails served. The last column lists trails served that are not top-to-bottom for that vertical.

Ski Area	Greatest Verticals	# Lift Rides	Trails Served	Trails Not TB
Killington	3050'	2	●■	♦ ♦♦
Skyeship Gondola	2520'	1	●■	♦ ♦♦
K-1 Gondola	1642'	1	●♦	■ ♦♦
Sugarbush Mt. Ellen	2600'	2	■	●♦ ♦♦
Lincoln Peak	2400'	2	■	●♦ ♦♦
Castlerock lift area	1600'	1	♦	■ ♦♦
Stowe	2360'	2	●	■
Gondola	2160'	1	■	♦ ♦♦
ForeRunner Quad	2055'	1	●■	♦ ♦♦
Jay Peak	2153'	1		●■♦
Flyer Quad	1614'	1		●■ ♦
Smugglers' Notch	2610'	2		●■♦ ♦♦
Madonna Mt.	2130'	1	■♦	♦♦ ♦♦♦
Mad River Glen	2037'	1	♦	●■
Sunnyside Double	1405'	1	●■	♦
Stratton	2003'	1	●	■♦ ♦♦
Okemo/Jackson Gore	2200'	4	■	●♦ ♦♦
Okemo Mt.	2053'	2	●	■♦
Northstar Express	1763'	1	●■	♦
Burke	2000'	2		●■♦ ♦♦
Upper Mt. Quad area	1600'	1	■♦	♦♦
Ascutney	1800'	2		●■♦ ♦♦
Upper Mt. Quad area	1700'	1	■♦	● ♦♦
Mount Snow	1700'	1	●■	♦
Magic	1650'	1	●	■♦ ♦♦
Bolton Valley	1634'	3		●■♦ ♦♦
Ricker Peak	1030'	1		●■♦
Pico	1967'	2	■	●■♦
Summit Express	1567'	1	■	♦
Bromley	1334'	1	●■	♦ ♦♦
Bear Creek	1300'	1	●■♦	
MC Snow Bowl	1050'	1	●■♦	
Suicide Six	650'	1	●■♦	

Glades/tree skiing

The term "glade" refers to skiing among the trees. By definiton a glade is an opening in the woods or forest, so you may still see some old trails named as a glade that are actually cleared trails (or being renamed to avoid confusion). Today, gladed terrain refers to forests with openings among the trees that allow skiers and riders to weave their way through. The trails designated as glades at ski areas have been brushed out and dead trees have been removed to create a skiing or riding experience. It is also commonly referred to as tree skiing. "Open" glades have a lot of space between the trees and "tight" do not—some areas differentiate by calling the latter tree skiing. Glades are not groomed; they offer natural snow and bumps often build up and in combination with the trees and any natural hazards create a type of skiing/riding that demands more skill, control, energy, and focus to successfully negotiate the run.

Off Piste and Backcountry

Off piste is French for off the trail. As used in this book, *off piste* refers to skiing off the ski area's marked trails and glades but within the ski area's legal boundaries. *Off piste* entails skiing the mountain in its natural state—terrain that's not been cleared of brush or anything else so it contains more obstacles like rocks, cliffs, frozen waterfalls, fallen branches, or dead trees that are snow covered or not.

"Backcountry" refers to out-of-bounds skiing or riding; that is, going beyond or outside a ski area's boundaries. See Appendix D for more information on *off piste* and backcountry options as well as risks and responsibilities.

All-terrain, boundary-to-boundary, or off-piste policy

An area with this policy offers the opportunity for skiing and riding within the ski area's boundaries, not only on its designated trails and glades (marked on the map) but also in all the forest and mountainous terrain that is within the boundaries *that is not marked as closed*. Such a policy will usually be found on the ski area's trail map. Note that you assume all responsibility for your safety and well being if you choose to take advantage of this option which comes with inherent risks. See Appendix D for some areas with this option.

Terrain Parks and Halfpipes

Terrain parks have features or elements like hips, spines, rolls, table-tops, and ramp jumps for freestyle skiers and riders to enjoy. They require advanced skills and should be learned in parks with smaller features before tackling the big parks. Halfpipes are snow or ground excavated U-shaped terrain that may be located in or near parks or off by themselves. They offer a way for skiers and riders to *get air* and do maneuvers that take the excitement and thrills up a notch. Superpipes are longer and have higher walls of 17 to 22 feet.

Appendix C

Helmets: Added Protection But No Guarantee

One of the hottest trends and issues in snowsports concerns the use of a helmet. Although helmets have been around for many years, the deaths of a young girl from a collision with another skier and those of Sonny Bono and Michael Kennedy (from hitting trees) brought national attention to their use for snowsports in recent years. The results include: studies that confirm helmets' injury-preventing and life-saving potential under certain conditions; more educational efforts; more recreational skiers and snowboarders wearing them; and debate over making them mandatory.

Snowsport head injuries can occur through a collision with another person or an object such as a tree or from a fall. During the impact, the brain's forward motion decelerates within the skull, deforming it as it does so, and then shakes back. It's an action with effects like those of shaken-baby syndrome, says Dr. Stewart Levy, a Colorado neurological surgeon and helmet researcher/advocate, who adds that little tears can occur during this process deep within the brain (the white matter) and shape changes can take place as well.

A helmet can protect against brain injury in two ways. One is by deflecting the blow and dissipating the energy. The helmet's EPS (expanded polystyrene) or Zorbium foam padding does this by absorbing energy and slowing the rate of the brain's deceleration. Dr. Levy stressed that "speed matters and by changing velocity, the helmet can reduce concussions, brain tears, and subdural hematomas."

The other way a helmet protects has to do with its "hard shell which can prevent direct impact skull fractures, contusions, and bone cutting into the brain," he said.

Noting, "It's not brain science to put helmets on kids," Dr. Levy said that because most helmets must be replaced after an impact, parents should:
1) inspect kids' helmets by peeling back the fabric liner and checking the EPS or foam padding for dents or cracks;
2) ask their kids if they had a big fall or collision;
3) explain to kids and teens that they are not invincible;
4) make sure the helmet fits properly.

A helmet should come to one or two fingers breadth above the eyebrows and fit snugly. It should not be loose or able to be pulled off. It should not move more than a half inch in any direction and should not fall down over the forehead, Dr. Levy warned.

This advice applies to adults also. Dr. Levy stressed that, "The older you get, the more severe the injury—subdural hematomas go up exponentially with age as do fatalities and recovery times. Inherent biological differences make you more susceptible—as the brain shrinks with age, there is more rattle room in the skull. Tolerance and recovery begin to be affected as early as age forty," he noted. Bottom line, adults can benefit from a helmet's added protection and need them, too, he said.

Dr. Levy also noted that in studies of head injuries seen at major trauma centers, helmets reduced the risk of brain injury among skiers and snowboarders by 65-75 percent. Those studies found that they did not increase cervical spine or other injuries and that they reduce the severity of brain injury even in major accidents.

Aside from being a "brain bucket" that could prevent a need for brain surgery, the pros of helmet use include being a warm and trendy head topper. The fastest growing groups to use them are "tree" skiers and riders. "Get one with good venting and it will be the warmest, driest hat you'll ever wear," advised a cool, young salesman who said he got one because "my friends in the trees were all wearing them."

With a host of makes and styles, all ages and head shapes can be assured a proper fit—not every make would fit every head shape so you might have to try a few to find the best fit and comfort level for your particular noggin. Also, there are helmets just for boarders with cutaway ear sections for keener hearing. Some helmets have removable ear flaps. Helmets come in a variety of stylish designs and colors, and there's even fleece-covered chin straps to avoid "chin rub."

Carl Ettlinger, president of Vermont Ski Safety, Inc. and a long-time ski safety researcher, stresses that we should "look for helmets with an ASTM (www.astm.org) or Snell (www.smf.org) certification." These certifications indicate that the helmet has met stringent standards.

The drawbacks to helmet usage include getting used to them and cost. My first time wearing a helmet I was sensitive to pings from tapping the chair or a ski pole on lift rides and a different hearing sensation. The next day I felt strangely vulnerable without one, which told me any adjustment period is brief.

Helmets cost more than a wool hat. Children's range from $40 to $80; adult's, from $50 to $150 and up. Once involved in a significant impact, most helmets must be replaced (because the EPS liner cracks when it absorbs energy). The exceptions are some new multi-impact models. Some manufacturers allow you to send a helmet back and discount a new one.

Since they are an investment, one of the best ways to decide on a helmet is to demo or rent one. Many ski areas have Helmet Demo Days where manufacturers or retailers bring their helmets to the slopes and let skiers and snowboarders try them out for free. This is a good opportunity to see how you like a helmet and which model or type is best for you. Another, is to rent one.

Aside from the issue of freedom of choice (potentially serious head injuries were only 2.6 percent of all injuries during the course of 30 seasons, note the researchers), there is major concern that requiring helmet usage will confer a sense of invulnerability and encourage unsafe behaviors. This happened with bicycle helmet usage. Despite increased bike helmet usage, head injuries rose and experts believe it was due to increased risk-taking (U.S. Consumer Product Safety Study finding as reported in the July 29, 2001 *New York Times*).

At a time when the number of skier injuries has actually decreased, people don't want to see them tick back up due to offsetting behaviors among helmet wearers. This is one of the main reasons that the ski industry has not been quick to push mandatory usage of helmets. The concern that helmets may engender a false sense of security and encourage skiers or boarders to take more risk is joined by a concern that "an improperly fit helmet may be able to do more harm than going without."

Additionally, there are some limitations to helmets. Helmets cannot protect the *body* in crashes so there is still a chance of injury or an organ rupture and death. Nor can they protect the brain in *every* crash/fall. There are limitations on their effectiveness beyond certain speeds, warns Dr. Jasper Shealy who has spent thirty years studying snowsport injuries and collaborates with Ettlinger. **"Speed is the worst enemy," especially among teenagers**, he said, noting that **the high risk group of ages 12 to 20 are going faster with a helmet.**

I asked Dr. Shealy, a professor of engineering at the Rochester Institute of Technology, "What is it that kills a person when they strike the tree or collide with another person or die in a car crash?"

He said that the human body is made in such a way that when we run, we can reach speeds of about 12 mph (trained runners being exceptions who can attain higher speeds). When we collide with something and suddenly stop our forward motion at higher speeds than that, our aorta bursts and we bleed to death. The human body fails due to its built-in limitations.

I have heard stories of excellent skiers who have caught an edge and hit a tree talking to their rescuers one minute and gone the next. The human body simply cannot sustain a direct impact beyond a certain speed and survive.

That's why some people don't use a helmet. My brother knows that if he makes a mistake when carrying speed, he would most likely be a goner so he doesn't wear a helmet. (A reason to stay away from trees when skiing fast.)

In response to a question of why wearing a helmet should be a matter of personal choice, the Lids on Kids Website includes not only the previously mentioned bicycle study data but also says that, "The latest data on ski helmets shows that while usage is up, head injuries have not decreased, and the severity of head injuries is significantly greater among the helmeted population than the non-helmeted population." This contradicts the protective effect of helmets found in Dr. Levy's studies—a reason that there is a call for more studies, but it also may reflect a demographic of higher-risk users of helmets who are traveling at higher speeds and hence skewing the results.

It's a factor in the debate to make helmets mandatory and why informed choice is currently the recommendation. Many ski areas recommend "helmets as a consideration for skiing and boarding participants and parents." They encourage parents and others to educate themselves about the benefits and limitations of helmets. They support individual and parental rights to choose to wear a helmet or not—"It's Your Choice."

The National Ski Areas Association supports this view and encourages education as key to long-term slope safety. They stress knowing the Responsibility Code and skiing safely and in control as a first line of defense and wearing a helmet as a second line of defense. They also stress education for an informed choice.

One way to do that is to visit: www.SkiHelmets.com; www. LidsOnKids.org; www.astm.org and www.smf.org .— all Websites that can help with the decision-making process). Another good step is to talk with a knowledgeable salesperson at your ski shop. "Salespeople are trained to fit helmets properly. They should come to the top of the goggles and be comfortably snug. Do not buy big for a growing child. Helmets are for added protection—they are not a guarantee of safety," noted one ski-shop manager.

Dr. Shealy and Ettlinger stress these points: "Helmets help under specific conditions. Under current standards, helmets will probably be very effective for glancing blows, but not for direct impact with fixed objects above 20 km/hour [12 mph], such as a tree, rock or lift tower, which is what typically kills participants. Do not have unrealistic expectations as to what a helmet can do *and* ski safely. *Ski as if you were not wearing a helmet.*"

Just because some people are taking greater risks while wearing a helmet is not a reason for anyone not to wear one. If you ski in control and don't ski too fast or recklessly, but do sustain a head impact from a fall or collision, a helmet could make it a glancing one and it could spare you from a concussion or other serious head injury.

If you are still debating the use of a helmet, visit the Websites and remember this advice from Dr. Shealy and Carl Ettlinger:

"Ski/ride in control; know your limits; obey the rules of the slopes; and don't forget to tune up your equipment."

That includes inspecting your helmet if you use one and considering a purchase if you don't.

Appendix D

Off Piste and Backcountry

In this book, the term backcountry refers to terrain outside an area's boundaries, which are always marked on the trail map. *Off piste* refers to skiing or riding off a marked trail or glades but within an area's boundary; it generally entails skiing woods or other mountainous terrain such as chutes that haven't been cleared or maintained in any way for snow travel. Both types of exploration have become popular (for reasons of beauty, solitude, powder snow stashes, and/or adventure) among some skiers, riders, and Telemarkers. However, it is a major concern for ski areas that have had to mount some very expensive (and at times dangerous) rescues for persons who have gone off the ski area's open trails and glades and become lost.

Since getting lost in the mountains can lead to serious injury or even death, spending the night on a mountain is *not recommended*. Temperatures usually drop to well below freezing and often sub-zero. If not properly prepared, frostbite can lead to the loss of fingers and toes, and the very real risk of hypothermia can be life threatening. Furthermore, Vermont law provides that anyone leaving a ski area's legal skiing boundaries or going *off piste* is responsible for the cost of their rescue should one become necessary.

Parents might want to have a discussion with their teens and young children regarding where they ski. Like adults, they need to understand the potential danger of going off a trail or glade or beyond the area's boundaries.

The majority of Vermont's ski areas do not allow and do not encourage *off piste* or backcountry exploration. However, Jay Peak Resort, Mad River Glen, Smugglers' Notch, Bolton Valley, and Okemo do have a boundary-to-boundary policy which allows *off-piste* exploration at the skier's own risk but not on any area marked closed. This policy is usually accompanied by a proviso to go as a threesome (at minimum), enter from an open trail, and not after 3 p.m. Read any warning on the trail map carefully and abide by the conditions if you are going to engage in this activity. A few other areas allow this exploration (they won't pull your lift ticket for it) but don't officially offer it or note it on their maps.

Bolton Valley Resort offers *off piste* at the downhill ski area as well as on the additional tract of 5,000 acres of wilderness which they own (i.e this acreage is within the resort's boundaries). Officials there add that "accompanying this activity, there must be an increased awareness by all parties concerned that the wilderness is a resource that must be shared by all user groups, and all parties must demonstrate basic respect for each other and their right to be there."

Some areas also have *backcountry* terrain which is visited by outdoor adventurers—some who are well versed experts and some who think they are but are not. Jay Peak, Sugarbush, and Bolton Valley offer guided tours of this type of exciting but potentially dangerous backcountry terrain.

Before deciding to explore *off piste* or backcountry terrain, you must be willing to assume the risk of becoming lost or injured. The following are some considerations culled from people who perform rescues:

1. Tell someone where you are going, with whom, and when you can be expected back.

2. Travel in groups of at least 3 or 4 — 4 is better because if anyone becomes injured, two can go for help and one can remain with the injured party. The buddy system is always a good idea in mountain adventuring; that includes on the trails, also.

3. Never undertake such a sojourn late in the day; timing will depend on the distance to be traveled but it gets dark in the woods earlier than on the slopes so err on the side of caution. It also gets COLD.

4. Be prepared to spend the night in the woods with a pack containing food, water, a source of heat such as compact thermal blankets, a first-aid kit, and ideally a source of communication. Because cell phones often don't work in the mountains, long-range 2-way radios, a source of light to signal to rescuers, and a whistle to call to rescuers should be included.

This is a partial list meant to help you survive by being prepared should you become lost or stuck in the woods. It is not meant to encourage anyone to undertake this type of risk. If interested, seek instruction and go with a guided tour to experience this type of activity before you decide to risk life and limb on your own. (Repeat: Jay, Bolton, and Sugarbush offer such tours and instruction.)

The following comes from an experienced skier, patroller, and rescuer:

> *Off-piste* policy is directly rooted in Vermont Law. Legally, any person who uses any facilities of a ski resort (parking, lifts, bathrooms, food, trails, etcetera) and leaves the open and designated terrain is 100% ON THEIR OWN. NO ski area in Vermont has ANY legal requirement to provide ANY rescue services for these folks. If the ski areas do voluntarily direct or participate in a rescue for these individuals, Vermont law allows them to bill and collect a reasonable fee. No ski area in this state has even the remotest responsibility for those who ski closed trails or go *off piste*.
>
> If you ever receive a call for help while skiing or riding at an area, always report it to management or the ski patrol. NEVER assume it is a joke. Do not use the 9-11 number unless you are having a serious emergency. And never program a personal radio (long-range 2-way radio) to use channel "9-11."

Appendix E

Nordic Areas

For après-ski fun or a day off, discover the challenge and joy of "skinny skiing" at one of these cross-country ski areas. Check out www.XCski.org or www.skivermont.com for more information on Vermont cross-country and snowshoeing opportunities or call one of the areas listed below.

Nordic Ski Area	Town	Phone
Blueberry Hill Ski Center	Goshen	802-247-6735
Blueberry Lake XC	Warren	802-496-6687
Bolton Valley Nordic Center	Bolton Valley	802-434-3444
Brattleboro Outing Club	Brattleboro	802-257-5292
Burke Cross-Country Ski Area	West Burke	802-626-8338
Catamount Family Center	Williston	802-879-6001
Craftsbury Outdoor Center	Craftsbury Common	802-586-7767
Grafton Ponds Nordic Center	Grafton	802-843-2400
Green Mountain Touring Center	Randolph	802-728-5575
Hazen's Notch Association	Montgomery Center	802-326-4799
Hermitage XC Touring Center	Wilmington	802-464-3511
Highland Lodge & XC Center	Greensboro	802-533-2647
Hildene Ski Touring Center	Manchester	802-362-1788
Morse Farm Ski Touring Center	Montpelier	802-223-6914
Mountain Meadows XC Ski Area	Killington	802-775-7077
Mountain Top XC Ski Resort	Chittenden	802-483-2311
Okemo Valley Nordic Center	Ludlow	802-228-1396
Ole's Cross Country Center	Waitsfield	802-496-3430
Prospect Mountain XC Ski Center	Woodford	802-442-2575
Rikert Touring Center	Middlebury	802-388-4356
Sleepy Hollow Inn Ski & Bike Center	Huntington	802-434-2283
Smugglers' Notch Nordic Center	Smugglers' Notch	802-644-1173
Stowe/Mt. Mansfield XC Center	Stowe	802-253-3688
Stratton Mountain Nordic Center	Stratton Mountain	802-297-4114
Timber Creek XC Ski Area	Wilmington	802-464-0999
Trapp Family Lodge XC Ski Center	Stowe	802-253-5755
Viking Nordic Centre	Londonderry	802-824-3933
Wild Wings Ski Touring Center	Peru	802-824-6793
Wilderness Trails Nordic Ski Area	Quechee	802-295-7620
Woodstock Ski Touring Center	Woodstock	802-457-6674

Book Order Form

Ski Chase books are available at Vermont Ski Areas and selected stores. To order books, please fill out form (*print legibly*) and mail to: Mountain Publishing, 1300 CCC Road, Shrewsbury, VT 05738

Name _____
Street Address _____
Town, State, Zip _____
Phone _____
Number of copies of *The Great Vermont Ski Chase*
    @ $25 which includes free Priority shipping   _____

                                      Total enclosed   _____

Please make checks or money orders payable to:
Mountain Publishing, Inc.

Ski Chase books are available at Vermont Ski Areas and selected stores. To order books, please fill out form (*print legibly*) and mail to: Mountain Publishing, 1300 CCC Road, Shrewsbury, VT 05738

Name _____
Street Address _____
Town, State, Zip _____
Phone _____
Number of copies of *The Great Vermont Ski Chase*
    @ $25 which includes free Priority shipping   _____

                                      Total enclosed   _____

Please make checks or money orders payable to:
Mountain Publishing, Inc.

This page may be photocopied as often as you like.

About the Author

Karen D. Lorentz grew up in West Hartford, Connecticut and graduated from the University of Connecticut in 1968. She taught English at Scotch Plains-Fanwood High School in New Jersey before moving with her husband John and their sons to a remote mountaintop in Shrewsbury, Vermont in 1978.

Here, they learned to heat with wood, plow four-foot snowdrifts, and survive long cold winters as John developed a law practice in Killington and taught college courses while Karen ran a bed and breakfast (Lorenwood) and became a freelance writer. Living in the Green Mountains, they raised their three sons to enjoy hiking, cross-country skiing, and visits to Vermont's Alpine ski areas as well as nearby Nordic areas.

The author and sons Jason and Jon after she completed her ski chase at Pico in March 2003.

The author has written over 2,000 articles for magazines, newspapers, and newsletters and is a member of the National Association of Snowsports Journalists and Eastern Ski Writers among other organizations. She has covered Vermont skiing since 1979 and authored books on Killington and Okemo.

As a young girl, Karen learned to ski at small areas in Connecticut and Massachusetts and has skied in Vermont since 1958. She delighted in all the chairlifts at Mount Snow at a time when most uphill transportation was still provided by surface lifts. After a move to New Jersey in 1962, she skied at the 'banana belt' areas (NJ, NY, and PA). However, during college she again skied at Mount Snow and enjoyed ski weeks at Stowe.

During her teaching years, Karen shared her love of skiing with the high school ski club which she advised and helped grow to 200 members. They took trips to Vermont, the Alps, and Colorado along with NJ and NY areas. The permanent move to Vermont stemmed from a love of skiing and a desire to bring up their sons in the Green Mountains. They reside at an elevation of 2,210 feet, surrounded by a sea of mountains and spectacular views of neighboring Killington, the Green Mountains, the Adirondacks, and the Taconics.

Karen is working on a history of Vermont skiing and invites readers to share early skiing stories and photos with her. Also, please consider donating early photos of the ski areas to the ski museums or ski areas. Areas with skimpy archives would greatly appreciate them as would the Vermont Ski Museum.

The Great Vermont Ski Chase Challenge

If you would like to participate in the challenge to ski all of Vermont's major Alpine ski areas, **fill in the form below (please print legibly), cut it out, and send it in with your receipt for the purchase of this book to:**

Mountain Publishing, Inc.
1300 CCC Road,
Shrewsbury, VT 05738

You will receive a **free Vermont Ski Chase Card**. Simply present it at the ticket window for validation when you purchase your tickets and be sure to get a receipt for your purchase. When you have completed the challenge to ski all the areas (you have 4 seasons from date of card issue), simply send in your card and receipts and you will receive a voucher good for a day at the area of your choice *for all the persons on your card who completed the chase.*

Because Stowe Mountain Resort is not participating in the reward of the free day, you are *not required* to ski that area. It is totally optional (being included in the book was not dependent on area participation in the reward). All other areas in this book are participating.

However, if you are a snowboarder only, you can't ride Mad River Glen as they do not allow snowboarding. Simply include a photo of yourself and your board (taken anywhere) and write your name and "snowboarder only" on the back. This photo is in place of a Mad River ticket.

The Ski Chase Card will be good for the persons you register on it but is limited to a family, couple, or small group of 6 persons or less. (Ski clubbers will need to have their own cards, not one for an entire ski club.)

Names of persons on card _____

_____

Street Address _____
Town, State, Zip _____
Phone _____
Have you skied Vermont before? Yes ___ No ___
Number of Days a year you ski _____ # days in VT _____
I purchased my book at _____.
My receipt for the book purchase is enclosed (staple here).

This page may not be duplicated. Book purchase is required to participate.